NEGLECTED
ALTERNATIVES

Portrait of Roy Wood Sellars by Joseph Maniscalco

NEGLECTED ALTERNATIVES

Critical Essays
by
ROY WOOD SELLARS

Edited by
W. Preston Warren

Lewisburg
BUCKNELL UNIVERSITY PRESS

© 1973 by Associated University Presses, Inc.

Associated University Presses, Inc.
Cranbury, New Jersey 08512

Library of Congress Cataloging in Publication Data

Sellars, Roy Wood, 1880–
    Neglected alternatives.

    Includes bibliographical references.
        1. Realism—Addresses, essays, lectures.
    2. Empiricism—Addresses, essays, lectures.
    3. Materialism—Addresses, essays, lectures.
    4. Worth. 5. Free will and determinism. I. Title.
    B945.S421W37   100   72-3453
    ISBN 0-8387-1232-0

MAJOR WORKS OF ROY WOOD SELLARS

Critical Realism
The Next Step in Democracy
The Next Step in Religion
Evolutionary Naturalism
The Principles and Problems of Philosophy
Religion Coming of Age
The Philosophy of Physical Realism
American Philosophy From Within
Principles, Perspectives and Problems of Philosophy
Social Patterns and Political Horizons

Printed in the United States of America

Contents

Editor's Preface   7

Acknowledgments   17

A Brief Biography of Roy Wood Sellars   19

Part I Critical Essays

1 An Important Antinomy   27

2 Realism and Evolutionary Naturalism   40

3 American Critical Realism and British
   Theories of Sense-Perception   47

        Part I: G. E. Moore and Gilbert Ryle   47

        Part II: Russell, Price, and Broad   80

4 Positivism and Materialism   104

5 Two Divergent Naturalistic Theories of Sense
   Perception: Pragmatism and Critical Realism   140

6 In Defense of "Metaphysical Veracity"   162

7 Dewey on Materialism   181

8 Reflections on Dialectical Materialism   185

9 Materialism and Relativity: A Semantic Analysis   214

10 Querying Whitehead's Framework   242

11 Existentialism, Realistic Empiricism, and
   Materialism   272

12   Foundations in the Philosophy and Theology
        of Paul Tillich   294

Part II Three Previously Unpublished Constructive Essays
13   A Conflation of Philosophical Positions   303
14   A Naturalistic Theory of Value and Valuation 341
15   Agential Causality and Free Will   361
        Index   385

Editor's Preface

Roy Wood Sellars's contributions to philosophy have been epochal. The originator and persistent elaborator of critical realism, he was the first full-scale exponent of emergent naturalism. He reformed materialism as a substantive naturalism, in the light of biology, psychology, and physics, in an era when the conception of substance was being summarily dismissed. In addition, his work on the brain-mind problem anticipated by more than thirty years a number of identity theories of the brain-mind relationship. As an exponent of religious and social humanism, furthermore, Sellars was a sophisticated yet down-to-earth theorist of human values.

Sellars first used the term *Critical Realism* in two articles on "Critical Realism and the Time Problem" in 1908, two years before the New Realists published their "Program and First Platform." It is worth noting that in these articles, Sellars made scant reference to the New Realists; they were incidental to his problem. Following the publication of Sellars's volume *Critical Realism* (1916),[1] Durant Drake visited Sellars to ask if six realists who were planning a volume on realism might use that same title. Sellars was invited to participate. The outcome was the 1920 *Essays in Critical Realism,* to which— besides Drake, Lovejoy, Pratt, Rogers, Santayana, Sellars, and Strong also contributed. The group was composed of three "Essence" theorists and of four who stressed the "intentionality" of experience. Sellars

1. This volume, first published by Rand McNally, was reprinted in 1969 by Russell and Russell.

7

found himself in the second group, but later distinguished his view from theirs on the ground that he alone had investigated the mechanism of perceiving and found a biological basis for the referential or "intentional" factor in perceiving. His "Reexamination of Critical Realism" (1929) and "Clarification of Critical Realism" (1939)—along with such later writings as "Sensations as Guides to Perceiving" (1959), "Referential Transcendence" (1961), and "Direct Referential Realism" (1963)—disclose the stages in the development of his realism.

Edward H. Madden has given Chauncey Wright the credit for articulating the conception of emergent evolution. But whereas Lloyd Morgan was the first to publish a volume titled *Emergent Evolution,* Sellars's *Evolutionary Naturalism* (1922) antedated Morgan's publication by a year, and the first of Sellars's articles on emergent naturalism antedated Morgan by five years. (Morgan's volume, consequently, devotes an appendix to Sellars.) Sellars's book also antedated by one year Samuel Alexander's article on emergence titled "Natural Piety" (1923). As Sellars states his own case, his theory of emergent evolution was more pluralistically naturalistic than either Alexander's or Morgan's. And he was more explicit and inclusive than Chauncey Wright.

Sellars's physical realism is evident in his *Critical Realism* and in his evolutionary naturalism, to which he devoted articles beginning in 1919. True, Sellars argued for a physical naturalism and against materialism as late as 1927 (in "Why Naturalism and not Materialism?"). Yet when he found the term *naturalism* preempted for a methodology, Sellars concluded that the time had come for a "reformed" materialism. His substantive naturalism was basically materialistic, yet his materialism was an *emergent* variety, which could affirm the reality of consciousness and of human values. In all, Sellars wrote some ten articles on modern, reformed materialism.

On the brain-mind problem, Sellars's work comprises a dozen major papers. Among these papers, "Is Consciousness Alien to the Physical?" "Evolutionary Naturalism and the Mind-Body Problem," "The Double-Knowledge Approach to the Mind-Body Problem," and "An Analytic Approach to the Mind-Body Problem" are four of the most significant.

Sellars's *Next Step in Democracy* (1916), *Next Step in Religion* (1918), *Religion Coming of Age* (1928), *Social Patterns and Political Horizons* (1970), and numerous articles all articulate his humanism, which he regards as the third facet of his philosophy, complementing his referential critical realism and his evolutionary substantive naturalism.

His work on human values includes "Cognition and Valuation" (1926), "Human Life and Values" (six chapters in *Principles and Problems of Philosophy* [1926]),[2] "The Nature and Status of Value" (1932), "Can a Reformed Materialism do Justice to Values?" (1944), "Valuational Naturalism and Moral Discourse" (1958), and "In What Sense do Value Judgments and Moral Judgments Have Objective Import?" (1967). Sellars succeeded in synthesizing the theoretical insights of axiologists with more practical and more functional conceptions of values.

Although Sellars has written a number of original books,[3] the bulk of his writing is in the form of articles, and the task of assembling these is imperative for future scholarship. I have previously edited a selection of Sellars's writings that exhibit the development of his referential physical realism, his identity theory of the mind-body relation, his theory of value, and his humanistic social and religious philosophy.[4] That volume did not include any of Sellars's predominantly *critical* essays, some of which are particularly noteworthy. Every philosopher, Joseph Blau has stated in correspondence, expresses his position in two ways: first, by direct statement of it; and, secondly, by contrast, by criticism of opposing views. In Sellars's writing, his own position is constantly tested against opposing ones. The finer

2. These chapters were published in revised form by the Pageant Press in 1970.

3. Cf. the list of Sellars's major publications on page two. The books that best represent the substance of his philosophy are: *Critical Realism, Evolutionary Naturalism,* and *The Philosophy of Physical Realism.* The most complete and updated statement of his philosophy is contained in his *Principles, Perspectives, and Problems of Philosophy.*

4. *Principles of Emergent Realism* (St. Louis: Warren Green, Inc., 1970).

and fuller development of his philosophy may be said to have been achieved through a dialogue with philosophical "isms" that were current in successive decades—idealism in the first years of this century, pragmatism over several decades, behaviorism in the teens and twenties, logical positivism and Whitehead's organicism in the thirties, existentialism in the forties and fifties. Although other realists became tired reformers and went on to tasks "more attractive and general,"[5] Sellars substantiated and refined his critical realism with evidence drawn from neurology, physiology, psychology, sociology, evolution and information theories. And he gleaned both material and insight from opposing positions. He demonstrated thereby not only the plausibility of critical realism but its probability. Thus he surmounted subjectivism, phenomenalism, and epistemological dualism.[6]

---

5. Herbert Schneider, *Sources of Contemporary Philosophical Realism in America* (Indianapolis: Library of Liberal Arts, 1964), p. 23.

6. Sellars's critiques cover all the chief developments in 20th-century philosophy. An early article, "An Important Antinomy" (1908) is directed especially against Bradley. His critique of James Ward's *Naturalism and Agnosticism* was, however, his *pièce de résistance*. Idealists generally come in for Sellars's intellectual rapier—for example, in his *Critical Realism*. Also reproduced in this volume is his reply to Hoernlé in 1927.

His writings on Dewey begin with an article in 1907 entitled "The Nature of Experience." They extend well into the sixties. One article, "Two Divergent Theories of Sense Perception," was accepted for publication yet never published. I have been able to obtain a copy for inclusion here.

Sellars's relationship with psychologists and neurologists has always been close. In his early days as an Instructor at the University of Michigan, Sellars roomed in the same building with the behavioristic psychologist John Shepard. Shepard's was a kind of Gestalt behaviorism, hence it was a discriminating variety of behaviorism that confronted Sellars in Ann Arbor. This accounts for his readiness to give the behaviorists credence without one-sided acceptance.

Sellars has written two substantial critiques of Whitehead's philosophy: "Philosophy of Organism and Physical Realism" (1941) in Paul A. Schilpp, ed., *The Philosophy of Alfred North Whitehead* (New York: Tudor Publishing Co., 1941), pp. 405-33; and "Querying Whitehead's Framework" in *Revue Internationale de Philosophie* (1961). The latter is included here.

Sellars wrote two major articles on positivism: "Positivism in Contemporary Philosophical Thought," *American Sociological Review* (1939), and "Positivism and Materialism," *Philosophy and Phenomenological Research* (1946). The latter is more critical, the former more descriptive. On existentialism and Marxism, he has chapters in *Reflections on American Philosophy from Within* (South Bend, Ind.: Notre Dame University Press, 1969) as well as articles such as those included in this compilation.

Certain critiques stand out not only as statements of Sellars's own position, but as searching analyses of others. "Querying Whitehead's Framework" (1961), "American Critical Realism and British Theories of Sense Perception" (1962), and "Reflections on Dialectical Materialism" (1944) are among these, also a series of critiques of Dewey's Experimentalism.

Other essays in this volume further suggest the range of Sellars's interests. Included here are his criticism, in 1908, of Bradley's idealism, and his critique of Hoernlé's critique of critical realism, his crucial essays on British theories of sense perception and on logical positivism. Finally, Sellars's statement of his divergence from Einstein; three essays on pragmatism; one each on dialectical materialism, Whitehead's organicism, and existentialism; and supplementary notes from another essay on this subject are included to provide a rounded view of the philosopher. (His critique of relational theories of knowledge,[7] and of metaphysical dualism,[8] his essays in debate with Sidney Hook,[9] and most of his writing on relativity[10] are not included.)

This volume of critical essays concludes with three unpublished constructive studies: "A Conflation of Philosophical Positions," "A Naturalistic Theory of Value and Valuation," and the case for "Agential Causality and Free Will." It has been typical of Sellars to recognize certain components of truth and value in divergent philosophies and to attempt to make full provision for these in his own philosophy. In one of his earliest essays he sought a realism that "passes through idealism,"[11] rather than one that simply stands in arbitrary opposition to it. In his treatment of behaviorism a few years later, he was neither entirely for it, as were some neo-realists, nor entirely against it. For him, behaviorism had much to offer toward a theory of mind, but it needed to be complemented by the

---

7. Cf. "Is There a Cognitive Relation?", *Journal of Philosophy* (1912).
8. "Epistemological Dualism Versus Metaphysical Dualism," *Philosophical Review* (1921).
9. Cf. "Does Naturalism Need Ontology?" and "Is Naturalism Enough?", both in *Journal of Philosophy* (1944).
10. "Materialism and Relativity: A Semantic Analysis," *Philosophical Review* (1946); "The Philosophy and Physics of Relativity," *Philosophy of Science* (1946); "A Note on the Theory of Relativity," *Journal of Philosophy* (1946); plus unpublished papers. Cf. n. 24.
11. "Consciousness and Conservation," *Journal of Philosophy* 5 (1908):238.

data of introspection. It needed, therefore, to be fitted into a more inclusive conception of the mind. Similarly, he saw the functionalism of pragmatism as an important truth, while its lack of substances that function was its basic deficiency. Sellars's philosophy was hospitable rather than exclusive. At one point, indeed, he went so far as to propose that his philosophy could accept the claims of a Kierkegaard if the Dane's views were sufficiently enlarged and made specifically empirical.[12] Yet there was no sentimental laxity in Sellars's thought. While inclusive, he was a tough-minded thinker. His treatment of the problem of freedom or determinism is typical of his "both and" findings.

What now is this perspective which is at once so critical yet hospitable? "Roy Wood Sellars," said one of my students, "seems to me to be a common-sense philosopher." What could he have meant by such a statement? Sellars's early writing concerned itself especially with the main concepts of a science that, he stated in 1916, turns ever more completely away from the pictorial language of common sense.[13] In 1922, as I have already indicated, he published an original formulation of emergent evolution, and, in 1932, an essentially scientific *Philosophy of Physical Realism*. In the mid-forties, he opted for a reformed materialism, and throughout his career, from 1905 to the present, he has been elaborating a social, moral, and religious philosophy that penetrates beyond common sense.[14] He is therefore not a common-sense philosopher in the usual usage of that phrase.

He is, however, a philosopher who believes that certain conceptions dismissed by recent philosophers express essential realities: that physical things are objective substances and that we can perceive external entities other than our own sensations or ideas;[15] that action

---

12. "Accept the Universe as a Going Concern," in H. N. Wieman, ed., *Religious Liberals Reply* (Boston: Beacon Press, 1947), pp. 171–72.

13. *Critical Realism* (Chicago and New York: Rand McNally, 1916), p. vi.

14. Sellars has never been sentimental in social, moral, or religious matters, although common sense is close to sentiment in all these matters. On the other hand, Sellars has never been negative or simply sophisticated. His social and religious philosophy are grounded in his substantive naturalism; his "Accept the Universe as a Going Concern" serves as an excellent example of his position.

15. Sensations are sensory responses to stimuli impinging on organisms. Perceiving is the identifying of objects from which stimuli come. Sensations

contributes to, and is indeed basic to, knowledge;[16] that the resonances in experience known as "feedback" are crystallizers of definiteness in both conception and perception;[17] that conception enters into the very process of definitive perceiving as well as into abstract thought;[18] that science, despite its special methodologies and metalanguage, does not disclose an entirely different world from that of ordinary experience and action, but rather the same world in different sets of references;[19] that minds are not ghosts within physical machines, but special organic capacities;[20] that human values are neither Platonic ideas nor mere objects of interest, but anything that makes a difference in the functioning human economy.[21]

The tie-in with common sense is evident, though the conceptions go far beyond what is assimilated from everyday experience or from tradition. "I start from natural realism or common sense," states Sellars, "but I quickly see that it has no theory of perceptual cognition. . . . I [therefore undertake to] analyze the situation and [come in course to] stress the from-to situation [in which] sensations are used as sources of information. . . . I stressed ways of getting . . . facts about the world. But science found it had to measure

---

are clues and indices of things and are not characteristically objects *per se*—Russell and many others to the contrary. (Cf. "American Critical Realism and British Theories of Sense Perception" in *The Philosophy of Physical Realism* [New York: Russell and Russell, 1966].)

16. Perception is, in the first instance and basically, built around physical action. It of course becomes variously conditioned and developed by other factors than physical action.

17. See "Levels of Causality: The Emergence of Guidance and Reason in Nature," *Philosophy and Phenomenological Research* (1959), together with chapter 4 of *The Philosophy of Physical Realism* (1932) and recent articles on perception.

18. *Ibid.*

19. *The Philosophy of Physical Realism*, pp. 97–98. Cf. "My Philosophical Position: A Rejoinder," *Philosophy and Phenomenological Research* 16 (1955): 78.

20. See "Evolutionary Naturalism and the Mind-Body Problem," *Monist* (1920), pp. 568–98, and Sellars's other writings on the conception of the brain-mind, referred to earlier in this preface.

21. Cf. especially "Cognition and Valuation," *Philosophical Review* 35 (1926): 124–44; "Can a Reformed Materialism Do Justice to Values?" *Ethics* 55 (1944): 28–45; "In What Sense Do Value Judgments and Moral Judgments Have Objective Import?" *Philosophy and Phenomenological Research* 25 (1967): 1–16.

things and events and to quantify,"[22] and to fit its findings into a conceptual and theoretical structure. An adequate bridging of the gaps between common sense and the sophisticated findings of both science and philosophy has therefore been an integral concern of Sellars. In this respect, he has a certain affinity with the critical common-sensism of C. S. Peirce, who upheld "the retention of the main body of our instinctive beliefs."[23] In Sellars's case there is an elaboration of the biological bases for "common sense" beliefs. They function in the protection and development of the organism, and, insofar as they are actually functional, they are capable of increasing refinement. Sellars's philosophy thus brings ordinary living and the conclusions of scientific research into a critical synthesis. He becomes, in consequence, a sophisticated epistemologist.

His philosophy is, accordingly, no less concerned with penetrating critical analysis than with ordinary, work-and-play conceptions. His papers on the principle of relativity are evidence of this,[24] as is his essay on "Reformed Materialism and Intrinsic Endurance."[25] He has ample place for all possibilities in the imaginative and speculative life of the mind, as his writings in cosmology and ontology not merely

22. A statement in a letter to the editor summing up a number of both earlier and later writings.

23. "What Pragmatism Is," *Monist* (1905). Cf. Justus Buchler, ed., *Philosophical Writings of Peirce* (New York: Dover, 1955), p. 260.

24. See n. 10. In stating his realistic position regarding the theory of relativity, Sellars wrote this editor: "There is a purely kinematic *Gestalt* of separating bodies. This is an absolute. Einstein put it in place of absolute motion with respect to an ether or absolute space. I don't think he was quite clear as to this ontological foundation. This *Gestalt* lends itself to the *cognitive construct* in kinematics of relative motion with respect to observers. This construct bothered people, especially idealists. Even Russell was perplexed. The relative motion is the same for both observers since it concerns the *Gestalt* fact of rate of separating. And so Einstein works out his equations using light as a factor. He then saw its dynamic import. Here we have induced uni-directional movement. The point I would make is that the *Gestalt* of the earth-sun situation was an historically achieved *Gestalt*. Russell keeps to the kinematic construct and argues that it is equally true to say the sun revolves about the earth as to say that the earth revolves about the sun. *My* ontology stresses the historical *Gestalt*. . . . I am not arguing for absolute motion with respect to an ether or absolute space. And I am not challenging his kinematics. Rather am I, an ontologist, *pointing out what underlies* relative motion as a cognitive construct."

25. *Philosophical Review* 53 (1944): 359–82.

illustrate but propose. There are continuity and comprehensiveness as well as critical realism to his philosophy. To surmount the restrictions that beset contemporary "isms" means to take adequate stock of work such as his, and, to use an oft-repeated phrase in Sellars's writing, to seek the *neglected alternatives*.

Acknowledgments

The editor acknowledges with gratitude permission to reprint several of the articles brought together in this volume:

Notre Dame University Press, for "Foundations of Philosophy in Tillich's Ontology," from *Reflections on American Philosophy from Within.*

Open Court Publishing Company, for "Realism and Evolutionary Naturalism." Reprinted from *The Monist,* Volume 37, La Salle, Illinois, with the permission of the publisher and the author. Also for the chapter "In Defense of 'Metaphysical Veracity,'" reprinted from Paul A. Schilpp, ed., *The Philosophy of C. I. Lewis,* with the permission of the publisher and the author.

The Philosophical Review, for "Materialism and Relativity: Semantic Analysis," Volume 55.

Philosophy and Phenomenological Research, for "Dewey on Materialism," Volume 3; "Reflections on Dialectical Materialism," Volume 5; "Positivism and Materialism," Volume 7; and "Existentialism, Realistic Empiricism, and Materialism," Volume 25.

Revue Internationale de Philosophie, for "Querying Whitehead's Framework," from no. 56/57 of the *Revue.*

Russell & Russell, Publishers, for "American Critical Realism and British Theories of Sense Perception," which appeared originally in *Methodos* and form Chapters XVIII and XIX of *The Philosophy of Physical Realism,* New York: Russell & Russell, Publishers, © 1966, by Roy Wood Sellars.

A Brief Biography of Roy Wood Sellars

Roy Wood Sellars was born in Seaforth, Ontario, the son of Ford Wylis and Mary Stalker Sellars. His ancestry included a great grandfather, David Wood, who was a patron of the arts at Queens University, Kingston, Ontario, and a Canadian hero of the British-American War of 1812. From him, Roy received his middle name. There were also Scottish, German, and Irish notables in his genealogy.[1] His father, Sellars reports, was a very able man, a school principal who had to give up teaching for reasons of health following the birth of the last of his three children. Nevertheless, the father then studied medicine at the University of Michigan, graduating with one of the Mayo brothers in the early 1880s. Faced with the necessity of quickly establishing a practice, Ford Wylis Sellars settled in Pinnebog, Michigan, where his children were raised.

---

1. The Sellars branch of his family, Sellars reports, migrated from the region of Glasgow, Scotland, to Nova Scotia, then to Ontario, where they intermarried with the Wood family of Canadian historical distinction. His grandmother on his father's side was of German descent. The Stalkers, his mother's family, came from Scotland, where they wore the Royal Stuart Tartan, to York (now Toronto, Ontario), intermarrying with the landed Stanley-Evans family from Ireland. A genealogy of the Stanley family compiled in 1943 by Earl Spencer Seeli-Armitage-Stanley of Lucan, Ontario, traces the Ontario, Canada Stanleys to Robert Stanleigh vel Stoneleigh, who was sheriff of Lancashire in 1123-1128. Robert Stanleigh, interestingly, is shown to be the great grandson of William, Count of Arques, and great-great-grandson of Richard II, King of Normandy. More distantly, on the male side, the lineage goes back to earlier British royalty. Sellars writes (in a letter dated November 11, 1971): "I think I am proudest of the fact that an ancestor of mine, Lord Stanley, appears in Shakespeare's *Richard III* . . . in Bosworth field."

All three children attended Ferris Institute at Big Rapids, Michigan, following the completion of their schooling in Pinnebog. Roy taught for one year before going to the University of Michigan, where he received his undergraduate degree and won the accolade of the Class of 1903 as one of its two most outstanding scholars.[2] His interests as an undergraduate were already wide-ranging. During his sophomore year, he discovered philosophy; in his senior year, comparative linguistics and comparative culture. He pursued the latter interest for one year at Hartford Theological Seminary, then accepted a fellowship in philosophy at the University of Wisconsin. Here he felt the influence of pragmatism and socialism, though he treated both critically. The pragmatist influence was to be assimilated to Realism and that of socialism to democracy.[3]

In 1905 Roy Wood Sellars accepted a teaching appointment at the University of Michigan while completing his studies for the doctorate. With the intellectual activism and energy that were to characterize him throughout his extended life, he proceeded constantly from one undertaking to another. In 1906 he attended a summer session at the University of Chicago; the outcome was a substantial essay plus a series of briefer papers.[4] The essay, "A Fourth Progression in the Relation of Mind and Body," critical of J. Mark Baldwin, was published by the latter in the *Psychological Review*. There followed a series of articles on the main concepts of science, and in 1910 he began teaching a reputedly notable course on this subject. Meantime, he had been in Europe for the year 1909–1910 and had broached his conception of emergent naturalistic evolution to Bergson, who referred him to Hans Driesch, with whom he studied.

Major publications began to flow. Between 1916 and 1926 he

---

2. *Principles of Emergent Realism*, pp. xvii–xx.

3. His affiliation with socialism, though not with its Marxist or it Utopian forms, is explicit. In *The Next Step in Democracy* (1916), he argues that socialism is a democratic movement, and that in its active concern for the reality of the social, it is the "next step" in democracy. It is democratic in its *concern for everyone*, and it is democratic in its emphasis on the *participation* of all in sociopolitical processes. It is opposed to any and all arrogations of prerogatives and power.

4. The briefer papers were: "The Nature of Experience," *Journal of Philosophy* (1907); "Professor Dewey's View of Agreement," *Journal of Philosophy* (1907); "Consciousness and Conservation," *Journal of Philosophy* (1908); "An Important Antinomy," *Psychological Review* (1908).

completed five volumes, and two additional volumes were published in the following years: in 1928, *Religion Coming of Age,* and in 1932, *The Philosophy of Physical Realism.* His writings on "reformed materialism" have not yet been compiled, though in 1949 Marvin Farber and Ralph McGill joined with him in publishing a volume of essays on materialism, two of which were written by Sellars.[5]

Professor Sellars has continued to write prolifically, with perhaps some let-up in the fifties. An article appeared as late as 1969.[6] Books recently published are: *Reflections on American Philosophy from Within* (1969),[7] *Principles, Perspectives, and Problems of Philosophy* (1970),[8] and *Social Patterns and Political Horizons* (1970).[9]

There have been two major developments in Sellars's philosophy: 1) from a professed epistemological dualism to a direct referential realism, and 2) from a more general naturalism to a specifically reformed materialism. I have elsewhere attempted to document these developments. Here I simply wish to indicate that to take some of Sellars's earlier statements as representing his later views is to lend oneself to the misconceptions of Montague and others.[10] Nevertheless there is a real continuity in Sellars's philosophy. The referential element in his realism is there from the start, but its mechanism and import are grasped only later. The substantive, physical character of his naturalism is also present in his early writings, but is perhaps not

---

5. "Social Philosophy and the American Scene," and "Materialism and Human Knowing," in *Philosophy for the Future* (New York: Macmillan, 1949).

6. He published at least one article in 1969 and sent a manuscript to the press. Shortly before writing this preface, I received the manuscript of another article. The list of his writings in the sixties is substantial. See my supplemental bibliography in *Principles of Emergent Realism* (St. Louis: Warren H. Green, Inc., 1970).

7. South Bend, Ind.: University of Notre Dame Press.

8. New York: The Pageant Press.

9. Nashville: Aurora Press.

10. W. P. Montague's statement that none of the critical realists went beyond the epistemological dualism of Locke has been challenged both directly and indirectly by Sellars (cf. also my own "Mote in the Eye of the Critic of Critical Realism," *Philosophy and Phenomenological Research* [1965]). Cf. Dewey's confession of the complete philosophical relativity of the issues of realism in his statement: "we did not solve the problem; we got over it" (Schneider, *Sources of Contemporary Philosophical Realism in America* [Indianapolis: Bobbs-Merrill, Library of Liberal Arts, 1964], p. 23).

obvious because of the difficulties with the traditional conception of matter.[11] Only after other thinkers had restricted the term "naturalism" to a purely methodological view, and consequently reduced substances to constructs, did Sellars clearly recognize that his was actually a materialism.

Sellars's earliest books (*Critical Realism, Evolutionary Naturalism,* and *The Next Step in Religion*) gained him status at home and abroad. He was invited to give a paper before the Eastern Division of the American Philosophical Association and elected a Vice President. He was invited to give a paper before the Aristotelian Society in Britain, and he was elected President of the Western Division of the American Philosophical Association. As for his work in the philosophy of religion, the New York critic James G. Huneker ranked his *Next Step in Religion* as one of the two best books of 1918. Sellars articulated religious humanism for the American mind, and his humanistic writing led to his being chosen to draft the "Humanist Manifesto," published in 1933.[12]

The coming of the foreign "isms"—logical positivism, existentialism, and Whiteheadian process philosophy—did indeed move Sellars's work from the mainstream of attention (or rather, move attention away from the main currents of American thought). But those who know Sellars's work can subscribe to his colleague DeWitt Parker's assertion that "No American has done more persistent and original thinking on fundamental philosophical problems . . . than my colleague, Professor Sellars."[13] That the output of his middle and later years needs more study is indicated by Richard J. Bernstein, who wrote this writer, "I have often felt that the neglect of R. W. Sellars has more to do with passing philosophical fads than with any substantial refutation or encounter with his views." Neglect of Sellars's work is not just neglect of a man: it is the neglect of fundamental contributions to philosophy.

---

11. Cf. "The Requirements of an Adequate Naturalism," *Monist* 30 (1921):249–70; "Why Naturalism and not Materialism?" *Philosophical Review* 36 (1927):216–25.
12. "A Humanist Manifesto," *The New Humanist* (1933).
13. In "Some Comments on Reformed Materialism and Intrinsic Endurance," *Philosophical Review* (1944).

NEGLECTED
ALTERNATIVES

PART I
CRITICAL ESSAYS

1

An Important Antinomy[1]*

In his chapter on nature[2] Mr. Bradley discovers an insoluble contradiction, which leads him, not unwillingly, to the altar of the Absolute. Without calling in question his other journeys to the same shrine, I must acknowledge that this one seems unjustified. Before going further let me state the antinomy and its meaning as nearly as possible in his own words. "(*a*) Nature is only for my body; but, on the other hand, (*b*) my body is only for nature." A slightly different form of this antinomy including the traditional Kantian emphasis on man's reason as the lawgiver to nature is given by Professor Royce:[3] "But we, of course, all recognize a sense in which man is to be conceived as a part of nature; while, on the other hand, nothing is clearer than that for us, all our beliefs about nature are determined by conditions which belong in one respect to the mind of man." Preparatory to the development of the two sides of his dilemma, Mr. Bradley points out what may be called the natural realism of common sense. We get the notion of a world consisting of primary and secondary qualities and extended in space and this world strikes us as not dependent on the inner life of any one. Our bodies with their organs are taken as the instruments and media which should

* *Psychological Review* 15 (1908) : 237–49.
1. The MS. of this article was received May 3, 1908.—ED.
2. *Appearance and Reality*, chap. 22.
3. *The World and the Individual*, vol. 2, Lecture IV, p. 158.

convey it as it is and as it exists apart from them (p. 262). But as
a result of the antagonistic growth of the physical and mental sciences
doubts arise, the physicist and the psychologist being forced by the
pressure of their data and methods to pass far beyond this naïve
position. The result is the conflict between impersonal scientific objectivism which knows no peculiar starting-point, such as the individual's
body and the tendency to a pluralism, on the part of the psychologist,
who deals perforce with individuals and their perceptions and ideas
as mediated by their bodies. In brief, this conflict is due to the fact
that physics knows nothing of the individual whereas psychology
does.[4] To sum up the difference antithetically: while things are
consciousness is considered a flux of presentations somehow cognizant
of these things; while physics deals with the extended in space,
psychology has to do with the unextended; while, in the external
world, individuality is unknown, the distinctive characteristic of
consciousness is its unity; while in nature, as the term is used,
mechanism seems provedly to rule, mind is teleological; while matter
in motion gives no heed to values and ideals, this heedfulness and
selectiveness are markedly true of mind. These groups of science,
dealing respectively with what is usually called mind, on the one
hand, and matter and energy, on the other, have developed naturally
enough, nay seemingly inevitably, different norms and categories that
clash relentlessly when brought in contact. And this antinomy of
Mr. Bradley seems to me to express this contrasted development.

Examining the two sides of the dilemma, we discover that "the
proper consequence of (a) appears to be that everything else is a
state of my brain" (p. 263). This brings out the prerogative character
of the brain as in some, so far unexplained, way the center of *my*
physical universe. It would be possible to use the metaphor of a hub
from which spokes radiate in all directions, or of a spider's web whose
strands run inward to where the spider awaits.[5] But if the world is
looked upon as at least relatively permanent collocations of matter,

---

4. "The material world shows us no real individualities; these are best
known to the psychological standpoint from which inner centers of memory,
action and endurance are discovered." Höffding, *Psychology*, p. 66 n.

5. "The consciousness of self is a relatively permanent factor of our experience and that important constituent of it, the consciousness of the body, is

my brain-state, then what is my own brain? "To me my own brain in the end must be a state of my own brain," or, combining the two sides with Mr. Taylor[6] "the physical order as a whole, must be a 'state' of my nervous system which is itself a part of that order." Turning now to the second thesis, facts as obvious and undeniable confront us. "Most emphatically, my organism is nothing but appearance to a body. It itself is only the bare state of a natural object. It is clear that for the existence of our organism, we find the same evidence as for the existence of outer objects. . . . Both nature and body exist necessarily with and for one another" (p. 265). Body and nature, then, are on the same level for this position, and naturalism might easily take the bit in its mouth, were it not for the warning voice of the psychologist who stands sponsor for the earlier thesis. We are obliged to include our own body as a member in this impersonal and common world of things which we have constructed in social intercourse, and the prerogative that attached to our bodies while we were looking at the first side of the antinomy disappears. For our perceptual experiences, nature focuses itself in our bodies; a certain perspective is shot through all our immediate experiences of the world; there is a definite "here" and "now" as a point of departure and this "here" is where my body is situated at the time. Logically this is witnessed to by the difference between perceptual and hypothetical universal judgments. Moreover, physiology, and in particular that of the sense organs, emphasizes the role played by the organism as the hero of the piece. In the distinctively conceptual view of the physical world, on the other hand, the "meanings" of "common" and "independent" attach; the "here" and "now" has been largely abstracted from, and the impersonal scientific "I" rules the outlook with the fixed stars as points of reference and even our body is engulfed in this continuous, all-embracing world.

To what conclusion does this antinomy, which seems so suggestive, lead Mr. Bradley? He infers that the "physical world is an appear-

---

perceived to be a condition of the occurrence in consciousness of other experiences. . . . The body—a something of which we are conscious—is perceived to be a condition of our having other experiences." Fullerton, *Metaphysics*, p. 199 n.
6. *Metaphysics*, p. 199.

ance; it is phenomenal throughout." Again, "the physical world is an abstraction which for certain purposes is properly considered by itself but which if taken as standing in its own right becomes at once self-contradictory" (p. 267). To me this is no satisfactory resting-place. Certain questions arise inevitably. Does it not signify that the physical world *as we perceive it* is not self-supporting apart from our perception of it, yet that we have strong motives to make such a hypostatization? On the one hand, the body is simply one thing in the world with no special primacy; on the other hand, for me the world can well be considered the adjective of my body, especially of my sense-organs and brain. Is it possible to do justice to both sides of this antinomy? I think it is. Suppose nature to have a different meaning in the two statements; they would, then, no longer contradict one another.

"Nature is only for my body." This judgment has its *raison d'être* in the fact that *my* conscious experience is, in some sense, an ultimate for me. On the basis of perception, by means of constructive inference and memory, I laboriously build up what I call my world. A great deal of this construction is either unconscious or else socially mediated, coming to me not in the raw but in a prepared condition. The facts of communication must be accepted but we must also never forget that each individual is active, that he must interpret what he receives through the eye and ear. The recognition of this apperceptive function is the achievement of logic and psychology that can be least disputed. Consequently, though each individual is aided in the formation of his world by others, yet he must be the main factor in the work and the final result, giving the perspective of his peculiar purposes and selective interests, has always a unique character that proclaims this fact.[7] The logic of value is especially insistent on this uniqueness of each individual's experience. "Nature is only for *my* body," then, stands for this pluralism of experiencers. Nature, here, must be looked upon *idealistically* as a construct of mine, based upon, and growing out of, my experience, which seeks to include all my experiences of physical things and all my possible experiences as indicated by the

7. Cf. Stuart, in Dewey's *Studies in Logical Theory*, p. 319.

statements of others. The desert of Sahara forms part of my nature because I have read about it and have no reason to disbelieve that it is continuous with the soil on which I now stand. That the extent of each man's "nature" varies directly with his education and training or, to put it succinctly, with his development scarcely needs detailed elucidation. But while the analysis of the obvious is not required, the import of the obvious is. And if evolution has any epistemological significance, it lies here, in the fact that the increasing complexity of the brain runs parallel with increasing intelligence and intelligence with the organization of the individual's experience in space and time, or, in other words, with his "nature." But what can this mean, if not that each individual has its own kind of nature? That of the fish gazing out of the pool must have hardly a semblance to ours, and the dog's "nature" constructed so largely on the data of scent, must also even in its elemental character differ widely from that of the fish or from ours. Cannot comparative psychology with all its labor force philosophy to a wider prospect in which human egotism may sink itself? Surely Buddhism would be more hospitable to this truer humility than Christian thought has shown itself, except, perhaps, in the mystic love of St. Francis for his brothers, the birds. The relativism, then, that comparative psychology teaches carries but to a more scientific expression the first thesis of our antinomy, "Nature is only for *my* body."

In this idealistic sense, then, there are as many "natures" as animals, even though in the more highly developed consciousness of man the meanings of "commonness," "betweenness" or "independence" may attach themselves so that nature is thought of as independent *in some sense* of *my* nature. It is this struggle of realism to be born from idealism that has so puzzled philosophers who could see only one side of this antinomy or who, seeing both sides, could not reconcile them. Not only does the solution of this apparent contradiction lie in the two meanings of "nature" but it focuses in the mind-body relation, giving an additional proof of what I have called the fourth progression.[8] By a study of the mind-body relation in

8. Cf. *Psychological Review* (September 1907)

connection with this antinomy, moreover, I think we can convince ourselves that realism involves personal idealism and that personal idealism would be meaningless without realism.

"My body is only for nature." It seems impossible to exclude my body from nature just because I learn of its existence in the same way that I learn of the existence of other things and other bodies. Furthermore, as the conceptual view of the world grows clearer, the impersonal standpoint, that of "experience-in-general," supersedes the concreter outlook, at least in certain reflective attitudes, and (may philosophy pardon my vulgarity!) the food question prevents hesitation. Every dish of porridge bears witness against any *alibi* for my body. More seriously, and with more academic dignity, let me refer to the exact experiments of Rubner and Atwater on the conservation of energy in the human organism. Admitting, then, nature's right to take my body unto herself in pursuance of her universal imperialism, we shall do well to ask ourselves some of the formal characteristics of this nature which engulfs the body. First, it is continuous. My body is in functional relation with the things around it and these, also, are in unceasing interaction with each other. Only the fairy-hand of science can reveal much of this delicate interplay and interdependence and only the eyes anointed by her can witness the subtle weaving of nature's living garment. The vital equilibrium of the organism with its surroundings, its stern struggle for ever fresh supplies of energy, its purposive self-maintenance, and, still more impressive, because more inclusive, the reciprocity of all parts of nature with all, deserve recognition better accorded in the term *dynamic continuity* than in that of monism with its vague idealistic inclinations or number symbolism. Second, conservation of energy, capacity or power of doing work, obtains in the transformations that unweariedly occur. This conservation makes meaningless any question of absolute origin. Third, nature is a universe in the sense that it is self-sufficient, no influx nor efflux being required or thinkable. Though Mayer and Helmholz, perhaps Joule and Atwater, have proved this as far as experiment can reach, yet only if this formally conserved universe can include consciousness will its complete self-sufficiency be assured. But how can this be done? Even while we are duly impressed by these tremendous and apparently proved facts, personal idealism as representative of the other side of our antinomy whispers doubt in our ear: "It cannot be the body as an experience of yours which is swallowed up in this 'macrocosm' called nature nor can this nature be identical with your construction which you have labelled with the same name." Harkening to this voice, must we not take a realistic attitude toward the body and toward nature in the second thesis of this dilemma? "My body is only for nature," yes, but for nature as "macrocosm," as reality. Does not this satisfy our antinomy and resolve the contradiction? But this was precisely the conclusion of a former study of the mind-body relation, where we saw that, corresponding to the psychical attitude toward another's mind, a realistic attitude toward his body must be taken.

What, however, is realism, and what is a realistic attitude toward a thing? This we are in a position to define more clearly. Starting, as I believe metaphysics must, from an individual's conscious experience, realism signifies that things are independent for their existence of his experience of them. In short, my experience does not affect the things around my body in any way unless it leads to an overt action on the part of my body. I may think about the book before me in any manner I choose but, until I take it up, an act mediated by my body, it is not changed. This does not mean that the book is as it is experienced as independently of my experience of it. That would be naïve realism, which, like idealism, is a stuff-theory of reality. Realism, as I have defined it, is not concerned, at least at first, with the character of the stuff of reality but with the relationship of the "microcosm" of the individual's experience with the "macrocosm" of reality, and the conclusion we have been forced to arrive at from a study of the dilemma is that nature has two meanings, my nature, a construct in my experience, and nature as *other than* my experience.

Now these "microcosms," or minds, seem to be intimately associated with certain peculiarly differentiated and organized nodes of this "macrocosm." This primacy of the brain was expressed above in the first thesis, "the proper consequence of (*a*) appears to be that everything else is a state of my brain." Consequently our problem has changed into the brain-mind relation, for, in the brain, microcosm and macrocosm meet. Can any clue be found to rede the riddle? I think so—*consciousness is a variant*.[9] An experience, once gone, is gone forever. The Heracleitean flux is surely true of the stream of consciousness. My approach, then, has led me to a possible solution of the old problem of change and permanence, or change and conservation. Reality is a process but a stereometrical and conserving process, and a careful reflection finds no reason why activity should involve destruction of the capacity for action on the part of reality, every reason, however, why activity should imply changes. As a matter of fact, conservation of the capacity of reality (conservation of energy) exists and there is also change, since transformations of energy are as evident as quantitative identity. Now change involves variancy of some sort. But consciousness, as we have seen, is a variant. Does this not lead us to the position that consciousness is the variant of the change-process of that part of reality called the pallium or cortex? The macrocosm thus embraces consciousness, does not reject it as alien. This result is further enforced by the facts of death and sleep. When the brain ceases to function, consciousness disappears. Such a functional identity is hinted at by Höffding, though his double-aspect theory prevented his realization of it. "Sensations, thoughts and feelings are mental activities which cannot persist when the definite individual connection in which they occur, has come to an end. *They correspond to the organic functions* (italics mine), but not to the chemical elements. If the organism is resolved into its elements, organic function is impossible."

It is highly probable that a question may arise in some reader's mind with respect to the relation of variant and invariant, so I hasten to make my position clearer on this point. It is, in a certain sense, the application of a double-aspect theory to reality. Reality is a process, everything in modern science cries this aloud, but it is somehow a self-conserving process. Dynamics precedes statics. "From motion we attain the notion of force or energy, by means of which equilibrium becomes intelligible."[10] But dynamics in no wise precludes change nor does it negate permanence and lawfulness. The category

---

9. Cf. *Journal of Philosophy* 5, no. 9, "Consciousness and Conservation."
10. Höffding, *The Problems of Philosophy*, p. 91.

of process, then, contains in itself both attributes in peaceful continuity. The invariant is not a thing somehow related to another thing called the variant in a most paradoxical fashion, it is not an atom or a piece of so-called energy, and any question as to whether the variant or invariant is effective in the process of reality is, therefore, absurd and results from a misunderstanding. Reality, as a process, may be regarded from the side of conservation, and this gives its invariant aspect, for us stated in terms of phenomenal energy; or from the side of change or variancy and here we are, fortunately, direct participators; we experience change immediately. We are, in short, dealing with distinctions, not with things, and there is no reason why we should reify these aspects of the reality-process and thereupon bewilder ourselves in the attempt at their relation.

What, however, is the consequence of this doctrine of functional-identity or variancy? It is that the question of the efficacy of consciousness has ceased to contradict the principle of conservation of energy. Conservation having become a formal characteristic of reality and this reality including consciousness, there can be no objection raised of influx or efflux. The first movement is toward what I would call temporal "parallelism." The old way of raising the problem of the effectiveness of consciousness was dualistic. Interaction was dualistic. The physical and the psychical, really abstractions of the impersonal scientific logic and methodology of physics and psychology, glared sullenly at each other across a yawning chasm. Even in so stating it I overreach myself and lapse into spatial imagery, for the gulf between mind and matter was one of quality, like that between the king and beggar-maid, and the marriage could be consummated only by God (Cartesianism). A restatement is now possible in this monism which I have advanced. We may ask, Is consciousness efficacious, has it any function? And this launches us upon the hitherto treacherous sea of ontological or real causation. I realize how impossible it is to treat adequately this extremely technical problem in brief space, so I shall content myself with a condensed outline.

Are there any facts that point toward the efficacy of consciousness? If so, an analysis of these may give us a hint of great value. First, evolution seems to demand the effectiveness of consciousness. Thus Darwin speaks of the sense of hunger and the pleasure of eating as, no doubt, first acquired in order to induce animals to eat.

He also thinks we may safely infer that the parental, filial, and social affections have to a large extent gained place through natural selection.[11]

Second, the relation of consciousness to habit seems to be that of changing function to fixed function. Consciousness, like attention with which it is closely related, attends the reorganization of habits. It thus allies itself with function-in-the-making and, at the present, the inclination of biologists is toward the temporal priority and molding character of function in relation to structure. Function, in the higher and more complex organizations, precedes structure and makes it possible. But, as we saw, consciousness as a variant corresponds to function.

Third, consciousness is selective and practical in its primary character. So much is this the case that everything points to its adaptive character and work in the economy of the organism, only the impersonal logic of science, which, at the expense of an infinite series, negates individual initiative, could for a moment believe that blind mechanism could react so effectively to a continually changing environment. Biology with its doctrine of "organic selection" reveals this necessity,[12] and modern sociology demands the play of intelligence even more earnestly.

Fourth, "it is a well-known fact that pleasures are generally associated with beneficial, pains with detrimental experiences. But if pleasures and pains have no efficacy, one does not see (without some such *a priori* rational harmony as would be scouted by the 'scientific' champions of the automaton theory) why the most noxious acts such as burning, might not give thrills of delight and the most necessary ones, such as breathing, cause agony."[13] So strong is this argument when examined carefully that so stern an upholder of the so-called physical world and its laws as McDougall concludes that "the

---

11. *Descent of Man*, 1 : 8 ff., quoted from J. Ward.
12. Cf. Baldwin, *Development and Evolution*, p. 117.
13. James, *Principles*, 1 : 143.

evolutionist finds himself confronted with the following dilemma: Either pleasure and pain are efficient causes of appetition and aversion and therefore have played in biological evolution a part of incalculably great importance, or we must postulate divine interference with the course of evolution at some early stage of the development of the animal kingdom."[14] Those who know McDougall recognize how much this admission means.

Fifth, the development of the trial-and-error theory in connection with excess-discharge or uncoordinated functions demands teleological selection.

We have gleaned two things, at least, from this enumeration. There are weighty reasons for belief in the efficacy of consciousness and the clue seems to rest in the relation of function and structure and thus to growth and organization. But death and disease or disintegration of any kind show that *organization is also a variant in the process of reality*. What could be more natural than to conclude that these are related directly? What stands in our way? Not conservation of energy, for we have surmounted that, but mechanism. And here is where the doctrine of grades of causal relation comes into use.[15] Reactions are undoubtedly selective in organisms, enzymes,[16] and even in chemical elements. I have not decided yet whether resonance in physics can be brought under the same idea. The type of causal process depends apparently on the organization of the interacting nodes of reality. This is what one would expect, and only the atomism of mechanical theory can have prevented its recognition for so long. Man, of course, with his tremendously delicate and complex functional organization presents the highest type of causal reaction, ordinarily called teleological. If we look at the process temporally and call the antecedent, conceptually delimited in a continuous process,[17] the cause, and the consequent, the effect, there is of course in such a system no loss or gain of energy or capacity. But this is true of any such system and represents the aspect of conservation in a process.

14. *Physiological Psychology*, p. 160.
15. Cf. "Consciousness and Conservation," *Journal of Philosophy* 5, no. 9.
16. Cf. *Science* (February 14, 1908), Chittenden.
17. Cf. Bradley, *Principles of Logic*, p. 488.

It, therefore, misses some vital aspect since it has no qualitative differentia for different processes, only differences in time coming to the fore. But if we pay attention to space and to the time during which certain amounts of energy are transformed and to the organization of the interacting "nodes" of reality in any causal process system, marked differences appear. Ostwald, quantitative mechanicalist that he is, cannot see this, though he has his hands upon it time and again.[18] Höffding also has this view almost in his grasp when he says, "Maxwell himself recognizes that geometrical as well as dynamic concepts are indispensable to the explanation of nature. In contrast to the dynamic, the geometric denotes simultaneity."[19] This explains in part why I have always called reality a stereometrical process with grades of organization and kinds of differentiation and, hence, degrees in selective reaction and influence. This in no wise conflicts with conservation, which is a temporal idea. Here is, I believe, a theory that may give articulation to the dissatisfaction with mechanism so widely current in late years among scientists themselves.

To sum up. By means of a study of an antinomy and the mind-body relation, I have sought to prove that we can handle reality as it is about our body even while it is independent for its existence, of our consciousness. This position affirms that the true starting-point for metaphysics is the individual and his experience, not experience-in-general, and that in the mind-body problem nearly all the critical questions can be seen to focus. The realism we obtained is not a stuff-theory and is perfectly compatible with personal idealism, since consciousness is embraced by reality. Just because it is not a stuff-theory, in the old sense, it cannot be called materialism or energism, for these are logical realisms, i.e., result from the reification of concepts. It is not an idealism, in the old sense, also, *because there may be kinds of variants* of which consciousness is but the one concomitant with that peculiarly organized and differentiated part of reality called the nervous system. Furthermore, this position is pluralistic in regard to the acknowledgment of separate centers of the experiencing.

---

18. V. *Vorlesung über Natur-Philosophie*, p. 325, "Regelung der Reaktionsgeschwindigkeit durch räumliche Bedingungen."
19. *Problems*, p. 93.

The doctrine of functional identity or variancy implies this. I cannot have your experience, i.e., my experience cannot be numerically identical with yours, any more than my body can be your body. This position makes *communication on the basis of interpretation* possible. The monads, if one wishes so to call these "microcosms," thus get their windows through the body and its dynamic relations to other bodies. This agrees with logic, apperception, language, and comparative psychology.

2

Realism and Evolutionary Naturalism
A Reply to Professor Hoernlé*

i

In a recent number of this magazine,[1] Professor Hoernlé selected the positions and arguments of Lloyd Morgan and myself for critical analysis from the point of view of idealism. It was almost hinted that the advocates of naturalism were more familiar with their science that with their philosophy. The article was, in truth, a challenge to the naturalistic movement to defend itself against the double charge of dialectical incompetency and lack of awareness of the rightful approach to theory of knowledge. And yet the article was fair and showed familiarity with much of the material.

The contrast of principle and method brought out by Hoernlé is one of those illuminating things which justify controversy. Sharp divisions in philosophy bring out the problems that must be subjected to exhaustive analysis. While in this instance much of Hoernlé's argument could have been anticipated by those who have read his books and have known his adherence to the main theses of Bosanquet,

* R. W. Sellars, *The Monist* 37 (1927):150-55. Reprinted with the permission of both the author and publisher.
1. *The Monist* (October 1926).

there was yet the advantage of detail. Idealism stands precisely for this and this; and it opposes naturalism on this count and this other count.

The article falls into two parts. The first part is concerned with dialectic or with the general nature of reality and the validity of certain categories, while the second part deals with epistemology. I cannot do better than follow his outline, and I shall quote where the argument demands it.

He begins with a sketch of the first epoch of evolutionism and shows that philosophy has concerned itself more with the *genetic* outlook than with the details of biological theory. He then proceeds to contrast the positions taken by Alexander, Lloyd Morgan, Bergson, and myself. On the whole, Alexander is the thinker who takes evolution most seriously. He has speculative scope and imagination. "What Sellars values in the evolutionary point of view is the aid it lends to a naturalistic theory of mind, by treating mind as a product of evolution in the context of the physical world."

May I point out in this connection that both Lloyd Morgan and Alexander have a more monistic tinge to their thinking than I have. For them, there is an underlying *nisus* to the whole cosmos and this *nisus* gives a unity that is alien to my more pluralistic outlook. I would refuse to say that I take evolution less seriously than they but would admit that I take it more empirically and distributively.

The first problem is this, Where shall we draw the line between the metaphysician and the naturalist? "Indeed, if it is the mark of a 'metaphysician' to go behind the scientifically ascertainable facts of evolution, whether on the biological or the cosmic scale, in the search for a source or cause (agent) of evolution, then even Lloyd Morgan is a metaphysician, and Sellars's type of theory the only genuine 'naturalism.'" Now I quite accept the reality of some such contrast. In an appendix to his *Emergent Evolution,* Lloyd Morgan was good enough to call attention to the difference in our outlook. But I don't like to be refused the name of metaphysician nevertheless. I am not a positivist, who limits himself to scientific facts, for I am a realist and a believer in categories. For me, the task of the philosopher is to analyze concepts and principles and to perform a labor of synthesis.

It is true that I regard nature as a self-sufficient system, that is, as reality. I see no reason to acknowledge an Activity back of the processes of nature as a patterned complex. But surely such an acknowledgment is not the differentia of a metaphysician!

Since I have not hitherto availed myself of the opportunity given me by Lloyd Morgan in his extremely just contrast between his position and my own, I feel it is only right to refer to it here. My query is this, Is not his acknowledgment of an Activity a holdover due to several causes? To what extent the traditions of past religion have entered, he can say better than I. I have a shrewd suspicion that an acknowledgment such as he works with must have a psychological basis, since it does not arise from the objective content of knowledge but is added to it. He seems to admit that the facts known are satisfied by naturalism. But there is a more technical point. Was not past naturalism supposed to be bound up with agnosticism? And it is well known that agnosticism easily allied itself with theism, witness Spencer. If you don't know reality . . . [there is something or somewhat unknown. This is a sort of inheritance that Lloyd Morgan receives and accepts from the Spencer period].* Note the following quotation from *Emergent Evolution* given by Hoernlé: "The more adequately we grasp the *naturalistic and agnostic position,* the more urgent is the call for some further explanation which shall supplement its merely descriptive interpretation." Does Morgan take descriptive interpretation to be penetrative knowledge? Or, in other words, does he look upon a physical system as an agent? Is the physical world a shell or a self-sufficient reality? For my part, the substitution of critical realism for agnosticism seemed to transform naturalism into a new naturalism, which may rightly be called physical realism.

I would reply to Hoernlé, then, that I am a cosmologist and ontologist if not a metaphysician in the literal meaning of that term.

That there are unsurmountable dialectical weaknesses in the admission of emergent novelties appears to Hoernlé a matter of common belief. But I take it that he is speaking here for the objective idealist

* Missing words in the published article make some such reconstruction necessary.

and that pragmatists and realists have long opposed this opinion. The evolutionist has good company. But, of course, this appeal to support is not argument for either side. And clearly the problem is so basic that I cannot do better than refer to my own detailed analysis of time and change in my *Evolutionary Naturalism*. Having this context in mind, I can point out wherein I deny the validity of his refutation of change.

"Creative evolution," writes Hoernlé, "clearly belies the old principle, *Ex nihilo nihil fit*. For it there is always more in the 'effect' (the later stage) than there was in the 'cause' (the earlier stage)." But it seems to me that this old principle is nothing more than the assertion of the principle of causality itself. It is the demand for a ground, or a sufficient reason, for an event. Taken in this general sense, it stands for the denial of the complete origination of being and against absolute beginning. But novelty in the modern sense is always relative beginning. It arises within a system as intrinsic to it. Let it be remembered that the evolutionist affirms only those novelties which are attached to organized stuff and are inseparable from it. Novelty involves its conditions and antecedents. Surely Hoernlé would not take this scholastic principle to be intuitive and unambiguous!

Hoernlé makes much of the phrase, "the universe as a whole." Being a pluralist in the general modern sense in opposition to singularism, I take the universe distributively in my thought as a spatio-temporal system. I would not speak of evolution as applying to the universe as a whole in a unilinear way. The universe is for me a stereometrical system in which changes with different directions may go on simultaneously. I would, indeed, admit that change applies to the universe collectively because it applies distributively. I would even admit that changes reverberate all through the universe in some degree, the degree to be determined empirically. But surely this does not imply organic evolution for the sun or for the sidereal system as a whole. There may be evolution in one locality and devolution in another.

With this introduction, let us examine Hoernlé's argument. "The whole cannot change. . . . It cannot change, because any change introduces something that is, and this, *ex hypothesi,* falls within the whole. The whole, if it changes, was not the whole, but something less." But change does not introduce anything new from outside. If the whole has four dimensions, it is of its very nature to alter. Development is within reality and has its conditions and continuity. This difference of opinion depends upon the starting-point, and I claim that the admission of change within the identity of a system is more in accordance with experience. Ultimately, I suppose, the divergence between critical realist and idealist turns on the acceptance by the former of identity of existence as other than logical identity of universals.

ii

Let us now pass to the problem of the nature of knowledge. Hoernlé is clearly right in his opinion that it is basic to naturalism as a philosophy and not merely a scientific generalization. However, he implies that the naturalist is more a scientist than a philosopher, and has misunderstood and confused problems.

It may be of interest to point out that many American thinkers are seeking to put mind in nature and to avoid the traditional dualisms that have teased philosophy. Hoernlé's charge found me somewhat incredulous, since I had felt myself more philosophic in this matter than Dewey or Woodbridge in that I stressed the importance of epistemology. Had Hoernlé read my *Critical Realism* or my *The Essentials of Philosophy* or the other work in which I devoted my attention to epistemology? In the essays to which he refers I had taken this prior work for granted and the stress was upon the naturalism.

I would put my argument in this way. I have worked both from the side of naturalism to theory of knowledge and from the side of theory of knowledge to naturalism or, if you will, physical realism. And I have found that these two ways of approach reenforced each other. Thus I quite agree with Hoernlé that "if the account given of knowledge as a phenomenon in nature is such that it throws doubt on our knowledge of nature . . . the argument destroys its own basis."[2] Only, I have found that the two ways of approach harmonized. Let me come to detail. "I draw attention, at once, to what is the crucial point, viz., the 'naturalistic' context in which the analysis of mind and knowledge is to be undertaken." But in critical realism my beginning was the context of natural realism, that is, the structure and meanings of experience at the level of perception. In this I have agreed with much of epistemological exploration in this country, England, and Germany. Does natural realism break down under persistent reflection, and does this breakdown lead to idealism or to a more critical type of realism? As a critical realist, I have concerned myself with the second query, which he outlines on page 571, namely, an inquiry into the truth-claim of perceiving, thinking, reasoning *as such*. It has been my endeavor to show that traditional representative realism made certain corrigible errors. And I was pleased to find that Professor Hoernlé was struck by the ingenuity and clearness of my correction. But if knowledge consists in the comprehension of the characteristics of an object by means of, and in terms of, characters held before the attention in the act of knowing, and if such a claim can be tested by such criteria as consistency, guidance, and prediction—and such is the outlook of critical realism as I champion it—wherein am I untrue to the standpoint of epistemology? Is not such knowledge, so tested and interpreted, something that can be sustained by individual minds in responsible relations with their environments? In other words, *knowledge* is inseparably connected with *knowing,* and knowing is a complex act that has its nature and conditions, which must be studied empirically. Will the naturalistic context or, if you will, the content of knowledge cast light on the act of knowing? I believe that it will.

In short, I am certain that I have never confused these two questions in my own mind. And the space I have given to both critical realism and to naturalism as separate investigations is my vindication. It is just possible that Lloyd Morgan in his first systematic work kept the two questions very closely together by his way of approach. I am sure, however, that he saw the difference between them.

May I, in conclusion, again express my belief that such frank

2. P. 570.

criticisms as the one I am answering are very valuable in philosophy. There are too few of them. I await Professor Hoernlé's reply with interest. I hope it will take the form of a criticism of critical realism along the lines sketched by Bosanquet, a criticism that I regard as about the best offered and that I have had in mind in my recent formulations. May there not be cognitional identity between content of knowledge and the characteristics of the object of knowledge without existential identity of thought and object? Had the idealist laid more stress on the existential side, upon the act of knowing and the object of knowing, he would, perhaps, have better understood both the nature of knowledge and its limits.

3

American Critical Realism and British Theories of Sense-Perception *

Part I: G. E. Moore and Gilbert Ryle

i

SOME INTRODUCTORY REMARKS

It is my considered opinion that the American realistic movement of the first three decades of this century explored possibilities as regards the nature of perceiving more systematically than had been the case hitherto. It was motivated by a conviction that idealism had an insecure foundation. And there had been advances in both logic and science. It was time for a fresh effort at foundations.

The new realism, which is usually regarded as the first stage of the endeavor to work out a realistic perspective, though critical realism was actually concurrent, sought to transform the radical empiricism of William James into a presentational realism. Berke-

* *The Philosophy of Physical Realism* (New York: Russell & Russell, 1966). First published in *Estratto Rivista Methodos* 14 (1962). Republished by Russell & Russell, New York, in the *Philosophy of Physical Realism,* chaps. 18 and 19, 1966. Reprinted here with the permission of the author and of Russell & Russell, Publishers, © 1966.

ley's ideas and Hume's impressions were given a new status. This radical move fitted in with the current rejection of Locke's conclusion that perceiving terminates on ideas and does not reach external things so that it must be supplemented by inference and, likewise, of Kant's postulation of things-in-themselves, a position akin to Locke's but more agnostic in import. The trend, in short, was toward an "immediate perception," as can be noted in James, Peirce, and Mach. There was, accordingly, a strong animus against any form of representationalism.

I cannot here go into any detail. It must suffice to say that the new realism was presentationalistic and along the lines of naïve realism. The realm of the "subjective" was excluded as tied in with the traditions of representationalism and the rising tide of behaviorism in psychology was welcomed. The new realism was a bold effort but foundered on its inability to distinguish between an object and its varying appearances. In short, it found it hard to account for error. It would seem that it was gradually adjudged a *tour de force* with good motivations. Somehow, perceiving must be direct and terminate, in some fashion, on external things.

Now it was with this thesis that the critical realists busied themselves. The so-called essence-wing, represented by Santayana, Strong, and Drake, postulated that, in perceiving, an essence was somehow intuited and regarded as embodied in the object perceived. Thus, veridical perceiving involved a literal identity of this kind. But how could this identity be substantiated? How could truth be verified? It is not surprising that those who identified critical realism with the essence doctrine were satisfied with neither the new realism nor critical realism. Something of a stalemate ensued. That is the way things often happen in philosophy.

But, as I have frequently pointed out, I who had given its name to critical realism and had begun to explore the *mechanism of perceiving* in the context of biology and psychology had a quite different theory of what takes place in perceiving. As the years have gone by, I have developed it in considerable detail. I want now to formulate the principles involved. And I shall try to show that epistemology has not been thwarted by an enigma but by retention of a one-sided approach to the mechanism of perceiving that emphasized the stimulus but did not grasp the use of it made by the organism in its response. But has it not been long clear to the biologist that the sense organs help to guide the organism in its adjustment to its environment? The brain, of course, enters the picture with its sensory centers and their interconnections.

As I see it, then, the act, or process, of perceiving rests on a from-and-to movement in which the brain, as an organ of behavior, uses the sensations under the control of the object as guides to the organism's response. This biological analysis corresponds to, and supports, the view that reflection on perceptual experience has long indicated, namely, that *sensory appearings* of the object that is stimulating us and toward which we are responding are used as cues to action and even as means for deciphering features of the object. There is a causal circuit here of the type called in cybernetics a feedback. We dwell upon what attracts our attention. Mental operations of noticing and what Ryle calls "heeding" enter the picture.

It is obvious that there are levels in perceiving. The ordinary animal level is dominated by instinct and the need for quick response. The human level is affected by delayed response, curiosity, and the advent of language and linguistically controlled concepts. What we perceive we can express in such symbols. We indicate position and describe features. Culture has gone on from there with frames and techniques.

But I want to come back to the role of sensations in perceiving. As I see it, they function as *appearings* of the object controlling them to which we are responding. In recent scientific terminology, this means that they are information-carrying. Certainly, they are so used in deciphering the thing to which we are responding. As I have elsewhere put it, we look *"through"* our visual field at the things before us. But birds and other creatures do this admirably. It rests on a biological technique. The camera type of eye focuses light-patterns coming from objects. This is the point of departure for guided response. What man is able to do is to organize this directed awareness in terms of conceptual, categorial distinctions and so have a world of a recognizably continuing sort which confronts him and in which he participates, a world of things.

The essential point to keep in mind is that the mechanism on which this rests makes use of sensations in a from-and-to operation so that they are not terminal but functional in a larger, directed operation. Not to grasp this setting was the mistake of the traditional causal theory of perception. Hence modern philosophy got off to a bad start in a fog of subjectivism, sensationalism, Cartesian dualism, introspectionism, and conceptualism. Sensationalism made sensations terminal in perceiving and so ignored their informational role as appearings of things. Conceptualism made concepts terminal in much the same fashion and so separated them from their applications. The ensuing framework set up quite unnecessary puzzles. Locke resorted to different theories of unperceived things, and Berkeley and Hume sought to reduce the objective import of perceiving to awareness of ideas.

We have already noted how the new realists by a *tour de force* sought to objectify sensations. The only alternative they saw to this was Locke's representationalism. What I am offering is a quite different framework. Critical realism, as I have worked it out, builds on a more adequate idea of the *mechanism* nature worked out. The information fed in through the sense organs to be of survival value had to lead to adjustment. It is clear that the organism in its environmental setting is the unit to keep in mind.

But I must make a long story as short as possible. What I am suggesting is a complete revision of outlook. I can put it this way: Directed perceiving is neither presentational nor representational. In place of presentationalism, which identifies perceiving with the inspectional presence of the object perceived, as in sensationalism, naïve realism, and the new realism, recognition of the mechanism of perceiving leads to a stress on the role of sensations as *appearings,* under external control, of the object we are responding to and, at the human level of delayed response and concern, *heeding* with various degrees of centrally aroused mental, or cerebral, activity. This functional role of sensations is to provide relevant information about the object.

It is better, I take it, to say that the object appears than that it is presented. Appearing is the kind of presentation made possible by means of the sense organs. It is really a remarkable achievement. Much of the condemnation of sense-perception as involving illusions rests on presentational notions. Perceiving is an activity in which cues of all sorts are used and involves learning and what Ryle calls *perception recipes*. But the point to bear in mind is that it is directed at the external thing and that we bring to bear upon it the resources of various sense organs and past experience. The resultant is a verdict—to use Warnock's phrase—or, as I have long called it, a claim.

Since it is the object we are deciphering in this mediated way, it is obvious that we avoid the pitfalls of Locke's kind of representationalism. It is not ideas that we know but the external thing itself. I have the impression that C. D. Broad has not yet quite escaped from the framework that was natural to Locke in a Newtonian age, that is, the traditional, one-sided causal approach. But, surely, the biological unit is the functional from-and-to operation in which sensory appearings are used for guiding and deciphering.

It should be clear now what I mean by saying that critical realism moves between presentationalism and representationalism. It asserts a direct, referential realism in which information is received and used. Unless both vectors are recognized, the act of perceiving, which rests on both, cannot be understood. The job of epistemology is to work out a satisfactory terminology.

If a framework is adequate, it should throw light on traditional puzzles. I shall merely mention here the controversies that have raged around the correspondence theory of truth. In modern philosophy, it has usually been connected with the framework of Locke's representationalism. How, indeed, could we know that our ideas corresponded to external things if we are shut into our ideas? But with our rejection of his representationalism, we secure a different setting. Information is fed to us through our senses, intelligently used. What we achieve in this way is knowledge of the object expressed in propositions about it. The question of truth is essentially that of verification. And there are two dimensions, logical consistency and coherence with other relevant propositions and adequacy of information bearing on the object. We should not set up a mythical comparison but stress the information relevant to the object gained by controlled appearings. The point is that the object discloses itself in observation and that this is the basis of *knowledge about* the object. Truth is but a term for the acceptance of knowledge-claims tested in this fashion.

I have allowed myself remarks on various thinkers, partly to bring out my own analysis by contrast. I am persuaded that Brand Blanshard's rejection of the correspondence theory of truth and his adhesion to the coherence theory reflects the fact that he does not have the kind of analysis of perceiving I have advocated, with its stress on the role of sensations as appearings used as information about the object to which we are responding. As I have said, this analysis moves between presentationalism and representationalism in that it puts controlled *appearings* in place of literal presentation and referential decipherment in place of a mythical relation between an idea as the object of knowledge and a supposedly inferred but unperceived object.

One of the tests of a new framework is the way in which it leads to reformulations of old problems. I have always been as ironic as possible. I have mentioned the rationalistic idealist Blanshard and suggested an improvement in his epistemology. It may be well to point out that Professor Donald Williams has adhered to the new realism because he regards critical realism as representational. But, as I have tried to show, it is referentially direct because it regards perceiving as a complex act in which sensations have a disclosing role to play as controlled *appearings* carrying information. To use the generic term, *ideas* are not terminal but functional. The biological unit involves—as we should expect—a concern for the object which is stimulating the organism and to which adjustment must be made. But the whole complex of early empiricism was, as noted, subjectivistic, introspective, and dualistic. The new realism tried to get objectivity but in too simplistic a fashion. This brings me to the final topic of transcendence. It should be clear by now that transcendence is no magical achievement by a disembodied mind using innate *intensional* capacity, but a resultant of the cooperation of directed response and the use of received information about the object. At the human level, this framework has been given a linguistic expansion in terms of denotative, or referential, terms and descriptive adjectives. But all this will not be understood unless the biological mechanism of the from-and-to complex is appreciated. The act of perceiving rests on both stimulus and response. Sherrington was quite right in emphasizing the importance of the motor element for the development of mind.

If I am right in my analysis of perceiving and its conditions, one can understand why Berkeley and Hume were unable to pass beyond their sense impressions and ideas. If these are taken out of their functional context and made terminal, one cannot get beyond them. Inference has no foundation. But once one supplies the natural framework, learning and inference, as activities, can carry on and give us perception recipes. Satisfactory perceiving is an achievement.

In this paper I am going to examine in considerable detail the positions taken by some outstanding British thinkers. If I take G. E. Moore, Gilbert Ryle, Bertrand Russell, and C. D. Broad as fairly typical, I do not think I shall go far wrong. I have studied H. H. Price carefully, but have the feeling that he is meticulous in description but represents no shift in base.

Now one of my purposes is to reinvigorate empiricism by making it more realistic and more in touch with science. That is the framework I shall have in mind. I think that John Passmore is quite right in pointing out that S. Alexander represented a similar approach. He was much influenced by the new realism, especially by Holt, as he told me. While Russell has kept in touch with science and is critical of the adequacy of the ordinary-language technique, he has been, I hold, too much of a Humeian. Several times in meeting him at Ann Arbor, I tried to get him interested in my analysis of perceiving as involving an integration of stimulus with response in which sensations play a guiding and deciphering role, but he was too dominated by the traditional idea that *percepts* are sensations plus images to get my point. But, surely, perceiving things is not having percepts. Reference, transcendence, and claims, or verdicts, are left out in such a translation. The subjectivistic curtain has come down.

I shall argue that G. E. Moore's type of analysis, which is the substitution of one sentence for another, missed clues that a more biological approach might have given. It encouraged him to set up sense-data as entities and to leave him with the puzzle as to how these are related to things. Thus a phenomenalistic note intruded in his realism. This was already foreshadowed in his famous article, *A Refutation of Idealism*. In 1904, F. C. Sharp and I analyzed it and decided it would not do. When all was said and done, the framework was still Berkeley's. In intention, Moore became increasingly a physical realist but was unable to see how the perceiving of things is achieved. I shall argue that some insight into the complex mechanism on which the act of perceiving rests is needed.

I am particularly interested in Ryle's framework. He makes much of the rejection of Cartesian dualism and flirts with "philosophical behaviorism." It is hardly needful to point out that Cartesian dualism has had small standing in the American realistic movement. J. B. Pratt was its chief defender. It may surprise Ryle to learn that his position resembles John Dewey's in several respects. I have recently written an article aimed at bringing out Dewey's reaction to the realistic movement that confronted his form of pragmatism or instrumentalism. He rejected critical realism as he understood it, largely in the Santayana-Strong-Drake version, and swung to a modified form of the new realism. It was his thesis that traditional epistemology had been tied in with all sorts of false assumptions, such as dualism, the realm of the subjective, representationalism, and so on. The thing to do was to make a fresh start with a new kind of presentationalism more naïve than that of the new realists, a merely experiential presentationalism, *prior to cognition,* which arises only with problems. There was no room in this set-up for the subjective and for any traditional sort of representationalism. The result is a pragmatic empiricism with stress on ideas as ways of reconstructing *experience*. It is clearly a naturalized form of objective idealism with all the latter's dislike of British empiricism. The interchange between Russell and Dewey in the Schilpp volume [on Dewey] is illuminating. I think that Dewey understands Russell's framework while Russell is perplexed by Dewey. Parenthetically, I shall argue that there are, at present, three forms of empiricism: 1) the Hume-Mill type extended into the new realism, Russell's neutral monism and logical positivism; 2) pragmatic empiricism of the instrumentalist type; and 3) realistic empiricism of the kind I have outlined, which I think is more in harmony with science.

But to come back to the agreements between Ryle and Dewey. Both are sour on epistemology in Aesop fashion. Dewey complains of "epistemologs" and Ryle seeks to deflate epistemology in the concluding sections of *The Concept of Mind*. Now I, myself, regard human knowing as a remarkable achievement that deserves careful study. It all begins with a biological technique in which sense organs and sensory centers in the brain receive information of import for behavior. That is their job. Controlled appearings are used to guide and decipher the objects appearing. The act of perceiving rests on this circuit. At the human level, the possibilities in this circuit are developed first by common sense and then by scientific method. I think that ordinary-language analysis gives an excellent reflection of the logic of language in this natural setting. But it seems to have no idea of its foundation. The tantalizing feature of Ryle's work is its linguistic acumen as united with puzzlement about "neat sensations," the role of sensations in sense perception and the reality of images. Like Dewey, he is afraid of the subjective and takes refuge in behaviorism. Now the only remedy, as I see it, is to appreciate the framework indicated by biological mechanisms and face up to the possibility that sensations and images are, quite literally, intrinsic to cerebral activity and function in perceiving and imaging. And behaviorism is a very equivocal term. It was usually methodologically motivated. I am persuaded that an adequate epistemology can aid in seeing the whole picture. If the act of perceiving is a from-and-to operation in which controlled appearings are used to adjust to, and even decipher, the object appearing, the cerebral location of consciousness must be thought out in categorial terms. There is an "in-ness" here of a special kind. I have myself spoken of consciousness as a natural isolate and postulated a double knowledge of the brain as functioning. Certainly, those who reject Cartesian dualism, as do Dewey and Ryle, must face these complexities. And the starting-point is an adequate notion of the biological foundation of perceiving, something that Berkeley, at his time, could not possess.

I have the impression that some Australian philosophers are shifting base and reaching a perspective similar to mine. Dr. Hirst of Glasgow seems to be making a similar exploration. The outcome will be an integration of epistemology and ontology along evolutionary lines. That, I take it, is what philosophy can contribute to the clarification of science. It is my thesis that realistic empiricism is more consonant with science than are phenomenalistic empiricism or Dewey's prag-matic empiricism. And if the scientific outlook on the world is to prevail, such an integration is essential. I do not think that philoso-phers need complain that they are left with no task of a magnitude sufficient to call out their energies and restore their self-respect.

My purpose, therefore, in writing this paper is to confront British theories of sense perception with what I regard as ignored develop-ments within the American realistic movement. Dewey's pragmatism was largely brushed aside in a conventional way without realization that the position he took was a part of the realistic debate. Attention was, thereupon, turned in empirical circles to such things as logical atomism, logical positivism, and the rather cryptic pronouncements of Ludwig Wittgenstein. In curious and devious ways all this led to ordinary-language analysis. It would take me too far afield to discuss Wittgenstein. Let us take the word *fact*. To me, a fact is a case of disclosed knowledge about things mediated by directed infor-mation. For Wittgenstein, facts constitute *what is*. I am quite aware of the greater flexibility in the use of language introduced by *meta* procedures. That logic and philosophy have been technically enriched I have not the slightest doubt. Nevertheless, it is my opinion that epistemology was, unfortunately, neglected. When Carnap jumped to physicalism, it was more a shift of base than an epistemology. Of the former logical positivists, Herbert Feigl seems to me best to sense the import of critical realism. Sensations are, for him, no longer terminal for meaning or for knowledge. I have great respect for Ayer's epistemological acumen and will look forward to any comment. I judge that he still sees no alternative between phenomenalism and Locke's unperceived things. But, if I am right, perceiving is a directed deciphering of things by means of sensations controlled to carry information. Ideas are put to use by the organism.

This whole discussion shows how many competing approaches there are. And how easy it is to get bewildered! The essential thing, as I see it, is to get an adequate framework. I shall now test mine by employing it in a series of running comments on G. E. Moore, Gilbert Ryle, Bertrand Russell, and C. D. Broad. The outcome will be important, for I quite disagree with such an able popularizer as Walter Kaufmann that the alternatives in philosophy today are logical positivism, existentialism, and ordinary-language analysis. I have the impression that logical positivism has shot its bolt, that ordinary-language analysis, healthy as it is, moves on the surface and needs supplementation, and that existentialism is a cultural emphasis with no clear epistemology and ontology to back it. Since this latter is chiefly a Continental affair, I must here disregard it. It, of course, rejects empiricism. To use Kaufmann's terms, I belong to traditional philosophy and, I hope, to its growing point in the present. My stress is on problems. As I remember them, none of my contemporaries thought of going back to Locke or to Kant, except as students. The idea was to press forward, to make a fresh start. If only a more adequate analysis of perceiving could be hit upon, Locke, Hume, and Kant could be bypassed. And I was gradually led to explore the possibilities of a position between presentationalism and representationalism resting on the referential use of sensations in the perceptual act.

Now I think that all this hangs together. It connects the function of the sense organs and sensory centers with the objective import of perceiving, and it shows how transcendence and correspondence are achieved. What the human mind has done is to develop the possibilities implicit in the very mechanism of perceiving.

ii

G. E. MOORE

In his little essay called *Visual Sense-data,* contributed to the book *British Philosophy in Mid-Century,* Moore speaks of a relation to be called R between sense-datum and object. And he concludes his essay by expressing his belief that no philosopher has explained clearly what the relation R is "where it is not identity."

There is much doubt these days as to the existence of sense-data as nonmental entities that are intuitable. Ryle, for instance, rejects them. And they have never had any standing in American realism. But the empirical base of the theory is that perceiving involves some sort of mediation. The physical object is not just intuited.

The analysis of perceiving I have offered in my introductory remarks suggests a reformulation. Sensations arise in the brain under the control of the external object and play the role of appearings of it in the setting of directed response. There is a causal circuit here so that the relation R of the sensation to the object perceived is a functional one expressive 1) of its informational status, and 2) of its referential use in perceiving. In this circuit, the relation R is that of causally controlled appearing and its application in a guiding and deciphering way to that which is appearing. All this represents a neat little device worked out by nature at the biological level. There is no need to dwell on the sensations for their own sake. Their role in the circuit is automatically assigned. Birds, bees, and humans look through their visual fields at the objects manifesting themselves. The traditional causal theory of perception isolated sensations from this functional setting. The emphasis should be upon learning and adjustment, upon perceptual recipes. And man lifts himself to a more reflective level in which guidance gives way to cognitive claims. But, as I shall try to show in connection with Ryle, sensuous deciphering of objects is a prelude to conceptual cognition.

I thought it wise to give some indications of my theory of this mediating relation, R, which baffled Moore, though speaking in terms of sensation rather than of sense-data. I am inclined to hold that

Moore did not immerse himself sufficiently in modern biological and psychological thought but trusted too much in an analysis of sense perception as something reflectively perspicuous. I do not think that biological and psychological knowledge alone is sufficient. There must be, in addition, the pressure of epistemological dilemmas. One must be harassed by the query, How do we *achieve* the perceiving of external things? One tradition in psychology stresses *percepts* (*Gestalt*) while another emphasizes behavior. My reply to both Dewey and Ryle in defense of epistemology is to the effect that there are unavoidable questions as to the nature, conditions, and reach of human knowing. One must show how referential transcendence and informational correspondence are achieved. The flaw in ordinary-language analysis seems to me to be that it ignores these foundations. The logic of grammar is important, but the insertion of language into perceiving must be explained. Realistic empiricism seems to me to bridge the gap and make science completely relevant. So I have some sympathy with Russell's protests, though I think that his own epistemology is quite inadequate.

It will be recalled that I stated that modern philosophy started with assumptions of subjectivism, dualism, sensationalism, and conceptualism. All this made a bad heritage. There flowed from it the twin problems of proving an external world and reaching other minds. G. E. Moore wrestled with these dilemmas, as in his famous proof of the external world by show of hands. But, as I see it, if perceiving attains it object by means of the from-to circuit and we are left more with the job of learning, that is, of assembling relevant information, there is really no such problem as that which Locke and Kant envisaged. Here I agree with Dewey but reject his *experiential presentationalism,* his modification of the new realism. If my analysis of the mechanism of perceiving is correct, perceiving is directly concerned with external things but is guided by information received from them. This analysis moves between presentationalism and representationalism in that the act of perceiving uses sensations rather than terminating on them.

My thesis will, then, be that Moore's common-sense approach was not analytic enough because it was not alive to cues of all sorts. Bluff common sense may guard against speculative vagaries, such as Bradley's, but tends to be dominated by a traditional framework. I have always felt that Moore's sense-data were a recognition that perceiving is mediated and were, thus, an obstacle in the way of the simplicity of logical positivism. Unfortunately, his sense-data got between him and the object perceived. But he wrestled valiantly with the situation.

What I have admired in British philosophy is not its scope and framework—these have been too limited—but its pertinacity. And I suppose that Moore helped to set standards here. But his character and attitudes have been so fully discussed that I need make no comment. He seems to have been a sort of institution. What value this paper may have will be, in part, the presentation of a divergent approach in another area of the English-speaking world. I shall now proceed to examine Moore's treatment of sense perception with this aim in view.

There has been considerable discussion as to whether Moore's emphasis was upon beliefs or upon the use of words. I find both factors present, as we should expect. For instance, in the essay I have mentioned, he points to the contextual use of the word *looks*. You may be able to say with truth 1) that the distant boat looks much smaller than the near one, and 2) that the distant boat "looks as if it were" much larger than the near one. In the first case, I suppose, looks is based on simple appearing while, in the second, more learning and judgment are involved. Language reflects the complexity of the act of perceiving.

One point Moore is clear about is that *two objects* are involved in such a statement as *"This* is a penny." He rejects Ayer's interpretation to the effect that the visual sense-datum is the only object about which I am making the assertion. To say a visual sense-datum *is* the penny would be silly. Here Moore falls back on the Russell gambit of a definite description as against acquaintance with. "This" is then short for a definite description and refers to two objects, though in different senses. I am referring to, and denoting, both the visual sense-datum and the physical penny. Hence the acuteness of the problem about R, the relation between them. Moore would have liked his sense-datum to be on the surface of the penny, but could not convince himself that such was the case. The consequence was a frank frustration.

We shall note that Ryle moves in the direction of presentational, or naïve, realism. He is inclined to play down sensations in vision except as dazzles. In fact, his paradigm for sensations appears to be something of the nature of tickles. Linguistically, he distinguishes between "neat" sensation words in the context of aches and pains and our sensory terminology when sensations are being used in perceiving common objects like haystacks. We catch glimpses of robins and of autos moving. The ordinary procedure is to describe sensations in this context. They are connected with looks and glimpses. But I have the impression that Ryle has no clear theory of the role of sensations in this objectively oriented perceiving. But of that later. Neat sensation-words do not here apply, and Ryle is somewhat skeptical of the sophisticated usage of physiological psychology. It is as though he holds that *seeing an object* is an achievement that just must be accepted. In this respect, he resembles Dewey and the new realists. Russell was to call him a naïve realist. But, of course, this is sophisticated naivité, as S. Alexander pointed out to me in defense of his new realism.

While, then, Moore affirms, again and again, both his common-sense beliefs and his conviction that there are entities to be called sense-data, though admitting that he cannot bring them together, Ryle launches out on a careful study of the logic of words in ordinary discourse. Now I, myself, think this is an excellent procedure, only that it should be supplemented by a careful study of the mechanisms involved. Seeing a thing in the sense of visually perceiving a thing is an achievement, analogous to winning a race. If my own analysis is correct, it involves the use of the visual field in a guiding and deciphering way connected with interested response. We look *through* the visual field at the object controlling it. There is learning and the application of conceptual meanings at the human level. Only then do we see haystacks. But a blind man cannot see them; he lacks the visual field. It should not be surprising that, since our interest is in the achievement, we employ such terms as looks and appears when our attention shifts to conditions. The act of perceiving is not a bare intuition but a complexly mediated achievement.

But to come back to Moore. What is the function of *this* when we say "This is a penny"? Surely, we have here perceptual language. It is connected with an achievement. I can expand the sentence and say that this thing which I am looking at and which I can point to and even take hold of is a penny. Reflectively, I may add that it is manifested through my eyes and the visual field and that I see it by the use of visual sensations. But this reflective addition concerns the mechanism of visual perceiving rather than the achievement. Only so far as *this* includes a sense of the activity of selecting has it this kind of thickness. But I can see no good reason to speak of two objects. It is because his sense-data are a kind of object that Moore has the difficulty. Ryle is more nearly right; but he does not tell us how the perceptual achievement is obtained. He is rightly afraid that scientific sophistication with its stress on the neurological base will lose itself in a form of Cartesian dualism. Dewey was similarly afraid of a *subcutaneous mind* from which one could not escape. In both cases the jump was to "philosophical behaviorism." What I have been arguing is that the alternative is to understand the role of sensations in the complete from-and-to act of perceiving.

Only once did I have the opportunity of talking over perceiving with Moore and then his position seemed to me a strange blend of phenomenalism and realism. We could not really communicate because he knew little about my position. I had the impression that he was a forthright sort of person who had felt that idealistic locutions were rather silly, if not monstrous. I do not think that he was much concerned with the light science could throw on perceiving. I agree that science has tended to take the causal-stimulus approach and reproduce Locke. It was well, therefore, to have Moore stress the fact that we do perceive things, even though sense-data got in his way. Ryle, as we have noted, stressed the achievement while dropping sense-data. How, then, handle sensations? He may not have noted it, but he was wrestling with the same problem that had bothered Woodbridge and Dewey. Both tended to do away with sensations in perceiving. Taken by themselves, they tended to be a *tertium quid,* to be termini rather than functional aids. What was needed was a shift in perspective.

The point is so important for epistemology that I shall press it at the danger of some repetition. Moore, I take it, was nearer right than the logical positivists with their phenomenalism. He was sure that perceiving concerned itself with things but was somehow mediated. But his theory of intuited sense-data was unfortunate. The truth is, rather, that there is a sensory factor playing an informative role in the responsive and directed act of perceiving. There are not two objects symbolized by *this,* but the one object that we call the penny. Yet the referential *this* is recognizably presented sensuously. It is not just, itself, intuited. Once we fully appreciate the foundation of external perceiving we grasp the technique involved and realize that it is the function of sensations to disclose objects. When this is realized, we see that we are *between* traditional presentationalism and traditional representationalism.

Warnock's little book on Berkeley is illuminating. He recognizes that Berkeley is engrossed with the immediacy of *looks* in vision and falls short of verdicts to the effect that it is an orange on the table that we claim to see. Like Ryle, he banks on linguistic declaration. But, like Ryle, he has no clear idea of the *mode* of the realistic achievement. That, I take it, is the shortcoming of the ordinary-language technique. But a linking of human perceiving with animal psychology might well have directed attention to the mechanisms involved. Man but embroiders this starting-point and develops its possibilities conceptually. In him, referential transcendence supports a world of atoms and of stars. But his peep-hole remains observation of a sensory sort.

A word finally on *analysis.* This became a slogan. It meant a rejection of airy speculation and a stress on careful scrutiny. So far, so good. Was it not equivalent to a critical attitude, a concern with carefully formulated problems? But the technique employed was, I think, too linguistic. In science, there is always the search for problems and hypotheses relevant to them. And, for me, philosophy was continuous with science. It, however, asked questions that no special science had taken up, such as the nature of perceiving and the standing of truth. But it would be foolish to ignore the framework of science. It was clear to me that something had been missed by philosophy, perhaps because of the holdover of old assumptions in it. The promising thing was to drop dualism, subjectivism, sensationalism, and conceptualism, all dated, and to try to develop a fresh eye. As I have tried to show, Dewey sought to do this in his reaction to the American realistic movement but did not get the right clue. In certain regards he was, I think, ahead of Russell, who kept to Hume too closely. What I tried to contribute was a better analysis of the mechanism of perceiving, which emphasized the mediating role of the subjective and the brain. The brain is an organ of behavior but can perform this function only as it is guided by the sensory centers and the messages that come to them. In point of fact, the brain seems to have developed as a locus of such integration. But it also had the job of adjustmental response to perform. I would not be surprised if neurologists would be aided by such a point of departure. It involves levels in which new capacities are added to old ones. Here the cortex becomes the organ of intelligence. I respect computers but I still respect the ingenuity of nature even more. But I must not here consider the mind-brain problem in detail.

With this outlook, it can be seen why I felt that Moore's analytic technique of translation was insufficient. It led him sometimes to speak as though the sense-datum was the grammatical subject in perceptual linguistics, sometimes as though the material thing was. I do not see how his technique could give the needed clue. I doubt that the act of perceiving, which seems to me very complex, is analytically transparent to common sense. I would recommend the philosopher to immerse himself in biological and psychological knowledge about sense perception while keeping his epistemological demands on the alert. His contribution will stem from that alertness. He will find that neurologists tend to think of ideas in Lockean terms while psychologists will talk of *percepts* rather than of *perceiving*. What I like about Moore and Ryle is their dogged stress on perceiving as an achievement. The fault I find in them is their lack of concern with mechanisms and modes. I suspect that engrossment with language has in some measure dulled their sensitivity to such traditional problems as information-base, reference, transcendence, and correspondence. That these tie in together and support one another when the proper framework is discovered is a confirmation.

To repeat. Phenomenalistic empiricism of the vintage of Hume and Mill never got a grip on the physical world and its categorial constitution. Pragmatic empiricism swung away from epistemology and ontology and devoted itself to the instrumental value of ideas. In its own setting, I have great respect for Dewey's logic of inquiry. It is its framework that I reject. Curiously enough, Russell's logic shows analogous limitations when it is confronted by "contrary-to-fact" statements and assertions about dispositional properties, as the logical positivists began to discover. These reflect our *categorial thought* about the world that we begin to explore in sense perception. I do think that philosophy has been showing a capacity for self-correction in these matters somewhat similar to that which exists in science. It would be my thesis that realistic empiricism will offer an adequate framework.

I am now going to examine Ryle's position. I have already indicated my line of criticism along with my recognition of his technical improvements on many points. The grammar of language must be taken seriously. I do think it reflects our responsive knowledge of the world. Language and thought are intertwined. Those who have envisaged an ideal sense-datum language, like Russell and some of the logical positivists, did not realize that sensations are only points of departure for considered exploration. They give cues in the service of learning. Even, as Ryle points out, perceiving involves learning and use of perception recipes. At the level of science, the use of observation is still more complicated technically. Theory is a conceptual affair directed at the world and employing observation in confirmatory decipherments and denials. As Galileo saw, science is an affair of interrogating nature.

It is with regret that I have had to set aside the careful descriptive work on perception of H. H. Price. As I understand it, he starts with sense-data, much as Russell and Moore did, and asks himself how they *belong* to material things. This is Moore's query of the relation R. If my analysis is correct, they do not "belong" but, taken as sensations, they are under responsible causal control by things via sense organs and sensory centers and are used as *appearings* in the responsive act of perceiving. I shall have something more to say about this when I come to discuss C. D. Broad.

iii

GILBERT RYLE

While I shall refer to points in Ryle's *Concept of Mind,* I shall concentrate on his analyses in *Dilemmas* and in his contribution to *Contemporary British Philosophy.*

He points out that we have the ordinary words of perceptual detection under very good control long before we leave the nursery. The primary emphasis is on *what* we perceive. Interiorization, as the psychologists call it, comes much later. There is no primitive prior stage of introspection. Ryle points out that it is a later stage when children begin to talk about the act of perceiving, the way things look and sound to us, and the conditions governing the different classes of sights, felt temperatures, and heard sounds.

In his *Concept of Mind,* he raises the question of the status of "glimpses" and "looks." It is clear that these are not entities but episodes in perceiving. We do not here use "neat" sensations words but terms in connection with what we are observing. I take this to be in harmony with my analysis of perceiving. Sensations are here functioning within a referential activity. But I do not think it follows that the psychologist cannot inhibit this activity and study the sensations involved, in a sophisticated way, under laboratory conditions. The sensations are then taken out of the context of perceiving something. I have the impression that Ryle is so concerned with perceiving as an achievement that he tends to ignore the factors in the achievement and comes near to the naïve realism of which Russell speaks. I suspect that the ordinary-language approach has this failing. It picks up results and examines their logical grammar and does not probe into the operations involved. The critical realist tries to hold the two perspectives in mind. Glimpses, looks and *verdicts* are two phases of perceiving. In verdicts, that is, in perceptual judgments, we denote and characterize the object perceived. But looks and glimpses are in solution, so to speak, as preconditions. As we noted, Warnock accuses Berkeley of never passing beyond sensory appearances. These constitute his sensible things. But the realistic empiricist recognizes that sensory *appearings* are used in the complete act as having objective import for guiding and deciphering. If they did not have this import they would be of no value to the organism. Certainly, the referential characterization of external things would have no responsible foundation. What I have been calling attention to is the ingenuity of the device developed in nature and exploited most fully by man. Explicit cognition is, of course, a human achievement supervening on guided behavior in animal life.

As a good empiricist, Ryle rejects the views of some mathematicians and of those who wish to "depreciate mundane beliefs in favor of supramundane beliefs" and defends a critical empiricism. I am one with him in this stand. While there is no hallmark stamped on veridical perceiving, the very notion of counterfeiting implies genuine coins. The appeal is to vigilance. I would argue that the stress should be on learning and self-correction. Common sense goes far in this direction and science goes farther still. C. S. Peirce challenged the Cartesian, unmotivated doubt. In this I think he was quite right. Russell went too far in the Cartesian direction, at first, under the influence of his mathematical rationalism. Santayana, likewise, pushed skepticism to the extreme and fell back on animal faith. I think that Ryle has moved in the right direction but that his treatment needs supplementation.

The job of the empiricist is not to prove an external world while starting with subjectivism. It is, rather, to confirm the beliefs involved in perceiving and action and to work out the mechanisms on which they rest.

Ryle seems to be a little afraid of the body. Somewhat like Dewey, he fears a subcutaneous mind. The idea is that there is danger in an approach that concentrates on what goes on in the body. The question too easily becomes: *What happens to us* when we see trees? But this is to neglect the fact that the body is engaged in adjustment to its environment. I am not one of those who ignore what goes on in the brain. But, surely, the brain has a job to do. It is in the circuit from stimulus to response. Ryle is quite right in maintaining that it is the trees that we see. The point is, how is this accomplished? It is not a case merely of something happening to us. Such an assumption was the flaw in subjectivism and the traditional causal approach. Instead, we are doing something, making use of the information carried to us, taking our controlled sensations to be glimpses of their external controls.

Just because he, somewhat like Moore, is not fully alert to this from-and-to foundation of perceiving, Ryle tends to shift to what may be called a disembodied "consciousness." He is, of course, quite right in his assertion that our ability to have perceptual experiences of the achievement-sort does not depend on esoteric knowledge about our insides. But our ability to understand this kind of experience may depend upon some knowledge of the mechanism underlying perceiving, and this involves some idea of the functional working of the nervous system as it connects stimulus with response. It has long been my thesis that early empiricism missed this clue and wandered in the mists of sensationalism. Even logical positivism started with this gambit. As nearly as I can make out, Carnap shifted his base to *physicalism* because of the scientific inadequacy of his former doctrines. But he still looked down on epistemology. Now I make no bones about it. I am professionally a philosopher who always kept in touch with science. The question I asked myself was this, What light can new developments in biology and psychology throw upon perceiving as an achievement? Can a new framework be set up that involves a "Copernican Revolution" from dualism and subjectivism? The point is that Kant resorted to *a priori* machinery in his own endeavor because he did not grasp the role of sensations as controlled disclosures of external things and was, accordingly, led to construct a phenomenal world. The stress, I take it, should be on exploratory learning rather than on construction.

But, to return to Ryle, I suspect that he is nearer to Moore and the British tradition than he realizes. Consciousness, as open to the philosopher's analysis, must give the answers. The transempirical and the esoteric cannot greatly help. At most, he compounds for a conjunction of psychological and physiological reports.

Of course, *having* a certain kind of experience, such as seeing an object, must be a point of departure for reflection. But reflection may well call attention to many *conditions,* such as the use of the eyes, esoteric knowledge of the working of the nervous system, and so forth. Only after all this has been noted, may a *theory* arise as to what goes on in perceiving. Such a theory does not displace the perceptual experience and its claims, but may well throw light upon it.

As we should expect, Ryle is well aware of the difficulties in the traditional causal approach, which made seeings and hearings concluding stages of a chain-process ending in the body. This perspective made sensations and images terminal. And it implied that these were the primary objects of knowledge. As we have noted, in the United States, Woodbridge and Dewey reacted by denying sensations, much as Ryle tends to do. But is there not an alternative? Do not visual sensations, in seeing, function in a directed activity in which they become glimpses and looks? That is, they do not stand out in this context as "neat" because they are being used in a directed act. We look through our visual field at the object that interests us. That is, we use our visual field as a condition of seeing the objects to which we are responding and to which we are alerted. We come here to the primary epistemological question of the information-giving capacity of sensations. If they are *appearings* they can be so used. But to so use them involves no denial of their existence. And a psychology not interested in epistemology arrives at percepts rather than at perceiving.

What I have sought to put in place of the traditional causal approach with its terminus in the body is the *circuit.* Surely, sense organs developed to be of use in the organism's adjustments to its surroundings. Sensations as appearings are surrogates of the objects appearing and give us cues of supplementary kinds. What a battery of sensory appearings we possess! There is integration, learning, the working out of "perception recipes." I have never liked the term, *messages.* It is too anthropomorphic. It assumes that there is something that receives them and decodes them. What we have is more of the nature of an exploitation of indications. At its lowest level, it is of the nature of integration of sensory currents with motor responses attuned to them. But the germ is there, ready to hand, for a more explicit decipherment. At the human level we easily pass from glimpses and looks to directed assertions. In both cases, there is operating the return circuit of concern for the external thing. It will, I hope, be remembered that this analysis moves between terminal presentationalism and postulated and untestable representationalism. It is the very nature of ideas to have cognitive value.

Ryle is, therefore, quite right in saying that there is something drastically wrong with the whole program of trying to schedule my seeing the tree as either a physiological or a psychological end-stage in the body. As a living thing, the body has the job of concern with, and adjustment to, its surroundings. The emphasis should be upon the role of sensations in this activity. My thesis would be that they mediate perceiving as a directed achievement. As I see it, this is a referential affair expressive of the cooperation of directed response and relevant information. Only as we understand the twofold mechanism involved, the receiving and using pertinent information under control can we appreciate the nature of the achievement in the seeing of the things around us, a framework upon which science builds microscopically and macroscopically. I am inclined to hold that the comprehension of this foundational mechanism is the point of departure for any adequate notion of *mind*. Only as we perceive things can we pass to the higher level of manipulable symbols about them.

This kind of realistic empiricism outflanks idealism, phenomenalism, and positivism. We are not shut into an envelope called consciousness, which we cannot transcend. The very unit of consciousness is an act of guided reference made possible by a biological mechanism. Language carries on from this starting-point so that we can talk *about* stars and atoms. The grammar of language has this setting. I think that very much is being done in the way of clarification. But I am concerned that epistemological foundations were not adequately worked out. The ingenuity of life was not fully appreciated. One still heard of the transempirical and of the meaninglessness of trying to transcend something called experience. But if we take the act of perceiving as a unit of consciousness, it is devoted to achieving transcendence in the only feasible way, a union of responsive reference and fed-in information. And not only does this approach help to solve traditional problems, such as those which stymied Locke, Hume, and Kant, but it gives clues for a naturalistic theory of the rise and role of consciousness. It is simply foolish for the empiricist to start out with the dogma that consciousness is alien to the physical world. It must be correlated with emergent activities. And so far as I can make out, feelings and sensations are "natural isolates" intrinsic to cerebral processes. Dualism has had many motivations, which must be carefully studied and done justice to. One of them, which manifests itself in "philosophical behaviorism" is the epistemological confusion of descriptive fact with the object. The act of perceiving is not, itself, the object perceived, though it achieves descriptive knowledge of it. I am one of those who hold that an adequate epistemology will be a great help in all these matters. It will give a framework for thought.

Now, as Ryle sees, language ties in with, and extends, perceptual achievements. These can be noted and confirmed by others. In this connection, his remarks on chess players and athletic coaches are illuminating and quite to the point. Mental activity is one with heeding and taking care. *Knowing how* is openly displayed, and it is recognized that it rests on learning.

But learning involves sensory guidance. And so we come back to the role of sensations again. These operate in both knowing how and knowing *that*. In knowing that, we are working with propositions about. We pass from looks and glimpses to referential verdicts.

A gambit dear to the heart of idealists is that of starting with sensations and adding interpretations. We are then supposed to get something objective. There are many variations on this theme. As Bosanquet put it, extremes meet. It is not a far cry from logical positivism, with its emphasis on possible sensations and the definition of meaning in terms of sensory confirmation, to idealism of the Berkeley type. In what sense can the table in the next room be said to exist if we do not see it? These questions have been threshed out in detail of late. I have argued that, even in perceiving what is present to the percipient, the object is not given in the way sensations are. These are given under the control of the object, but the object, itself, is regarded as appearing and as being responsively selected and described. This gives the object standing coordinate with the percipient. I take this to be the basis of what Berkeley calls absolute existence and rejects.

Ryle proceeds to demolish the "interpretation" move in the following way. The initial sensations, the colors and sounds, collapse into internal states. And, as such, they become *screens* between observers and external things. Woodbridge and Dewey rejected sensations for much the same reason. If a primary cognition terminates on them, we are left with a subjective, cortical, subcutaneous mind. As Ryle puts it, they come to have the status of internal events and so cannot be equated with the attributes of external things.

Now I would argue that sensations are used in a complex perceptual act as having informational value. They are treated as relevant appearings and thus points of departure for decipherments of their external controls taken as objects. As I see it, this is the mechanism nature worked out. It seems to have been too subtle for philosophers to grasp. The reason for this was that their minds were dominated by preconceptions along dualistic, subjectivistic, and introspective lines. As I see it, Ryle has sought to cast these aside but has not yet quite grasped the alternative.

Intent on bringing out his dilemma, he argues that we cannot conceptualize perceiving along lines suitable for optics and neurology. I take it that he means that these sciences concern themselves with sensations as events, not with the *use* made of them in perceiving. This may well be the case, for scientists are specialists. But biologists and psychologists must, surely, have in mind the full economy of the situation. Ryle rightly maintains that "seeing" is an achievement concerned with what is outside the body. But he seems to have no clear idea of how this achievement is consummated. He even seems to take the body as a sort of enclosed volume. But it is a complex of functional activities concerned with both internal conditions and external conditions. The special sense organs are devoted to the latter. The sensations in the visual area are points of departure for motor response. Primitive eyes are merely directional in function, while camera-type eyes present detailed patterns. The act of perceiving rests on the use of this information to guide the organism. It is an integrated act that could hardly get going if it were broken into two separate steps: 1) a cognition of sensations as terminal, and 2) the further step of inferring that these entities had import for something outside the organism. No; there is a unified movement from stimulus to response. Even like the birds, we look through our visual field at the objects. Our primary concern is not with the visual field but with what it discloses. As Ryle himself points out, children first learn the vocabulary of what is perceived, just, as I may remark, the baby looks around for the rattle he has dropped. In short, perceiving rests on the use of sensations in response to external things. If they had no relevance to use, of what value would the sense organs be?

The traditional causal approach was misleading, for it did not have in mind the complete circuit. Entities were set up, or abstracted, and the quite false problem, such as Moore's of the relation, R, between sense-data and material things ensued. Or Price's of how sense-data *belong* to things. As I see it, the complete act of perceiving uses sensations as appearings of the object being responded to, which means that they are taken to be informative and of value in deciphering it. It is this role which traditional presentational theories missed. To recognize the informing role of sensations is to move between presentationalism and representationalism. Kant did no better by regarding the sense-manifold as having no deciphering import for things-in-themselves.

But to come back again to Ryle. The next point he makes is that sense impressions do not represent a factor that is a component in what we perceive and in the content of perceptual judgments. We do not regard ourselves as perceiving our sensations. Quite right. But it does not follow that they are not components of the *act* of perceiving, functioning in the decipherments achieved. There are, of course, levels here. The lower animals are guided in their behavior, while man rises to the stage of conceptual descriptions founded on sensory cues and indications. The sense impression as such does not function as a component of the object but as a factor in the complex act. We read off, as it were, features of the object from indications in the sensory appearance. It is in this way that perceiving, as an achievement, is mediated.

As we should expect, Ryle is dubious with respect to the present appeal to camera plates and phonograph records. The reason for this doubt, of course, is that there is seldom any indication as to the role of such patterns in perceiving. If there are records produced in the brain, how are these used in perceiving? My analysis of the from-and-to circuit involved in perceiving gives, I take it, the proper clue.

This dilemma is clearly similar to that which confronted the old telephone-exchange metaphor. How are incoming messages received and used? There is no mysterious operator within to make connections. To use Ryle's phrase, there is no ghost within the machine. The answer is that there is a functional unity operating here. It is the very nature of response to be guided by the stimulus-pattern. In looking, for example, my eyes are adjusted to foveal demands, so that I look sharply at the external thing through a definite visual field. Much of this achievement is automatic, but I can seek the best distance and point of view. It is in this context that an interiorized self with criteria and demands supervenes. Adjusting a microscope illustrates the techniques that go with "perception-recipes."

Having been frustrated in his analysis of perceiving by finding no role there for sensations in seeing as an achievement, Ryle is led to challenge the technical theory of sensations in the biological sciences. He admits tickles, pains, feelings, and the like. But these are more or less acute and localizable in particular parts of the body. We have them as episodes. In this connection he has some good remarks on Berkeley's tendency to oversimplification. But as regards the special senses concerned with the outer world, my objection still holds. He thinks of the organism more as a volume than as a center of guided activities. But perceiving through distance-reception is the crux. And he is so nearly right in noting looks and glimpses rather than "neat" sensations. In other words, in perceiving our vocabulary reflects the functioning of the sensation in the perceptual act.

What all this leads up to is the fact that, for some reason, sensations have been looked upon as *screens* rather than as having the function of disclosure. Traditional empiricism tended to make sensations terminal as mental objects. Deciding that this stance supported subjectivism, Woodbridge and Dewey threw out the baby with the bath. They rejected sensations and turned in the direction of naïve realism. Ryle is, as I see it, doing much the same.

But why should sensations be looked upon as screens? Is it not more plausible to hold that they carry information and are actually used as *appearings* relevant to what is being perceived? I have argued that this was the device nature worked out. Recognition of it enables epistemology to move between presentationalism and representationalism in that controlled appearings disclose the object of the act of perception. It is, from the first, the external thing that we are concerned with. This gives us the *epistemological monism* the American new realists demanded, but not in a presentational form. The act of perceiving is referentially direct but mediated by sensory factors that have cognitive value. This cognitive value rests on their causal connection with the object. In this context, the recent stress on camera and recordings has point. It is the role of sensation in the perceptual act that has not been understood.

It follows from this analysis that we are on the wrong track when we start with sensory data and either regard them as screens or as bases of inference to an external world. Both moves result in blind alleys.

But, in one place, Ryle hints at what he calls sensuous thinking as a possibility. What I speak of as guiding and deciphering is, as I see it, of this nature. Sensuous thinking is the employment of sensations in the task of the disclosures for which they are fitted. To use a metaphor, it is sort of reading off indications contained in the sensations. When I look at this table before me through my visual field, I can spell out patterns and relations and positions. This sensuous thinking rests on the cognitive value of my sensations. It automatically gives perceiving objective import. Conception supervenes to make this explicit and predicative. And man is launched into the logic of assertion and description. Language begins to dominate. But I do think that sensuous thinking, or the use of sensations as indicative in a referential response, is the foundation.

Ryle is really turning his back on old gambits such as the one-way causal approach into the organism, the use of sensations as bases of a mysterious inference to an outside world, and the rest. In his brief flirtation with sensuous thinking he is, I believe, on the right track. In the directed act of perceiving, sensations are used as informative. Learning and perception-recipes carry on responsibly.

Like Dewey, Russell, and myself, Ryle is opposed to Cartesian dualism. But the danger here is that of oversimplification. It is so easy to lapse into "philosophical behaviorism." Much depends on one's epistemology. I have long argued that Dewey's attempt to reform philosophy resulted from an inadequate epistemology close to that of the new realism and, like it, fearful of the subjective. Much depends upon one's analysis of perceiving as an act able to achieve external reference. One can then do justice to the complexity of the act and interiorize our knowledge of it, while recognizing its objective import. I suggest that such an epistemological advance will aid the neurologist.

In the continuation of this study of British theories of sense perception, I shall take up Russell and C. D. Broad. I shall argue that Russell is still too much of a Humean and Broad too much of a Lockean. The implication is that neither has quite grasped the biological mechanism of perceiving.

iv

CONCLUDING REMARKS

Epistemology has been frustrating to many empirical thinkers because they missed the essential cue that connects in with ontology or *what is*. The function of sensations was not fully realized. It was not ability that was lacking but the recognition of the technique nature had worked out from the stage of instinct. Instead of sensations being considered appearings, manifestations, and indications, controlled by the object and relevant to it, they fell into the disastrous mistake of thinking of them as terminal screens. Phenomenalism, sensationalism, and agnosticism followed inevitably.

What I have stressed is the circuit from the object and back to the object. It is this basic framework which intelligence presupposes. What it does is to develop the possibilities of the situation. The sensuous deciphering of the object becomes the point of departure for explicit assertion and conceptualization. To further this effort—even, perhaps, to make it possible—language supervenes. Man enters a world of enduring things lending themselves to remembrance and expectation. And his activities are correlated with them. Vision anticipates a confirming handling, as Berkeley, himself, realized in his famous essay on vision. What I wish to stress is the cooperation of the various senses in dealing with things confronting the body and the central role of the body in perceiving.

I do not think that it is difficult to appreciate the rise and growth of categorial meanings, like thinghood and causality, in this setting, something that puzzled Hume with his eyes fixed on Cartesian rationalism. The point is that perceiving, as an act, is concerned with objects and their decipherment and characterization. As Ryle sees, sensations are not components of the object perceived. Their role is in the act, giving cues and indications to thought. He is, of course, quite right in maintaining that knowledge about the mechanism upon which explicit knowledge supervenes is not essential to the act of perceiving any more than knowledge about the digestive process is essential to digestion. And it will, probably, take neurology a long time yet to trace out neural connections and activities. But I am persuaded that the points I have outlined as basic to directed perceiving may give clues. The old, one-way causal approach fostered blind alleys.

Another point. It seems to me clear that language can be understood only in this activist setting. Its framework is that of perceiving. It goes with the categorial distinctions native to it and the actions that it supports. Only in this setting can we appreciate the logical grammar of speech as a public affair and with the otherwise perplexing enigmas of contrary-to-fact conditionals and dispositional terms. Those who have sought an ideal language in a return to neat sensations are, in my opinion, being misled by a false epistemology. Human knowing is an achievement that reaches the external world by means of the use of sensations and concepts having primary cognitive value. And that is why the grammar of speech is molded on what is. Because of his too-Humean epistemology, Russell set the problem of the objective import of language wrongly. Language is a tool developed to work within cognitive achievements, such, for example, as the simple one of my *seeing* this table and this typewriter. Denotative terms like *this* and *that, here* and *now,* go with direct cognitive acts and are ostensive therein. There are not two objects involved.

Such a review makes us realize that epistemology is no easy affair. Without the right cues, frustrations are inevitable. Locke with his "way of ideas" got off to a bad start. But I need not ring the changes. If I am correct in my analysis of the mechanism of perceiving, sensations play a role in the circuit for which they are prepared. They are appearings, which have cognitive value in deciphering the object that appears. That is, the stimulus-object is likewise the response-object and becomes the object of the perceptual act. It is really quite an ingenious device. It is in this referential framework that concepts emerge and are tested.

Now those who saw only frustration in epistemology took some royal road. Dewey resorted to "perspective realism." Carnap fell back on "linguistic frameworks." Quine sought to ground ontology on the techniques of mathematical logic. But I do not believe that the problem of the epistemology of perceiving can be thus sidestepped. Even the ordinary-language approach explicates achievements rather than explaining how they are achieved. Ryle comes very near with his stress on perception-recipes and learning but is still too obsessed by the traditional type of causal approach. He is almost fearful of getting into the body. The answer, as I have tried to show, is that the sensory centers are not terminal but, rather, aids to response. One must keep the whole circuit in mind. I take it that, once this roadblock is removed, the rich resources in analysis of present-day philosophy can take over. The result will be an adequate realistic empiricism.

I may remark in passing that consciousness seems to me a term for the alerted activities involved in the various, and complex, cerebral circuits. That sensations, images, and feelings are components of these circuits strikes me as the most plausible hypothesis. I see nothing in our external, descriptive knowledge about the brain that conflicts with this idea. As I see it, each one is on the inside of his acts and participates in them. That there should be this intrinsic sensory, imaginal, and affective richness to cerebral activities seems to me a fact to be accepted. But this is a big subject, which requires systematic exploration.

The present paper represents an attempt to confront British thought with a continuing development of the American realistic movement. Both, I think, have made contributions. It may well be that these can be integrated. As I have remarked, an outlook that promises to find a way between presentationalism and representationalism and to make perceiving referentially direct has much in its favor. If to this is added a new foundation for the correspondence theory of truth based on the cognitive value of sensory observations relevant to the object, the persuasive appeal is increased. In my opinion, such an approach deserves careful study. It may well give an empirical philosophy sympathetic with science a new life and remove the scandal of a presumed choice between logical positivism and a vague, and rather romantic, existentialism. In all this I speak as a professional philosopher concerned with perennial problems and their possible solution.

Part II: Russell, Price, and Broad

i

INTRODUCTORY REMARKS

In a prior paper, I analyzed Moore's and Ryle's position with respect to sense perception, noting their likenesses and difference. In this one, I want to concentrate on Russell and Broad, while taking note of Ayer and Price. In my opinion, an adequate analysis of perceiving might well be the point of departure for a systematic advance in philosophy. So much has been done in the way of careful analysis! What seems to be lacking is the proper framework.

My memory goes back to F. H. Bradley's presentationalism and his rejection, in favor of logical monism, of singular, designative judgments. Russell's development of definite descriptions never seemed to me quite to meet the difficulty. The present shift of emphasis to context and communication strikes me as an advance, and I shall try to show how it fits in with the view of perceiving I advocate. I stress the role and function of sensations in a responsive, directive act resting on a from-and-to circuit. It is this circuit which I put in the place of the traditional causal approach, which is biologically incomplete. I take it to be evident that this framework gives us a referentially direct view of perceiving and bypasses Locke's representative perceptionism with its frustrating effect on epistemology.

One more introductory remark. While the job of epistemology is different from that of psychology, since it explores cognitive claims from perceiving onward, primarily with respect to *validity,* I am persuaded that it demands a psychological perspective compatible with itself. The kind of associational psychology to which Bradley opposed his logic with its universals is now outmoded. In a sense, I move between *Gestalt* and behaviorism. As will be seen, I take perceiving to be an informed responsive act guided by controlled sensations, usually integrated interpretatively. But *I would stress perceiving rather than percept,* as Gestaltists tend to do, since I am concerned with objective import and activity. As I sometimes put it, we look through our visual field at the object which is stimulating us and to which we are responding and adjusting ourselves. It is this setting which makes possible the emergence of cognitive deciphering of objects. As I see it, sensory data are *informational* and are so used in both adjustment and cognition. That is, *sensations are not terminal, as they were for traditional empiricism, but have a* disclosing *role to play.* But more about that later. I would remark that any theory of perceiving should stress the centrality of learning. We follow cues and indications in our gradual adjustment to, and cognizing of, things. At the level of human perceiving, we regard ourselves as dealing with external things, which are the objects of our directive response. It should not be surprising that, in this context, sensory *qualia* are but indices of objective qualities and properties. It is evident that, in looking at objects through our visual field, the role of sensations is to be informative in the work of cognitive decipherment. It is in this fashion that categories and their implications arise. As is being realized now, language and its logical syntax involves this context. All this is very condensed but I hope to make it plain as I proceed in my studies of Russell and Broad. I cannot forbear quoting a passage from Russell's account of his mental development: "But it seems clear that whatever is not experienced must, if known, be known by inference." Again, "I find that the fear of solipsism has prevented philosophers from facing this problem." Now it will be my thesis that the role of sensations in perceiving is informative and that they function in a referential setting. If so, we escape between the horns of Russell's dilemma. The primary framework of perceiving is responsively referential, and it is within this framework that we ordinarily make explicit inferences. Traditional empiricism—and I must add logical positivism—made sensations terminally experiential. In my opinion, it is only as we appreciate the informative role of sensations within the framework of responsive reference that we can understand the rise of cognitive transcendence. This is an achievement based on what I have called the from-and-to circuit involved in perceiving. Russell's Humean setting had no clue for this achievement. But animal psychology is realizing that the unit in the nervous system is a stimulus-response or S-R pattern. But, I think, to do justice to learning as a factor, we should add a central element and speak of an S-C-R unit. Centrally aroused integrations play a part and become increasingly conceptual in nature. There is, also, a measure of feedback in behavior and in perceiving. All of which returns me to my thesis that psychology must be such as to give a framework for cognition. Russell is quite right in his suspicion that traditional empiricism was linked with a psychology weighted in the direction of solipsism. One recalls that Bradley tried to transform image into *ideas*. To my way of thinking, cognizing is based on the informative value and role of sensations and images. The development of verbal symbols represents a technique that presupposes this base. Psychology is just beginning to tackle such problems, which logic and epistemology show to be imperative.

So much in the way of preliminaries. I hope that some of these points will be kept in mind.

Since I am concerned to contrast the outlook on perceiving represented by critical realism in the United States with that prevailing in England, I shall now run over some issues. As regards Moore, the crucial question was that of the relation, R, of *sense-data* to material things. Back of this issue was the problem of the status of sense-data as against sensations. Like Ryle, I was skeptical of the standing of sense-data as intuited entities. On the other hand, Ryle swung nearer to naïve realism, as Russell also asserts. One reason for this stance was the difficulty of fitting visual and auditory sensations into an act of perceiving objectively directed. It is not easy to handle sensations epistemologically if they are isolated technically from their role in the human economy. They tend then to become terminal and to have the status of *screens* between the subject and the object. Like Dewey and Woodbridge, Ryle takes the gambit of naïve realism. The alternative seems, under these circumstances, to be a phenomenalistic positivism. One motive for positivism, as comes out clearly in the writings of A. J. Ayer, is the assumption that *appearances hide* the physical world. The thing to do, then, is to reject the physical world, so conceived, and to make the sensory factors primary and elementary. As Ayer puts it, "Statements about physical objects are theoretical with respect to statements about sense-data." Much linguistic ingenuity has been exercised on this point. The relation involved does not seem to be either deductive or inductive. And, as we saw, Moore remained puzzled. My suggestion is that we explore the role of sensations in the referential act of perceiving by showing their function as informative. They are used as appearings of the object perceived and thus as cognitively relevant. The relation involved is neither deductive nor inductive but something more elementary. Here nature showed its ingenuity. I do not think that statements about physical objects are theoretical with respect to statements about sense-data, but that they are based on the information carried by them. It is because perceiving is dominated by directed response and the activities that go with it that we think and talk in terms of the qualities and properties of physical objects. Sensory appearings mediate this achievement. The analogy with reading is sometimes employed, but here the marks are conventional symbols for meanings. As I see it, we must develop a terminology that does justice to the role of sensations as informative and mediating. They must be understood within the circuit. They are tools of disclosure. That is why we sensuously decipher through them. In this referential setting categorial meanings of thinghood and of properties emerge. And it is a percipient who perceives. The flaw in sensationalism has always been its tendency to abstract from the biological context.

I have already mentioned Bradley's presentationalism. His was a world of appearances. My point would be that he did not appreciate the mechanism of perceiving and, therefore, could not do justice to the function of presentations and their role of disclosure. With this went his rejection of designative judgments with their contextual *this* and *that*. James Ward felt that something was wrong and introduced a semi-Kantian self. As I see it, *the self emerges in the activity of perceiving* as awareness of these activities. Such is the locus of the subject-self symbolized as the "I." But into this question I cannot here enter in detail. The point is that *feelings* have an informative role of their own. The human economy has many dimensions.

ii

RUSSELL'S OUTLOOKS

But I must not prolong my introductory remarks. Russell is a slightly older contemporary of mine and I have followed the movements of his thought with great interest. I, myself, honor him for his flexibility, though many hold it against him. But this flexibility had its limits. Fundamentally, he has remained a Humean in his view of perception. His neutral monism showed the influence of William James's radical empiricism, which was somewhat like that of Mach. This perspective was the basis of his attack upon materialism. It seemed to him to bring the material and the psychical together in a neutral way. The alignment had much in common with American new realism.

But, increasingly, Russell has been impressed by the implications of the causal approach to perception. This led to what Lovejoy called the "under-the-hat" view of mind. Because of his neutral monism, Russell has tended to identify the brain with terminal *percepts*. This terminology should be noted since I stress *perceiving* as referential and objective in import. As I have indicated, the transcendence involved rests on the working together of directed response and the cognitive relevance of sensations as controlled appearings. Nature was very ingenious. Lacking the idea of this from-and-to circuit, Russell has to resort to *postulates* to get outside the brain. Sometimes I have the suspicion that Russell's logical equipment played him false, for it may have prevented him from analyzing perceiving along new lines.

It may be well to recall that I, also, *unify mind and brain and regard consciousness as literally "in" the brain as functioning.* In my first book, *Critical Realism* (1916), I gave a chapter to the topic, "Is Consciousness Alien to the Physical," and there I examined various meanings of "in." In point of fact, I had advanced the notion in my first writings in the first decade of the century. Ultimately, I defended a double-knowledge approach and held consciousness to be a natural isolate. But, at the same time, I emphasized the point that perceiving, as an experience, reflected the neural mechanism as concerned with both stimulus and response and as an S-C-R affair. Consciousness thus has objective import. It goes with locating and characterizing external objects. I would call attention to echolocation in both bats and dolphins. Thus, I do not need Russell's postulates. Taking this view of perceiving as tied in with response and designation, I see no good reason to prove the existence of the external world, a problem which came down from Descartes and Locke. The very fact that G. E. Moore sought to give a proof of sorts went with the touch of phenomenalism involved in his sense-datum theory. The relation of sense-data to material thing remained to the end an unsolved problem for him.

In his account of the development of his philosophy, Russell asserts that he gave up sense-data in 1921. Since then, he speaks of sensations and locates them in the brain. As I have indicated, I think that he is quite right in this shift but does not realize how they function in perceiving. It may be recalled how Ryle was so puzzled by the job of linking the causal approach in sense perception to the achievement-consummation of *seeing* an external thing that he fell back on naïve realism, a stance that Russell deplores. The danger here is that epistemology tends to be belittled rather than mastered. I saw the same development in Dewey.[1] The fashion of "natural language," so popular at Oxford, has its dangers, as Russell asserts. One danger

---

1. I am publishing a paper contrasting Dewey's form of naïve realism, which has been called "perspective realism," and my form of critical realism . . . [in this volume of critiques].

is that of becoming a philosophy without tears. It seems at present to go with a kind of behaviorism. I am, myself, all for the linkage of epistemology with ontology. This involves not only a theory of human knowing as a remarkable achievement, but its extension into a study of the categorial constitution of nature. Starting with perceiving, we explore and decipher the constitution of things. As I see it, natural language takes us only a little way in this task. We must work with the sciences. I shall have more to say about this in connection with my study of C. D. Broad. I shall argue that Broad is still too much of a Lockean.

Perhaps it would be well to stress a point here. The problem is to make perceiving direct and yet mediated. *Philosophical naïve realism* falls back on intuition, a kind of immediate seeing of the object, its givenness in person. And then the alternative is conceived as some kind of representative perception. Those who think in terms of sensa, or sense-data, *as objects* have somehow to pass beyond these to the material thing. As we shall see, H. H. Price, who has specialized on the subject of perception, adheres to the sense-datum theory in what J. O. Urmson calls a moderate form, since he postulates an *occupant* at the locus of what we call a material thing and holds that sense-data somehow *belong* to it. And, as nearly as I can make out, Broad still believes in sensa as primary data, though he has begun to qualify the nature of our awareness of them. Now my position puts sensations within the *act* of perceiving, having there a role of disclosure. They do not, in perceiving, stand out as primary objects. Their function is to mediate the act. We decipher the object of our objective concern through them. This can be called sensuous thinking. As I see it, conceptual thinking needs this base as a point of departure. Otherwise we would be lost in conceptualism, that is, the making of concepts into primary objects.

These various gambits are interesting and one must choose between them. Ayer, the positivist, dwells on sensations and makes statements about material things secondary and theoretical and is afraid that appearances hide the world. I, on the other hand, hold that it is their function within the act of perceiving to disclose the world. They are appearings of the object perceived and informationally relevant to it. Of course, much activity of piecing together and of constructing is necessary. Perceiving is no passive affair. Common sense, perceptual knowledge, is, itself, an achievement resting on sensory and intellectual resources. But the point I want to make is that it is referentially direct and the mediations are *within the act.* In this fashion, we move between phenomenalism and variations on Lockean representative perceptionism.

But let us return to Russell. His first book, *The Problems of Philosophy,* is still a classic. I have inscribed on my copy Santayana's famous comment to the effect that "It might rather have been called 'The problems which Moore and I have been agitating lately.' " We are fortunate in having his retrospective judgment in chapter 9 of his book *My Philosophical Development.* There he states that his opinions at that moment had a clear-cut definiteness that they did not have earlier or later. As yet, he accepted matter as it appears in physics. But he was increasingly puzzled by "the uncomfortable gulf between physics and perception, or, in other language, between mind and matter."

It would seem that Russell identified perception with what we actually and directly *experience,* and held that it is only what we directly experience that gives us reason to believe in the world of physics. But may not what we directly experience—say, the visual field—have a function of disclosure as the controlled *appearing* of the object perceived? The term *experience* does not do justice to this function. And yet it connects up with the adjustmental value of the sense organs. Russell had on his hands perceptions or percepts. To use his own words, "We cannot, therefore, suppose that the physical thing is what anybody *sees.*" That is, seeing terminates on visual percepts.

Now we have noted that Ryle takes such an achievement as seeing a material thing as an accomplishment, though he is not clear as to how it is achieved. It fits in with natural language. Russell calls it naïve realism. But is not critical realism, with its analysis of the act of perceiving, another possibility, also agreeing with natural language? But, of course, I see no reason to expect that reflective problems, such as that of the mechanism of perceiving, can be answered by a mere inspection of language. It may, however, indicate that the perceiving of external things has *somehow* been achieved. Something of the same order stands out in the formulation of laws and in the presence of the assignment to objects of dispositional properties. As I see it, language sets problems that carry us into epistemology and ontology.

I shall only sketch the essentials of Russell's first outlook. And I do so largely because he continued to circle around it.

At this stage, he stressed knowledge by acquaintance and had a relational view of sensations. "Every sensation, according to this view, was itself a cognition and consisted in awareness of what I called the sense-datum." Under the influence of William James he gave up this view and concluded that sensations are not in themselves cognitive. With James, he likewise gave up the belief in a special "mental entity" to be called the *subject*. He was, accordingly, on the road to his neutral monism. It may be recalled that James was attacking Kantianism. All this led Russell to explore knowing and experiencing in a more analytic way. But both in his writing and in my conversations with him, I got the impression that he conceived knowing and experiencing as involving accretions of habits and images. "The total occurrence is always an interpretation in which the sensational core has accretions involving habits."

This approach led him to conclude that "perception" is something less direct than it seems to be. Thus Russell remained impressed by the gulf between sensations and their supposed external causes. In *The Problems of Philosophy* he saw no reason to regard sense-data as *signs* of the existence of physical objects. He is ready to recognize our motives for belief in public, neutral objects and admits our "instinctive beliefs." But the question for him was this: can we find, in our given experiences, characteristics that tend to show that there *are* external things? Reflection leaves us short of proof.

Let us appreciate his dilemma. Sensations are given and we have, apparently, no logical right to infer physical things from them. Here he is one with Berkeley and Hume. But he cannot ignore physics so easily. The situation that ensued was to the effect that physics exhibits sensations as functions of physical objects, science being able to tell us more about this causal sequence than can philosophy. Thus Russell got into the brain in a causal way. But he goes on to say that *verification* is possible only if physical objects can be exhibited as functions of sensations. Empirical statements must be capable of being verified.

Moving within this circle of ideas, Russell sought to give a *logical construction* of matter out of sensations and sensibilia. He also brooded on the possibility of a nondemonstrative inference from sensations to the external world, arriving in his book *Human Knowledge* at a series of postulates. But, so far as I can make out, sense perception remained intracerebral. The gulf still remained. But Russell took comfort in his identity form of solution of the mind-body problem. In itself, the brain consists of percepts. The external observer perceives only his own percepts.

Since I am concentrating on perceiving I shall neglect Russell's logical atomism, which is just one possible form of logical pluralism. Atomic facts were of the sensory sort, like *this being red*, symbolized as *a*. The *a* here would stand for a short-lived entity. Urmson believes that there was operative in the background a combination of hope for an indubitable starting-point with the belief in the primacy of sense-data or of sensations. Sentences picture the atomic fact in terms of its internal structure.

Analytic philosophy has been exploring Russell's suggestions about a sense-datum language or an ideal language. But, as I shall try to show, a different view of perceiving supports the framework of ordinary language with its use of direct reference. It will be recalled that I think of perceiving as resting on the complete circuit of stimulus and response with room for sensations and ideas as guiding the response. The unit I symbolized as S-C-R. Learning and meanings make the responsive reference more adequate. But an essential point is that perceiving is directly concerned with the external thing and that sensations and images have cognitive value, even though they are not, in themselves, cognitions. It does not seem to me that Russell does justice to the informational value of sensations or to their role in sensuous thinking or deciphering. They may be said to function within the *act*, which has referential direction.

It is in this fashion that I bridge the gulf that bothered Russell and that goes with the simple, causal approach. Transcendence is an achievement resting on directed response and the concomitant, informational value of externally controlled sensations. Vision, hearing, and touch cooperate in this basic framework. But, of course, the human economy involves alertness to proprioceptors and feelings. Russell is quite right in rejecting a "mental entity" kind of self. It is a functional growth developed around the pole of action, trying, motivation, and decision. But that is another story.

Needless to say, I have great admiration for Russell's achievements. His range was far greater than mine. But we had much in common. On the whole, he seems to me to have worked within the presentational perspective of Hume, Mach, and William James. This took the form of neutral monism. I, on the other hand, was more of a physical realist, inclined to stress levels of causality, emergence, and a new, or nonreductive, materialism. My view of perceiving as referentially objective enabled me to locate consciousness in the brain while linking it with a biological mechanism. Thus I escaped the twin evils of introspectionism and mere behaviorism.

I am going to close this brief study of Russell with some comments on his six "prejudices," as outlined in his book *My Philosophical Development,* pages 128 ff. I do so because they were largely mine.

First, as to the continuity between animal and human mind, I think that both continuity and discontinuity should be stressed. Knowing, as Ryle says, is a polymorphous term. Several of my friends were animal psychologists. The idea of stages in the development of mind was common to them. Snails showed no capacity to learn. Chickens, rats, and cats did. Norman Maier believed that he showed something like reasoning in rats. J. F. Shepard proved the use by rats of auditory, floor cues in learning a maze. At this level, there is, I take it, some degree of sensuous thinking, that is, the use of sensations as indications of objective situations. But, with man, concepts become explicit with language. I am persuaded that broad, categorial meanings, such as thinghood, properties, causality, time, and space, become explicit at this stage and are enshrined in language. Given the objective import of perceiving, this seems a quite natural growth. Hume's empiricism was too elementary, and he was fighting rationalism in its intuitive, anti-empirical form.

Russell's second prejudice was in favor of physics. All of us, I suppose, are these days impressed by physics as a type of knowledge reflecting scientific method at its best. But I do think that common sense has, from the start, been interrogating nature and experimenting with it. But into the points of novelty in science I cannot here go. I simply want to indicate my feeling that Russell has a tendency to *reduction,* while I would stress levels of causality and even admit a kind of free will in the sense of relative self-determination. In other words, I do think that intelligence makes a difference.

Russell's third prejudice is against the overstress on the concept of experience. This went with idealism and still remains in Dewey's pragmatism. Russell admits that there are difficulties in explaining how we acquire knowledge that transcends experience, but holds that the denial that we have such knowledge is utterly untenable. I have argued that transcendence rests on a natural mechanism of directed response and the concomitant use of information-carrying sensations. Logic makes use of this framework in its formulae, All A is B, if anything is an A it is a B. Logical thought has objective import.

His fourth prejudice is against any *a priori* method of proving the existence of anything. I do think that this is the heart of empiricism and appears in scientific empiricism as the principle of confirmation.

Russell's fifth prejudice concerns the correspondence theory of truth. My comment is that the escape from Locke's representational view of perception and its replacement by a mediated, referential act in which information about the object is drawn from sensations controlled by it makes correspondence an explicable achievement and not something tied in with an impossible comparison between idea and object. My divergence from Russell reflects our differing views of perception.

Lastly, I share his sympathy with analysis. Only I do think that analysis takes place within a framework and that his has been too atomistic. Something of Hume's assumptions remain. My kind of logical pluralism concerns itself with information about things and their relations. Synthesis, if you will, goes with analysis.

What I have here offered is of the nature of suggestive contrasts. It may call attention to elements in the American realistic movement that have been neglected.

iii

SOME REMARKS ON H. H. PRICE

The framework that I want to emphasize is that of the human level of perceiving. As I see it, there is explicit in this developments reared on animal response and the guiding use of sensations. The percipient is set over against what is perceived. And to sensuous decipherment is added the application of concepts. All this comes out in perceptual judgments and their linguistic expression. It is a tree that I see over there, a thing that has grown through the years and is quite distinguishable from myself as a percipient. I live and move among recognizable objects in space and time. And the "I" here is the active and informed body that I call myself. There is, of course, no need to postulate a special mental entity. Let us forget Cartesian dualism.

The point I want to make is that philosophy was puzzled because it had no clear idea of how such *referential transcendence* was achieved. We saw how Russell was torn between his belief that it was attained and his inability to explain it. According to my analysis, it had a humble enough beginning in the very mechanism of perceiving, with its movement from stimulus to guided response. What guided animals became for man the point of departure for decipherment and conceptual description.

Without this clue, philosophers found themselves confronted by what they called the subject-object *relation*. And this was a mystery. Was it internal or external? I, myself, concluded that there was no such entity but that the act of perceiving was referential and of objective import and that cognition rested on the informational value of ideas. This meant that perceiving was directed and mediated. It, likewise, indicated that it was a unique achievement evolutionarily prepared for. One had to think it through on its own terms.

Let us turn now to Price, who has done such meticulous, descriptive work within a Hume-Russell perspective. We may call this his foreground. I judge from his contribution to the Schilpp volume on Broad that he is a trifle nettled by those critics who emphasize the background in a more realistic way. What he seems to be concerned with now is the way in which sense-data (the foreground) *belong* to the material thing with its occupant, *matter*. It is much the problem with which G. E. Moore was left.

As Urmson shows, Price was a moderate and was not satisfied with phenomenalism. He wanted more than a picturing of sensuous data by sentences. In this, he was more in line, as I suggested, with Moore. But if sense-data do not belong, in some fashion, to the external thing, how can they further our knowledge? But, within his perspective, the best he could do was to define a material thing as a complex of sensed sense-data and a localizable occupant. The sense-data occupy the foreground and are generated in some fashion. Hence the problem of distinguishing the *private* from the *public* arises. What impresses one is the pressure of problems within a perspective. Price shows great ingenuity. But it reminds me a little of the ingenuity of the defenders of the phlogiston theory in chemistry. According to my way of thinking, *sense-data have no more reality than phlogiston*. We saw that Russell fell back on sensations. But these are "in the brain." I have argued that Russell did not realize their role in the referential act of perceiving. Now, as I see it, visual sensations, though private, can do much the same job for me as yours do for you. What we usually talk about is *what* we perceive, as Ryle recognizes.

For Price, the *perceptual object*—this term is significant—is, strictly speaking, a complex group of sense-data. These are thought of as belonging to an occupant somehow. But if sense-data are private, how can the perceptual object be public? Of course, they are not private in the way Russell's and my sensations are. They are objects of a kind of cognitive intuition. Price's answer is to the effect that many people's sensa are constituents of the public perceptual object and that it is neutral as between the various sense-modalities. Hence, it is not as *ghostly* as his critics maintain. He finds much in common between his position and Broad's. I think he is right on this point. We shall see that Broad's perceptual objects are ambiguous.

What I am trying to bring into the scene is an element of cultural contact. S. Alexander was, I take it, aside from Russell, the last major British thinker affected by the American realistic movement. He told me in 1922 that he was much influenced by Holt along the lines of the new realism. He spoofed me in his gentle way by saying that my critical realism implied that his realism was naïve. I replied that philosophical theories are always sophisticated. The question was whether his position did justice to relevant facts. I had found that all the new realists considered Locke's representative perceptionism as the only alternative. I denied this and argued that the act of perceiving was referentially direct but informationally mediated. Even in critical realism I represented a minority stance. Santayana's essence doctrine received the chief consideration, perhaps, because of his deserved prestige. R. J. Hirst, who has recently published an excellent book on perception much along my lines, has written me that critical realism meant for him the essence-wing. It should be clear by now how basically different my conception of the act of perceiving is. Cognizing emerges as a conditioned achievement.

What, then, is a material thing? It does not seem to me to be reducible to an occupant plus sense-data, as Price would have it. It is what we directly perceive and gain facts about. Our common-sense categorization is supplemented by the additional results gained by scientific method. While knowledge is never equivalent to being, it reaches it and discloses it on its own terms. Thus, I take the physical world to be much as modern science describes it.

Such a realistic empiricism is full-blooded and ontological in import. In this respect, it seems to me an improvement on both phenomenalistic positivism and pragmatic empiricism. Like science, philosophy must have stamina. I have not been unduly impressed by those who, like Carnap, derogate from epistemology and just leap from solipsism to physicalism. Linguistic frameworks are indicative. But, if I am right, the thing-language has its foundation in the mechanism of perceiving, a mechanism that is the gateway to action and exploration.

iv

C. D. BROAD

I am now going to touch on some strategic points in C. D. Broad's outlook. He began his publications shortly after I had laid the foundations for critical realism. I think that all of us have had respect for his competence in the physical sciences and for his powers of exposition. I am not so certain that he had a *feel* for biology and psychology. There is often a kind of suspicion of the latter in British philosophical circles. I think that this attitude partly accounts for the prevalence of sensa and sense-datum theories. These are generated entities that are somehow apprehended. But the recurrent problem is how to pass from them to the external object. A few years ago, Professor John Wild classified Broad as a critical realist.[1] Wild's purpose was, in part, to bring out what he regarded as a basic short-coming of critical realism, the lack of cognitive contact with external objects. This is a crucial question and I have already tried to show how cognitive contact is achieved in perceiving. I have argued that the *transcendence* rests on the integration of responsive reference and the informational value of sensory and conceptual material. As I see it, nature laid the foundation for this development in the guidance function of the sense-organs for adjustment. The linkage is sensori-motor.

Broad seems to make a sharp distinction between empirical concepts, closely linked with sensa, and categorial concepts, such as substance, causality, and dispositional properties, reached by what he calls nonperceptual intuition. These latter are *a priori* in an almost Kantian manner. It may be remarked that Broad has an apprehensional theory of universals, making our cognition of them a kind of "seeing." This is continuous with Platonism. Of late, a more linguistic approach to universals is being developed. But we enter here into

---

1. In an article in the *Philosophical Review*.

the problem of the status of *meanings,* so much discussed these days. When I say that I see a chair over there, I am applying a conceptual meaning within the setting of sensuous decipherment of an object.

I am going to argue, accordingly, that Broad has fused elements of Locke, Kant, and Plato in his epistemology. There are two topics to keep in mind: 1) sense-perception, and 2) nonperceptual intuition.

Like Price, Broad stresses sensa, or sensa-data, though he is increasingly skeptical of the "consciousness of" feature of the sense-datum tradition. To this extent, he would seem to be taking the path of Russell in 1921. However that may be, cognitive contact must be made through sensa or sensations. These are related to each other as constituents of the same "perceptual object." But the danger here is that we only have percepts rather than perceiving. Broad adds that in *ostensible perception* there is a factor of perceptual acceptance. This seems at times to fade away into mere behaving-as-if, accompanied by certain feelings and images.

The question now is whether this perceptual acceptance is equivalent to my analysis of perceiving as involving responsive reference and the role of sensations as instruments of sensuous thinking of the referent. I doubt that it is. Broad is led to make a distinction between an epistemological object and an ontological object. And it is hard to see how he brings these together. This is the problem of cognitive contact. Now I unite the ontological object and epistemological object in that it is what we are referring to and cognizing. Separate them and one has Locke's *idea* on one's hands.

It is a bit of history that the American critical realists debated this problem. The new realists had opted for presentationalism or naïve realism in fear of Locke and Kant. They called this position epistemological monism. Epistemological dualism meant, for them, Locke's representationalism. But was there not another alternative? I held that the act of perceiving is referentially direct, not presentationally direct. It is connected with response and flows into action upon the external object. But it is guided and mediated by sensations and images that are used in the act in a disclosing way. We may call this another form of epistemological monism, which avoids Locke's dilemma and Kant's thing-in-itself.

On the whole, I think that Broad's perceptual acceptance does not quite make the needed cognitive contact. As I see it, he recognizes, as does Russell, the causal moment in perceiving, which makes mere presentationalism impossible, and he desires to avoid Locke's kind of representative perceptionism, which makes ideas terminal and only postulates some degree of representationalism. Such was the problem the American critical realists were wrestling with. I have argued that the complete act of perceiving is dominated by referential response and that sensations and images operate in it as sources of information about the object. We see objects through our visual field and feel them through our tactual sensations. But if we set up a *perceptual object* we get into difficulties. If this is made up of generated sense-data, or sensa, we are obliged to ask how they *belong* to the material thing. Price has explored this gambit and he apparently thinks that Broad has made the same move. My own thinking has led me to put cognitively used sensations within the act of perceiving, with its objective import. Cognitive contact rests on the informational value of the sensations that are under the control of the object perceived. Nature has been more ingenious than much of philosophy.

I want, finally, to say a few words upon the subject of what Broad calls nonperceptual intuition. As I see it, this is the problem of the rise of meanings, categorial and otherwise.

I think that it all begins within the framework of perceiving. The percipient is concerned with the object to which he is making adjustment. And he is using sensory indications in his explorations. The object is set over against the self. All this is very concrete and involves attitudes and activities. It is bipolar. There is, clearly, an awareness of felt endurance supported by recognitions and memories. It is in this setting that the categorial meanings of thinghood and selfhood emerge and bring with them the ideas of properties and characteristics. Logical thought rests on this development.

I cannot here go into details but shall only draw conclusions. Categorial meanings, as I see it, emerge with experiential activity and are expressed linguistically in tenses, nouns, and adjectives. I see no reason to believe in a supplementary intuition of abstract entities. What is going on is the participative decipherment of the categorial constitution of things based on cognitive contact in the interplay of organic self and surrounding things. It is in this fashion that the outlook and categories of common sense emerge, something that so long puzzled Russell with his Humean assumptions. What science does is to carry on from there with new techniques.

A few words now about Broad's handling of the category of substance. Such a category I consider empirical in its own fashion as an element in the framework of perceiving. But it is not empirical in the way that sensations are. The point is that the particular color, shape, and size of an object must be worked out on evidence. The categorial constitution, on the other hand, is a framework that emerges and is of an overall sort. Because it is so basic and because there seems no alternative to it, it operates as an *a priori,* though not in the Kantian sense. Culturally, it is still developing.

Perhaps I can best bring out my meaning by considering the outlook of Brand Blanshard, as expressed in his paper in the Broad-Schilpp volume. Now Blanshard is an idealist whose thought is linked with that of Joachim. It is quite right, therefore, to discuss him in connection with British thought. His rejection of substance goes with his rejection of the correspondence theory of truth and his acceptance of coherence as giving the essential meaning of the term. All these things hang together. It has always been my thesis that idealism never did justice to epistemological problems. The American realistic movement was motivated by this belief and by the idea that pragmatism was a sort of half-way house.

It is one of the merits of Blanshard that he puts his cards face up on the table. "A particular," he writes, "seems to me a pattern of characteristics and nothing more." A particular here is essentially what we ordinarily call a thing or an object. Again he writes, "What makes a pattern, in any given case, particular does not lie in an 'unthinkable it' [his view of substance] but in a set of relations which at once links this group with others and distinguishes it."

My divergence from Blanshard begins here. The "it," thought of as enduring and substantial is, in my view, quite thinkable, because we have referential cognitive contact with it so that it is located and characterized. If Blanshard means that a table is just a pattern of characteristics, it seems to me that he is confusing an object with descriptions of it. But it all comes back to the analysis of perceiving. I hold that, even at this level, we have cognitive contact with our referents. There is no unthinkable of the Lockean, or the Kantian, sort involved.

There is much in Blanshard's theory of truth with which I can agree. Thought does have what he calls two ends, one immanent and one transcendent. In the one, we seek satisfaction of systematic vision; in the other, what he calls fulfillment in the object. I would call the second knowledge about the object. This is based on received evidence.

To make a long story short, *true seems to me to mean the acceptance of a proposition as a knowledge-claim about an object.* And such knowledge implies cognitive contact achieved through controlled information. I take it that "correspondence" has through the ages stood for the recognition that a distinction must be made between the proposition and what it is about. The job was to show how cognitive contact was made and how it could be endorsed. The coherence theory, as I see it, rested largely on idealism as an alternative to realism. Its strength lay in the inadequacies of past epistemology. As for coherence as a metaphysical category, that is another question. As an empiricist, I find pattern and organization in nature. But there is nothing dictatorial in this constitution. There may well be some measure of conflict and disorder too. Darwinism and Marxism have their talking points.

Let us look back for a moment to Blanshard's rejection of substance on the grounds that it is an unknowable "it." This leaves him with an apprehended surface and, of course, nothing for thought to correspond to. The dichotomy of thought and things has been set aside. But I have argued that it must be mastered rather than dismissed. Thought but follows the example set in perceiving of guided reference and the use of informational evidence. But I quite agree with Blanshard that thought is successful and finds fulfillment in the object. That is, that it has objective import. On this point, objective idealism and critical realism agree as against pragmatism and positivism.

v

SUMMARIZING REMARKS

I have been encouraged recently by the publication of two books on our topic, namely, Chisholm's *Perceiving* and R. J. Hirst's *The Problem of Perception,* both of which defend a position similar to my own. Of the two, Hirst is the more inclined to give a cortical status to sensations and thus defend an identity theory of the mind-brain problem. We use our sensations in perceiving but, as Ryle points out, they do not figure as such in the perceptual judgment. Russell and I have long sought to analyze the kind of "inness" in the brain involved. I take it that our divergence stems from different views of perceiving. I am more of a physical realist than he is. That is why I have always sought to enlarge materialism along evolutionary levels rather than to reject it, as Russell does.

Mental terms have both occurrent and dispositional import. Ryle has made a linguistic study of the dispositional phase. As I recall it, both Hobhouse and McDougall had this phase in mind, though inclined to animism and dualism rather than to behaviorism. I note that Russell queries Ryle with respect to the term *brittle.* I am inclined to think, following my analysis of perceiving, that sensations, images, and conventional symbols play a guiding role in complex habits and dispositions of a mental order. We should, I think, speak of mental activities. It remains to be seen how neurology is going to envisage such activities. But I do think my analysis of perceiving should be relevant.

It has been stimulating to make this study of British theories of sense perception. I had already gone over the earlier, American debate as represented by Woodbridge, Dewey, and the new realists. Aside from Russell, the British have turned their backs on this trans-Atlantic phase and had become engrossed in the challenge coming from Vienna. Logical atomism and phenomenalism were highlighted in the ensuing debate, which moved in the direction of concern with language. Analysis of a high order ensued; and yet I felt that something was lacking, namely, a more naturalistic and scientific study of the mechanism of perceiving. It is this feature that I have tried to add. I think it was a feature of the American phase. I have the impression that European philosophy, both in positivism and existentialism, has been somewhat divorced from science. Under pressure, positivism swung to linguistic physicalism, but existentialism strikes me as still unintegrated with the scientific approach to the world. But I hope to take up this issue shortly.

I shall now summarize my reflections on the outlooks of the very able men whose positions on sense perception I have studied.

Ayer is clearly aware of difficulties he had first ignored. He is more inclined to recognize the objective import of statement about physical objects. But, like Russell, the foreground of sensations, or sense-data, looms as primary for him. Like Russell, again, he does not see how physical objects can be reached from sensations by deduction or by induction. Hence, he holds that statements about physical things are theoretical, with the cash value in sense-data. Now, in contrast, I hold that, in perceiving, the reference to the physical object is direct and connected with response. The function of sensations in the act of perceiving is that of disclosure. That is, they have information value, and their role is to aid the deciphering or sensuous thinking of the object perceived. It is for this reason that they do not constitute elements in the perceptual judgment, though we are aware of their operative presence in sense perception. Their function, however, gives them verificatory or cash value. Such an analysis, I take it, puts a bridge across the gulf which so impressed Russell and with which Ayer is still wrestling. The answer is neither deduction nor induction, but the ingenuity of nature in using sensations to guide behavioral response. Man lifts such guidance to cognition and description. In this context it is better to speak of *perceiving* than of percepts or perceptual objects.

Since I have dealt with Russell in detail, I have little to add. My comment I have partly included in my remarks on Ayer. Russell still seems to me to think in terms of percepts rather than in terms of perceiving. The consequent puzzle is that of *transcendence,* of somehow getting outside the head. This also perplexes Ryle in his reflections on the traditional causal theory of the rise of sensations and leads him to adopt a position akin to naïve realism. My answer is that there is no literal stepping outside the brain and its activities. Rather does perceiving rest on a circuit of stimulus and guided response and the information gained is used referentially so that the sensory appearing is directed at the thing appearing. The stress must be put on the behavioral function of the brain. The traditional causal theory ignored this role of the brain and left us with sensations in the brain as introspective entities. I cannot see that *Gestalt* psychology has done more than show the inadequacy of associational atomism. It still leaves us with *percepts* isomorphic with cerebral integrations. But epistemology must stress external perceiving and its mechanism. I have argued that transcendence, with its resultant cognitive contact, is an achievement resting on responsive reference and the informational use of controlled sensations.

While I have great respect for G. E. Moore, I do not believe that he had the cues for the proper analysis of perceiving. But his candor was such that he formulated his puzzle in his own terms of a supposed relation, R, between sense-data and material thing. Like Russell and Ryle, I do not believe in entitative sense-data. Hence the problem becomes for me the role of sensations in the referential act of perceiving. As I see it, we think referentially *through* them. But they do not appear in the resultant judgment. I cannot help thinking that this may satisfy Ryle.

For all his meticulous care, I am persuaded that Price, likewise, missed the correct framework. He seems to have thought of sense-data as belonging to material things as parts of them, to which he added an occupant. I imagine it is the old story, so frequent in science, of the need of a new perspective.

All of us, I suppose, have great respect for the knowledge and acumen of C. D. Broad. And yet I have been compelled to argue that he never succeeded in making cognitive contact between his perceptual object and the external material thing. That is, he could not get his epistemological object and his ontological object together. Now it seems to me clear that it is the ontological object, chair, table, or tree, that we are perceiving. I hold also that categorial meanings emerge in this referential activity. If they function in an *a priori* way, that is because they are so basic to the framework of human thought and so well founded. This does not imply that categories cannot be improved. But Russell made the mistake of trying to do away with them, the Humean note.

The outlook I am defending can be called a *realistic empiricism* in contrast to phenomenalistic empiricism and pragmatic empiricism. I think it has more body and promise to it than these other forms. I agree with Richard Aaron that no hard-and-fast line can be drawn between empiricism and rationalism. Reason is not a faculty but a term for activities that elicit possibilities in the human situation. At a high level, thought moves from perceiving to a stage in which it recognizes logical constants and logical syntax. Sensuous thinking seems to me the point of departure for concept formation.

I may say, in conclusion, that the fact that this analysis of perceiving enables me to give a base for the correspondence theory of truth and knowledge is an added point in its favor. A position that has an explanation for both transcendence and correspondence along naturalistic lines promises to undercut both Locke and Kant and to restore epistemology to its fellowship with science as an equal. Human knowing is an achievement of such a rare quality that it deserves exploration and comprehension. It inevitably has a terminology of its own. The lesson I have learned through the years is that a philosopher has to have both stamina and persistence. If he has something novel to say, it will take him a long time to work it out. There can be no better method in the end than that of contrast. It is this method I have used here.

4
Positivism and Materialism*

One of the dramatic events of the period after the first World War—so far as philosophy was concerned—was the incursion into the perhaps too-tranquil atmosphere of English and American thought of that industrious, somewhat clannish, and self-confident movement originally spoken of as the Vienna Circle. It has by now achieved various aliases, such as logical positivism, logical empiricism, empirical realism, and scientific empiricism. It might also be called neo-Machism or neo-Humeanism. In accordance with this linguistic vivacity, I shall at times refer to it as logical phenomenalism.

Now it has so happened that I have found myself both agreeing and disagreeing with the movement. While I do not desire to lean on the prestige of science, I do think that scientific method is the most promising procedure for attaining knowledge about man and the universe. On the other hand, I am still convinced that there are formal questions in epistemology that are important and that philosophers are as yet best trained to analyze. It is also my opinion that epistemology inevitably ties in with ontology and with basic categories. The query in my mind, then, is whether these enthusiasts have sufficiently considered realism and materialism or whether they were not chiefly fighting speculative idealism. These are matters of

* R. W. Sellars, *Philosophy and Phenomenological Research* 7 (September 1946) : 12–40. Reprinted with the permission of both the author and publisher.

cultural setting. In any case, it will surely be worth while to contrast positivism and the kind of nonmechanical, *depth materialism* I, as a physical realist, have come to favor.

i

What I am going to undertake in this article is a job of probing and exploration. I have a strong suspicion that the sodality of the logical positivists has not, as yet, a clear notion of Anglo-American realism, particularly of physical realism, and that they are ridden by certain assumptions. I shall argue that these go far back to the origins of the movement and antedate modern forms of realism, *so that logical positivism was, to a certain extent, outdated before it began its campaign of enlightenment.* One important task is to discover what notions of realism and of materialism are entertained by the logical positivists and what assumptions inhibit them from taking a more constructive attitude toward them. From reading the literature I have the suspicion that, aside from the momentum of their own traditions, there operates the conventional fear of the transcendent or transcendental—usually thought of in semi-Kantian terms, as with all good representatives of Middle Europe—a fear of the more mystical formulations of emergence, and a sworn allegiance to the operational notions of relativity, with an accompanying disbelief in the possible reconstruction by philosophy of the "absolute" or ontological interpretation of the spatial and the temporal characteristics of the physical world.

The union of the tradition of empirical immanentism with such operational emphases can, I think, well account for the characteristic attitude of the positivist toward realism. What I shall try to do in the present paper is to explore, to clarify new possibilities in, physical realism, and to institute contrasts. As a result, the alternatives should be clearer and some misunderstandings lessened. Because of my personal acquaintance with Feigl and Bergmann and my belief that they have a fair general knowledge of my position, I shall treat them as proponents of what I shall call logical phenomenalism; one more alias should not hurt. I employ this descriptive term because the status and merits of realism and ontology are in question. In the case of Bergmann I shall chiefly use articles of his that have appeared in *Philosophy of Science* and *The Scientific Monthly*. Feigl's contribution to the volume called *Twentieth Century Philosophy* will be drawn on. The writings of Ayer and of Carnap will also be kept in mind. I shall, however, be chiefly concerned with contrasts and alternatives.

ii

There seems little doubt that logical positivism took over and developed, in terms of modern logic and linguistics, the tradition of *empirical immanentism* associated with the names of Mach, Avenarius, and Cornelius in the German-speaking world, and linked it still more with the Anglo-American empirical tradition of Hume, Mill, and James. Comte, Poincaré, and Duhem were regarded, I take it, as having a certain general kinship. In the development of mathematical logic, a new catalytic agent was introduced; and here the work of Russell, mediated by Wittgenstein, was outstanding in its influence—though Russell has been something of a disappointment because of flirtations with realism.

It must be remembered that, even in the United States, excessive hopes were once aroused by Russell and his admirers as to the epoch-making effect upon the perennial questions of philosophy of his technique. His slogan, scientific method in philosophy, carried conviction to many. To me, this appeal to science as the savior of philosophy has always had something of the savor of Christian Science. It tends to degenerate into sycophancy to the prestige of science. As I see it, the great advantage of philosophy, its contact with the whole of human experience and its chance to work both up and down the hierarchy of the sciences, tends to be lost. In my opinion, the gateway of philosophy is epistemology and its courtyard is the clarification of the categories. And so I believe that science and philosophy should cooperate, but that the one should not try to reduce itself to the other. Yet if, as we were once told, epistemology and ontology are *sinnlos,* what else could poor philosophy do but shift to language? I shall try to give reasons why I think its case is not so hopeless. But the physical realist has found philosophical territory in recent decades first inundated by a speculative fusion of Platonism and subjectivism and then excessively drained by linguistics. *C'est un peu trop fort,* as the French would say. I hope we can come back to a good mean. And this paper is written in the belief that an equilibrium can be reached between such extremes.

Russell was too big a man not to have had some qualms as to the correctness of his use of Occam's razor and his principle of logical construction taken over in the *Aufbau* of the world from data.[1] But is perceiving a matter merely of sensing? Is it not intrinsically denotative and descriptive?

The point is that logical positivism conserved this original, empirical immanentism and gradually added new logical and linguistic techniques as a consequence of further contacts. We may speak of two poles to the movement, the empirical and the logical. In what follows my concern is more with the empirical pole, that is with the sphere of extra-linguistic reference, and that for two reasons: 1) I am inclined to think that the hypertrophies in linguistics will gradually be reduced, with certain distinct gains remaining, and 2) the basal problems of perennial philosophy lie in the empirical pole, at least, as soon as one gives up any *a priori* knowledge about nature.

As regards this empirical pole, I shall argue that positivism must come to terms with realism in its modern forms. I believe that it would be correct to say that the Vienna Circle was not acquainted with the American realistic movement, which was, in many ways, more incisive than the corresponding English development. Their references to G. E. Moore concern more his method of analysis than his realism. As Professor Donald Williams suggests in a recent number of *The Philosophical Review,*[2] it is high time for this con-

---

1. I shall not try to take on Russell in this paper. Suffice it to say that my divergence from him stems in large part from a different theory of perception. This affects both the organic self and things. Hume was puzzled by the self and, no doubt, realized how his view would be affected by a realistic theory of the organic self. Bergmann is becoming aware of the self, as I shall note.
2. "Naturalism and the Nature of Things," 53 (1944):417–43.

tact to be made, and it is one of the purposes of this article to complete the electric circuit.

iii

Into the early history of the current of thought I need not enter in great detail, for it has been carefully documented by both friends and opponents. Under Schlick the Vienna Circle drew to itself philosophically inclined scientists. He, himself, was trained in physics and was once, I understand, something of a realist. Was it the influence of Mach permeating Vienna? Was it the impact of relativity physics? In any case, Schlick swung to *Erlebnisse, Kennen,* and *Erkennen.* I have been told that Einstein was much affected by Machism. I can well believe that it helped him escape from the intuitive rationalism of Newtonian physics, that is, its uncritical attitude toward basic concepts like space and time.

Now, as I have already indicated, it is well to remember that empirical immanentism was a conspicuous movement in the early part of this century and in the decade or so before. It seems to have had much in common with James's radical empiricism and Russell's later neutral monism. I still remember how I wrestled with Mach and Avenarius and Pearson when, in 1908, I was working at my doctoral thesis, some of the material of which was published in the succeeding years in the *Journal of Philosophy* as articles on space, time, and causality. In spite of having been introduced to relativity by Tolman, who was then teaching at Michigan, I kept to my realism and began to work toward the distinction between the categories of knowledge-about and ontological categories, which I stressed in both *The Principles and Problems of Philosophy* and in *The Philosophy of Physical Realism.* Time, I held, was ontologically only local activity, but physics needed mensurational, *factual knowledge* about the order and temporal distance of events for its laws. Thus I took a different direction from Schlick and called the resultant realism *critical realism,* a term some ten years later adopted for the *Essays* at the instance of Durant Drake.[3]

---

3. I had a great admiration for Drake as a man and as a thinker, but I

Now I do not believe that modern logical positivism can be accused of intentional affiliations with fideism, for it has sought to show that theological and ontological propositions—hardly separated seemingly—are *sinnlos*. But alas! criteria are apt to be arbitrary, as Carnap has implied in his famous aphorism, and certainly Maritain has shown that Christian Aristotelianism dislikes logical positivism less than it does Marxism with its forthright materialism. How can you prove that what is meaningless to one may not be very meaningful to another? And even Ayer's emphasis upon the difference between psychological and logical meaning does not quite answer. It is for this reason that I would qualify Professor Hall's suggestion that Thomism and positivism are the extremes today. That is a belief whose causes are fairly obvious. As a matter of fact, logical positivism is in between Thomism and materialism. And the same, I think, holds for pragmatism.[4]

The rejection of the epistemological dispute between idealism and realism was an accepted, and quite logical, phase of past empirical immanentism, as Lenin pointed out. Europeans had not yet thought out Perry's clever dodge, using the magic of the "new logic" and "external relations" to enable ideas to be things and things, ideas, *and so keep immanentism and realism*. What immanentists were excluding was the *transcendent* as something outside "experience." I shall argue that critical realism, by its reanalysis of perception, as a more complete, organic activity than sensing, and as involving the opposition of percipient and object perceived, draws off the mystery and venom from transcendence and reduces it to denotative reference.[5] It is because perceiving as a cognitive act involves directed reference to things that I do not altogether like the expression *epistemological dualism,* which was used in contrast to Perry's *immanentist*

---

did not agree with the essence doctrine. My stress was upon reference and conceptual disclosure.

4. To bring this out was one of my reasons for a recent debate with Professor Sidney Hook in the *Journal of Philosophy* 41 (1944) : 533–44, 544–51.

5. See *The Philosophical Review* 53 (1944) : 534–56, for the article "Causation and Perception." I am inclined to think that sensing is an abstraction from the complete S-R cycle. In awareness of sense-data, we are on the road to signs and symbolism.

monism. It seems to have suggested, to nearly every one, Kantianism and mysterious things-in-themselves. That is one reason why I have used the term *physical realism.* I am perceiving chairs and tables, but they are not immanent in the tradition of empirical immanentism. Ayer makes them constructs in the technical sense that statements about them can be translated into statements about sensations. I want the alternatives to be thoroughly explored, for I am very skeptical of the equivalence of such translations. They are, I think, quite evidently founded on the rejection of perception as a cognitive activity with its own justifiable categories, a rejection that goes back to traditional notions of transcendence and the trans-empirical. A clearer notion of the status of the organic self in perception is also involved. Obviously, the precise significance of the expression *thing-words* is in question. Is "I" a thing-word?

Let me illustrate. Bergmann is very careful to assert that no analysis of the empirical language rests upon epistemological assumptions, nor has it anything to do with perception or a theory thereof. That is, language analysis is strictly formal. He then proceeds to recognize the differences between a sense-data language and a physicalistic language. The primitives in the two cases are diverse. There is the suggestion that that scientific level is still higher, and, within limits, I am ready to agree with him. The divergence will probably appear in my rejection of operationalism and my stress upon factual knowledge about physical entities and processes, a knowledge in terms of mensurational quantities. But more important for my present purpose is the attitude taken toward a theory of perception and what Bergmann calls an *epistemological subject.*

Now I have never been clear as to the epistemology of methodological solipsism. Did it presuppose an epistemological subject dealing with *Erlebnisse* and engaged in *Kennen* and *Erkennen,* in *Aufbau?* Well, if it did not, it might easily suggest such an almost Kantian notion. I do not wonder, however, that Carnap and Bergmann are firm in their denial of such an implication. After all, they are empiricists of the immanent, or the *completely given,* school of thought. As we shall see, Bergmann thinks hopefully in neo-Humean terms of mental elements and passing thoughts as adequate to the self. This analysis of self and awareness by Bergmann is important.

I come now to the empirical theory of perception as against linguistic forms. Bergmann states that it is the task of psychology to give such a theory. I would agree with him to this extent, that an epistemological analysis of the directions and claims of perceptual knowing must not conflict with the psychological analysis. What is more, I hold that psychological analysis of perceiving best accords with the physicalistic language, and that a better analysis than behaviorism usually accords it must be made of the organic self as both knower and agent. But this point can be better taken up in connection with logical behaviorism and what Bergmann calls the *mentalistic mass*. Here is where the double-knowledge of the organic self must be confronted with the double-language theory of Feigl. I think that we can locate the total "mentalistic mass" within the organic self but that it requires a subtle epistemology and ontology. I have, I may say, written extensively upon these points.[6] The interesting feature of the situation is that Bergmann appears to suppose that *intuitionism* of a semi-Kantian type is the only alternative. I can put it this way: The "I" lies on the perceptual horizon on which we live. *The trouble has been that so much of behaviorism has ignored interpersonal discourse and reflexive self-awareness.* Linguistic analysis should assist here. "I" is at once a subject term and a thing term.

iv

Let me try to summarize the drift of the argument thus far. I have pointed out that the tradition of logical phenomenalism is essentially that of empirical immanentism and that the emphases of this outlook were *relative to the then-dominant ideas of transcendence and realism.* Physical realism, on the other hand, expresses an attempt to get away from both Kantianism and Lockeanism. Historically, it is more nearly tied in with Reid and his efforts to escape from Hume by questioning

6. *Critical Realism,* chap. 9; *Evolutionary Naturalism,* chap. 14; *The Philosophy of Physical Realism,* chap. 14.

his assumptions. It represents a *direct referentialism* in which the minded organism is reflexively aware of itself as over against other things: persons, animals, and inorganic masses. It differs from presentational, epistemological monism in that it does not hold that things are literally presented, or open to inspection. It stresses a directed reference and cognitional interpretation. It is thus *between* traditional notions of epistemological monism and Lockean representationalism. The emphasis is upon guided denotative reference and characterization, all of which can, naturally, be formulated linguistically.[7]

Now I do not know into what metaphysical theories of consciousness Bergmann will ultimately get. It is clear that they are on the horizon for him because of his increasing interest in the self and because of his recognition of the pluralism of consciousness. Even Feigl is apparently haunted by the need to escape from solipsism. The suggestions are that it will be along the lines of a nonromantic idealism. Will there be another development of panpsychism?

But, unless something of this sort is done, the tried gambit is that of phenomenalism, that is, *a stern acceptance of sensations and a refusal to account for them.* We shall have Mill over again, with the absurd reduction of matter to the permanent possibility of sensations. Or we shall have a *strong* phenomenalism, which refuses to ask the *sinnlos* (a valuable word when one gets into difficulties) question of the causal origin of sensations and the ground for their expected recurrence. The very fact that Lewis, Ayer, and the logical phenomenalists have fought shy of this question is revelatory. They are Berkeleians without a God as a substitute for matter. Or, to put it more decorously, they are Humeans with the proper mixture of phenomenalism and skepticism. The supporting tradition of empirical immanentism is now so old and self-sustaining that most of its representatives feel little need for Berkeleian substitutes or Humean shrugs. To them empiricism just means phenomenalism or, to be correct, phenomenalism has been fused with empiricism. And, as though to make assurance doubly sure and to calm any rising doubts, operationalism has made its timely appearance.

Let me not be misunderstood. One cause of the strength of phe-

---

7. Language guides realistic analysis.

nomenalistic empiricism has been the past weakness of realism. But I am arguing that Anglo-American realism is something that should now be confronted.[8] By distinguishing between the level of perception and the level of sensing, we can have a causal theory of sensation that does not lead to Lockeanism, for perceiving is a directed and interpretative response guided by sensations. Bergmann has a clear linguistic recognition of these levels but he, as yet, refuses to develop an *epistemology with a concrete, human knower.* He apparently associates epistemology with the tradition of a mysterious "epistemological subject" or with a transcendental ego below the level of sensations. But is it not the concrete percipient self that makes knowledge-claims?

Empirical immanentism, as I have indicated, represented a strong tradition at the beginning of the twentieth century. It argued for an outlook that bypassed the controversy between idealism and realism. I wonder whether Ayer realized what an old song he was singing. Materialism was too strong meat, culturally, and also had not been ably developed by academic philosophers.[9] It was at that period quite the usual thing for men like Mach and Ostwald to speak of atoms as fictions and conceptual shorthand. In short, materialism was scarcely on the academic horizon. Even today Carnap evidently thinks of absolute idealists as his primary opponents. But, surely, positivism must face the issue of ontological materialism—and that in a sophisticated form.

It is none too easy to regard atoms as fictions in these days of microscopic physics and electronic microscopes and x-ray photography. Only operational logic offers any escape; and, as we shall see, that is the general way taken by pragmatists and positivists, with a little help from the devices offered by Russellian logic, that is, to construct rather than to refer. Now, of course, all this is a kind of inverted Kantianism, that is, it is merely a kind of experiential constructionism *that avoids Kant's synthetic a priori.* It is to the credit of C. I. Lewis that he recognized this fact and grasped the nettle boldly. To the

---

8. In the broad sense in which I am using this term, Parker is clearly a realist. He also has a causal theory of sensations. Russell, also, accepts a causal theory of sensations.

9. This point is taken up by me in a recent article, "Reflections on Dialectical Materialism," in this journal, 5 (1944) : 157–79.—And science was too immature.

physical realist, Russell's dictum was a begging of the question, for the denotative reference of perception is not an inference, though it can be supported by a study of the external and internal conditions of perception.[10] Logical phenomenalism is, in other words, a revised Kantianism with the thing-in-itself left out, just as it is Berkeleianism with God omitted. As I have already indicated, the New Realism was also dominated by the tradition of empirical immanentism but, in its case, radical empiricism was reconstructed, not so much by means of turning sentences about material things into *just as good sentences* about sensations, as by the magic of the phrase *external relations,* so welcome to offset the idealist's internal relations. Just a bit of legerdemain, of course. My thesis has been that there is no cognitive relation at all, only a denotative reference and conceptual characterization in which the organic self, as percipient and knower, responds to, and becomes aware of, a *Gegenstand,* something other than itself in its environment, an awareness deepened by action and emotion and memory. There are two poles in perception.[11]

Now the upshot of this historical alignment is, as I see it, to the effect that the time is ripe for the confrontation of this long maturing and technically sophisticated development of empirical immanentism with the revision of realism that physical realism represents. Let logical phenomenalism meet, in fair debate, a critical form of physical realism. Let the positivistic, immanentist tradition grapple with a sophisticated type of materialism. And let there be no misunderstanding about the basic postulates of the two alignments. If I am at fault in any of my historical and descriptive explorations, let me be put right. I take it that both sides are, in intention, naturalistic and empirical in persuasion. There is no need of quoting Hegel or

---

10. I have the impression that Broad, Ewing, and Stebbing support this contention, though they seldom do justice to American critical realism as regards priority, perhaps because it means to them essences. It may be recalled that Pratt always appealed to my thesis that, in perception, we regard the objective of perception as as real as the percipient self. But he was a dualist with respect to the self-body question.

11. Propositional attitudes and the use of the word *I* must be taken seriously. I judge that Bergmann is exploring these factors of a linguistic hierarchy.

Heidegger at me; it can be just a family discussion. It is important to grasp the point that I have sought to revise the whole idea of transcendence by making denotative reference coordinate with the organic self and relating knowing to the complex activities characteristic of perception and judgment. Consciousness is held to be personal and intrinsic to the brain-mind of the percipient; and there is no *existential transcendence* by the individual of either his organism or his consciousness. Any epistemological use of the term *transcendence* is *sui generis* and refers to the mechanism and nature of knowing through denotative reference and conceptual disclosure. It does not imply any existential transcendence. But, of course, one who analyzes in this fashion does not regard epistemology as *sinnlos*.

It is also evident that the nature and status of the self are involved. Why? Because the percipient is to have the same objective status as the object perceived. The physical realist materializes both as coordinate. That is why, for me, the self is the minded and conscious organism. Self-awareness, likewise, must be analyzed somewhat along the lines of sense perception with, however, the recognition of such differences in the data employed as are obvious, such as feeling attitude, desire, intention. But I am increasingly inclined to think that the self is from the first felt as bodied, and that this identity unifies the external and the internal reference to the organic self, especially in the thought of attitudes and capacities. All this amounts to the deepening of our conception of the organism and an outgrowing of Cartesian dualism.

Increasingly, then, I take self-knowledge seriously and refuse to follow phenomenalism's traditional breakdown of the self into presentations. The reflexive self is as public as the organism, denotative reference to which can be publicly verified. It is merely the additional knowledge[12] that each of us has of himself which makes self-awareness richer in content than other-awareness. The framework remains public in the denotative sense. The psychical is intrinsic to the functioning organic self, and any discussion of *Fremdpsychische* must be

---

12. And, of course, the preferential position for self-knowledge. *This difference of height,* as Bergmann calls it, will come up later.

given this integration of epistemology and ontology. The very fact that physical realism can straighten out these traditional puzzles is, I take it, very much in its favor.

Suppose, then, that I bring to a head this preliminary exposition of the contrast I am building up before I begin the work of controversial analysis of such questions as the status of ontology, behaviorism, operationalism, the double-language theory of the mind-body problem, and so on. I want to reduce ambiguity to a minimum, for I suspect that the logical phenomenalists with their tradition of empirical immanentism are fighting a theory of transcendence I do not endorse. Perhaps some of these complexes can be lifted from the subconscious. Ayer, as a good Berkeleian, I am sure can never forget that Berkeley never had identical thing-ideas but merely similar ones. In my opinion, only a theory of perception that stresses denotative reference can get numerical identity and genuinely public, linguistic reference. Reflexive self-awareness merely deepens this public pattern.[13]

Now it should not be forgotten that the American realists were at least as well acquainted with the British empirical tradition as the logical phenomenalists were. They were trying to break through it to physical realism, having completely given up absolute idealism with the aid of the pragmatists. I feel rather oldish when I think of this period and recall that my first immature efforts to explore the mind-body problem were published in the *Psychological Review* and consisted in part of a criticism of Baldwin's position, he being then the editor.[14] But to the main point. Most of the New Realists were what I would call *presentational epistemological monists,* except Montague, who saw difficulties—his merit—and straddled. The way the terminology was set by Perry with his magic of "external relations," built on James's astonishing essay and Russell's new logic, induced those working along the lines of critical realism to call themselves epistemological dualists. As I see it now, it was a terminology leading

13. I still think my chapter in *Critical Realism,* "Is Consciousness Alien to the Physical," has been too much neglected.

14. It was entitled "A Fourth Progression in the Mind-Body Relation." The terminology followed Baldwin's. It was the beginning of my double-knowledge theory. This goes back to 1907.

to associations in the minds of many with Locke and Kant. We should have spoken of ourselves as *referential, epistemological realists. The dispute was really over the nature of perception.* Is it of the nature of a presentation? Or is it of the more complex nature of reference and interpretation? Of course, Pratt and Lovejoy, being ontological dualists, would probably still prefer the suggestions of dualism.[15] Physical realism, in this article, is a form of referential, epistemological realism. Chairs, tables, and persons are direct objectives of characterization. But they are not immanent in consciousness.

The decks are now cleared. Suppose I examine the following topics: empirical statements; testability and truth; ontology and theology; the body; behaviorism and double-language; operationalism with special reference to relativity and atoms; and the unity of science. My essential queries and questionings can be brought within this range of topics.

v

Much water has run over the dam since the first challenging formulations of the positivist's meaning of meaning. The emphasis was at first upon the method of verifying and often gave the impression that we do not know what we mean apart from the actual process of verifying what we mean. The animus was clear, that of leading back into experience in an operational sort of way. It was, as I see it, a quite logical device for empirical immanentism. But, as the debate proceeded, verifiability in principle and even the weaker form of testability were substituted. The complicated logical aspects of hypothesis-testing were fully recognized by Carnap and Ayer. The question remained, however, as to whether empirical statements could be framed that had meaning, although none of the recognized sciences had methods of testing them. Can we think of a life after death, of a transcendent God, and so on? If we can, then meaning extends beyond "scientific" testability, and, at the same time, the

---

15. I have the impression that Ledger Wood thinks of critical realism more in the Lovejoy fashion. As nearly as I can make out, Stace merely enlarges sensing to perceiving, in the Bosanquet fashion, and neglects what I call external reference and interpretation.

traditions of empirical immanentism are being challenged. I am myself little interested in such statements; in any case, such objects must tie in with the physical cosmos. I am satisfied with empirical statements. The question is this, What are they about? Things or possible sensations? The other side of the moon involves the essential points.

Now, as I read them, the formulations by Feigl, in his essay entitled *Logical Empiricism,* are excellent. They have assimilated Peirce's heuristic rule on how to make ideas clear. Also they include the impact of all known ways of testing *factual* statements and bring out the difference between the logical and the empirical. Satisfactory, also, is the criticism of Hume's rule, which emphasized a one-to-one relation between thoughts and sensations, and the stress upon language. It would appear that, like Ayer, he recognizes that questions of genesis are different from questions of validity. However thoughts may have developed, they cannot claim much cognitive value unless they can be brought into some coherent connection with the region of well-tested beliefs about ourselves and the observable world in which we live.

How, then, do I diverge from logical phenomenalism? Why, with respect to its phenomenalism, of course. It is my thesis that physical things—in the quite literal meaning of that term, that is, the realistic meaning—are observable *through* sensory data and that we can make confirmable statements about their structure, probable endurance, and behavior. In other words, I do not think that science is, as Bergmann seems to assume, reducible to predictions. I am inclined to take constitutive and dynamic *theories* fairly literally. While I do this, I recognize the role played by implicative predictions in the testing of theories, but I doubt that the theories are merely equivalent to the predictions. The chemical structure of molecules is a case in point.

It follows, of course, that I take *categorial meanings,* such as those which appear in thinghood, to be empirical and testable, once the realistic theory of perception, which I have called the referential, is adopted. Things perceived have the same status as the percipient, organic self. Hence, the struggle is not between empiricism and an anti-empirical view but one between two empirical theories of perception. Epistemology is not *sinnlos* but crucial; and the tradition of empirical immanentism from Mach and Avenarius to Carnap, Ayer, Bergmann, and Feigl—I leave out the terrifying cloud of witnesses that Feigl has summoned, which almost overawed me—can only reject physical realism by dogmatism and by repeating the old formula that there is no difference between idealism and realism. Now I assume that Bergmann and Feigl will not dismiss the analysis of the conditions and nature of perception which I have indicated and which I have explained in detail in articles and books. And so I assert that the claim that ontology is unempirical rests upon a sensationalistic thinning of perception which, in my opinion, is outmoded.

My conclusion is that physical ontology, that is, materialism, is an empirical affair and has nothing in common with the sort of mystical transcendence that, probably, Schlick was opposing. To emphasize this point, suppose we glance just for a moment at natural theology. Here we have a theory that, except perhaps in certain forms of pantheism, postulates an ontological deity linked with, but transcending, the physical cosmos. Abstractly speaking, I do not see that such a deity is inconceivable, for his existence is, supposedly, in some sense *continuous with* the physical universe. But, since such is the case, we must try to make statements about him empirical. Now theology as its best has tried to do so through natural theology. In my opinion, one of the weaknesses of recent neo-supernaturalism has been its break with this empirical tradition. I would agree with Laird that cosmology is essential to theology and that, for the theist, the universe must be in some sense *deiform*.[16] I must postpone to another section even a brief consideration of the nature of the more subjectivistic, empirical tradition of Protestant thought, deriving from Schleiermacher and moving to the outlook of Macintosh, Brightman, and Garnett. I have not found their propositions convincing because I could not agree with their epistemological and ontological arguments, which were more of the idealistic type. While Garnett is a realist, his ontological position is dualistic after the manner of Stout, Pratt, and Lovejoy. But I cannot sweep all their arguments away whole-

---

16. As it is for the neo-Thomist.

sale, as the logical phenomenalists seek to do, by fiat. If the tradition of empirical immanentism is faulty—as I have tried to show—then realistic empiricism must fight out all these traditional debates. The humanist argues that the physical universe is self-sufficient and that there are no indications of its deiformity or its inability to include all human experience and values. Here, as I see it, is the struggle of the future, which both Protestant empiricism and Catholic Christian Aristotelianism must meet. In short, the physical realist has an ontology on the base of realistic empiricism and he challenges the epistemological thesis of the logical phenomenalist. Ultimately, as I have tried to show, the pyramid rests upon the correct analysis of perception and the percipient self.

Let me turn next—and very briefly—to the question of truth.[17] Now empirical statements, whether referring to future experiences or to physical things, observable through sensory contents, must be testable or verifiable, directly or indirectly, through experience. Here I am, of course, in agreement with the great empirical tradition to which, after all, even Aristotle was not alien. It is the predictional, nomic side of science, which has been added to the more qualitative and classificatory outlook of Aristotle.

As is to be expected, logical phenomenalism, or positivism, is quite in touch with logic and scientific methodology, perhaps not so much to the exclusion of other philosophies as some seem to suppose. For example, I never thought of myself for a moment as not an empiricist. Struggling with Hume and Berkeley, while rejecting *a priori* rationalism of the Cartesian, Augustinian sort, was the inevitable set-up for my generation. But, as I said before, we were undertaking to do what Reid surmised was necessary: *Escape from phenomenalism, not from empiricism.*

To give the gist of the matter, the adjective "true" applies to empirical propositions, or meaningful statements, which are claims to

---

17. A discussion of truth is appearing in this journal (vol. 4 (1943–1944), pp. 236–284; 317–419; vol. 5 (1944) pp. 50–107. Ducasse and I have reached a fair measure of agreement. Vol. 4 (1944), pp. 317–340; vol. 5 (1944), pp. 98–103. Our divergence seems to stem from the fact that I hold that denotative characterizations *through* conceptual descriptions apply only to what is the case. Error is an abortive attempt and involves no subsistential realm.

know referents. Now that the logical positivists have got to semantics, pure and conceptual, there is no need to review those scholastic debates about whether propositions exist. Let us put our men-of-straw away in cold storage or make a bonfire of them. Fewer beginners in philosophy will be bewildered if we do so.

To say that a statement is true is to say that it can correctly be asserted, that it is *such that* it can perform its cognitive function, it will express facts about the referent, that it will disclose, or give knowledge about, the referent, that it will tell us what is, or was, the case. Such seems to me the *meaning* of this little adjective. Hence to assert *p* involves the belief that it is true, that is, gives factual knowledge. If *p*, "It is raining," is true, then it *is* raining.

But the complication enters with respect to the conditions of knowledge and the testing of empirical statements. It is here that the dispute about correspondence and coherence has had its animus. And we must remember that these controversies have been tied in with complex epistemologies, even with ontologies.

Let us forget Truth and Absolutism. Now, as I have long argued, the tests of empirical statements are both empirical and logical. I have tended to suppose that there was pretty general agreement here among all those who have analyzed scientific method. There is coherence and consistency; and there is the responsibility to data. I judge that the divergence between the logical phenomenalists and the realistic empiricists is that the latter regard the data as disclosing the state of affairs in the physical world that science and common sense are concerned with and that we are *perceiving through* data and concepts. In other words, statements are not primarily concerned with the data but with the objective state of affairs. Such statements will not be accepted as true unless they undergo these logical and direct, and indirect, tests of empirical responsibility.

I do not, I believe, need to go into the questions about "protocol sentences" or statements and their corrigibility. Ayer has, I take it, made sufficient qualifications. As I see it, the logical phenomenalists have matured and recognized the part played by concepts. And my present interest is not so much in knowledge-by-acquaintance as in knowledge-about, that is, reference and characterization.

Within the context of empirical immanentism, there can only be varying emphases upon coherence of statements and the agreement of observational statements with sensory data. The realistic empiricist, on the other hand, has all this to bear in mind and something else, namely, the capacity of descriptive statements, from the level of the perception of physical things to the level of theories about their constitution and behavior, to mediate knowledge about the physical world. Such is the cognitive function they must perform.

So far as I can see, the tests used are experiential and of the sort indicated above; but the claims and import are different. We do not try to translate statements about physical things into statements about possible sensations. Categorial meanings are retained as significant and as filled out by facts about structure, position, behavior, capacities. The context is that of the concern with things and organic selves. The difference of context and import should by now be clear.

What, then, does the attainment of well-tested statements as candidates for the accolade of trueness signify? Merely, as I said, that they disclose, or give knowledge about, what is the case. But philosophical theory can hardly restrain itself from asking how this result can be accomplished, through what mechanisms and correspondences. And it is only at this stage that the physical realist theorizes about the mechanisms and conditions of knowledge. He accepts the fact of human knowledge as guaranteed by *praxis* from the level of guided perceptual adjustment to scientific prediction. The claim is there; and skepticism seems to him valid only against naïve conceptions. But if we have knowledge, its conditions must be achieved. To make a long story short, correspondence becomes, for him, a term neither for the tests of truth nor for the meaning of truth but for the nature and mechanisms of knowing. It deals with the *theory* of such things as how sensory data can have the capacity to disclose something about the properties of extra-bodily states of affairs and how concepts can do the same at a more abstract and synthetic level; and how the facts, so grasped, can fit into categorial meanings at the respective levels of common sense and science, for categories require refinement with finer facts, that is, facts resting on scientific, and not merely organic, techniques.

It is, I take it, clear that this additional level in the theory of truth spells the difference between logical phenomenalism and physical realism. Both, I think, are quite logical within their respective contexts. The materialist says "both—and," while the phenomenalist tends to cling to his implicit solipsism. His is the spirit that denies, possibly because he has phobias connected with traditional notions of speculative philosophy. The materialist, on the other hand, has plowed through to an ontology of a naturalistic sort and offers a hand to the scientist, urging him to be no longer afraid of ontology, for it offers him a firmer foundation than phenomenalism ever can. And so I think that even logical phenomenalism is dated and even outdated. Nevertheless, in spite of some rather irritating features of this incursion, when the realists were completely ignored and extreme pronouncements the order of the day, it must be acknowledged that much has been clarified. But I do think it is about time for positivism and materialism to thresh out their differences so that people can see in just what the divergence lies.

vi

The ontology of the critical materialist seems to him in no wise to conflict with scientific facts. In truth, he thinks that most scientists who have not been indoctrined by phenomenalism or by strained interpretations of operationalism tend to look at things much as he does, though he will probably ask questions additional to those of the specialist in science, questions bound up with the categories and with the mind-body problem.

Hence he is somewhat startled when Feigl loads ontology *per se* with all the incubi of cultural thought.[18] Thus, "Finally transcendental metaphysics in its attempt to uncover the basic categories of both thought and reality may turn out to be nothing else than an unclear combination of epistemology and cosmology, which is then dignified with the name 'ontology.' " The *patient empiricist* knows that he has to do with emotive terms. Now the materialist is an ontologist but not much given to emotive terms. Let the positivist

18. Especially pages 385–86.

forget the religionist and the speculative, romantic idealist for a while and take on someone as hard-boiled as himself. . . .

I always admit that I do not like the word *metaphysics,* because so many associate it with doctrines about an ultimate reality lying beyond anything physics can tell us about. Referential epistemological realism knows nothing about meta-physics. On the other hand, it seems to me that the physicist today is a little puzzled with respect to epistemology and the categories; and, if one is an honest philosopher believing that he has some professional competence, he will feel that it is his duty to make suggestions for what they are worth.[19]

It is also clear that Feigl, like Russell, wants to give up absolute space, time, causality, and substance as examples of metaphysical bondage. I, on the other hand, following the logic of physical realism, want them revised and put into their proper context. I am not a Newtonian for both epistemic and ontological reasons. Space and time are for me adjectival and not substantival. About this I have written much elsewhere; and I shall have something to say when I discuss relativity. Again, even decades ago, I never dreamed of regarding numbers as Platonic entities. They are obviously only concepts developed around operations like counting.[20] While, then, I applaud the lead Einstein has given to the mensurational interpretation of physics, I am skeptical whether it involves more than a better understanding of s and t; and, of course, the consequent recognition that there is no preferred position in the formulation of scientific laws. That is, of course, technically magnificent. But it concerns what I call knowledge-about.

The gist of the matter is, accordingly, that the physical realist must clarify ontology while the logical phenomenalist escapes responsibility. It seems to me that Feigl skims over thin ice like a graceful skater.*

---

19. It is obvious that Bridgman, Eddington, and Jeans do not see eye to eye. And Levy and Haldane would differ from all three.

20. There are no *threenesses* in nature—only pluralities. Until Russell is clearer about the nature of a class, I prefer to think of number as an applicable concept connected with symbols and their rules.

* In more recent years, Sellars has been crediting Feigl with becoming a critical realist. Evidence of this development in Feigl's thought appears in his prefatory article, "Philosophical Tangents of Science," in *Current*

vii

I feel there is very little need to say more about theology in its relation to ontology. In intention, theology can, I believe, be empirical. My doubt concerns its ability to make the necessary linkage with man and nature, the empirical foundation. St. Thomas had the right approach but his natural theology rests upon assumptions that do not accord with facts and categories as the physical realist sees them in the light of scientific knowledge. Here is where the struggle between Christian Aristotelianism and reformed materialism is engaged. Protestant empiricists usually depend upon a mind-body dualism if not upon complete idealism. As for the dialectical Calvinists, I am unable to see that they have any clear natural theology or even desire one. I am ready to give them over to the tender mercies of the logical positivists; but I judge it would be a case of rhetorical cudgeling; and who would get the better of the other in the use of such weapons? Perhaps it would result in one side intoning the magic word *science,* while the other side, not to be outdone, evoked the magic word *revelation.*

viii

Let us turn next to what may be called the context of the mind-body problem, that is, to what the body is, how the term *behaviorism* is used, the status of consciousness and the *Fremdpsychisch.* All this ties in together, and the main contrast between the materialist and the logical phenomenalist is not hard to draw.

Now it is quite obvious that, for me, "I," "you," and "thing" lie on the same level and that both I and you are organic selves and both knowers and practical agents. Moreover, I am skeptical of the entity Bergmann constantly refers to disapprovingly as the "epistemological subject." Such an entity does not enter into my economy. Furthermore, I do not think that either the perceiving of the things

---

Issues in the Philosophy of Science (New York: Holt, Rinehart, and Winston, 1961) pp. 5–6; cf. also Feigl, *The "Mental" and the "Physical"* (Minneapolis: University of Minnesota Press, 1958 and 1967), pp. 79–80, 86–87.

around us or self-awareness is an affair of givenness. Rather is it an affair of guided reference and characterization. As regards the cognitional status of sensations, I would hold that it is that of activity plus a supplementary knowledge-of-acquaintance. And knowledge-of-acquaintance does not have the *same* kind of objective and interpersonal reference that perception and scientific knowledge have. Self-awareness needs more careful study than it has yet received.

It would carry me too far afield to take up the whole question of introspection and its assumptions. I presume that what Bergmann calls "the mentalistic mass" is connected with this problem. In the strict sense, introspectional *reports* seems to me necessarily public in import but to concern data that are open only to personal knowledge-of-acquaintance. Such reports presuppose, in other words, referential knowledge and interpersonal discourse and are recognitions of factors that guide and mediate such discourse for each one. The point is that objective knowing is a complexly conditioned operation and that we quickly become aware of that fact. I do not see why Bergmann refers to this mentalistic mass, open, first, only to intuition supplemented by knowledge-of-acquaintance and then to public knowledge-about as being "above" the thing plane. I suspect that his empirical immanentism and his hankering after methodological solipsism enter here. As I see it, the essential thing is to recognize that referential cognition is not reducible to intuition and knowledge-of-acquaintance.

His strictures upon the "double-language" formula as a formalization of the *brain-mind* of my view are interesting. In what sense do these two languages speak about the *same*? Linguistic analysis should, of course, help empirical analysis.

Now I see no reason to let Bergmann escape by the channels of an appeal to the present limits of psychology. What is the ineffable but what symbols are about? I think that I can talk about anything I experience or claim to have knowledge-about. As for my formulation of the mind-consciousness-organism complex, I think it is philosophically clearer than Koehler's phraseology just because it has a more explicit epistemology and ontology. Though Koehler appeals to Lovejoy's formulation of epistemological dualism, it must be remembered that Lovejoy is a psychophysical dualist in the ontological sense, whereas I have always contended for a double-knowledge of the brain-mind—and by brain-mind here I have always signified the thesis that mental activities and experiences are rightly assignable to the brain. The precise way of thinking *consciousness* with respect to the *minded brain* was, for me, a very delicate problem in ontology, which I approached in terms of the thesis that in consciousness alone is the individual on the inside of the brain-mind system, that is, participating experientially in its working. *This involved no crude theory of isomorphism.*

The epistemological upshot of all this is that the so-called common-sense core of solipsism represents a confusion between intuition of data and knowledge-of-acquaintance, on the one hand, and referential knowledge with interpersonal intercourse on the other. Psychological behaviorism has always, as Russell pointed out in *Philosophy,* been epistemologically naïve. What it has really had in mind is referential knowledge of the sort we have in the physical sciences with neglect of the complexities of self-awareness and knowledge-of-acquaintance. It began with Watson's rats with whom he could not chat. I leave out the reaction against the scientific adequacy of the introspective tradition. My psychological friends here tell me that the proper integration is proceeding. In my opinion, such a theory as mine of the proper epistemology involved and of the organism, mindedness or *mentation*—to use Coghill's term—and consciousness would throw light upon the situation.

Now I have the impression that Bergmann might not essentially disagree with me but that his incomplete comprehension of the realistic theory of referential knowledge together with an assumption that it involves a quite literal givenness of the self in self-awareness may have misled him. The tradition of empirical immanentism is still too strong. Perhaps my thesis that the "I" is a thing—that is, the organism—but a thing minded, conscious, and capable of both public, referential knowledge and language and of reflexive reference, which can then be reported back into public knowledge and the corresponding language, is now clearer. But it involves realism and a more flexible and critical materialism, that is, ontology. Bergmann seeks to get to structures below the intermediate plane of interpersonal discourse and realistic epistemology. But the danger here is reductionism.

It is noteworthy that Ayer, in discussing other selves, takes refuge in the body as the overt phenomenon involved. But what can a good Berkeleian really do with the body? It becomes only a phenomenal *point de repère*. Even this compromise he seems to have given up.

ix

We come now to the problem of other selves and the *Fremdpsychisch*. In some measure, this question should be a test case as to the comparative power of the intellectual instruments set up.

To the realist, other organic selves are, quite obviously, referential things on the same level as himself. Like himself, they differ from inorganic things and the lower animals in the way of conduct. Here we have the application of a referential realism that reduces transcendence to otherness, to guided selection of loci in the environment. Other organic selves are no more hypotheses than are other physical things.

Social psychology has thrown much light upon the growth of self-awareness and other-awareness so far as these awarenesses go beyond the basic perceptual reference to public things, including the bodied organic self. Cooperation, conflict, adjustment, signaling, communication, all play their part. Royce, Cooley, Mead, and others were pioneers. As I see it, all this merely signifies a deepening of the notion of what selves are, but presupposes the realistic framework. Mind-body dualisms and nonrealistic epistemologies have created false problems.

But reflection forces the individual to admit personal consciousness with its intuition and knowledge-of-acquaintance as an essential *condition* of realistic, referential knowledge. Having built up to the realistic belief in other selves on the perceptual basis outlined above, it is to be expected that he will assign to others what he finds about himself, that is, the personal conditions of reference and communication. He finds he can even communicate reports about his personal data and meet corresponding reports; and, where there are differences, these can be largely correlated with physiological differences.

In other words, he finds no reason to believe that he differs from other people or that other people differ from him, along the lines of James's automatic sweetheart. *It follows that other selves are no more inferences than are other physical things.* Social behavior plays more of a role than does analogy. And, of course, analogy presupposes realism. There must be at least three terms, two organic selves, publicly aware of each other, and one aware of his own conscious data about which he can report.

The basis of the usual problem is that the self is equated with consciousness and it is suddenly realized that one person cannot intuit and have knowledge-of-acquaintance of another self's consciousness. And, so far as I can see, that's that. But he can certainly talk in a public way about such data and gain descriptive, referential knowledge about them. When, therefore, the ultimate doubt assails him, of which philosophy has made so much ado, the answer cannot be that of achieving acquaintance with other consciousnesses of other selves but of recognizing the situation as a factual one and realizing that there is no good reason to suppose that he is unique among all these organic selves. Now, so far as I can judge, Bergmann's emphasis upon difference of height is just *the recognition that each one must do his own knowing* and that knowing involves personal consciousness, though referential knowing is concerned with public objects and interpersonal communication. Traditional idealism, by excluding referential knowledge, identified the organic selves with their consciousness and so constituted at best a pluralism of separate consciousnesses. And it strikes me that this is just about where Bergmann is with his nonromantic idealism. Realism changes the venue.

And that is where I shall leave the problem of the *Fremdpsychisch* for the present.

It follows from this analysis that all of us have a double knowledge of ourselves: knowledge through external perception of our bodies and our behavior, including our language habits, and knowledge guided by our feelings and desires and thoughts as data for what I call reflexive self-awareness. These flow together and form a living concept of the self. But we also have, as an unavoidable factor in the mind-body problem, *the allocation of consciousness*—that is, how to think its insertion in the functioning brain ontologically. Here critical realism permits a *depth* materialism that the new realism does not. Montague apparently thinks that, if consciousness is in the brain, we should be able to see it. So far as I can make out, it is a *natural isolate* connected with the brain's functioning. That is, it is confluent with the active brain and is the one factor that is intuitively given. It is a unique part-whole affair and the self's only conscious participation in the life of the evolved, organic system that it is. If this is not empiricism, then I regard empiricism as a form of sensationalism, blind to the depth and ontological quality of being.

x

I come next to operationalism, fictionalism, and relativity. Here, again, it is, for me, a case of "both—and" and not of "either—or." I recognize to the full the operational and constructional methods of physics. Knowledge is not given on a platter or by means of intuition. The divergence between the logical phenomenalist and the materialist concerns the question of the cognitive import of science. Do these operations and concepts mediate knowledge *about* a material world? Or do they merely enable us to build up physics, for example, as a set of observations, operations, empirical constructs, theoretical models, empirical laws, and predictions?

May I say, to begin with, that I find, in the main, nothing but desirable refinements in the logic and methodology of science so much emphasized by logical positivists, though I really cannot discover much that is basically new, or revolutionary, in the technique. After all, reflection on science has a long logical and philosophical history. The logical self-consciousness of scientists in these latter days has made considerable difference. And much of this is due to the impact of the relativity theory. To this has been added the continuing influence of the tradition of empirical immanentism, pugnaciously regarding itself as the only true form of empiricism.[21]

21. I am a little inclined to think that empiricism has become for many an emotive—or shall I call it pragmatic—term? Historically, empiricism declared that *knowledge* must rest upon experience. It did not say that it can only concern experience. What is meant by asserting that physical things are either reducible to sensations or are trans-empirical?

The preceding sections give us a foundation on which to build and enable us to see the alternatives quite clearly. I have been arguing for a realistic empiricism, that is, for human experience as a basis for knowledge about a material world. And we can see that when Bergmann, for instance, talks about the observation of physical things, he does not mean by that phrase what the realist means. Pointers and instruments are, for Bergmann, derivatives characteristic of the medium plane of discourse. For me, they are material things *observable through* sensory appearances. The watershed is here and is epistemological.

The philosophy of science is, in my opinion, not reducible to logic and methodology without a remainder, but also involves the issue whether science is both knowledge and knowledge-about. This is more than a linguistic question. I can quite understand how a physicist, like Bridgman, may for various reasons become anti-ontological and desire to keep within the context of physics as a system of observations, operations, and theories. He will then be satisfied with factual information and prediction without concern for the material world. Now this myopia, which logical phenomenalism encourages, is, I take it, based upon a premature rejection of the possibility of a better ontology of space and time than was postulated in Newton's strange mixture of physics and theology. Surely space and time—as against *s* and *t*—are adjectival characteristics of the physical world and not things-in-themselves, capable of being intuited in terms of an outmoded mathematical rationalism. Moreover, operations prepare the way for observations, and observations are not reducible to operations. In the human organic technique, even, such operations as comparison do not modify the data obtained but merely make their discovery possible.

To make a long story short, the material existence of atoms is *meaningful* for a physical realist, for he has a different conception of physical things than has the logical phenomenalist. They are literal constituents of material things, corresponding more or less adequately to the physicist's concept. But, to Bergmann, such a conception is naïve and resort is made to the mystic of the movement, Wittgenstein. He should merely assert that if there are only material things in a Pickwickian sense—as he holds—then atoms can only be unifying fictions.[22] To the physical realist, the concepts of atoms are unifying and *also* disclose the atomic constitution of material things.

Which gambit will the philosopher take for his game? That depends, as I see it, upon his epistemology.

This watershed applies to "reduction of an abstract term to the physicalistic verification basis" likewise. Abstract terms should have their verification basis, of course, but their reference and significance are not so reducible. Entropy, electrical fields, and currents, all these seem to me to involve statements about physical processes. It is my suspicion that Bergmann is in the tradition of Mach and Ostwald and of the science of that era. It is just empirical immanentism and the undercutting of the idealism-realism controversy by fiat working itself out. I have high respect for the sophisticated technique employed. It is admirable. But the crux of the affair is epistemological. It is for this reason that I do not consider such further topics as ontological causality and empirical laws. The opposing doctrines are consistent. The materialist says "both—and," while the logical phenomenalist says "either—or" and affirms his alternative, the Humean.

What is absolute simultaneity? Merely the order of co-actuality as against the order of before and after. In any locus the "before the actual" is the past and is, of course, nonexistent. The recognition of that fact is the basis of tense. The same holds for the "after the actual," which is the future and the not-yet-actual. It follows that knowledge about events must seek to approximate, as nearly as possible, these orders of co-actuality, beforeness and afterness. It is also clear that there are no *temporal relations* but only a temporal order of events.[23] The aim of science is to gain as approximate a knowledge of that order as possible by means of operations and *s-t* measurements.

Recently I have ventured to reject the assumption that light moves in ether or space and to regard it as an extensity-activity. Even more than time, space needs analysis.[24]

---

22. I am referring to his *Scientific Monthly* article, 59 (1944) : 145.

23. Similarity and simultaneity are not relations but bases for factual statements of the relational type.

24. A semantic study of relativity has appeared in the *Philosophical Review*. I there argue that we should expect the zero result of the Michelson-Morley experiment when we give up ether and space.

While, then, it is foolish to reify the abstractions of physics, it is not unjustified to hold that they mediate genuine knowledge about the nomic routine of the cosmos. The interest is primarily in the routine and the possibility of prediction and control rather than in metaphysical questions. That is why, for instance, the distinctions between past, present, and future in physics concern primarily only order and temporal distance and not the startling difference between actuality and nonactuality. It is in history, human life, and practical application that the moving finger of actuality, that is, of *activity*, stands out. Prediction, on the other hand, can work as well backward and forward; and space-time has often been thought of as a Platonic sort of fixed continuum.[25]

xi

And now I wish to say something about the "Unity of Science" program. Of course, I, who had worked all my intellectual life to break down the barriers in nature that James Ward had so emphasized, the chasm between the organic and the inorganic, between living things and minded things, had my interest aroused. But evolutionary naturalism with its theory of the connection between novelty and integrative causality and organization was disregarded. It was to be merely a matter of the primacy of the language of physics. Optimism or provincialism? The primacy of physics is an ancient tradition.

Now in the last chapter of *Evolutionary Naturalism* (1921), I argued that mind is a physical category, that is, can be expressed in the setting of behaviorism. In an article in the *Journal of Philosophy*[26] I asserted that mentation is physical, much to the scandal of my good friend Pratt. The more difficult problem, as I saw it, was bound up with the status of consciousness. Now Bergmann and Feigl are likewise aware of the crucial nature of this factor, as we have seen. Since I have already indicated my way of inserting it into the functioning organism, I need not go over the grounds again. Consciousness is indispensable for the physicist as conscious knower but has no

---

25. At least, Minkowski suggested such an outlook.
26. "Is Consciousness Physical?", 19 (1922): 690–94.

place in his statements about the world. It is the job of the psychologist and of the philosopher to handle it.

I judge from Bergmann's remarks that he associates the idea of emergence with Koehler's Gestaltism. Now I am quite aware of the history in Germany of the notion of *Gestaltqualitäten* from Ehrenfels to Wertheimer. But the conception of emergence developed in England and the United States in a less merely psychological medium. The foreshadowings of it from Mill to Lewes have been pointed out by Lloyd Morgan. Those who are interested in my own connection may be referred to Lloyd Morgan's discussion of my position in the appendix to his book and to McDougall's treatment in his *Modern Materialism and Emergent Evolution* (1929).

But questions of priority are beside the point. I only put it in because so many Americans ignore the part played by Spaulding, Lovejoy, Wheeler, Jennings, and myself.[27]

Now the heart of the ontological theory of emergence is the conception of integrative causality and the development of new action-patterns or functional wholes. As I see it, it expresses a rejection of old-fashioned mechanism with its rigid atoms and empty space and mere positions. But physics has outgrown those notions. The primary principle of my concept of emergence is the belief in the active self-directedness of physical systems from the cosmic, inorganic floor upwards. I postulate, in other words, the *generic* characteristic of all physical systems to be relatively self-directed activity or immanent directedness, taking this latter term and robbing it of the dualistic implications of active form and passive matter of Platonic Aristotelianism. Evolution, or emergence, postulates the rise of new wholes having new properties expressive of their integrative unity. Integrative causality prepares the way for immanent causality, that is, for internal functional togetherness.

May I say that I could never see why so much ado has been made over the boundary line between physics and chemistry so long as molecules are not shown to be merely *aggregates* of atoms. As I have

27. See his "The Status of Emergence," *Journal of Philosophy* 39 (1942): 486–93. His analysis of the logical conditions of prediction seems to me excellent. But the ontological question is that of rules of composition, or togetherness, in physical systems, if we relinquish old-fashioned mechanism. What kind of unity shall we give integrative systems?

followed work in physical chemistry, I have noted that merely additive notions have been undermined. A molecule is a unitary system; electrons express in their position the fields of force operating. Need I refer to the delicate work done in physical chemistry by Professor Fajans? In other words, I find it hard to grasp just what is meant by the glib statements about the forthcoming reduction of chemistry to physics. The only discontinuity I believe in equally holds of atomic physics, that is, the importance of the sort of integrative causality that manifests itself in the atom as against the electron. And I suppose an electron is a phase of some dynamic pattern or field. All of which means that the theory of emergence, as I conceived it, was directed against the old barrier notion of Ward. The novelty would be a rejection of mechanical uniformitarianism. It is really a question of the *texture* of nature. Basic concepts are changing.

Bergmann seems to me to be handling the problem of vitalism in much the same terms as Jennings, Wheeler, and I conceived it, that is, the rejection of classical atomistic, mechanical notions and the adoption of organismic ideas without any mystical holism. The crucial question here is that of the operation in some patterned way of a systematic complex of chemical controls. Vitalism, as dualism, we reject. The need is for biochemistry and philosophy to achieve more adequate categories in connection with integrative causality.[28]

A conception of mindedness, or mentation, as a physical category, follows along the same lines. As I see it, we simply have, in the brain, a physical system, which integrates and accumulates action-patterns and is plastic and, in its measure, capable of new patterns. I cannot take seriously Russell's coinage of mnemic causation if it means literally that the past affects the present. For me, the past has only a vicarious existence in the brain-pattern laid down. Here is where the materialist has an advantage over the eventist. Time, activity, is in nature and not nature in time. The basis of memory must be in effective organization.[29]

---

28. I think that Professor Ralph S. Little has done excellent work in accounting for directive action. But I am not quite clear as to his use of the term "psychical."

29. Here, again, I am astonished at Professor Montague's assumption that the mind contains the past in a fashion the brain cannot. Surely, only traces of the past continue to exist. These are the basis of memory judgments.

The place of consciousness in the theory of emergence is a special one because we must then shift from physical categories of knowledge-about to something literally experienced. Here, and here alone, as I have always remarked, each one is participating in the activity of his brain, his locus in nature. It is out of this fact that the pluralism of consciousnesses, which so intrigues Bergmann, arises; and by it is this pluralism explained.

Now the emergence of consciousness, as we experience it, cannot be tied in with the physical categories, for these never contain an intuition of the content of a physical system. In that sense, matter is factually cognizable but not intuitable; it is that which has structures and is quantitative and acts nomically. But, for the ontologist, matter cannot be empty. It must be something *concrete* justifying the *facts about it* that science discloses. It is, however, not reducible to these facts.

The panpsychist, in my opinion, is simply one who assigns more existential weight to consciousness than it can carry. I have argued that consciousness is an existential isolate from a functioning brain-mind system, having, so far as I can see, guidance value. But I am an existential, *intuitionalistic agnostic,* so far as the existential context of consciousness is concerned, not an agnostic in terms of descriptive knowledge-about. Going down the scale of animal organization, I am as skeptical as Bergmann is of the consciousness of ants. Even analogical intuition in large measure fails us. And I have not the ghost of an idea as to the "feeling" of the protein molecules of the tobacco mosaic-disease virus. All I hold is that there must be some concrete filling to the activities of the molecular system. Thus consciousness emerges not out of something alien to the possibility of consciousness, as the traditional type of materialism seemed to suggest, but out of an internal quality of being, which I cannot intuit because I am limited to the emergent level of mindedness for my intuition and knowledge-of-acquaintance. It may be just too bad, but this seems to be the human situation. And thinking of the immensity of the cosmos and how rare the gradient level we occupy on this little planet, this limitation strikes me as quite the thing to expect. And this is what I call *intuitionalistic agnosticism.* Our *knowledge* about nature is very abstract. But nature is not itself abstract.

While I am at it, it may be advisable to make a brief comment on two points frequently raised in connection with a materialistic form of emergence theory. I think Henle is quite right in his analysis of prediction as involving at least four relations and as being, logically, a very complicated and human affair. It is relative to the theory of the level for which predictions are being made. I suppose the denial of predictability in much of the theory of emergence was due to the reaction against La Placian notions of almost *a priori* deducibility. There are complex questions about the relations of mathematics to science involved here, into which I have no space to enter. So far as I can see, mathematics is merely used by science and the empirical element is inescapable. Integrative causality involves new types of wholes, but these presuppose the properties of the parts that help to constitute them. Thus we have neither an aggregate nor a mystical and unconditioned whole. And so the hierarchy of integrations moves upward to new abilities. I should like to see a discussion of *negative predictability*. Can the physicist predict what cannot emerge?

For instance, Garnett argues against the emergence of mind on the assumption that mental acts are cognitive acts and that cognitive acts are linked with their objects in a fashion no physical activity could parallel. But this argument rests on the belief in a *cognitive relation* between a mental act and its denoted objective, a belief that I reject. There is no cognitive relation.[30] And so, as I see it, Garnett's chief argument against materialism falls to the ground and, with it, one of the main supports for his empirical theism, that is, psychophysical duality.

xii

What I undertook to show in the last section was that the Unity of Science campaign was rather superficial from its inception. Where are you to draw the line between the philosophy of science and the

30. Parker has come to the same conclusion. Reference and symbolic disclosure suffice.

philosophy of nature? Logical phenomenalism had fewer problems than physical realism because it had sliced off ontology.

And here I shall make my suggestions with respect to the categories. I take it that they develop around perceiving just because denotative reference and symbolic interpretation go together. And that is why the sensationalist, or Humean, has so much difficulty in handling categories. He seeks to explain categories away because he cannot find them adequately represented in sensations. From his point of view categorial meanings are not hard data. If we take referential perceiving and reflexive self-awareness as the basic interpretative acts, then the categories express meanings inseparable from this frame of reference. Bergmann, quite rightly, recognizes common-sense realism and the physicalistic language it involves, but, like Hume, wants to explain it away. I, on the other hand, want to clarify and develop it. And that is, essentially, what critical realism is.

The gambits are now before us. Both claim to be true to the empirical tradition, namely, the rejection of *a priori* rationalism as a means of knowing the world. The one gambit works along the line of neo-Humeanism and achieves a high level of analysis. The other commends much of this analysis but seeks to give it a more adequate framework. Like Reid, it holds it necessary to escape from the "way of ideas." One more remark. Categorial meanings do not permit *a priori* entailments, for the empirical, cognitive value of categories must be established experientially. Thus causality is a categorial fact about changes and not a particular descriptive fact. To say that Brutus killed Caesar is to state a descriptive fact involving the categorial fact of causality.

I suggest, then, that a fuller exploration of the "I" and of the linguistic domain that the positivists call pragmatics will indicate that it is the minded and conscious organism that is so symbolized. Hence the realism that the phenomenalist avoids in external perception will confront him in the exploration of the self. And is not realism, *prima facie,* the most plausible position? I take it that phenomenalism presupposes the inability of the realist to expand and clarify common-sense realism. And it has been my thesis that the

Vienna movement was not sufficiently aware of developments within American realism. It is, at least, time for such a confrontation.

A critical, *depth* materialism is not so appalling. It surrounds us with immensities; but these immensities are self-regulating and without malice. The ethical metaphysics of oriental asceticism, which regarded matter as evil, has little authority in a scientific age. We know that even the lilies that raise "their pure, white heads above the dirt" have vital roots that just adore the good humus and manure gardeners dig in around them. And the true artist feels in his fingertips the plastic quality of the materials that he is shaping. It is man's glory that, in him, these self-directed forces have at long last combined on this dear, cantankerous planet of ours to culminate in him and his works. The advocate of reformed materialism does not look upon nature merely from the outside, as traditional, mechanical materialism did, but has a feel, however dim, for its categorial nature and immanent force and vitality. That is why I call it a qualitative, evolutionary, depth materialism.

I most emphatically protest the arrogant claim of those who, by fiat, identify empiricism with phenomenalism. Empiricism is, historically, a rejection of *a priori* rationalism. But, to me, even the categories are empirical. It is around the axes of *reference* that they develop, self-reference and external reference.

5

Two Divergent Naturalistic Theories of Sense Perception: Pragmatism and Critical Realism*

i

It is my intention, in the present paper, to examine John Dewey's "perspective realism" and to contrast it with the direct, referential realism that I have long advocated under the designation *critical realism*. In these positions we have alternative, philosophical gambits of considerable importance. My main task here will be to distinguish them.

Any adequate estimation of Dewey's philosophy demands an appreciation of his main drives and interests. On the whole, I think that Professor Gail Kennedy's summation is essentially correct.[1] Dewey's stress was upon the role of intelligence in relation to values and human living. I take this to be the view of Professor Sidney Hook likewise. And, as I look back at my long years of interaction with American pragmatism, I find myself agreeing with, and also appreciative of, the combination, in Dewey, of emphasis on method and on goals.

---

* An unpublished essay printed with the authorization of its writer.
1. Gail Kennedy on Dewey, in Fisch, *Classic American Philosophers* (New York: Appleton-Century-Crofts, 1957).

And yet, in my opinion, there is a flaw in Dewey's outlook that tended to vitiate it and rob it of its full impact. This was his attitude toward knowledge. I think Dewey was aware of this fact and somewhat puzzled by it. He tended, I think, to get even a little emotional about it and to fall back on phrases such as the "spectator theory of knowledge," "mirroring reality," and "antecedent reality." These expressions symbolized for him the alternative to his own instrumentalism. They get much of their meaning in this light. But I do think—and I shall try to show—that these expressions connect up with his belief that they are tied in with muddles in epistemology and ontology of the sort found in Descartes, Locke, and Kant, which had produced a kind of stalemate in philosophy. Hegel had tried to re-route philosophy along the lines of his objective idealism. What Dewey did, I shall try to show, was to transform this kind of idealism with its *constitutive reason,* by stressing activity in a bio-logical and naturalistic setting. Here he was influenced, as we all know, by Darwin and by William James. He kept the covering term *experience,* for lack of a better, though he flirted with the term *culture* as an alternative.

A bit of the history of American philosophy will be involved, though I shall try to keep it subordinate. Let me say at this point to those who belong to the tradition of American pragmatism, that it has always been my purpose to supplement it and enlarge it rather than to replace it or cast it aside. It has so many valuable insights and emphases. But the inadequacy of its epistemological and onto-logical framework—and I hold that these two philosophical disci-plines are interconnected—have prevented its spread to Europe. There, the tradition emphasized the theoretical investigation of nature and, rightly or wrongly, subordinated practice to it. But, surely, the ideal would be to relate the two together. Justice could be done to both dimensions of human thought. Having this in mind, I was encouraged by a statement by Professor Warner Wick who, quite clearly, has a well-informed feeling for Dewey's whole range of thought. I quote: "But nevertheless conformity to an antecedently given object does seem to make sense when we are engaged in a theoretic investigation of nature, in spite of Dewey's strictures about the 'spectator theory.' "[2] Woodbridge had the same conviction, and was led to hold that Dewey moved too much within the context of a dialectical, logical reconstruction. I shall argue that Dewey saw no alternative. In his eyes, antecedent reality and the spectator view of knowing were inseparable from epistemological muddles.

I believe that it is historically correct to say that Dewey, who had been moving away from idealism to a sort of pragmatic naturalism with no great concern for epistemology, was confronted by the realistic debate between the new realists and the critical realists, and had to work out his own theory of sense-perception in distinction from their positions. William James had already anticipated the shift and had sketched a development of his premise of "immediate perception" along lines of two contexts, outer and inner, or auto-biographical. As I see it, this move rested on a rejection of Locke's and Kant's schematisms, which favored agnosticism. In Vienna, Mach was doing much the same sort of thing.

As is well known, the new realists made much the same move, but in different logical terms and more incisively. The result was a combination of presentationalism and panobjectivism with behaviorism. Anything savoring of Lockean representationalism was tabu. The object perceived had to be open to inspection. I emphasize this point because, in my own theory, which takes perceiving to be referential, I hold that the role of sensations is to *disclose* the object perceived in an information-carrying way. The object *appears* in the sensation it controls and *the appearing* is used in a referential way [to guide organic responses] back to the object. This circuit seems to be of the feedback type, so much studied these days in cybernetics. I shall argue that we have, in this analysis, the possibility of a position *between* presentationalism and representationalism. The emphasis will be upon the role of sensations as information-carrying *within an act of perceiving* directed at their objective controls. This is neither presentationalism of the traditional type nor representationalism of the Lockean sort. The stress now is upon the *function* of sensations

2. Warner Wick in *Self, Religion, and Metaphysics: Essays in Memory of James Bissett Pratt*, Gerald F. Myers, ed. (New York: Macmillan), p. 216.

in the animal economy. As I see it, man uses this function as a point of departure for cognition, with the use of concepts and criteria. Perceiving is guided and referentially direct.

To come back to Dewey, I shall argue that the position he adopted was akin to that of the new realism, that is, it was a modification of presentationalism. Like the new realists, he was fearful of subjectivism and of what would follow from any subcutaneous starting-point. It is amusing that he was as much opposed to the "under-the-hat" theory of mind as his great opponent, Lovejoy. Both were horrified at Russell's light-hearted acceptance of the implications of the causal approach to sensation. Once you got into the brain as a terminus, how could you ever get out?

How I get out should be clear, in outline at least. The unit is a circuit, or feedback, a from-and-to affair. The sense-organs and nervous system are parts of an adjustment affair involving guided response. It is upon this foundation that objective cognition is reared. I fear that a combination of introspectionism and mind-body dualism long obscured the situation from philosophers, who worked zealously and analytically *within* their assumptions. I suppose that is one reason why I have been a little skeptical of the vogue of analysis *à la* G. E. Moore. There are always assumptions in the background, and it may well be that these should be revised.

Following Savery in his paper in the Schilpp volume on Dewey, I shall call Dewey's modification of the new realism *perspective realism*. He argued, rather reasonably, that sense perception is not an affair of constant, searchlight cognition, but a reactively achieved slice of objective *experience*. *Things are as they are experienced as.* In Dewey's eyes, the correct outlook was that of an even more naïve realism than that of the new realists. Cognition would start from here with the rise of problems. But the whole schematism of an antecedent reality that had to be mirrored and grasped in a spectator sort of way was to be discarded. Now this does not mean that Dewey gave up the world as science and common sense conceive it. It simply means that he redefined cognition along instrumentalist lines. True ideas are ideas that truly work, warranted ideas. As I see it, it is a case of what Professor Paul Edwards calls *high redefinition.*[3] Edwards is concerned with the treatment of induction by Russell. I have regard to the issue of truth. The point is that Dewey was led to turn his back upon the classical perspective, which took its point of departure from the knowledge-claims of propositions with respect to objects—what C. I. Lewis has come to call, disparagingly, the metaphysical theory of truth—and devote his attention to the instrumental value of ideas. This meant a redefinition. I think that Dewey was more aware of this fact than was Russell in his remarks on Dewey. But it is an important point and I wish to explore its context. My thesis will be that Dewey's development from objective idealism to pragmatism blinded him to a more basic lead, which I sought in a reanalysis of perceiving, as indicated above.

I shall now proceed to show that he had a very good excuse in what he called *traditional muddles.* As he saw it, these stood in the way of the whole genus of such things as "antecedent reality," "being a spectator," "mirroring." Now it is obvious that all these expressions are tied in with the logic of the correspondence gambit. It may be well to indicate, at this point, that I regard correspondence as an implication of any knowledge-claim and hold that, *as an achievement,* it rests on the information-carrying role of sensations. It is, as it were, the *converse* of this operation. Ideas correspond to their objects just because the very mechanism of perceiving furthers it. The feed-back circuit of perceiving develops a situation in which the objects *appear* in the sensation it controls and this *appearing* is used in a referential way back to the object.

It is not surprising that Locke never thought of this mechanism. The idea of it is a modern development. Dewey missed it and was led to attack Locke's formula of terminal ideas and hypothetical objects and an impossible camparison of them. I have always been a little surprised that Russell missed the circuit. I take it that he was too Humean, and the best he could do was to put sensations in the brain without grasping their guiding role in perceiving.

---

3. See his paper entitled "Bertrand Russell's Doubts about Induction," *Mind* 48 (1949); reprinted in *Logic and Language,* Anthony Flew, ed. (Oxford: Blackwell, 1951).

I am now going to study Dewey's reaction to critical realism. It is very illuminating. When he rejected it, the road was barred for him to anything but instrumentalism. He carried through instrumentalism very ingeniously. But—and here I agree with K. R. Popper[4]—there is something very anthropomorphic about instrumentalism that allies it with engineering and the application of rules.

Any move has its inevitable consequences. I shall try to show that Dewey's led to ambiguities about the status of sense qualities and to vagueness about the ontological status of atoms and electrons. Are these merely constructs? Fictions? The term *experience* symbolized a sort of straddling on many topics. It is the same sort of thing that manifests itself in Mach, Whitehead, and logical positivism. As I see it, the only cure lies in an adequate epistemology that feeds realistically into a materialistic ontology. And much depends upon one's analysis of perceiving.

Very understandably, in his critique of critical realism, Dewey had chiefly in mind Santayana and Drake. If he studied my position —and I have no reason to suppose that he did—it undoubtedly seemed to him more amorphous. As a matter of fact, I was still exploring new possibilities, though the general setting of perceiving seemed to me clear and connected with guided response. I had early put sensations in the brain. The job to do was to grasp their role in perceiving. Charles Morris's assessment of my position in his book *Six Theories of Mind* was fairly typical. The problem was, How could you get objective import for perceiving if you put sensations in the brain. Lovejoy, Dewey, Bentley, and others were clamorous in their denunciation of "under-the-hat" and subcutaneous notions of mind. Philosophical behaviorism was of the same ilk. It was clear that a new lead was needed. What was the *unit* in perceiving? Just to be aware of sensations in a Humean way would do no animal any good. And man, essentially, was a higher animal.

It is not surprising, then, that Dewey rejected critical realism as inextricably bound up with all sorts of traditional muddles that had not been—and, in his opinion, could not be—mastered. Montague

---

4. "Three Views Concerning Human Knowledge," *Contemporary British Philosophy* 4, 3d. ser. (New York: The Macmillan Co., 1956).

and Perry were of the same opinion, though they took the path of the new realism. Terminal ideas, representationalism, correspondence were the giants in the path. They would not have been presentational new realists if they had glimpsed a new lead, something midway between presentationalism and representationalism, such as the role of sensations in the controlled circuit, from-and-to the object. In both science and philosophy, advance usually comes from grasping *an ignored alternative*.

Dewey went all out. He identified the traditional muddles with traditional epistemology and the kind of metaphysics that went with it. These two ghostly Siamese Twins had to be exorcized by anathemas. The Greeks had begun it, and the only health lay in a complete reconstruction of philosophy along practical and instrumental lines. Now this strategy was entirely logical, given his assumptions. Metaphysics is a natural scapegoat. We find much of the same thing in logical positivism. If you have an inadequate epistemology, you are certain to have a mysterious ontology.

I do think that epistemology and ontology—a term I prefer to metaphysics for semantic reasons—are interconnected, in that cognitive-claims from perceiving upward involve something to be known. But, since I am a realist in my epistemology and a materialist in my ontology and a thorough believer in scientific method, I do not find the connection disconcerting. To speak of atoms and chemical bonds does not seem to me at all wicked. But this is because I regard perceiving as having objective import.

Had I the space at my disposal I should like to go into the *use* of sense-organs by various animals. The navigational activity of bats is, for instance, astonishing. The thermic guidance of snakes is remarkable. In all this we have a from-and-to circuit. What man, as I see it, adds is the ability to use the information involved, especially visual information, in a cognitive way. He explores and develops concepts and adds language. So far as sensory equipment is concerned, man is not outstanding. It is the cortex that comes into play in this already-prepared setting. It is the thesis of all empiricism that primary concepts cannot be made out of whole cloth, though, as time goes on, sensory data play more of a checking and refuting role. The hypothetico-deductive method has then come into its own. Man has become the cognizing, historical, acculturated animal, and, in this way, unique, as Walter Everett and Sir Julian Huxley maintain.

ii

A man of Dewey's stature demands a study of his development. It was somewhat different from that of James, since objective idealism furnished its background. James belonged more nearly to the British empirical tradition, which he tried to modify. Objective idealism represented an attempt to conquer the dualism and subjectivism that threatened philosophy when confronted by physics and astronomy, by going Kant one better. It postulated a *constitutive reason* of an absolute sort. I have long argued that, if Kant had regarded his sense-manifold as information-carrying with respect to his things-in-themselves, he would have come out at a different point. But neither he nor the Newtonian world was quite ready for that new framework.

Dewey's reorientation was a step-by-step affair. The point of departure was largely set by the outlook of G. S. Morris. Morton White's book *The Origin of Dewey's Instrumentalism* indicates the steps taken. These, I believe, fit in with Dewey's biographical statements in the Schilpp volume. One of my teachers, Alfred H. Lloyd, was a friend of both Dewey and Mead and reflected something of their perspective. Common to all of them were such ingredients as dislike of dualism, stress on the organic, doubt of the value of British empiricism, and impatience with formal logic. White calls attention to Dewey's rejection of the correspondence theory of truth in its usual tie-in with Locke and his growing doubt of the adequacy of the coherence theory. The path opening up was an emphasis on ideas as plans of action pointing to the future. Peirce and James had already been exploring this avenue. Dewey now gave his energy to what he called experimental logic within the schematism of doubt-inquiry. A constitutive world-reason faded out of the picture.

What I am trying to bring out is a certain direction and momentum in Dewey. Mead took much the same stand. He was, in this period, opposed to metaphysics, because it involved one in epistemological questions of the traditional sort, the query as to the status of consciousness, the so-called problem of the external world, and the mind-body issue. Why get into such a mess if it can be sidestepped?

As we all know, the logical positivists had much the same motivation and put their faith in stipulations and sidestepping [epicycles]. I think it has again been shown that it simply won't work. One must grasp the nettle. That does not mean that nothing is accomplished in these efforts.

What I have been trying to bring out is the presence of a certain continuity as Dewey moved from Hegelian logic to experimental logic. That is, he retained the objective idealist's antipathy to Cartesian dualism and to the Lockean view of ideas with its implication of correspondence. Experience is, in some sense, the universe of discourse. What Dewey was seeking was a more naturalistic setting for experience. This perspective did not, of itself, lead to any particular interest in epistemology. It is interesting to note that Morris had long before this regarded the question of the existence of an external world as a problem not worth discussing; in 1915, Dewey concurred.

And now Dewey is brought sharply up against the American realistic movement and is compelled to take a stand on sense perception. He finds himself between the new realists and the critical realists. As I indicated, he finds himself more in sympathy with the new realists, but enters some *caveats*. The result is what I, following Savery, have called perspective realism. Like the new realists, he will argue that the critical realists are really reactionary and engulfed in traditional muddles. *There is no new way out.* Once you grant sensations and the subjective, you are in the bog waist deep. I have been told by an old friend of Perry, Professor Demos, that Perry regarded the critical realists as reactionaries. In his eyes, they were in the Lockean gambit with no way out. That was, also, the view of Montague. Now we shall see that Dewey had much the same idea. In its way, it was quite logical. If sensations and the psychical are terminally given and, perhaps, assigned to the brain, how can you get beyond them? Have not all the changes been rung on this move?

It is well to recall, at this point, that I have advanced a different notion of perceiving, which gives a role to sensations in a stimulus-response unit of a circuit, or feedback, type. In this, a sensation functions as an *appearing* under external control, which guides the adjustment to its control and can, at the human level, be used as information-carrying and evidence.

The traditional causal approach to perception [contrarily] made sensations terminal and subjective. Philosophers had become desperate as they reflected on the conclusions drawn by Berkeley, Hume, and Mill. Now American thinkers, in the period under consideration, had begun to revolt against idealism and phenomenalism. Why not give up sensations? they had begun to ask themselves. Woodbridge, for example, had come to the conclusion that sensations as mental entities should be rejected, despite the psychological tradition in their favor, because they got between the percipient and the object. He was quite daring and suggested a relational view of consciousness as an alternative. With much the same motivations, the new realists made a high redefinition of Hume's sense impressions and got their panobjectivism. The idea of the tulip, said Perry, *is* the tulip. William James had, actually, given the lead in his radical empiricism, founded, as I have pointed out, on "immediate perception" as undercutting Locke and Kant.

Now I have great respect for the acumen with which this line of thought was worked out. It, of course, got into insuperable difficulties but it was worth trying. The question was whether a novel alternative would open up.[5] The critical realists undertook to do so along three, somewhat different, lines. I shall be concerned here only with my own analysis of perceiving.

Given his development, as I have outlined it, and the situation, Dewey's stand followed pretty logically. The first thesis was to give

5. See my paper "American Realism: Perspective and Framework" in the Pratt book, already referred to [*Self, Religion, and Metaphysics*, Gerald E. Myers, ed. (New York: Macmillan, 1961.)]

up subjective sensations and the idea of the subjective that went with them. The whole idea of a subcutaneous mind was misleading. If one started there, one could never escape to the outer world. It should be remembered that I give a *role* to sensations in an act of perceiving that has objective import. This analysis did not occur to Dewey. What he did was to modify the new realism by rejecting its assumption that perceiving is a knowing of a searchlight sort. No; it is a natural event. *Knowing* comes subsequently, when problems arise. It is forward-looking and reconstructive of experience. It is in this context that we can understand his rejection of antecedent reality, mirroring, the spectator attitude. Instrumentalism was in the saddle. The danger, as Woodbridge warned his colleague, was that of confusing a logical construct with the object science is investigating. By the way, it is not surprising that Russell and Dewey could never understand one another. One should read Russell's contribution to the Schilpp volume and Dewey's reply. But I do think I have worked out the logic of Dewey's modification of the new realism and the framework of his perspective realism. Savery is quite right in his comment, "In Dewey's definition (of mind) nearly everything which is ordinarily called *psychical* is excluded." The motivations, as we have noted, are those of panobjectivism and philosophical behaviorism.

We have, I take it, enough insight into the direction along which American thought was moving to realize that a *direct realism* was being sought. Locke, it was felt, would not do. If Hume, then his sense impressions must be reified. The *gay phenomenalism* of later logical positivism was not even considered. But was it possible to find a position *between* presentationalism and traditional representationalism? What was the role of sensations in the act of perceiving? As I have already indicated, it was this line of thought which I was exploring. If objects control sensations as their appearing, and if such appearing is used in the reflexive act of perceiving directed at the same object, then we can be said to sense and image objects in terms of sensations and images so used. In recent terms, it is a feedback affair, a biologically operated circuit. At the more explicitly developed level of human cognizing, it might well be that we develop and apply symbols and concepts in the same direct fashion, with perceiving as our framework. The flaw in traditional conceptualism was that it made concepts terminal, and did not see how it could get beyond them to apply them. I wish to acknowledge how suggestive to me has been the work of Professor Wilfrid Sellars with respect to language. It had been so easy to assume that the Reason intuited, or grasped, *entities* to be called universals.

iii

A year ago I had occasion to chat with Professor Sidney Hook on the subject of Dewey's view of sense perception, and he called my attention to a paper of Dewey's that first appeared in the *Journal of Philosophy*[6] and later was reprinted in his book, *Philosophy and Civilization*. I undoubtedly read it at the time but had forgotten about it. I note that Savery regarded it as basic. Dewey here spoke of his own position as a naturalistic theory of sense perception. The outlook that he contrasted it with and that he was attacking, critical realism, he called the "epistemological theory."

Now this terminology is important, for from this contrast stemmed Dewey's repeated attacks on epistemologs and metaphysicians. This is one of his themes in the popular book *Reconstruction of Philosophy*. I note that Professor Morton White, in a recent exposition of "analytic philosophy," has allowed himself the same sort of facile denunciation. As a physical realist, I cannot help asking myself what is so mysteriously and reprehensibly metaphysical about bread-and-cheese and sunlight and atoms? There is need of semantic clarification, and it is the job of the technical philosopher to do it. But, as we have realized, it is not an easy job. A correct analysis of perceiving is involved.[7]

Now what, precisely, is Dewey's idea of the "epistemological theory"? It is a mixture of the following items, just the ones I had

---

6. Vol. 22 (1925).
7. The similarity between Ryle and Dewey is evident, though Ryle takes the linguistic path. Both approach philosophical behaviorism. [See the 1966 edition of the *Philosophy of Physical Realism*, chap. 18.]

long been wrestling with: 1) the belief that sensations are "psychical entities"; 2) a puzzling ontological dualism of the Cartesian type; 3) the view that *empirical things* are *not* directly perceived; 4) the faith in a peculiar kind of inference from the given psychical to the not-given physical; and 5) the taking of empirical things, now as causes of qualities—the traditional causal theory of perception—and, again, as correlated groups of qualities.

This is not at all a bad summary of the mess with which the new realists and the critical realists had been confronted. But it is not a statement of the solutions offered.

Dewey's recipe, like Perry's, is to do away with the subjective and the "psychical." Make them cognitively terminal, to begin with, and put them in the brain and you will be shut up in the brain and be left with a subcutaneous mind. You will have all the traditional problems on your hands, a mysterious inference, the relation between the psychical and the physical, and so forth. The thing to do is to shut your eyes and bring in the old axe to cut the Gordian knot. The new realists had prepared the way. Dewey but modified their pan-objectivism in the way I have already indicated. The [better] thing to do is to be *just a little more naïve* in a sophisticated fashion linked with the traditions of objective idealism. Things are as they are experienced as. But experiencing is not cognizing.

The move to make, Dewey argued, is to go back to sense perception, in its primary and unsophisticated use as a term for the observation and the recognition of objects by means of the bodily organs, such as eyes, ears, hands, and the like. One then keeps one's objectivity. The stress is now on what is perceived, namely, *empirical things* and their qualities. And we should not be surprised to find that causal connections in the way of antecedents and consequences are noted. And if we are careful we can relate *color out there* to its conditions as electromagnetic vibrations, and not fall into dualism. The secondary qualities are not subjective in any invidious sense. We just make distinctions. How about atoms and such things? Well, they are *constructs,* scientific objects.

Now, as Guthrie might say, this is a sophisticated form of pre-

Aristotelianism. It has no place for sensations.[8] As we have noted, sensations had gotten in the way of direct perceiving. The neglected alternative I have advanced is that sensations play a role in a referentially direct act of perceiving. . . .

Dewey makes much of a linguistic caution. The adjectives *sense* and *sensory* are prefixed to the qualities perceived as well as to the act of perception. But this use is metaphorical. The qualities perceived are not sensory. This term but designates an important *condition* of their occurrence but does not apply to their nature. It is a similar usage when we speak of a house as a building because it is the outcome of an operation of building.

All this is rather magnificent in its way. It was Dewey's way of avoiding the traditional muddle. And it is quite in line with philosophical behaviorism. He was convinced that the epistemologists (the critical realists) were doomed to the old runaround. Besides, as I have noted in my study of Dewey's development, the contrast between thought and things and the problem of the external world had never ranked high for him. As a matter of fact, objective idealism had been able to sidestep them. What he did was to devolute, or descend, into transactions. Perceptual perspectives are natural events. Mind and matter are just different characters of natural events. The correspondence theory of truth is mistaken in its aspiration because there is nothing extra-experiential to correspond to and, even were there such a transcendent reality, it would be impossible to make a comparison. The thing to do is to stress warranted verifiability and the future. Ideas are instruments. To express all this, one needs a new vocabulary. One speaks of contextualism, transactions, the reconstruction of experience, consummations, working, warranted ideas. All this overlapped scientific method, or paralleled it. It had, however, a dialectical flavor that puzzled Woodbridge, for example. But soon many were adept at it. And they were sure there was no alternative. Epistemology and metaphysics were outworn delusions. How similar it all was to logical positivism!

8. W. K. C. Guthrie, *The Greek Philosophers*, pp. 146f. A Harper's paperback.

iv

Well, the only thing for a dissident to do is to face up to Dewey's challenge and show a way out of the muddle. Let us take up his five points one by one.

Are there sensations? And are these *psychical* in a special, intrinsic way? I, myself, do not doubt that there are sensations of all sorts connected with the functioning of sense organs and central nervous processes. But I want, first of all, to find out what their role is. They seem to go with guidance in a stimulus-response setting. At the human level, they are dwelt upon, especially in delayed responses, and lend themselves to the very human, cognitive enterprise, since they are information-carrying and under control of the external object. But there seems to be no good reason to hold that they are intrinsically alien to the brain and the kind of activity that goes on there. I have called them "natural isolates." We are here at the level of awareness, that is, of participation in guiding and signaling and the use of symbols. Hence, all these factors stand out from the total cerebral setting. But there is every reason to believe that oxidation must go on and all sorts of chemical activities are needed as a condition of guided response. Something quite analogous can be said of modern computors. But it is just a fact that there is this presence of feeling, sensation, and awareness in cerebral activity. It is a fact to be adequately categorized, and I think that epistemology can help a lot.

One thing to do is to clear away dead timber. Some of this dead timber is due to the tradition that sensations are terminal in perceiving. We have noted that many American thinkers of great acumen were led to reject sensations because they were regarded as intervening in a *tertium quid* fashion between the act of perceiving and the object. Then there was the introspective tradition, more or less continuous with the belief in a substantive mind or soul. It was assumed that sensations and images were "mental states" in an intrinsic way. That is, they were *psychical*.

Now I would cut out this dead timber. The *act* of perceiving is, as I have tried to show, complex and involves the referential use of sensory appearings to that which is appearing. At the cognitive level, we are trying to describe the object in terms of concepts founded on these appearings. We do not intuit, or participate, in the object. In point of fact, I think that perceptual knowledge is a remarkable achievement resting on a complex mechanism. Even if we perceived a brain, why should we expect to penetrate it and have its *act* of perceiving participatively disclosed? I have long advocated a materialism, epistemologically competent and accepting levels in nature.

It is in this fashion that I eliminate the first bit of muddle that Dewey puts on the debit column of the "epistemological theory."

With respect to his second point, I would simply say that no more than Dewey was I seeking to retain Cartesian dualism. I argued that objective idealism had won its victory over dualism too easily and that Dewey had kept something of this tradition. My quotations from Savery's paper illustrate what I have in mind. As I see it, his perspective realism was quite akin to the outlook of the new realism. Both were designed to eliminate the realm of the "subjective."

I come now to the third point in his indictment. Are "empirical things" directly perceived?

I hold that they are, but I have a different idea of perceiving from Dewey's. His is more what I would call presentational. Mine develops a position *between* presentationalism and representationalism. I hold that it is because sensations are appearings and information-carrying in the from-and-to operation of perceiving that we know by means of them. It is this *cognitional relevancy* of sensations that I put in place of the desperate return to naïve realism of the new realists and of Dewey. I put stress on the mechanism that nature worked out as a foundation for the act of perceiving. Objects are, so to speak, presented not in their own person but by a controlled substitute. On the other hand, it is the object, itself, toward which the act of perceiving is referentially directed. What is usually called transcendence and treated as a mystery is really an achievement based on guided reference and causally controlled cognitional relevance. We know through ideas of this sort. I conclude that, in this sense, external things are directly perceived. Critical realism, as I understand it, moves between presentationalism and representationalism. It has a feeling for the mechanisms and operations that nature developed, and that reached their consummation in human cognizing. Scientific method was culturally added to this basic framework.

I come then to the fourth point in Dewey's indictment of the "epistemological theory," that it is a peculiar kind of inference from the given psychical to the not-given physical.

It should be clear to the reader that the analysis of the act of perceiving I have made undercuts this traditional problem of which Berkeley made so much. I stress the role, or function, of sensation in the from-and-to movement of perceiving. Perceiving is referential and not inferential. Sensations are not cognitively terminal as in the old empirical tradition so that we must start from them and wonder how we can get beyond them. Berkeley had it altogether too easy. Given his premises, he is irrefutable. But his premises are not well-founded in the outlook of today. Even philosophy must ultimately change its assumptions.

The fifth point in the traditional muddle turns on the confusion between the causal stage in perceiving and the use of the sensations caused. I suppose Dewey had Mill partly in mind. To my way of thinking, we should distinguish between sensory *qualia* and ascribed qualities and properties. The thing perceived (Dewey's empirical thing) is a cause but is not, itself, a correlated group of *qualia*. Dewey gets around the complexity of perceiving by resorting to a presentational immediacy. Sensory qualia are out there, and the thing to do is to check on our language.

As I see it, there is no contradiction between the statement "That thing is red"—redness being a property ascribed more or less dispositionally—and the statement "That thing reflects light rays of a certain frequency to the eye." There had to be some guiding and informational *mark* if objects were to be distinguished at the perceptual level of knowing. Disputes about primary and secondary qualities seem to me to rest largely on an inadequate epistemology. Locke confused matters, and Berkeley went back to the sensory base. But into the details I cannot here enter. It must suffice to say that

Dewey's type of naïve realism does not meet the complexities of the problem. It is a kind of *tour de force* set up in despair of traditional muddles.

The question, then, is this, Can critical realism work out an epistemology that avoids them? If so, we shall have a naturalistic epistemological theory that shows the mechanism of perceiving and that indicates how human knowing emerges from guided response. It keeps the same objective import as response has, but builds it up to reference and aboutness. The growth of manipulative curiosity leads on to experimentation. Human beings develop attitudes, expectations, and beliefs. In all this the object perceived is regarded as coordinate with the percipient, who is also an agent.

I have always argued that something of the nature of naïve, or presentational, realism is the natural outlook because there is no innate knowledge of the mechanism involved. Hence the result is given in an unanalyzed way. It is *as though* the external thing were open to inspection. But reflection has forced the majority of philosophers and scientists to recognize difficulties. When the causal lead, alone, is taken, one gets in to such positions as idealism, phenomenalism, and positivism. I have tried to show that the causal *from* must be supplemented by the guided *to*. The theory of perceiving that comes out is neither presentational nor representational. It puts stress on the mediating role of sensations in a from-and-to movement. Perceiving is a very active affair. Sensing and imaging objects in this framework leads on to the development and application of concepts. But neither sensations nor concepts are, in themselves, terminal. That is why both sensationalism and conceptualism have been inadequate solutions.

I conclude that the new realists and Dewey turned their back on these complexities because they did not envisage the analysis the critical realists were trying to explore. For them, it was just Locke and Kant over again. As I see it, Dewey tried to improve on the new realism in terms of a naturalization of objective idealism.

When I consider the efforts made by him and by the logical positivists, I must conclude that the problem of perceiving is, after all, a difficult one. What is difficult about it is to get an adequate lead. After that, it is not so difficult. But that is the sort of thing that is always occurring in science. And I would be hard pressed to distinguish what, in my theory, is science and what is philosophy. It is philosophy largely because that discipline has concerned itself with the question about the nature and conditions of human knowing in a way that science, in its specializations, has not. But the *facts* appealed to should receive scientific approval.

v

In conclusion, I want to draw things together and, if possible, to weaken certain phobias that are recurrent.

As I see it, this analysis of perceiving gives language a natural, public, and objective framework. We point to what we perceive and may be led to name it and to describe it. All these activities have objective import. Many artificial problems that have engaged philosophers, such as that about an external world and about other selves, have followed from a bad starting-point. I am persuaded that Hobbes had it over Descartes here. Nevertheless, the Cartesian gambit drove problems home. It was well to explore self-consciousness.

Within the ambit of naturalism, I take epistemology—the study of the nature, conditions, and reach of human knowing—very seriously. Knowing is a magnificent achievement. I do not like Dewey's decrying of it, though I quite understand what he had in mind. In much the same manner, I regard ontology, or metaphysics, as the complementary term implied by epistemology. To know involves something to know. Science is engaged in filling out our knowledge of nature. I can see no sense in philosophers castigating epistemology and metaphysics. I admit there is a semantic job of clarification involved. Philosophy has had a devious history.

Let me turn now to the motives back of Dewey's rejection of antecedent reality, mirroring, and the spectator outlook. Surely, these rejections but symbolize his perspective. This, I have pointed out, had been a growth within objective idealism. There are no things lying *beyond experience*. There is no basic duality between thought and things. He was all for the organic in thought. There is really no problem of an external world. It is presented, is as it is experienced as. The correspondence theory of truth is self-contradictory, since it assumes something to be known that cannot, by its definition, be verified. Since he was dissatisfied—as were all the pragmatists—with the coherence theory of truth, what remained but instrumentalism. His "high redefinition" of truth became "warranted assertibility." Those who accuse him of practicality alone do not do him justice. And, of course, he was a naturalist, believing in the world of common sense and of science. His denial of "antecedent reality" is purely a technical affair with its context, as indicated above.

And so we come to the famous correspondence theory of truth as a sort of final test.

It is obvious that the critical realist would not put it in Lockean terms. I have made perceiving direct, though the act is mediated by sensations and supplemented by applied concepts. I have called this referential realism. As I indicated, this view is *between* presentationalism and representationalism. The thesis is that sensations play a controlled role of guiding and information-carrying, in a responsible setting of a circuit type. Thus I look at the very thing that is causing visual sensations in me. I use its *appearing* to characterize it. Hence the corresponding has a natural base. Our ideas of things are founded on information supplied to us by them. When we analyze knowledge, we realize that it implies a foundation in information; and we now recognize that it carries us back to the technique nature worked out with the development of sense organs. This was its humble beginning.

We can work all this out as a sort of logical equation. Knowledge is other than its object but implies its disclosure, which implies, in turn, an agreement, or correspondence, base that can rest only on information given. So we are led from knowledge, as an achievement, to a consideration of its conditions. And, as I have noted, this points back to the information-carrying role of sensations. It is, ultimately, as simple as all that. And nature began it in the development of sense organs and the locking in, within one circuit, of stimulus and response so that the appearing of the object is applied to the same object. There is no Lockean nonsense here of an impossible comparison of idea and object, for the idea is not terminal but of import to the object. The traditions of dualism and of introspection disrupted, for philosophy, the natural circuit.

The terminology follows as we return to the objective import of perceiving and thinking. To say that a statement is true is to say that one endorses it as a case of knowledge of what it is *about*. Knowledge is here the primary category as an achievement. But knowledge can be attained because it is founded on the communication of information. Because the term *true* is an endorsement, it demands verification, that is, attention to the informational base. And this rests on the informational function of sensations established by the mechanism of perceiving. Such information is now labeled *evidence*. We are now at the human level of the operation.

It is interesting to note that language has already worked out the essentials. We speak of *what is the case,* of beliefs about it, of evidence, of verification. But it is well to have the whole situation analyzed. And it is this that I have tried to do.

It was because Dewey despaired of mastering the traditional epistemological muddle induced by dualism and by stress on the first stage of the mechanism of perceiving, the causal one, that he cut the Gordian knot and fell back on presentationalism and his perspective realism, and thence upon instrumentalism. His own idealistic training, as I have shown, made this move easier for him. But I have tried to show that it was a mistake and did harm to American philosophy. . . .

I take the above analysis to be a satisfactory exegesis of the correspondence theory of truth. It has an epistemological base and metaphysical, or objective, import. On both these points, I differ from the handling of the question by C. I. Lewis and by Dewey. I must leave it to the logicians to do justice to Tarski's semantic theory of truth, which is a form of the correspondence approach. It strikes me as somewhat of a dodge, though a statement is true if what it is about is the case.

A word, in conclusion, about science. What it has done is to build on common sense, and its critical use of perceiving, by means of an interlocking complex of new instruments, such as clock, balance, microscope and telescope, theory, and relevant observation. An increasing role was assigned to theory but it was always to be checked by observation. This disconfirming role of observation is basic. Creative imagination becomes theory only as this control is kept in mind. This interlocking complex of method and technique constitutes science. As I see it, it fits in with, and extends, the technique nature had already worked out in the development of sense organs and the controlled use of sensation as a carrying of information about perceived objects in a from-and-to circuit.

I am persuaded that this approach, while entirely naturalistic, throws greater light upon sense perception and upon the emergence of human cognition than does Dewey's modification of the new realism. The job of philosophy is to size up the whole situation; and it often needs new leads. . . .

6

*In Defense of "Metaphysical Veracity"**

. . . Lewis and I belong to much the same period of American philosophy. Pragmatism had attacked idealism only to find itself confronted with various forms of realism. It was not surprising that pragmatism, in its turn, had some variations. Lewis's variation is often called conceptual pragmatism and showed some Kantian influence. As I recall it, one of the queries of the time was where his concepts came from. Dewey, as I shall try to show rather incidentally, met the realistic challenge in terms of a noncognitive presentationalism of "things are as they are experienced as." Cognition is a special affair pointing toward the future. As Woodbridge and others have pointed out, Dewey met the common belief in "antecedent reality" in a rather dialectical fashion, making knowledge concern itself with results and consequences. In any case, pragmatism stressed prediction and the future and tended to shrug off the past and the coexistent. This perspective went with a negative attitude toward the category of substance and the correspondence approach to truth. All this, as I see it, stands—or falls—together. Suppose we call this perspective *experientialism.* I am not certain that I want to call it phenomenalism.

Expressions like observability, verifiability, if-then, seem native to this outlook. But, if the more realistically inclined seek a framework

* *The Philosophy of C. I. Lewis,* Paul A. Schilpp, ed. (LaSalle, Ill.: Open Court, 1968), pp. 287–308. Reprinted with the permission of both the author and Open Court Publishing Company.

in which to locate these "abilities," he is assured they are basic. Any such search is motivated by ideas of transcendence, correspondence, and what Lewis calls "metaphysical veracity." As we shall see, he argues that this line of thought is self-defeating. Is he right? I shall try to introduce some novelty that is meaningful to me. If he makes the necessary effort, I think it will be meaningful to him. At least, I want him to try. The alternative would seem to be a supplementation of the "given" in a conceptual and predictive way. Thus is attained that *thick experience* of the world of things which is the *datum* for philosophical reflection. And "thinghood means a stability or uniformity of appearances which can be recovered by certain actions of our own." Now I do think that things appear and give evidence of themselves in our sensory experiences and are, in that sense, observable. I do not see how one could be an empiricist otherwise. But *appearance* seems to me an elliptical expression for the *function,* the way a thing appears to an observer, which involves a complex mechanism, a mechanism that I shall later examine. If appearance is thus taken, it presupposes a thing that appears to an observer and the thing cannot be reduced to its appearances. But this gambit points to the kind of epistemology that Lewis thinks is self-defeating. It is well to have a debate on it. I expect something solid and not an affair of arbitrary definitions and stipulations, such as the logical positivists indulged in. After all, Lewis is a trained philosopher and not a specialist in logic or physics who, in his pride, has gone amuck. As I pointed out, Lewis belonged to the same historical period in American philosophy that I did. And I think he had respect for the work done in it. Like Dewey and myself, he is naturalistic and humanistic in his outlook. The divergence is, accordingly, a technical matter.

In my book *The Philosophy of Physical Realism,* I wrestled with Lewis's type of experientialism and I am now returning to the encounter after these many years, during which I have sought to clarify my own analyses and during which Lewis has had the opportunity and incentive to expand his position. I think we have much in common. I imagine he is as tired as I am of deontological intuitionism and the "naturalistic fallacy." But to work. It is, then, a question of alternatives. It may not be amiss for me to devote considerable space to the exposition of the epistemological position that I offer as an alternative to Lewis's experientialism. I have reason to doubt that he has ever quite understood what I was driving at. The fault was, undoubtedly, partly mine. *But a basic difference in frameworks easily holds up communication.* It constitutes a barrier not readily broken down. And I do want Professor Lewis to understand my form of realism, the more so that I find myself sympathetic to his stress on concepts and on rationalism in ethics.

I am, of course, an empiricist. I would call myself a *realistic empiricist* in that I think that knowing of the world rests on the evidence of the senses, worked over and used in an inductive and deductive way. When I speak of the *evidence* of the senses, I mean that our sensations are information-carrying, not themselves terminal in perceiving, as the tradition in British empiricism held. From the standpoint of realistic empiricism, much of modern empiricism can be called *phenomenalistic empiricism.* But a point to be kept in mind in this terminology is that the phenomenalistic empiricist is usually convinced that there is no realistic alternative to his analysis. Therefore, he does not consider himself to be a phenomenalist in this contrasting mode. Or, to put it in another fashion, appearances *are* the thing, a position close to naïve realism.

Critical realism, as I sought to develop it, was a form of realistic empiricism. It explored the possibility of a *direct realism* of a new type. Its aim was to overcome the Lockean gambit, which made ideas terminal and resulted in a tantalizing kind of untestable representationalism. The thing to do was to reanalyze perceiving and to bring out its response and referential base. For this approach, sensations would be guiding and evidential and direct perceiving as a complex operation. Existentially, they might well turn out to be intracortical. But the operation of perceiving itself would be tied in with response and concern itself with the objects to which the organism was adjusting itself. The unit would, accordingly, be of the sensorimotor type. At the human level, perceiving would rise to the stage of concern with, reference to, and descriptive characterization of, the things man had to deal with and talk about. This was a direct realism of a referential type, which recognized the mediating role of sensations and concepts. The point was that these were not terminal cognitively but played a role in the achievement of knowledge. We know through and by means of them. The interplay of sensations and concepts in this operation needs careful study. Concepts, it would seem, take up and develop the information carried by sensations with their eye, so to speak, on the object. One speaks of conceiving the object or of applying concepts to it. Here again, we have direct realism. But it is not of the intuitional kind. Yet the directness of concern and the dominance of the attitude, reference, or intention involved encourages the belief in a sort of givenness, or intuition, of the object perceived. This is not surprising, since the complex mechanism operates more or less automatically.

Historically, the traditional, causal approach to perceiving expressed an incomplete analysis of its mechanism. It got as far as the arousal of sensations and made these terminal. Theorists were handicapped by lack of biological knowledge and by the prevalent mind-body dualism. The lack of biological knowledge led them to ignore response and adjustment and prevented them from seeing the operation as a whole. The mind-body dualism induced a stress on introspection and states of mind. Thus the historical setting gave support to traditional empiricism with its view that sensations are terminal for perceiving. As we are beginning to see it today, the brain is an organ of adjustment and its elementary unit is sensorimotor. Sensations are *factors* within perceiving as a complex and directed operation. Their location *in* the brain does not mean that we are perceiving brain states. Russell seems to have gotten himself into this impasse. The escape is to realize that sensations in the brain guide response and play a role in outwardly directed perceiving of the referential type. One must emphasize the fact that the unit of the mechanism of perceiving is sensorimotor. As we shall see, it is upon this unit that the human mind develops, adding cortical and conceptual complications.

Now I am inclined to hold that this framework will throw light upon the import and reach of human knowing. If sensations are information-carrying, the job of the brain-mind is to elicit this information and to use it in deciphering *facts about* external things. Later I shall connect up this approach with a new formulation of the so-called correspondence theory of truth, giving human knowledge a correspondence-foundation in the mechanism of its attainment. I shall, also, have some remarks to make on the status of so-called universals, connecting them with the operative use of evidence in knowledge-claims. As I see it, they are not entities, *ante, in,* or *post,* but terms involved in the import of knowing as an achievement. I am sure that I should not have readily grasped this view of the status of universals as tied in with cognitive acts and their conditions had it not been for Professor Wilfrid Sellars's treatment of the topic in his study of "Aristotelian Philosophies of Mind" in the book *Philosophy for the Future.*[1] If one concentrates on sensations and images as entities and ignores the use made of them in perceiv*ing* and conceiv*ing* as cognitive acts, then their information-carrying role is ignored. To conceive an object or to apply a concept to it is not just to *have* a concept, just as perceiving is not just to have a supposed psychological entity called a percept. The fault in much of psychology is to disregard knowing as an operative claim and achievement. Traditional empirical epistemology must take part of the blame for this.

Now I was never persuaded that Professor Lewis grasped what I was driving at in critical realism as a form of direct, referential realism connected with an analysis of the mechanism of perceiving. It had elements of novelty and its clarification took time. But I still think he was a little impatient with Pratt and myself. If one has a well-worked-out framework, it is hard to grasp an alternative. That requires a complete reorientation. The debates between idealists, pragmatists, and logical positivists illustrate this fact. They go on within different sets of assumptions. To my way of thinking, these assumptions are inadequate and are all tied in with the initial mistakes of Descartes and Locke, which tended to make *ideas* terminal in human knowing. I have found myself more sympathetic to the framework of neo-Aristotelianism, though I have not discovered it

---

1. *Philosophy for the Future* (New York: The Macmillan Co., 1949). Hereafter cited as PF.

in the sort of analysis of the mechanism of perceiving to which I was led by my study of modern biology and neurology. Moreover, my schematism fits in with ontological materialism and the movement from molar things to all sorts of particles. The information-carrying capacity of sensations seems to me to connect up more with the reproduction of pattern than with the transfer of an entity called "form." Aristotelian teleology seems to me outmoded. I prefer to work along evolutionary lines and to stress levels of causality with emphasis on immanent causality and the development of guidance and direction. It will be remembered that I speak of sensations as guiding perceiving.

But to return to Professor Lewis. Let us take the idea of transcendence and the revised notion of the correspondence-foundation of knowledge and truth as typical of the framework I am asking him to understand as an alternative to his experientialism. I have been rereading Professor Pratt's *Personal Realism* and find that I agree largely with his principles but that his mind-body dualism gave a slant somewhat divergent from mine. While I sought to explore the mechanism of perceiving to give a basis for external reference, Pratt was more inclined to appeal to mind and the self as the source of transcendent reference. Suppose I put it this way. If perceiving, as founded on a sensorimotor mechanism, displays itself as a guided reference to the things around us, we have the base for denoting, symbolizing, and characterizing. All that is needed is the operative insertion of conceptual intelligence. The assistance given by language is, of course, immense. But I take the sensorimotor framework to be foundational. Denotative and descriptive meanings develop within it. At the human level, the percipient points, means, relates, compares, and describes. He confronts the world actively.

What, then, about transcendence? It seems to me that there is nothing mysterious implied. All that is involved is the tested use of the information carried by the senses. This is developed and applied in terms of concepts. Guided reference is half the battle; the use of the controlled information, given by the evidence of the senses, is the other half. Transcendent reference is thus an achievement rooted in organic life and its concern for its environment. Starting from guided responses, it is lifted to the level of conscious reference and the symbolic application of concepts drawing on the resources of sensory evidence under the responsible control of patterned stimuli. I shall have something more to say about this perfectly natural situation later. It will have bearing upon Lewis's rejection of "metaphysical veracity."

Traditional empiricism, I have argued, tended to make sensory appearances terminal. As I see it, Professor Lewis continues this tradition. In contrast, I am arguing for a view of perceiving that connects with response and lends itself to the employment, by the organism, of the evidence furnished by the senses. As we pass from the lower animals to man, this framework is increasingly exploited because of the addition of emergent abilities. Man finds himself *looking at things out there* and describing them without much idea of how he is able to do it and just how the ability is achieved. The result is what philosophers call naïve realism. Puzzling at it, epistemologists got lost, as Locke did, by concentrating on the causal approach to sensations without grasping *the whole sensorimotor circuit*. This approach also made it difficult to understand the nature and import of concepts and conceiving. Surely, conceiving is an operation that has, so to speak, one eye on sensory appearances but the other on interrogating the object. That is, the evidence of the senses is made use of in the interest of asking questions about the object being perceived and conceived.

Now I see nothing mysterious in these directed operations. What I am trying to do is to rob the notion of "transcendence" of the mysteries read into it inevitably by those who start with sensations as terminal, as Locke did, and do not appreciate the relevance of the response and the *circuit* it makes possible. When I look at this chair before me, I am looking at it *through* my visual field. The "looking at" is of the nature of a guided response involving the interplay of stimulus and attitude toward. "Feedbacks" are, undoubtedly, operating. That is why I call it a circuit. But it is a circuit dominated by a basic concern with the object. This concern operates in delayed responses when we take time to size up the object. It is, perhaps, well to begin with the idea of reference and note how it is supported by the mechanism of perceiving. *Transcendence* calls additional attention to the cognitive claim as saying something about an object other than the act with its propositional content. Here, I take it, we need to appreciate the information-carrying function of sensations and their evidential use in the building up of concepts regarded as having objective import in conceiving things. As cognitive acts, perceiving and conceiving are quite complicated affairs. It is, as I see it, quite necessary to get an adequate framework, and I do not think that Berkeley and Hume had it. Biology and neurology and psychology were not sufficiently advanced. But that is no good reason why philosophers should refuse to grasp the import of this new knowledge and the reorientation it makes possible.

Thus far, I have largely concerned myself with what could be called an operational clarification of "transcendence" with the intent to show how cognitive acts are built up and directed at external things. It is *this chair* which I am looking at and pointing to that I am talking about. Speech clearly moves within the framework set by guided response. It is in this context of perceiving and speech that we can take external things to be terminal for cognitive acts. They are what we mean, refer to, identify, and describe. Of course, this outlook breaks completely with Lockeanism. How significant the break is one can realize when one recognizes that Russell and the logical positivists made sensations terminal and sought to construct things out of them and their possibility. To the critical realist, this endeavor largely displayed misused ingenuity. Logic is a powerful instrument, if you will, but it cannot replace sound epistemological analysis. Recently, Stace has formulated the axiom of this traditional empiricism to make statements terminate on sensory factors, *not as their evidence but as their meaning.* I shall say nothing here of that explosion called German romantic idealism. Great ability was exhibited but the foundations were weak. If Kant had realized that his sense-manifold was information-carrying, he would not have fallen back on things-in-themselves. But this would have meant the enlargement of the causal view of perceiving I have desiderated.

I suppose that philosophy is a difficult subject just because it is mixed up with foundations and orientations. Because of this fact, I shall not hesitate to repeat myself. What I want to do is to get Professor Lewis to understand the alternative I am offering. Since I began working in the subject in the first decade of this century I have noted many fashions and winds of doctrine. What I have sought to do is to carry through an integration of epistemology and ontology in an adequate framework.

* * *

. . . I have tried . . . to show that referential direct realism can give empirical meaning to transcendence and to correspondence by working out the mechanisms involved. The brain is an organ of adjustment into which patterned stimuli feed and which, thereupon, directs a guided response. It is within this setting that acts of perceiving emerge. The information carried by sensory factors under control of patterned stimuli, themselves under the control of the external thing, is, as it were, read off and developed by cortical equipment into concepts that can be cognitively applied to the stimulating thing in a circuit-like fashion. I have no doubt that neurologists will soon be exploring these mechanisms and equipment. In point of fact, they are. What philosophy can do, in aid, is a clarification of the nature of human knowing in an up-to-date fashion and not linger in the cultural era of Locke, Berkeley, Hume, and Kant. These were great thinkers but limited by the knowledge of their time.

The import of all this is that it is very function and task of human knowing to have "metaphysical veracity," *Anglice,* import for the world around us of which we are a gifted and distinctive part. The alternative, for me, would be agnosticism, which hardly has point in these days of mounting scientific knowledge of our world. Besides, the word was used by its coiner to express a theological stalemate. My dispute with Lewis turns on the contrast between "immediate perception," however thickened, and direct perceiving. In a way, I am not defending what he is attacking—Lockean representationalism and Kantian things-in-themselves. I am just indicating a somewhat novel alternative. My point is that British empiricism made sensations terminal in perceiving and that they are *not* terminal. I have intellectual respect for Bradley's sentiency and centers of experience and for Whitehead's version of it. My colleague, DeWitt

Parker, even tried to acclimate substance to this climate. But I think that this gambit was mistaken and outmoded. I must confess that the King Canute role of philosophy does not awaken my enthusiasm. . . .

One other point. An attempted solution of the mind-body problem was involved in this view of perceiving. The role of sensations as guiding and as *between* stimulus and response indicated that they were, in some sense, *in* the brain. Thus arose my double-knowledge approach and my view of consciousness as a "natural isolate" in the functioning brain-mind. I note that Professor Donald Williams in a recent number of the *Review of Metaphysics*[2] associates me with Russell. As a matter of fact, I have priority on this thesis, since I defended it in 1907 against Baldwin, to whose lectures I listened at a Summer Session at Chicago in 1906. He was then the editor of the *Psychological Review* and was good enough to publish my paper. With Watson's advent as editor, such philosophical nonsense was excluded. Recently I found biologists and neurologists more friendly [*]. . . .

I do hope that Professor Lewis will now understand the alternative framework that I am offering. Later I shall give my understanding of his outlook, which strikes me as a logical expansion of the tradition of "immediate perception," of *givenness,* as an alternative to the impasse of Lockean representationalism. What we critical realists were seeking was a *via media*. We wanted directness with mediation. As I increasingly saw it, this required a mechanism involving information-carrying on the part of sensory factors and objective import on the part of perceiving as an operation. It was as though Kant's sense-manifold disclosed facts about his things-in-themselves. In our biological and naturalistic era such a role would seem to be a natural one. In intention, then, I have sought to naturalize human knowing as an achievement made possible by the directed operations of the brain-mind, operations in which we consciously participate the more complex they become. The circuit is there as a

---

2. "Mind as a Matter of Fact," *Review of Metaphysics* 13, no. 2 (December 1959).

[*] Most notably C. Judson Herrick.

foundation, and the conceptual level emerges as capacities and problems require it. The result is a responsible intercourse with the things around us. This is the level of common-sense realism. And it is from this that scientific method took its rise, as culture made it possible. I shall have something to say about this in connection with what I call the *epistemology of atomism*. Atoms and their constituent particles are, in my opinion, not scientific constructs but physical realities, though our concepts of them are efforts at conceiving them.

I suppose that I have always regarded pragmatism as a half-way house between idealism—subjective or objective—and physical realism. It was not that I did not see merits in its emphasis upon meaning and verification and the use of knowledge. But I was persuaded that it had not faced up to epistemology imaginatively enough. The antagonist pragmatism had in mind was idealism. The rise of realism was unexpected by both James and Dewey. Woodbridge is an interesting figure in this connection. I was, at the time, somewhat irritated by his attacks on epistemology but I have come to realize that, like Dewey, he had in mind the tradition of Lockean representationalism, just as Lewis has. Woodbridge sought to return to presentational or naïve realism. Curiously enough, Dewey finally did the same, things are as they are *experienced* as. This is the gambit of "immediate perception," of the given. The alternative I have been developing is to grasp the role of the given as disclosing and the use made of it in perceiving as a directed operation. Woodbridge—quite rightly, I think—criticized Dewey's resort to dialectic when rejecting the notion of an "antecedent reality" and stressing knowledge as terminating on results of inquiry as such. For what is inquiry about? Its own results? There is ambiguity here. On his part, Woodbridge falls back on *sensing* external things (naïve realism), while arguing that sensations are a myth.[3] Dewey took much the same gambit. Both these able thinkers were afraid of a subcutaneous mind and the subjective. *Make sensations terminal for perceiving* and in the brain-

---

3. J. E. Woodbridge, "The Promise of Pragmatism," "Experience and Dialectic," "Deception of the Senses," *Nature and Mind* (New York: Columbia University Press, 1940).

mind and one cannot get back into the outer world. What both these able thinkers did was to ignore sensations and the subjective and jump into the external world by sensing or experiencing. They did not work out the difference between *having* sensations and perceiving. I cannot see that Russell did either.

* * *

Now I have the impression that Lewis is prepared to accept Santayana's essences as synonyms for the "given." But, in my form of critical realism—and I had some priority here . . .—essences were rejected in favor of sensations and concepts. It may be recalled that, following the suggestion of Professor Wilfrid Sellars, I have connected *universals* with cognitive activity in which information is used and developed and applied. In the strict sense, they are not entities. On the whole, I think that Pratt and I had most in common, but he worked within a dualistic framework. He appreciated what he was pleased to call the subtlety of my double-knowledge approach but did not think it did justice to the "self." Now I think that the *self* develops around the act of perceiving and the attitudes involved, drives, desires, and the need of direction and choice. Here I bring in agential causality as a high level of emergent causality. But this would take me into the metaphysics of ethics. I am persuaded that "directedness" is a characteristic of immanent causality. I was very pleased when my friend Herrick took this idea over to replace teleology.

It is obvious from all this that I suspect that Lewis took the path of presentationalism and is as much a naïve realist as a phenomenalist. Things are *experienced*. Thinghood means a stability of uniformity of appearances that can be recovered by certain actions of our own. Thickening comes from nonterminating increments. There is always more to *experience*. In contrast, I shall argue that things, *made objects,* are referred to and *known, not experienced*. And they are known through and by means of sensory factors and concepts developed in the exploratory acts of perceiving and conceiving. Both perceiving and conceiving involve the use of indications, discriminations, constructions, the solving of problems, and not a mere work of abstraction from the given. Appearances furnish evidence. But things are clearly other than their appearances. It is in perceiving and conceiving that we work out such categories as thinghood, space, time, causality, and dispositional properties. Such categories are cognitive achievements and are capable of improvement and clarification. They are neither innate in the Kantian sense, nor subjective as for Hume. They have cognitive import and are of the nature of decipherments of the constitution of the world.

That Professor Lewis's position is a logical development of the tradition of "immediate perception" is evident. The choice, as he sees it, is between immediate perception in which the appearance *is* the thing and a Lockean sort of representative realism, which starts with a qualitative datum as terminal in the first step of perceiving and then *somehow* moves to an object other than itself, which it *somehow* signifies. That is, he has in mind the traditional difficulties of this approach. By what right do we *infer* an external object from the given? And what guarantee can we have that the datum can mediate ascriptive knowledge of the inferred and nongiven object? The contrast is put succinctly on pages 14 to 16 of his book *An Analysis of Knowledge and Valuation*.[4] As he puts it, theory of knowledge "has puzzled itself for centuries and still continues to do so as to the authenticity or nonauthenticity of this mediating function."

I am not going to attack the details of Lewis's construction, though I shall point out now and then the tenets to which it leads him. The result hovers between phenomenalism and naïve realism. Judgments terminating on the given are supplemented by judgments of a nonterminating sort, which thicken the former. For expository purposes I shall indicate how Dewey and Woodbridge tried to meet the problem of perception along lines of naïve realism. My own conviction is that the only way of escape is the one I have outlined, which brings in the whole circuit of referential perceiving, makes sensations information-carrying, and considers the act of perceiving direct in import. This approach brings me out into the company of Aristotelian and dialectical materialists but, I think, with advances in technical equipment linked with developments in modern biology and lin-

---

4. C. I. Lewis, *An Analysis of Knowledge and Valuation* (LaSalle, Ill.: Open Court Publishing Co., 1946). Hereafter cited as AKV.

guistics. It is, if you will, a return to perennial philosophy with a difference. I do not here attempt to assess the contribution of idealism and objective rationalism. They, undoubtedly, loosened the texture of thought and brought the human self into the picture. But they built on insecure foundations and usually nourished a suspicion of science. Neo-Thomism, of course, had similar motivations for escape from naturalism and materialism and rested its case on the soul and on "active reason." In connection with a brief discussion of the epistemology of atomism, I shall pay my respects to "dialectical materialism." As I understand it, it builds on the "reflective" import of sensations for the material world. In its controversy with positivism, it saw that, without some such reflective import, sensations would be epistemologically terminal, as idealists and positivists held. My own ontological materialism rests on a reanalysis of the mechanism of perceiving to bring out the dominance of response, attitude, and adjustment. It is in this framework that language develops. I suspect that Lewis's subordination of language to the *primacy of appearance* goes with his epistemology.

To my way of thinking, many of the traditional problems of philosophy, such as solipsism, the external world, the status of other minds, vanish in this new kind of objective framework. Simplification and unity are usually signs of advance. There is nothing mysterious in *having* sensations as events. Their assignment to the brain is indicated and is held back by epistemological confusions, which I have tried to meet by my double-knowledge approach. I really think that psychology and neurology would be the better for an adequate epistemology. I must confess that I do not think that Ayer and Ryle quite came up to their opportunity in their handling of the questions raised by the galaxy of brilliant neurologists in the book *The Physical Basis of Mind*. As I see it, the proper cues were missing. Brilliance is not enough.

Since I am trying to see Lewis in his setting, I am now going to turn to Dewey's reactions to the rise of realism in American thought. He was too able a thinker just to say, as I have heard some smart young philosophers quip, that the new realists could not account for error and that critical realists could not account for truth. It will be recalled that I have completely restated the correspondence theory of truth, making *true* an endorsement of a knowledge-claim and showing how knowledge is achieved through sensory information explored conceptually. If sensations are regarded as terminal and having no information function, then knowledge must become an intraexperiential affair. Such is the strategy of both Lewis and Dewey. Hence the denial of the "metaphysical veracity" of cognitive claims. Hence Dewey's shift to warranted reconstruction and prediction. It is all quite logical. It is, if you will, a bypass, a detour. Ontological materialism was escaped and atoms became "scientific constructs." As is well known, Mach took the same stand. If one makes sensations terminal, one must. Whitehead's rejection of "vacuous actuality" is similarly motivated. Like Bradley, he was immersed in sentiency.

I suppose I should apologize for handling Dewey as brusquely as I do. But it must be remembered that I began thinking in a realistic way in the first decade of this century and was always confronted by Dewey's detours. His cultists, or epigones, followed his bypassing with loud acclaim. I do not put men like Sidney Hook and Ernest Nagel in this class, for both are outstanding thinkers. And these are difficult problems involving orientation.

* * *

Now I think that Lewis has been a little more *rusé* than Dewey. But Dewey's *things are as they are experienced as* is similar to Lewis's identification of things with appearances. And both regard *traditional* representationalism as the only alternative. In this I think they were both mistaken. A more adequate analysis of perceiving was required. Sensations are *in* the brain but they are not terminal for perceiving.

* * *

Some twelve years ago in a chapter I contributed to the book *Philosophy for the Future,* I pointed out how realistic Lewis could sound.[5] He affirms that we know *through and by means of presentations* some objective thing or event. Is he, like Dewey, a naïve realist with pragmatic intent or a phenomenalist? But I have the conviction

---

5. PF; see the chapter "Materialism and Human Knowing," p. 96.

that he regards these presentations as constituents of the object known. This fits in with "immediate perception" and the rejection of critical realism. Sense-meanings are thus part of the object. In other words, appearances have an objective status and are inseparable from the thing. I quoted his definition of thinghood on this point. For me, appearances operate in sense-perceiving as information-giving. Like Dewey, Lewis wants an experiential participation in the external world as an alternative to traditional representative theories. Objective knowledge is a kind of thickening of experience in a predictive way.

Now all those who accept a causal foundation for perceiving—from Aristotle to the present—must hold to what Feigl calls a nomological account of sensations. The sense organs have an adjustmental function. At the animal level, they guide. At the human level, the data they contribute can be used as evidence and serve in building up concepts. If so, they are not terminal but of objective import. In other words, perceiving is quite a complicated achievement. Much is made these days of the reproduction of pattern.

The pivotal question comes to be this. What is the import of objective statements? It is asserted by Lewis on page 189 of AKV that it must be *translatable* into predictive statements of terminating judgments. This thesis fits in with his conception of sense-meanings. For him, as I understand it, sense-meaning is the most important element of significance, epistemologically, in intention or connotation. Sense-meaning constitutes the criterion by which what is meant is recognized. Linguistic expressions of what is meant and what is apprehended are dependent and derivative phenomena. Now I do not deny that we perceive *through* sensations and images and so decipher objects. I am an empiricist.

To make a long story short, we are back to the question of the meaning of empirical statements about things. When I say that there is a piece of white paper before me, am I talking about the operation of perceiving it and what this operation would involve? I cannot see that I am. Of course, I can shift my attention to the seen appearance and what would happen if I turn my eyes to the right. Surely, the meaning of an objective statement is not identical with the method of its verification. Even the logical positivists—now largely scientific empiricists—have gotten over this stance. A cognitive claim is normative and statable in facts about, that is, items of knowledge. Though Lewis criticized logical positivism and emphasized a certain autonomy in concepts, he still wants to connect them up with sense-meaning in a terminal way. Now I want empirical concepts to be responsible to sensory factors but to go beyond them in import. When I say this valise is heavy, I am not saying that I am having certain kinds of muscular sensations. I am assigning a property to the valise and I am not surprised when the technique is adopted of weighing on the scales with numbers coming up. I have already indicated how biological technique is supplemented by scientific technique. But, peace to Eddington, it is the same table I am dealing with. I just know more about it.

Now I have been very impressed in recent reading on Lewis's appeal to a sort of conceptual apprehension. I do think we know through concepts. But that means metaphysical veracity, as I see it. Perhaps Lewis is fighting an outworn battle.

Recently, Chisholm has been moving toward physical realism under the guidance of Brentano. He wants to make appearances mediate knowledge and yet not be constituents of it, as Lewis holds. In a review of Chisholm's book in the *Journal of Philosophy,* Baylis hovers uncertainly between the two positions. I think he is quite right in holding that appearance is a complex term involving the role of sensations in perceiving, as in the *appearance* of this table from this angle and distance. Cognitional reference is already at work. If this is all that Chisholm has in mind, then I would agree with him so far. But there is no need to eliminate sensations in noting how they function in perceiving. Perceiving is a more complex level.

I suppose one difficulty in handling perceiving came from the mixture in it of two levels, the sensory and the referential cognitive. The traditional causal approach stressed sensations and took them as terminal. The term appearance may well be taken as symbolic of the cognitive, referential supplement that goes with response and brings in the circuit. As we have noted, Russell gets sensations into the brain but has no clear idea of perceiving. In the famous note on page 187 of AKV, Lewis speaks of presentations as ingredients in objects, the bent stick in water is an ingredient of the really straight stick, the term ingredient here showing Whitehead's terminological influence. Woodbridge met the same difficulty, as did the new realists. The correct answer, as I see it, is to recognize the internal complexity of the act of perceiving. This is the line taken by critical realism.

I pointed out how Dewey's jump to external presentationalism simplified for him the mind-body problem into behaviorism. I have never been able to get clearly in my mind Lewis's solution of the psychophysical problem. He certainly seems very vague about it. My attention was called to it by the fact that Professor Kuiper appealed to it to avoid my location of consciousness *in the brain*.[6]

As a sort of epilogue, I want now to say a few words about the *epistemology of atomism* within materialism.

When Aristotelian physics and cosmology broke down, it was replaced by the experimental interrogation of nature wedded to applied mathematics. As I have indicated, the biological technique of perceiving, which had led to common-sense belief in external, material things, was now supplemented by instrumental techniques of measurement. Quantities and laws were discovered. The ancient Democritean and Lucretian theory of atoms was entertained, but empirical evidence for chemical atoms and molecules had to wait until Dalton and the principle of combining units. Chemical technique improved until we have now the ability to synthesize such complex molecules as that of chlorophyll. I refer to Woodward's achievement. Here we have a terrifically complex pattern built up bit by bit with one magnesium atom surrounded by four nitrogen atoms with carbon, hydrogen, and oxygen atoms added.

Looking back at the development of modern science, I find myself agreeing with Conant that new concepts developed in intimate relations with problems and techniques. And I take these concepts to

---

6. See the Symposium on my philosophy in *Philosophy and Phenomenological Research* 13 (September 1954).

have cognitive significance. Today, atom smashers are classified as belonging to the genus of microscopes. And, as Bridgman puts it, scientific knowledge is tied in with the use of instruments.

As a physical realist, I take the concepts, thus evolved, as having denotative import. I do not say they are adequate or final. But they are continuous with the fact of divisibility, which the ancients had already noted. In other words, I take the particles already in some measure reached by photographical technique as literally existing. Of course, I recognize fields, relations, patterns as supplementary.

What I am calling in question is the tradition in philosophy from Mach to Dewey and Whitehead to speak of such particles as essentially "scientific constructs" within experience. Of course, all concepts are, as such, constructs. When I say there are lions, I am saying that the concept lion has application in the world of animals. I presuppose the existence of things. To say that things exist is a tautology. Russell could—and, of course, would—ignore this primary ontological meaning. The point I am making is that the tradition in empirical philosophy was to make ideas terminal. Bradley and Whitehead are immersed in sentiency and so material things are vacuous. Dewey moves within "experience" and makes logical constructs therein. The logical positivists want to translate material-thing statements into statements about actual and possible sensations, and so on. Lewis wants to stress appearances and sense-meanings. Now I do not think ideas are terminal in either perceiving or conceiving. We identify, refer to, and characterize, material things, and by means of techniques supplementing our biological equipment, get information about them. So far as I can see, accordingly, the epistemology of even ultra-microscopic particles is but an extension of the epistemology of perceiving chairs and tables. We must be careful in the use of language, of course. After Ryle's warning against muddleheadedness, even philosophers can learn to speak the language of science.

The upshot of all this is that philosophy should come back to the old tradition that its job is to do for human knowing and valuing a work of theoretical explanation that enables us to naturalize it. Now I believe that Professor Lewis, as a naturalist and humanist, has been concerned to do such a job, which might well put the capstone on science. . . .

7
Dewey on Materialism *

iv

. . . Either Dewey is right in his perspective with its rejection of epistemology, or else pragmatism is a sort' of makeshift and its *pseudo*-problems are not such at all. If the latter is the case, we should expect ontological questions to have a reach and depth that pragmatism is blind to.

There are four problems that can be used to illustrate this point. These are the problem of an external world, the correspondence theory of truth, the mind-consciousness-organism problem, and the question of the meaning and status of substance. To the physical realist, all of these have a significance they cannot have for Dewey. Take, for example, the connection between the idea of an external, material world and the correspondence theory of truth. If you call the first *sinnlos,* you will be well on the road to casting a pitying eye upon the correspondence theory of truth. What is there for propositions to correspond to? And if you give up the correspondence theory of truth, a really external, material world tends to become ghostlike, unknowable, unthinkable. In this fashion, the two denials support one another and a thinker must fall back, as Dewey does, into plans of action and mere temporalism.

* *Philosophy and Phenomenological Research* 3 (1943) : 389–92. Reprinted with the permission of both the author and publisher.

If, again, the external material world, of which the organic self may turn out to be a member, and the correspondence theory of truth are discarded, then substance likewise departs. It is then useless to explore such categories as simple endurance, organization, and the emergence of new capacities. In short, any meaningful development of an evolutionary and qualitative materialism is precluded.

And, of course, with the vanishing of the category of substance, any basic context for the mind-body problem disappears. The ontological depth of this truly profound issue is no longer apparent. All the pragmatist needs is to talk of functions of the organism, just as all the positivist needs to do is to speak of a double language. The reason for this is obvious. The organism is no longer a genuinely material whole, and consciousness is not an intra-organic complex of *qualia*. The full impact of the traditional mind-body problem ceases when a personal consciousness is rejected because it gets you into difficult problems in epistemology and ontology. The reformation of materialism lies in recognizing that consciousness is a "natural isolate" intrinsic to mind-brain activities. But then you are really immersed in both epistemology and ontology.

Is it not clear that these four windows on fundamentals are so connected that he who draws the blinds down on one does it simultaneously on the others? And Dewey is quite aware that he has rejected all four as *pseudo*-problems. Are they? The physical realist emphatically denies the allegation.

v

As an ontology, materialism has had a checkered career. Our cultural history with its Platonism and supernaturalism has not been favorable to it. It was left, in the main, to the tender mercies of amateurs who reified classical physics or a purely mechanistic physiology. There was little philosophical finesse about it. It had in its armor little epistemological acumen and still less categorial insight.

But, as I have already suggested, the time is ripe for a fundamental overhauling and reformation. Evolutionary theories have indicated the importance of emergent, or integrative, causality. The growth of naturalism has been a necessary preparation. But naturalism is not enough. A theory of existence is required, an ontology with all the paraphernalia of the categories. Just to utter the magic words *science* and *scientific method* is not sufficient.

After all, the intention of the materialist has always been honorable. He could never see the evidence for immaterial things. A human being was, of course, complex and gifted; yet, when all was said and done, he was but a living, acculturated organism granted a brief span of years. And have not technical philosophers made even more inexcusable pronouncements in arguing that material things do not exist, that to be is to be perceived? I suggest that the technical philosopher should be willing to let bygones be bygones. There are some rather absurd skeletons in his romantic and anthropomorphic cupboards.

vi

After this lengthy, but necessary, preamble, let us return to Dewey and his refusal to go beyond an experiential naturalism.

After recognizing that emotional causes often dictate preferences for one word over another, he proceeds to state his primary reason, which turns out, as could be expected, to be his rejection of substance. This was already implicit in his treatment of "scientific objects" and in his neglect of a knowing directed toward a material world. He remarks that he has been chided for not developing an ontology and replies that science is enough. I have attempted to show that his whole approach to philosophy practically precluded an ontology.

"If", writes Dewey, "the term 'matter' is given a philosophic interpretation, over and above its technical scientific meaning—e.g., *mass* until recently—this meaning, I believe, should be a functional relation rather than a substance. Thus, in case there is need for existential conditions in their function *as* conditions of all special forms of socio-biotic activities and values, *matter* might well be the appropriate word. But recognition that all these activities and values are existentially conditioned—and do not arise out of the blue or out of a separate substance called spirit—is far from constituting materialism in its metaphysical sense. For it is only by setting out from the activities and values in experience just as they *are* experienced that inquiry can find the clues for discovery of their conditions. Denial that the former are just what they are thus destroys the possibility of ascertaining their conditions, so that 'materialism' commits suicide. It is quite possible to recognize that everything *experienced,* no matter how 'ideal' and lofty, has its own determinate conditions without getting into that *generalization beyond limits which constitutes metaphysical materialism."* Such is the essential part of his reply to Savery.

But why is metaphysical materialism a generalization beyond limits? I suspect that Dewey has in mind old-fashioned, reductive materialism. Certainly any ontological materialism of today must be appropriate to the setting of evolutionary naturalism. It must stress relations, organization, levels. It must be willing to recognize new organic wholes with correspondent capacities, properties, and activities. In this sense it must be qualitative and permissive of differentiation. Again, no philosophical materialist would deny for a moment that, from the epistemological standpoint, we must take our point of departure from the experiences and cognitive claims of human knowers. In contrasting the theses of physical realism with Dewey's fluid experientialism, I have, I hope, made this clear. As Professor Parker has admitted in his recent book, *Experience and Substance,* a materialism that proclaims an inside to nature and has a critical theory of knowledge and an evolutionary approach cannot be toppled over by dialectics.

And so I am persuaded that ontological materialism of a reformed type deserves more careful examination than it has received. Nor should we be afraid of the category of substance which, after all, only stands for the recognition of existence, endurance, wholeness, executive capacity, relative independence. The human, organic self is substantial in this sense. Matter is dynamic and organizing in its own right. . . .

While I have emphasized my divergence from Dewey and have not hesitated to declare why I thought his long attack upon epistemology has been most unfortunate, I cannot close without expressing my admiration for the intellectual and moral stature of the man and for all that he has accomplished over such a wide field.

8

Reflections on Dialectical Materialism *

Since it has long been my opinion that the philosophical possibilities of a critical form of materialism have been too much disregarded by technical philosophers, I welcome this opportunity to participate in a symposium on Russian philosophy and psychology. It is especially timely to consider the context and alignments of that form of materialism to which Soviet thinkers have naturally given so much of their attention.

I am going to assume that dialectical materialism is not reducible to some abstract formulae found in Engels's *Anti-Dühring,* whose precise meaning and reference are by no means always obvious. In other words, I am not going to allow myself to be too much intimidated by the term *dialectic.* In a general way, it is clear what the term stands for. It symbolizes dynamism, movement, relations, conflict, development. The dialectical materialist rejects, as inadequate, a materialism of an Eleatic type, such as easily went with classical physics and Newtonian ideas of fixed, natural harmonies. In his own romantic and idealistic fashion Hegel was, of course, expressing his dissatisfaction with certain aspects of eighteenth-century thought and finding suggestions in history and personal psychology for principles emphasizing struggle, irony, relations, and growth. And these

* *Philosophy and Phenomenological Research* 5 (1944) : 158–79. Reprinted with the permission of both the author and publisher.

he was led to formalize triadically in his effort at panlogism and to project into nature in his speculative *Naturphilosophie.*

Now I think it is only fair to Engels to point out his interest in the development of the empirical sciences. He was one of the first to welcome Darwinism, for instance. And if, along with this contemporaneity, he carried with him many Hegelian *clichés,* it can rightly be pointed out that, as we recognize today, the science of the nineteenth century was too mechanical and atomistic in its principles. When I read his recently published notes on *Dialektik und Natur* I take this contrast into account. I do not expect any special revelations but I find some shrewd remarks.

The present paper is, accordingly, the product of an attempt to press beyond formulae and to reconstruct the context, emphases, and philosophical alignments of dialectical materialism. Since I am not as yet well acquainted with the kind of technical thinking in epistemology and ontology that is developing in the Soviet Union, I must content myself with the light thrown upon the assumptions and perspective of the movement by a study of the classics of Marxism. It will be noted that I make good use of Lenin's *Materialism and Empirio-Criticism,* the more so that he calls himself a "seeker" in philosophy, a designation I should like to call to the attention of dogmatic dialectical materialists. His attack upon Machism and positivism likewise has its appeal for me. It should also be noted that Lenin refers to the popularizations indulged in by Engels, such as the growth of a seed as illustrating the negation of a negation. This is not the spirit of an *epigone.*

It is my purpose, then, to elicit the leads and general alignments of dialectical materialism and to bring these out by comparisons with current philosophical movements in the United States and by contrasts. The comparisons will be with pragmatism and physical realism and the main contrast will be—following the lead of Lenin—with positivism. It may thereupon be possible to find some major community between the principles and problems of dialectical materialism and those of physical realism, emergent evolutionism and what I have called reformed materialism. I am going to stress technical problems in epistemology and ontology. In all this I am going to treat dialectical materialism as, in intention, a systematic philosophy and not reduce it to the level of the limited emphases of some Marxian-inclined biologist, physicist, or chemist, interesting as these may be as cultural countermovements to the speculations of theologically inclined physicists, such as Eddington and Jeans. I am going to write as a technical philosopher who has pride in his subject; and it is my hope that the dialectical materialist will find my analyses stimulating.

i

Now the general *leads* of dialectical materialism are to be found in Heracleitus, Locke, Kant, Diderot, eighteenth-century materialism, Hegel, Feuerbach, and Darwin. In intention it is, as I have already suggested, a dynamic materialism stressing movement and process. To illustrate, not long ago I was reading Garrigou-Lagrange's defense of Aristotelian principles in his criticism of Le Roy's Bergsonian theory of *devenir*. For Le Roy, movement is primary and is not an affair of successive replacements of fixed forms. This, remarks Garrigou-Lagrange, is pure Heracleiteanism. Now in recently reading Lenin's *On Dialectics,* I find Heracleitus the point of departure. By emphasis upon struggle he is defending Heracleitus as against Aristotle. The intention is a philosophy of movement. Somehow, new structures and relations must arise within what is an expression of tensions. I grant that I would not use quite the same terminology as the dialectical materialist, for I distinguish more sharply between being and existence.[1] But it goes without saying that dialectical materialism is opposed to the postulates of Neo-Thomism.

But, again, while stressing process and movement, dialectical materialism differs from Bergsonism and pragmatism in that it has accepted materialism. To me, one of the intriguing things about it is that it is a philosophy that is dominated by cultural alignments and leads. *Its perspective comes first; its solution of technical problems in philosophy is secondary.* And that is just what we should

---

1. Those who may be interested in my dynamic ontology will find it sketched in a forthcoming article in the *Philosophical Review* entitled "Reformed Materialism and Intrinsic Endurance."

expect. After all, Marx, Engels, and Lenin were not primarily philosophers by profession. But they had a strong sense of cultural realities.

The problem of change, of generation and corruption, has been indicated. In epistemology dialectical materialism has been confronted by the puzzles connected with representative realism and the so-called correspondence theory of truth. Here, again, the lead was inescapable but the solutions of traditional problems were not adequately worked out. And, on these matters, I shall make suggestions different from those made by pragmatism, suggestions along the lines of critical realism. Once more, the lead with respect to the mind-body problem was inevitable. Somehow the brain must be conceived as the organ of consciousness and mentation. But how was it to be stated? Here, again, the requirement was more evident than the correct analysis. I shall make bold to offer my own theory, called the double-knowledge and emergence approach.[2] It may well be that Soviet philosophers have developed analogous theories, for they seemed to me logical implications. This is a plea for communication and cooperation.

One other historical point. The importance of Feuerbach for an understanding of dialectical materialism should be more fully recognized. In reading Lenin's *Materialism and Empirio-Criticism,* the influence of Feuerbach stands out. He is the primary point of attachment in epistemology. Now, as Jodl shows, Feuerbach had clearer ideas than popular expositions have indicated. He was an empiricist and his so-called sensualism was very much like Stuart Mill's empiricism, doing justice to both sensation and thought. It was a protest against Hegel's panlogism.[3] And many of Feuerbach's aphorisms have been misunderstood because taken out of this context.

It should not be forgotten that technical philosophy throughout the nineteenth century was—to its discredit, be it said—in the main on the conservative side. The great seventeenth century in Hobbes and Spinoza had been far more daring. The eighteenth century was enlightened and skeptical. The nineteenth century got under way

---

2. Probably my best formulations are in *The Philosophy of Physical Realism* and in the article in the *Philosophical Review,* 1938.

3. *Feuerbach,* Fromanns Klassiker, chap. 2.

in a period of reaction, which was reenforced and curiously continued in intellectual matters by the rise of the middle class with its conservative tendencies in religion. Recall what happened to Tom Paine and Ethan Allen in this country. Though only deists, they were classified as horrid atheists. Now, as the latest edition of the Überweg *Geschichte der Philosophie* points out, there arose after the middle of the nineteenth century "a strong epistemological opposition to metaphysical materialism not only on the side of philosophy but also within the natural sciences so that it had no longer scientific validity."[4] Neo-Kantianism had much to do with this development. As I see it, positivism was a sort of compromise in this cultural matter. And I think it is so still. The problem was a deeper one than might at first appear because of the dominance of naïve mechanical ideas in science. I know from my own experience that epistemology was long the Maginot line against naturalism and ontological materialism. It was not until the twentieth century that realism was born again in Germany, England, and the United States. But, all this time, dialectical materialism represented a protest—seldom heard in the universities—against the epistemological opposition to ontological materialism. Engels has some scathing remarks to make on Lange's famous *History of Materialism* from the Neo-Kantian viewpoint. And so I think it is fair to say that Marxism stuck to its *leads*—despite revisionist movements—and has in large measure been justified by the course of events. As I suggested above, it was not so much that it solved technical problems in philosophy as that it had a strong sense of realities.

ii

Any systematic study of dialectical materialism requires a breakdown into at least four subdivisions: a) epistemology, b) ontology, c) the status and import of dialectic, and d) the relation between theory and *praxis*.

---

4. 2:286. This tradition is still operating in Eddington, Jeans, and Bridgman. I wonder how much longer it will continue. That, I suppose, depends upon directions in Western culture.

Let me state, at the very outset, that I find I can agree with much in the general perspective. As Carritt points out, dialectical materialism is realistic in its epistemology. This is ignored and belittled by Professor Hook because of his pragmatic bias. But much water has flowed under the bridge in epistemology since the days of Engels or even of Lenin. The revival of realism in the twentieth century has led to the exploration of the distinction between sensing and interpretative perception, with what seems to me significant results. It is now possible to replace the traditional causal theory of perception with the causal theory of sensation and to stress the objective import of perception as a complex, and fairly high-level, cognitive activity. In his own myopic fashion, G. E. Moore has obviously been working in this direction in his distinction between the direct apprehension of sense-data and the cognition of material things. It is the primary thesis of critical realism.

The bearing of this development upon the "mirror theory of knowing" and "the correspondence theory of truth" will, I think, become apparent. What I largely find in dialectical materialism is a *stubborn lead*. It was not ready to make the suave compromise with *experientialism* that pragmatism and positivism made. Here I am ready to lock horns with pragmatists and positivists and defend the insights of physical realism, which are undeniably confirmatory of the basic lead of dialectical materialism. There are subtle distinctions to be made and inherited confusions to be cleared away.

Uncertainty in exegesis and interpretation reaches its maximum in connection with the third subdivision, namely dialectic. So far as the dialectical approach represents a rejection of what is called "metaphysical" thinking, that is, thinking in Eleatic and unhistorical ways, the divergence appears to be largely terminological. But I take the problem to be more than this would imply. For the Marxist dialectic applies to both thought and being. For Hegel, of course, these were essentially one, as they must be for the idealist. The materialist does not quite escape this demand for unity, though it is the material world that dominates the picture. Thought is a differentiation within the material world, to be accounted for in terms of historical evolution. I shall, accordingly, try to find out the ontological import of such expressions as the unity of opposites, the negation of negation, and the change of quantity into quality. Does their meaning largely flow from the principles the dialectical materialist is rejecting? In these matters a sense of historical relativity helps to give perspective. It may at least be interesting to see how an American thinker, approaching such matters as the inadequacy of Eleatic atomism and the need of taking evolution seriously, in a non-Hegelian atmosphere, formulated his own rejection of "metaphysical" modes of thought. Do such expressions as organization, togetherness, functional unity, dynamic integration, emergence correspond in any degree to the import of the dialectical terminology? Even if a sort of parallelism can be found here, there would still be the question of the meaning of dialectic for logic and scientific method. Granted that logic and scientific method have a formal structure, it may still be the case that their application is conditioned by cultural assumptions and the dominance of fashionable categories. Moreover, culture and society are ontologically real and must have a texture and a "go"—to use Lloyd Morgan's term—that cannot be ignored. For instance, has not the liberal been too much influenced by the ideas of natural harmony and of "natural law" historically underwritten by Stoic and Christian theism? It is my opinion that the very clearing up in recent decades of the notion of the logical and the linguistic *a priori* may bring the empirical and the real into sharper perspective. As usual, the positivists have been more enlightening in their affirmations than in their denials.

Suppose we now glance in a preliminary way at the other three subdivisions. The purpose will be that of indicating perspective.

In epistemology, I take it, dialectical materialism involves realism. Accordingly, anyone who has been thinking along the lines of critical, physical realism will find points of interest. Our old friends, the thing-in-itself and the copy theory of knowledge, will be on parade. The important thing here is not to jump to hasty conclusions or to be misled by *clichés*. Any battle-scarred American realist who has had to lock horns with pragmatists and idealists has inevitably become both canny and a wee bit cynical. He finds that his opponents have fixed ideas, which they make no effort to change. Even as acute a

thinker as Professor Hook has so lived into the dialectics of pragmatism that he refuses to admit that the critical physical realist is
not just reproducing Locke or Kant.

Now, as I see it, dialectical materialists refuted Kant somewhat
in terms of Hegel. It is the very nature of essences to appear; or
things-in-themselves become things that appear, things-for-the-knower.
In other words, cognition does not terminate on appearances but
works through appearances to what appears. Now I think this argument has points, but it, of course, conflicts with the whole machinery
of Kantianism. Moreover, it manipulates the idealistic assumptions
of Hegel, which dialectical materialism rejects. There is the other
approach, which is more Lockean and which founds itself upon the
causal theory of sensation and the representational view of knowing.
This approach is more native to the materialistic tradition from
Hobbes to Diderot and harmonizes with physiological psychology.
The job is to give the proper external reference to cognition at its
various levels and to meet, firmly and intelligently, the usual objections to the correspondence theory of truth, the notion of transcendence, and the category of stuff or material substance. As I see it,
dialectical materialism finds itself in opposition to pragmatism, idealism, and positivism on all these points. Now it so happens that I
have spent much of my philosophic life in defense of a realism that
seeks so to restate the nature and conditions of human knowing that
the traditional formulations of correspondence, transcendence, and
stuff, used by pragmatists, idealists, and positivists in their attacks
upon materialism, are undercut. Perhaps dialectical materialists will
be interested in this epistemological development, which explores the
possibility of a *realistic empiricism* as against the dogmas of phenomenalistic, or "radical," empiricism.

Ontology should also raise interesting topics. I would, almost as
a matter of course, take dialectical materialism to be, quite literally,
a form of materialism, differing on certain points from the materialism of the eighteenth century and opposed to the rather casual
pronouncements of the German scientists turned materialists in the
middle of the nineteenth century, such as Vogt and Moleschott.
Marx, Engels, and Lenin were aware of the subtleties involved in

theory of knowledge in a fashion that Vogt apparently was not. They knew that consciousness is not a secretion but something bound up with the functioning of the brain-mind in a rather unique way. If consciousness and cognitive awareness are to be assigned to the functioning brain, how shall we formulate their status?

Now while many statements by dialectical materialists indicate the contours of the problem, I have not found the sort of handling of it that I have outlined in my double-knowledge approach. But I shall have more to say of that later and of the doctrine of emergence or novelty through integrative causality. That there is a sort of parallelism of intention between the theories of emergence and of the Marxist formula of quantity changing into quality there can be no doubt. The suggestions for the latter are to be found in Hegel; and their validity depends in part upon one's view of the intrinsic coherence of Hegel's development of the categories. Hegel set himself a problem suggested by Kant and Fichte. The empiricist who feels that he *discovers* categories in their natural relations rather than deduces them from some mental principle approaches categories in quite a different fashion. But Feuerbach was one of the first radical critics of the Hegelian deduction of the categories; and it is an historical fact that Feuerbach remains the point of attachment of dialectical materialism to the academic tradition.

Just how the line is to be drawn between naturalism and materialism remains debatable. All materialists are naturalists but not all naturalists are materialists. Professor Hook, as a pragmatist, fights shy of overt materialism and wants to retain Marx, at least, as a naturalist and not a materialist. But this topic can be better discussed after I make it clear what I mean by materialism and what its differentia is. This is not a simple matter and is inseparable from one's handling of points in theory of knowledge, such as transcendence and correspondence, and of the interpretation of the category of stuff or substance. I need merely remark at this stage that one can have an entirely dynamic conception of stuff and that our conceptions of matter are not fixed but may increase in adequacy, a principle of which Lenin made much in his discussion of the crisis in physics in his day. It has often seemed to me that academic philosophers have been very unimaginative in their handling of material existence or being. More time has been spent in showing the weaknesses of traditional conceptions of matter than in creating new ones. Following Hume, *empiricists by profession,* that is phenomenalistic empiricists, positivists, radical empiricists, neutralists, perspectivists, have preferred to discard the category rather than to reform it. Realistic empiricists, on the other hand, have the imperative job of rethinking being or stuff in the light both of modern science and of epistemology. I rather expect that dialectical materialists may be ready to cooperate with the realistic empiricists in this task, judging from Lenin's attack upon Mach and Avenarius. But more about this in a later section of this paper.

In considering the relation between theory and praxis, it may be well to bear in mind the distinction between historical materialism and dialectical materialism. Strictly speaking, of course, dialectical materialism gives the principles common to "nature" and human affairs. But certain laws have emerged at the human level that must be regarded as relative to that level.

For historical materialism the emphasis is upon the evolution of human society, the strategic role of the conditions, forces, and relations of production, and upon the class struggle. Here the unity between social ideas and action makes itself manifest. The very perspective and strategy of a class determines its ideology, its way of looking at events, institutions, and desirabilities. Unity of theory and action is demanded if the world is to be changed as well as interpreted. Here we are concerned with conscious programs and purposes looking to the future. Much the same sort of unity, or integration, is required in all moral action with wide horizons in which knowledge and appreciation of ends and means are blended in decisions as to what to do.

But the relation between theory and praxis has another context in epistemology, where we are asking ourselves whether the successful guidance in action, which a scientific theory apparently contributes, is a usable criterion of its truth. As against skeptics and agnostics, Engels and Lenin both use this criterion. The fact that science works, in that it enables us to predict events and control our environment, *justifies* the belief that we humans are achieving *knowledge* about our world. Let the agnostic meet this argument, which can be connected up with growth of human culture on both its theoretical and its technological side.

Now I had been led to emphasize this argument in connection with a debate I had with pragmatists and idealists without being aware how fully it was developed by the Marxists. It was my purpose to distinguish between the categories of truth and knowledge and to make the term *true* mean *a case of knowledge*. That is, I took the claim to possess knowledge to be the primary claim of the human mind and sought to define the term *true* with reference to it. To say that a proposition is true is to assert that it is actually a case of knowledge, that it discloses what it is about, its referent. With this base I could then show that the so-called correspondence theory of truth should rather be designated *the correspondence theory of the propositional conditions of knowledge*. A proposition must have what it takes to mediate knowledge. And so we are led to investigate the cognitive value of sensations and concepts.

It follows from this way of approach that we can distinguish between the intraexperiential criteria of truth, such as coverage of data, consistency, coherence with other empirical propositions, and what may be called the behavioral, or praxis, test, which concerns the capacity of the proposition to guide the concrete human being, or group of human beings, in adjustment to, and control over, the objective state of affairs.

Now I first became cognizant of the Marxist theory of praxis as Hook interpreted it along the lines of pragmatism. So taken, practice became at one and the same time an added criterion of the truth of ideas and a constitutive element in the meaning of truth. As is well known, for the pragmatist, knowledge is equated with the process of the validation of ideas within experience. The context is always that of solving problems and establishing firm bases *for the future*. For the realist, on the other hand, propositions that are validated are to be considered cases of knowledge about things and events other than themselves. Here, of course, the notion of transcendence is the point at issue.[5] Do we in our thoughts claim to refer to, and know, things that can never be literally parts of our conscious experience, so that knowing involves the use of the technique of denoting and description? The realist is convinced that human knowing rests upon the use of such a technique and that all that transcendence signifies can be connected with it. The pragmatist, like the idealist, is fearful of the notion, for it calls to his mind the weaknesses connected with the Lockean set-up, which means that any adequate realistic analysis must deal, at one and the same time, with knowledge, truth, coherence, and transcendence.

As I read more fully in Marxist literature I became convinced that Hook's pragmatic interpretation of praxis did not do justice to what Engels and Lenin had in mind. I take both of them to be realists and materialists. Praxis, accordingly, was directed against agnosticism and was used to confirm the belief we humans in general have that we do achieve knowledge about the world around us, knowledge being here taken in a realistic sense. And it is quite clearly the opinion of Lenin that this achievement is one of degrees, so that our concepts of matter become more adequate to their goal by a process of cultural approximation. I may remark that I had independently arrived at the notion of levels of knowledge connected with improvement of methods and operations. At the level of science human beings are engaged in the process of getting more and more adequate concepts. The goal is presumably set by the determinate nature of things. Perhaps it would be better to speak of approximations in knowledge rather than relative and absolute truth. But, so long as the situation is grasped, terminology is of secondary importance.

While Lenin was acquainted only with the early forms of pragmatism, he saw that its affiliation was with experientialism. In fact, he sensed its logical connection with positivism. In *Materialism and Empirio-Criticism,* he writes: "Pragmatism ridicules the metaphysics of idealism and materialism, extols experience and only experience,

5. I have come to dislike this ambiguous term. It should signify only the fact of objective cognition.

and recognizes practice as the only criterion of truth. . . . The difference between Machism and pragmatism is as insignificant and subsidiary from the viewpoint of materialism as is the distinction between empirio-criticism and empirio-monism."[6] In another passage he pays his respects to those who believe that by means of the word *experience* they are able to overcome the "obsolete" distinction between materialism and idealism.[7]

I was amused by these passages because they fit in so well with the course of events in our own time, when we see pragmatists and positivists drawing together with much this platform. The logic of physical realism, on the other hand, directs its advocates to explore epistemology and to develop the natural beliefs of common sense and science in the ability to decipher the pattern of things. Has not materialism been too much scorned by academic philosophy? Besides technical reasons for this attitude dating back to Berkeley and Kant, have there not been cultural ones?

I conclude, then, that dialectical materialists have had a vigorous sense of the realities of the human situation due to their biological and social realism. It is interesting to note that Feuerbach—in many ways their technical mentor—starts with concrete human beings eating, drinking, living. To this Marx adds the cultural note, changing their environment through work, while Engels makes much of the achievements of chemistry in producing dye-stuffs from things-in-themselves, which are, in his opinion, thereby shown not to be mysterious things-in-themselves. In replying to Fichte, Feuerbach points out that a human being is not an abstract ego but must be either a man or a woman. Before perceiving we breathe; we cannot exist without food and drink. To Lenin this signifies that already Feuerbach has absorbed the sum total of human practice into theory of knowledge.

All in all, then, I am inclined to maintain that there was a great deal of shrewdness and concrete realism in the making of dialectical materialism. What the academic philosopher can add is analysis. He

---

6. P. 296.
7. This is still Dewey's view. See his reply to Savery in the Schilpp series, and my article in this Journal, vol. 3, no. 4, p. 381, entitled "Dewey on Materialism."

may be able to press beyond the enigmas associated with Cartesian dualism, the correspondence theory of truth, transcendence, and substance. It may, perhaps, be found that the majority of philosophers have been too fainthearted in these matters, too ready to give up physical realism and materialism, too prone to fall back into the arms of phenomenalism and positivism.

iii

Let us make a brief historical survey. In order to bring home the situation to Americans if may be well to divide it into two parts, the development of philosophy in the United States and the growth of positivism in Europe. In such a brief survey I must inevitably oversimplify and leave much out of the picture.

I need not go into the story of the slow development of technical philosophy in the United States. Suffice it to say that, after the Civil War, Locke and Reid were gradually subordinated to Kant and Hegel. By the nineties, Anglo-American idealism, which was a blend of German thought in the spirit of T. H. Green, had secured prestige. On the whole, it should be spoken of as an idealism of the center. It was politically liberal but religiously conservative, though not orthodox. America was a dominantly middle-class and religious country with little of the deism of the eighteenth century remaining. In other words, it was not the Hegelianism of the left that migrated to these shores, or to England either, for that matter. Royce, Bradley, Bosanquet, and the Cairds were absolute idealists. And it is noteworthy that, although other strains of philosophy survived, this type of idealism largely held the stage.

But by the beginning of the twentieth century new ideas and attitudes expressing at one and the same time the growing influence of the sciences and the revival of the empirical tradition began to appear. The brilliant but erratic James defended theism to the last, yet moved in the direction of a radical empiricism and pragmatism that was in many ways akin to Machian positivism. He sought to reconceive knowing as a pointing forward in the stream of experience to future sensory data and to redefine the physical and the psychical in terms of relations of the same neutral elements. The parallelism with Mach and Avenarius is too complete to be accidental. James thought of himself as escaping from souls and transcendental egos of Kantian vintage and, in the process, improving upon Hume's atomistic sensationalism. But it is evident that he does not seriously reconsider physical realism. The influence of traditional idealistic arguments against Locke's mishandling of perception is still too strong. It is not without interest that Russell was confirmed in his phenomenalistic empiricism by James's neutralism. It became the fashionable thing to decry what were called nonempirical entities, which were also characterized as unobservables and inferred entities. *It seems hardly to have entered the minds of these thinkers that they were begging the question.* The realistic empiricist holds that physical things are observable in that they are directly denoted[8] in perception and are disclosed through sensory data and concepts, and that they are not inferred from sensation as a basis but denoted through the response of the percipient organism. It remained for the critical realists to try to explore the possibilities of a reanalysis of perception. Unfortunately, they were divided among themselves on many crucial points. Drake was one of the most brilliant ones and was fast moving toward materialism when cut off prematurely by death. Because of a too-atomistic physics he did not see the importance of organization and functional unity at the biopsychological level of evolution and did not grasp the significance of the theory of emergence. Accordingly, he kept to the mystical conception of "essences" associated with Santayana and refused to admit that the perceptual experience with all its cognitive distinctions could be intrinsic to the functioning brain as this responded to the stimulus-response situation of the organism.[9]

---

8. Though not directly apprehended.

9. Those who are interested in this divergence between Drake and myself will find his discussion in *An Invitation to Philosophy* relevant, especially chap. 10. He rejects no. 4, namely, that sensa exist in the brain of the perceiver, which is my position, and makes fun of the "under-the-hat" theory of mind. It goes without saying that I never think of landscapes as being squashed up in my brain. What is in my brain is my complex perceptual experience with its references and descriptions. Drake seems to me to use the term *sensum* rather oddly for what I would call a descriptive reference. These internal conflicts have inevitably helped to blunt the effect of the movement. It should also be noted that, for me, emergence does not involve the rise of a new kind of being to leave one with a new sort of Cartesian dualism. The minded brain is a physical system.

Even in a brief survey one cannot neglect Dewey, a monumental, somewhat perverse, thinker who followed James's suggestions as to the future reference of knowing and, taking it for granted that a private consciousness was tied up with Cartesian dualism and with all the false enigmas of correspondence, transcendence, and stuff, boldly developed a logic of experientialism.

The interesting thing is that Dewey approaches Marxism in many ways but keeps this side of it in terms of a liberalism and an evolutionary, experientialistic naturalism. His disciples, Eastman and Hook, seek to mediate in terms of social engineering and the rejection of materialistic metaphysics.

I have left myself little space for the treatment of the realistic revival. The new realism sought to press beyond pragmatism to realism, but did so not so much by a reanalysis of perception as by the power of two principles: the James-Mach doctrine of neutral elements, and the doctrine of external relations, which Russell had popularized. The result was, in the main, what is called panobjectivism. In England, also, neo-realism flourished for a time, but there the tradition of Cartesian dualism remained stronger than in the United States.[10] Consciousness was made much of, even though reduced to a transparent act of awareness. It is impossible to go into details and to do justice to shadings of opinion. On the whole, I have found myself most sympathetic with the epistemology of Ewing, Stebbing, and Broad, none of whom, however, seems to realize that their defense of representative realism parallels that of American critical realism. And it should be noted, of course, that none is an overt materialist.

What has happened largely, as a consequence of the stalemate into which the realistic movement fell, has been the revival of positivism. This re-revival was hastened by the enthusiasm of a group of "scientific" philosophers hailing from Vienna and Berlin, many of whom were specialists in mathematics and physics and, for that reason, all the more immersed in their theses. In America the linkage has been made—as one would expect—with hospitable pragmatic experientialism. The result has been almost a new Scholasticism of terminology

---

10. This fact comes out strongly in both G. F. Stout and G. E. Moore.

and technique. Yet it cannot be denied that it has initiated exploratory work in logic and linguistics, which has led by both action and reaction to a clearing up of ideas. To the realist it has been least successful and least original in its treatment of empirical statements.[11]

And so we have come full round to positivism, which is now international. On the whole, idealism has waned in its prestige and influence. Perhaps, as regards secular philosophy, the movement that parallels the developments discussed above and that has international significance is that of phenomenology. Here delicate analyses have been made in many fields on a background of abstraction from existential questions. There can be little doubt but that technical philosophy will owe much to the detailed descriptive work carried forward by the phenomenologists, though, I take it, the connection with existence must again be completed. However, in the present study of dialectical materialism I am led by historical and cultural factors to select the basic conflict with positivism, a conflict begun by Lenin in his attack upon Avenarius and Mach. As a critical materialist I agree in his rejection of positivism with Lenin, though it is my opinion that the advance in technical philosophy enables us to phrase some of the issues with more precision.

iv

Both dialectical materialism and positivism may be said to belong to the general class of philosophies which, as Professor Perry has pointed out, dominated Germany and France in the middle of the nineteenth century.[12] Materialism, naturalism, and positivism had much in common as reactions against romantic idealism under the influence of science. Positivism and materialism represented the extremes, overlapping to some extent in the universe of discourse of naturalism. All three are to be set over against spiritualism and idealism, positions that were to gain, for technical and cultural rea-

---

11. This sounds paradoxical, but it is owing to its neglect of epistemology. There are signs that the ambiguities of "physicalism" are being seen. Feigl has got as far as saying things *are* as they are known as. But are they reducible to concepts? Ontology begins to loom.

12. Perry, *Philosophy of the Recent Past*, pp. 2f.

sons, renewed influence and prestige in the second half of the nineteenth century. Not all German idealists when they died went to Oxford; some came to the United States; and others were reincarnated in Germany itself, where they were put to good use, as, for example, Fichte has been recently.

There is good reason to believe that spiritualism and idealism reached their zenith by the end of the century in both Europe and the United States. They were once more confronted by tendencies in the direction of realism, positivism, and naturalism. It is intriguing to note that materialism lagged behind, so far as academic philosophy was concerned. It was clear that no simple revival of eighteenth-century materialism would do. And the vague and often self-contradictory assertions of scientists turned philosophers for the occasion, like Vogt and Moleshott, could scarcely meet philosophical standards. Kantians like Lange and Windelband were able to cross-examine them and make them contradict themselves flagrantly. No; a realistic revival was necessary, as also a more evolutionary approach. This time the whole gamut of philosophy from epistemology to axiology must needs be run, with positivism offering its formal analyses as a way out. In the meantime, little was heard of dialectical materialism which, so far as academic circles were concerned, was largely a *terra incognita*. I have the impression that its Hegelian format was partly responsible, for it is usually hard to separate what is living from what is dead in Hegel. Perhaps Marxist interest had been largely in economics and politics until the awareness of the lure of Machism made Lenin explore philosophy from Berkeley to Poincaré. I have already indicated my opinion that the task before materialism is a Herculean one. The mastery of the mind-body problem, the reformulation of the so-called correspondence theory of truth, the correct analysis of perception as against sensation, the proper notion of denotative reference and cognitive transcendence, the exploration of emergent novelty in evolution, the clarification of the empirical status of categories like causality and matter in terms of realistic empiricism, all these tasks were presupposed. All the positivist had to do was to shake his head and murmur *sinnlos*. All this was, and, I suppose, still is, meaningless to him, though I think I have recently noted some signs of uneasiness. But whose fault is it? If people begin with the conviction that there is no such valid discipline as epistemology, they can hardly be expected to know much about it. And, as we have seen, all the "experientialists" begin with this assumption.

Because positivism has a tantalizing ambivalence, it has played a peculiar role in the intellectual life of modern times. It is, I take it, ambivalent because it leaves so much in the shadows, or, rather, it plays in the sunlight and stoutly affirms there are no shadows, no cosmic immensities and dooms. And yet, human nature being what it is, it often furnishes the point of departure for fideisms when there is some slight change in the moral balance of the human picture. It is this point which Lenin already noted and which gave animus to his attack. Even today its sophisticated descendent, logical positivism, enjoys much the same ambivalence. Thus we find the Neo-Thomist Maritain far less suspicious of logical positivism than of dialectical materialism. To assert that ontological propositions are meaningless may mean little more than that they are irrelevant for certain logical, or scientific, purposes. A philosophy that has no clear-cut epistemology and builds upon empirical elements ranging variously, and rather arbitrarily, from neutral elements to ineffable *Erlebnisse,* from sensations to things, has a shifting foundation on which to build. Materialism, on the other hand, is by its very nature forthright and unambiguous. This does not mean that its task is simple. Quite the contrary. It is ordered by its very principles to achieve an adequate epistemology and an ontology that will do justice—but no more than justice—to life, mind, consciousness, and human values. But, hitherto, because of the defection of technical philosophy, in part because of cultural reasons, in part because of complications and historically conditioned blind alleys, it has come about that materialism, the philosophy that most needs technical equipment, has had too little of it at its service. The consequence has been that Lange, Windelband, Pratt, and Hook—to mention only a few—have been able to circle it like nimble picadors. It is to me astonishing that this philosophical outlook, which, by its very genius, is cosmic in its scope and which tries to see the foreground of human life in its relation to its immense and impersonal background, should have awakened so little interest in academic philosophy. Even the seventeenth century had its Hobbes and its Spinoza.

v

Suppose, then, that we pay some attention to the life histories of these two philosophical movements which, in the main, speak for the naturalistic view of things. I take it that, for our purposes, pragmatic experientialism lines up more nearly with positivism than with materialism.[13] As I have already pointed out, both reject cognitive transcendence, that is, disclosures through concepts, the correspondence basis of knowledge, and the category of stuff. These define a watershed in philosophy.

Comte, the French founder of positivism, had little interest in, or concern with, epistemology, that is, the investigation of the nature, conditions, and reach of human knowing. Rather was he concerned with science as a cultural development superior to theology and to medieval metaphysics, as he conceived this latter. In science alone was to be found tested and verifiable knowledge. Human culture had at last risen superior to the belief in mythological agents behind the scenes and had outgrown formulations in terms of substances and forces somehow veiled from observation. In this latter point we make contact with the Humean thesis, which denies that we can observe *through* our sensory data. The physical realist of today rejects the arrogant assumption of the positivist that empiricism implies that sensations are the termini of cognition. In fact, as I have tried to make clear, it is perception with its objectives and meanings that is the elementary datum of cognition, and not sensation. But to proceed. The positivist holds that, at this third, and highest, stage of human thought, attention should be turned, once and for all, to the human scene. Genuine knowledge is now to be regarded as relative and human in its texture, categories, contents, and concern.

To the epistemologist the irritating feature of positivism is its mixture of validity and irrelevance. Let it be granted that scientific

---

13. See in this connection my article, "Dewey on Materialism," this Journal, July 1943.

knowledge is superior in standing to the guesses and surmises of pre-scientific eras, for no philosopher of standing questions the proposition. And let there be a symbiosis of the sciences within the free play of their differences. Is an artificial unity cultivated from outside in terms of assumptions that may well be alien to the genius of science, as Meyerson has suggested, desirable? The real issue is that of the reach and reference of empirical statements, factual and theoretical. Are there such things as atoms, photons, chemical substances, living organisms, transcendent to these empirical statements but not beyond their cognitive reach? As I pointed out, Comte did not put the question in this form so central to the struggle in technical philosophy between realism, on the one hand, and idealism, experientialism, and phenomenalistic empiricism on the other. It remained for Mach and Avenarius to link up Comte with Hume and give to positivism its epistemological affiliations. These, acknowledgedly, are Humean. And, as we should suspect, just as Hume represented a swing away from Berkeley's spiritualism, so, as Lenin points out, the positivistic phase of Mach and Avenarius expressed a quite similar deviation on their part *from a priori idealism*. The question then remains, Why stop at this point? Why not an outright realistic empiricism? And here we come, once again, to the technical stumbling blocks: cognitive transcendence, the correspondence basis of knowledge, and the category of stuff. Can empiricism be pushed through these obstacles? The realistic empiricist, or physical realist, affirms it can be, while the positivist, experientialist, and neutralist deny that it can be so harmonized with realism.

Let us now turn to the fortunes of dialectical materialism. It is scarcely deniable that Marx and Engels were as fervid in their admiration of science as was Comte. But they kept their attention fixed upon the constitutive theories of science rather than upon scientific procedure as such. And it is interesting to note here that, while German and French thought was constantly affected by the Kantian revival, Marxism fought it off, refusing to turn back from Hegel to Kant and preferring to press forward from Hegel to realism and materialism. To the realistic empiricist this was a healthier direction to take, bringing Marxism, as it did, into a position quite analogous to that which dominated the realistic revival in England and the United States in the twentieth century, as can be observed in Prichard's early book on Kant.[14]

Now one reason for this firm rejection of the phenomenalistic maze of Kant's so-called Copernican revolution, which was in effect a counterrevolution preparing the way for Romanticism, was the Marxist allegiance to the best traditions of the eighteenth century. I confess that I, also, have always had a firm sympathy with much of the thought of the eighteenth century while granting the need for more stress on relations, growth, organization. And it should be pointed out to the positivist that Comte was strongly affected by a reaction against the eighteenth century and developed a conservative perspective in social and political matters while Marxism expressed in its own fashion a *reaction against the romantic reaction*.

But the academic philosopher must not forget that Marxism, as a revolutionary movement, was to some degree forced underground, that is, was isolated and, accordingly, in large measure ignored by philosophy. In English-speaking countries it is only very recently that Marxian economics has secured fair and objective examination by competent economists like Lange, Sweezy, Dobb, and Robinson. It should not be surprising that it has had much the same fate meted out to it on its philosophic side. Here, again, it must, I think, be considered a challenge to subjectivistic and merely descriptive tendencies. Just as sociological realism rejects the overemphasis on the market, so materialism queries the self-sufficiency of fact and convention. There is something just a little pathetic in Lenin's report of the tendency of scientists and philosophers, when confronted by the crisis in physics following the discovery of radioactivity, to speculate in terms of Kantianism, idealism, and positivism, altogether ignoring dialectical materialism and the fruitfulness of the distinction between relative and absolute truth, or, as I would phrase it, between the approximating adequacy of scientific knowledge and the deter-

14. Pritchard, *Kant's Theory of Knowledge* (Oxford: Clarendon Press, 1909).

minate goal for human knowing set in the determinate nature of things.[15]

It is now time to bring our conclusions to a head. In the main I have tried to show that the naturalistic trend in philosophy has been so shaping up that the choice lies between positivism and some critically formulated type of materialism. It is not, I take it, unfair to say that positivism rests upon certain, not always clearly expressed, assumptions with respect to epistemology and ontology. Its affiliations are with phenomenalistic empiricism, experientialism, radical empiricism, and sensationalism, though it may veil this context by conventionalism and by stress upon logical and linguistic technique. Following Comte, there is an admiration for scientific culture and a readiness to enjoy the prestige of science, a readiness exemplified today in the "unity of science" movement. Materialism, on the other hand, has had less than justice done to its philosophical possibilities. It presupposes realism in epistemology and an ontology able to do justice to basic categories. It is undeniable that an adequate materialism involves a comprehensiveness of philosophical analysis that, hitherto, has been largely lacking. Instead of being an easy thing, to be dashed off by some physiologist in an odd moment of leisure, materialism of a critical sort demands the focusing of many lines of thought. But it, too, is second to none in its confidence in scientific method and scientific achievement, though less inclined to confuse philosophical questions with those of the special sciences and to advocate scientific method in philosophy, whatever that may mean.

I shall now adopt an affirmative approach and say farewell to positivism, whose strength, when all is said, rests upon the lack of clear development of realism and materialism. The task before this concluding section of this article will be that which I indicated in

---

15. The rise of relativity brought a quite analogous swing toward idealism, positivism, and operationalism. I have stood against the current to consider relativity epistemic and mensurational.

my opening paragraph, to translate the general insights of dialectical materialism into the terminology of physical, critical realism, emergence, and nonmechanistic materialism. I do not know how far Russian philosophers will agree with me in my suggestion of parallelisms and promising points for analysis. But I assume that they are, as Lenin called himself, "seekers" in philosophy and that they will agree that we must press beneath formulae which, for the non-Hegelian, can have only indicative, or symbolic, significance. It seems best to link my epistemological remarks with praxis and my ontological discussion with the status and import of dialectic. I shall take them up in this order.

I take it to be obvious that materialism presupposes the truth of physical realism. Now I think that physical realism can be best formulated as a realistic empiricism which, by making the distinction between sensing and perceiving, undercuts the traditional formulations of representative realism. Perception is the most elementary level of cognition and rests upon organic and interpretative responses *in the direction of* the stimulus that is conditioning sensations. Thus perception is intrinsically referential and cognitive, but does not involve the literal and immediate inspection of the objective denoted. It is not the sensation we know in the case of empirical judgment—though we may become conscious of it by an effort—but we perceive *through the sensation* the object that we, as percipients, are reacting to and concerned with. In this fashion sensations are the point of departure for symbols and concepts of properties.

Now this analysis signifies that empirical statements are about the things around us and, in the case of self-perception, about our organic selves. The result is a direct, nonnaïve realism that maintains that cognitive reference is transcendent only in the sense that it concerns selves and things and is not reducible to the sort of acquaintance with states of mind that Locke suggests by his purely causal approach to "ideas." Locke got things badly stated. Once we understand the nature of perceptual reference, we are on the level of cognition and have escaped subjectivism and sensationalism. Cognition becomes the disclosure of denoted things by means of symbols and concepts. Knowing is not a mysterious reaching out of a thing called mind but a directed operation resting upon *denotative response and the disclosure capacity of sensations and concepts.*

I take it that the position adopted by Engels and Lenin in defense of the reflection or "mirror" theory of knowing is explained by this analysis.* It is not a passive reflection but rests upon organic activity and the cognitive value of sensations and their intelligent use in deciphering the structure, behavior, and relations of things. Representation and depicting are an achievement. Let the pragmatist note this point. This undercuts the whole family of radical empiricism, neutral elements, and phenomenalism.

But how do we test these directed claims-to-know contained in empirical statements? Surely, by the generally accepted methods of induction, deduction, and verification. These methods presuppose the cognitive value of the data of observation and the validity of logic. But the ultimate test of the human power to know is the guidance it gives to the concrete human being and to the social group. It is this final test of praxis which defeats skepticism and agnosticism, and forces the thinker to admit some kind of correspondence to things in the materials of knowledge, sensations, and concepts, as the condition of knowledge, as that upon which their cognitive value rests. Thus, correspondence is neither a definition of truth nor a criterion of truth but a condition of knowledge. It is a condition implied by the tested fact of human knowing and supported by the organic mechanisms evolved to enable man to adjust himself to his environment. It emphasizes the *cognitive value* of sensations and concepts.

As I see it, then, the dialectical materialist showed his persistent sense of the realities of the human situation, even though much remained to be done in the way of clarification. Material things are denoted and described *and become objects*[16] *for us.* Their structure, behavior, and relations are actively deciphered by us and thus our

---

* Sellars does not here call attention to the limitations (and actual merits) of the Marxist reflection theory of perception. Cf. therefore chap. 8 in *Reflections on American Philosophy from Within* (South Bend, Ind.: Notre Dame Press, 1969), especially p. 116. Also, *Social Patterns and Political Horizons* (Nashville, Tenn.: Aurora Press, 1970), chap. 13, especially pp. 211 and 212.—Ed.

16. Denotables, *Gegenstände.*

thoughts come approximately to reflect them and disclose them. Such is the teaching of realistic empiricism.

One final point in epistemology. The puzzling paradox of transcendence, of which positivists, pragmatists, and radical empiricists in general make so much, is a reflection of their own faulty approach. By not seeing that perception is a cognitive act denotatively directed at an objective correlative to the percipient, they do not realize that cognition is by its very nature *objective* in motive. Not sensations but objects are the terminal intentions *of knowing.* To understand cognition is to understand transcendence and rob it of its mystery. All that is needed are an organic act of denoting and thoughts capable of disclosure.[17] And I take it that one of the errors of phenomenalistic empiricism from the time of Hume has been the neglect of the organic self and its role in both external perception and in self-awareness. Cognition is a complex organic activity.

Let me now turn to ontology. Here the first problem to confront us is the category of stuff or matter.

It should be clear that physical realism, or realistic empiricism, makes it possible to give meaning to this category while phenomenalistic empiricism with its false conception of cognition precludes it; so important is epistemology. In other words, if sensations are the termini of cognition, matter is an obscurantist verbalism and the job of the ingenious empiricist is to take the path of Mill, Russell, and Ayer and to speak of "permanent possibilities" of sensation, perspectives, and sensibilia or translations. But if things are the termini of cognition, we can understand that all sorts of meanings and categories have been built up within organic acts of cognition connected with organic adjustments to the environment. And here, I think, self-awareness has worked hand in hand with external perception. *The nuclear meaning of matter is that which endures and has being in its own right.* This nuclear meaning applies to the organic self as much as to the things around it. But this nuclear meaning is expanded and supplemented by detailed knowledge of spatiality, causal activity, texture—all categories as empirically found-

---

17. Language gets its attachment from pointing, and is both objective and social.

ed as could be desired, once one is past the myopia of sensationalism. Berkeley was fighting the windmills of inert matter by means of the resources of sensationalism and the echoes of Cartesian dualism. There is little excuse for that sort of thing today, once we press toward a realistic empiricism and brush aside the cobwebs of Kantianism and the puzzles instituted by Locke's unfortunate formulation. Matter is that which endures and has being in its own right, that which we can handle and shape, that which explodes and blows human beings to bits. We are ourselves made of it.

Such is the new materialism. But how far is it one with dialectical materialism? The best I can here do, perhaps, is to indicate a generic likeness and leave it to the protagonist of dialectical materialism to draw his moral.

Surely the preestablished harmony of Leibniz and the cosmic rule of rational natural law of Stoic and Churchman must be foregone. Eighteenth-century perfectionism and Newtonian deism likewise bow out. Struggle, dynamic relations, causal integration and disintegration, generation and corruption are the categories that science is filling out. The "unity of opposites" and "the negation of negation" seem to have been Hegelian recognitions of this moving compresence of conflicting tendencies. The ironic romanticist had his insights into the turbulence of life.

I have, however, the decided impression that Engels took Hegel's *Naturphilosophie* too seriously, despite his interest in the growth of the empirical sciences. That is, of course, quite understandable. But is it not better to elicit the categories from the results of the scientific picture of things than to fall back upon formulae? But here we come upon a point in ontology that the ordinary empiricist neglects, that of the basis and genesis of ontological categories. The empiricist easily becomes a Humean and is satisfied with descriptions. The materialist must explore categories such as endurance, force, causality, tension, togetherness, organization, conflict. I agree with the dialectical materialist that causality is an ontological category and is not reducible to regularities in experience. And so I can regard these Hegelian phrases as at least symbolic of the dynamic togetherness and relations of physical fields. There are conflicts, incompatibilities, integrations in what Locke called the "real essences" of things. And these may well rise at the human level to struggles and maladjustments. It is a darker world than liberalism conceived it to be. And I think that dialectical materialism is nearer the truth in these matters than the dialectical theology of Niebuhr with its supernaturalism.

It is, in short, the inalienable right of the ontologist to achieve categories, on the basis of human experience, which penetrate in some measure into the *Gang der Sache selbst.* The identity of being and thought of Hegel was too idealistically and mythologically conceived. But, surely, thought, while local and emergent and arising within human organisms, has the task and the capacity to grasp in outline at least the texture and "go" of being. We are a part of the world and not alien to it: and in our lives we apprehend its temporal, spatial, and causal texture. It is thus, as participants in existence, that we elicit the ontological categories. They are bone of our bone and flesh of our flesh and not *a priori,* rational forms *à la* Kant. It is this theory of ontological categories that phenomenalism and positivism have never appreciated. I take it that dialectical materialism would not find such an approach alien to its intentions.

It would be absurd, then, to reduce human thought to the formulae of symbolic logicians concerned with logical constants and deductive validities. And I do not for a moment suppose that these logicians postulate such a reduction. Logic must be distinguished from psychology. And yet positivism has encouraged a thinning of thought to the conventions of syntax and the reduction of valuations to the inarticulate feelings of the moment.

But I must hurry on. The formula, the transformation of quantity into quality, taken from Hegel, seems to me to limp. Hegel was dealing with concepts and, since, as one commentator puts it, he could not deduce quantity from quality, he tried the reverse. Now I take it that the theory of emergence when interpreted, as I have always done, as involving *integrative organization,* is a less ambiguous concept. The addition of energy may well involve changed relations and therefore changed qualities. Marx, however, was one of the first to emphasize novelty and temporalism.

Living systems and minded systems are, then, emergent systems with new qualities and abilities. I judge the dialectical materialist would agree on the essential point. There is evolutionary novelty.

It will be remembered that I stated that the working out of an adequate materialism requires extreme philosophical sophistication and cannot be the by-product of either a physiologist's or a physicist's leisure. The mind-body problem stands out particularly, and it is not enough to assert that consciousness and mind are functions of the brain as an organ of intelligent adjustment. The resources of epistemology and ontology must be applied to the question. Unfortunately, I am not acquainted with the present-day approach of dialectical materialists to this subtle problem. My own thinking has been along the line of a double knowledge of the brain and organism. At any rate, I imagine the dialectical materialist will not be satisfied with double-language formulas or with a position like Dewey's, which denies a private consciousness. If I am right in my interpretation of the implications of the epistemology of dialectical materialism, the correspondence theory of the conditions of knowledge involves the rise in the knower of sensations and concepts having cognitive value and the use of such sensations and concepts in cognitive acts directed at material things and organic selves. In fact, technical philosophy comes to a head in the mind-body problem.

Whatever may be the technical divergence between my own thinking and that of the dialectical materialists, I think we can take pride in being representatives of a very old and very healthy philosophical tradition including such names as Democritus, Lucretius, Hobbes, Cabanis, and Diderot. And when I read the table of contents of a recent work on the physics of the twentieth century and note a chapter called "The Liquidation of Materialism," I shrug my shoulders and say, "My positivistic friends, materialism is very much alive and is exploring the technical possibilities opened up by a realistic empiricism. It is not physics but philosophy that must decide the fate of materialism as an ontology."

9

Materialism and Relativity:
A Semantic Analysis*

"Analyzed, relativity turns out to be a logical question of either-or. It is the separating that is determinate."**

i

There can be little doubt that much uncertainty as to its full import has been left in the wake of the theory of relativity. Assuredly realistic philosophers have not been satisfied as to its significance when taken as more than a technical device in physics. It is not surprising, it needs scarcely be said, that positivists and pragmatists have been the least skeptical and critical of all, for these philosophical groups do not really believe in a material universe. The positivists,

---

* *The Philosophical Review* 55 (1946):25–51. Reprinted with the permission of both the author and publisher.

** From a postscript to an unpublished 1970 paper. The postscript continues: "The relational lagging light, which I emphasize, signifies that light can overtake less of the moving rod the faster it is moving. This, also, is a relation question. The *limit* is when the rod approaches the speed of light. This is *a Denk-experiment*. If something were found going faster than light, the same method would have to be used with respect to it. The speed of light is not an *a priori*. Light does not move absolutely in an absolute medium as frame. What I try to bring out is relational movement and spatial patterns in nature."

particularly, have made a fetish of expressions, such as observation and observables, while ignoring the realistic thesis that we can observe material things *through* the data of observation. May it not be a dogma, associated with an inadequate theory of perception, that we observe only the data themselves, that human cognition terminates on the data?

Now, the point I am making is this, namely, that the theory of relativity has been less examined than it should have been, because of the philosophical fashion it harmonized with, supported, and, in no small degree, was itself the expression of. We must not forget, as most English and American physicists do, the methodological influence of Mach and Avenarius upon Einstein's way of thinking. His device fitted in with positivism and was, in many ways, a peculiarly elegant development of that mode of thought. That was one reason why an English or an American physicist would have been unable to conceive it. Nor is it surprising that relativity has helped to bolster up positivism and give it moral support. The resulting state of affairs can be compared to a circular reflex in which the response reenforces the stimulus.

It seems to have become a fashionable dictum that the unobserved has no meaning for physics. But this is, obviously, nonsense; for an eclipse calculated for the past can never be observed by the scientist. He can only assert that he believes that it could have been observed by an observer living at the assigned date. And it is well known that many submicroscopic entities are more inferred than observed. As I shall endeavor to show, much of this language represents the emotional reaction of the modern physicist to his recognition that he was unbelievably naïve in respect to problems in theory of knowledge before the new developments woke him up. He seems to have believed that he could observe points in a Newtonian Absolute Space and locate moments in a corresponding Absolute Time. It is not at all surprising that, in his confusion, he has swung to the other extreme and delivered himself into the welcoming hands of positivists and idealists. The truth of the matter is, as I see it, that he is naturally only an amateur in theory of knowledge and is easily misled. When pressed, he is prone to take refuge in the expression, "Only observables have meaning *for the physicist,"* thus retiring into his citadel.

As a physical realist I am not dealing in unknowables. I can know things and events only by means of my observations and inferences therefrom. But that does not reduce things and events to my observations. Otherwise we confuse existence with human knowledge and its conditions. In talking with scientists recently, in order to check up on their language and modes of thinking, I was impressed by their neglect of this, to the philosopher, obvious distinction. They evidently concentrated on magnitudes and numbers rather than on what was being measured, on symbols rather than on what was being symbolized. It seems likely that the development of mathematical physics as against the old mechanical physics has increased this mode of thought. Relativity with its *s-t,* that is, its numbers that are interconnected and transformable from one frame to another, has, I feel, assisted this tendency. As one astronomer frankly said to me, I never bother about existence; my concern is with space-time magnitudes. To the physical realist, of course, this means that knowledge and its categories have crowded out any thought of existence and its categories. The philosopher sees that there is need for semantic analysis. It is possible that he is the only one who can carry it through and do justice to all the necessary distinctions.

Now the need for such a semantic analysis is peculiarly apparent to the materialist. He finds that pragmatists and positivists hide behind the theory of relativity like doughboys behind a protecting earthwork. There is no getting around it. The materialist must storm the position and reduce it to its proper significance as a technical device.

ii

Suppose it is the case—as I presume everyone not mentally corrupted by sophistications would tend to believe—that there are a multitude of events throughout the universe simultaneous with the beating of my heart or the ticking of a clock, though we are not in a position to give them a temporal assignment or dating; does it follow that the conception of such *absolute simultaneity* is meaningless? It is surely meaningful for anyone who accepts a material universe, who accepts existence. And if a physicist really is concerned with material things, then it is meaningful for him. Naturally this does not mean that we must accept the Platonic reification indulged in by Newton under the suggestion of the Cambridge Platonists of his day and his own theological proclivities. Since his day, philosophy has become empirical in its attitude. After all, Locke, a contemporary of Newton, began the shift in that direction. As I see it, the difficulty was to overcome ontological dualism and, by moving onward to an adequate materialism, to get rid of the horror of "metaphysics." In other words, the job was to get back to physics as knowledge about the material universe at its basic level.

Such a clarification of the situation required an adequate theory of knowledge and some rudiments of ontology. Out of their union could have come a framework for a natural philosophy superior to that of Newton's. Instead, as I see the situation, physics and positivism have tended to move away from such a desirable consummation toward operationalism and a kind of factualism hanging in the void. And I cannot help but feel that the theory of relativity has encouraged this emphasis.

In this paper, then, I am going as usual to "stick out my neck" and defend materialism by making space and time adjectival and by discriminating different meanings—I find at least three for both space and time and I am led to distinguish sharply between motion and movement. In all this, I shall write as a philosopher, although I hope that some of my distinctions may have significance for physics, which, after all, is not such a mysterious science, even though it deals with very small things and events and often in a statistical fashion. While I am full of admiration for its achievements, these have never thrown me into a mystical condition, ready to say good-bye to common sense and to proclaim "free will," either because photons affected electrons and made certain calculations uncertain, or because we have only statistical knowledge about the probable paths of radiations. Nor was I surprised that very small things acted somewhat differently from massive aggregates; that seemed logical enough, since I was well aware how sketchy the knowledge gained in sense perception is, just because sense perception is the most elementary level of external knowledge. In other words, I could hardly be a competent philosopher and not be a little sophisticated in such matters. One reason was that in the first decade of the twentieth century I had been telling scientists that matter could not be the sort of thing they believed it to be; that, if it were, organization, evolution, and naturalism would be precluded. The new physics was a relief—the sort of thing a critical materialist would expect.

A few more words about "natural philosophy" are in order, because I believe that it is time to give physics the context of a natural philosophy; not, of course, of the romantic speculative sort in which philosophers tried to discover fact *a priori* and spin scientific theories out of *Geist,* but a natural philosophy that has an adequate theory of knowledge and some notion of categories like being, existence, causality, space, and time. One of the purposes of the present study of relativity is to further such a natural philosophy.

It is because of the lack of such a clarified physical realism, I believe, that men like Eddington and Jeans—and they are not the only sinners—wander abstractedly, though confidently and brightly, between theology and tales of philosophic lore picked up here and there. Now, only Mind is real. Next, we hear of a Platonic demiurge. In another mood, hints are offered of Kantian things-in-themselves, of Spinoza's double-attribute thesis, the whole sprinkled with suggestions of Berkeley and Hegel. The lightheartedness and irresponsibility of it all rather shocks the technical philosopher who has been trying to do careful analytic work and integrate epistemology and ontology. On the whole, I prefer the positivist tradition because of its economy and lack of piety. One can at least know what their philosophy is. Pious Englishmen and pious Americans are neither fish nor fowl nor good red herring when they seek to harmonize science and theology.

In connection with the present study I was reading Eddington's book, *The Expanding Universe,* and came across the following delightful passage, which I must share. Aware that the assumption of an absolute origin to the material universe got science into difficulties, he proceeded to do some dialectical steps to the effect that *absolute same-*

ness and *nothingness* cannot be distinguished philosophically, and then added: "I do not picture a worn out world careering forlornly through the rest of eternity. What is left is only a few *conceptions* which we forgot to put away after we had finished using them."[1]

So far as I am aware, Einstein does not do this sort of thing. All the more honor to him. In his recent contribution to the Russell-Schilpp volume he seems to plead for "metaphysics" and propound something that looks like Kantianism. But it is all very sketchy, only suggesting a certain dissatisfaction with positivism.

It really seems that, until the Michelson-Morley experiment came along to perform the Humean job of arousing them from their dogmatic slumbers, physicists tended to think that there were points and positions in an Absolute Space and in an Absolute Time of a receptacular sort. The scheme was that of seventeenth-century intuitionalistic rationalism, quite analogous to that of the corresponding conception of Euclid's axioms as intuitive truths about the universe. Modern theory of knowledge seems scarcely to have affected them. Of course, Euler had wavered after reading Berkeley, and Ernst Mach had gone over to the Humean extreme. But these men were exceptions.

The result was that, when physicists saw the absurdity of their antique rationalism, they stampeded to this other approach, while scarcely realizing what was involved. The stress now lay upon observation, observables, and operations. These became the empirical factors that alone had meaning for science. Now, as against those mythological realities, Absolute Space and Time, there was sense in this emphasis. Unfortunately, the material universe tended to be like the famous baby poured out with the bath. The very idea that a physical universe could be known *through* their observations and thus become observable tended to rank as a heresy. Thus do pendulums swing.

In line with this fashion, we are constantly told that Einstein has *analyzed* the concept of time for the physicist. It is my considered opinion that this statement is extreme. What he did was to define a *time-interval* in terms of an operation involving the passage of light

---

1. P. 82.

over a distance, at a velocity invariant for any frame of reference. It was an affair of definition and stipulation. In the same connection, he supplemented an operational definition of a time-interval by the conception of *relative* operational simultaneity. To an observer in one frame it would be *as though* events simultaneous in his own frame would not be such for the other frame. It is a philosophy of the *als ob*. Numbers are to be assigned in accordance with these principles.

The least consideration of the way in which experimental data are secured shows us that Einstein kept for the laboratory the traditional instrument of scientific time, namely, clocks, and with them local absolute simultaneity. Clocks must be synchronized. And it is assumed that they tick away merrily. It is distance that brings with it epistemic difficulties, requiring the use of light signals. Operational simultaneity does not conflict with absolute simultaneity.

It is when the sea-change of the postulational scheme is thrown over physical systems moving uniformly with respect to one another that we have numbers assigned in accordance with relative operational simultaneity. Such numbers are assignable to the moving system with respect to the observer at rest. In each physical system, by itself, proper magnitudes are obtainable by measurement and, presumably, represent absolute facts, granted the units. There is no change in laboratory technique and assumptions.

iii

So much in the way of review was necessary. It should be noted that clocks and scientific time are presupposed. What is added is a definition of a time-interval in terms of an operation using the passage of light over distance with an invariant speed of some 186,000 miles per second. This velocity is, in the laboratory, empirically measured.

My intention is not to attack the logic of the stipulations and definitions but to raise the question of the meaning of the entire set-up. It will be my thesis that there has been confusion between physical systems as parts of the material universe, and frames of reference for observers, *a natural confusion just because it was generally supposed that the Einstein formula was the solution of the paradox of the*

Michelson-Morley experiment. I shall argue, on the contrary, that it was *not* such a solution and that it is only an ingenious kinematic device using stipulations and giving space-time numbers for certain cognitive purposes. Naturally, I shall offer my own solution by showing that, once we give up the preconceptions of past physics, we should expect no interference in the M-M experiment.

Another point is important. As a result of the tendency to reject absolute simultaneity as meaningful for the material universe—no one is more vociferous about this than the positivist, except his companion, the pragmatist—physicists became convinced that the observational time assignments were of exclusive significance. The job was to keep the laws of nature invariant with respect to different frames of reference. The extension of dating and time-intervals had become a hazardous, and yet necessary, undertaking, whereas in classical physics no one bothered about it. Now lengths and time-intervals were equally relative and physics had become sophisticated with respect to observers. Hitherto, of course, observers just noted coincidences and simultaneities in the laboratory and worked out ratios as absolutes. They then dropped out of the picture. Now they became part of the picture itself. The set-up relativized all magnitudes.

Needless to say, I am not attacking the logic of the postulational set-up, and, if the physicists find the method of value, they are, of course, judges of its usefulness. All I am going to do is to show that we can get back our material universe and again conceive extensities as absolutes.

The philosophical background of my semantic analysis is, as I have indicated, physical realism. I shall try to define time as change, rejecting Newton's Absolute Time. That is, time is a characteristic of a dynamic universe. A time-interval becomes factual knowledge about a process of change in terms of some clock or uniform movement, and requires for its achievement a mind able to note simultaneities, past and present. In other words, a time-interval is always a case of knowledge and not of intuition. It demands technique, comparison, memory. Nevertheless, it constitutes genuine knowledge about a process having duration. It should not be forgotten, however, that, in nature, the past has ceased to exist, that there is no literal interval in nature waiting to be measured. It should be a commonplace of philosophy that the *categories of knowledge,* interested in routines, durations and predictions, are different from the *categories of existence.*[2] The precise nature of this divergence leads into the heart of ontology. There are no ready-made cosmic time-intervals as for Newton.

Scientific time would be badly conceived as an intuition of Newton's Absolute Time. It is, instead, knowledge about the durations of processes in terms of some accepted standard duration, such as the movement of the earth around the sun, divisible into units so that magnitudes, called time-intervals, can be assigned. Calibrated clocks are ordinarily used; and it was generally assumed, before relativity, that mere change of place without alterations in temperature made no difference to the rhythmic working of the clocks. There was a lot of nonsense written about the isotropic character of abstractions called Space and Time, but that, again, was merely a mode of speaking. There is no such thing as Space and no such thing as Time. Back of this mode of speaking lay lack of analysis of the expressions "in space" and "in time." Because of that lack of semantic analysis, these expressions were taken too literally, as though things and events were located in empty absolutes. It will be one of my purposes to show that physical space and time are adjectival and that "in space" and "in time" are technical expressions signifying that geometrical principles and chronometric methods are applicable. The lingering influence of Newtonian cosmology has confused both scientists and philosophers.

The concept of simultaneity is as important as that of time-interval, and implied by the latter. Since I am going to defend absolute simultaneity as meaningful, I must make a few remarks on the subject at this point. There has been much confusion between awareness of simultaneity and the fact of simultaneity. It is true that awareness of simultaneity of an intuitive sort only occurs when there is the compresence of two events in the consciousness of an observer. What

2. I pointed this out in *The Principles and Problems of Philosophy* (1926), chap. 17.

is intuited as simultaneous consists of co-actual changes in the field of consciousness; but, since people are apt to be naïvely realistic, they are prone to believe that the external events that are the causes of these changes are likewise simultaneous. A little reflection leads to the rejection of such a belief. We conclude that neither external simultaneities nor time-intervals can be intuited. Before Einstein, there was no great interest in determining simultaneities beyond the earth, for the correlations between t and $s,$ as in Galileo's law of falling bodies, were supposed to hold elsewhere. Simultaneity was not regarded as a significant variable but as an absolute. Of course, after Ole Roemer's discovery of the finite velocity of light, it was recognized that a calculation would have to be made to determine when the light that reached our eyes had left a star. But that was a simple idea.

What, then, do I mean by absolute simultaneity? Merely the fact about the members of a class of events to the effect that they have actuality in common. Of events that have ceased to be and are past, we can say that they *were* simultaneous. That signifies that, when they were actual, they had their actuality in common. In the strict sense, only actual events are events, that is, existing changes in some region. Past events do not exist for nature. It is the human mind with its capacity for memory and historical knowledge that peoples the universe with ghosts. And because science is interested in calculations about what was, and in predictions as to what will be, it tends to live in the realm of knowledge and to have too slight an awareness of the texture of existence. Past, present, and future tend to become of the same type—*as they are for knowledge.* But it would be a poor philosopher who would not point out that only the actual state of affairs exists, that existence is a process within enduring being.[3]

Such a conception of absolute simultaneity does not depend upon the ability of the human mind to know what events are simultaneous. Nor does it depend upon an appeal to some cosmic mind. To the

---

3. I would call attention to my article, "Reformed Materialism and Intrinsic Endurance," in this *Review* (July 1944). For absolute simultaneity as co-actual events, see *The Philosophy of Physical Realism.*

realist, what is does not depend upon any act of awareness. The job of the scientist—if he finds such knowledge important for his purposes—is to work out a technique, just as he has worked out a technique to measure time-intervals. So far as I can see, Einstein's operational method of determining the synchronization of clocks is a satisfactory one. But there is no great mystery about it. In fact, it can be checked within a physical system by moving a clock from one place to another. It is the conception of relative operational simultaneity that is the novelty, together, of course, with the redefinition of time-interval in terms of the passage of light over a distance, a preparation for the relative type of operational simultaneity.

To sum up these preliminaries. In the first period after the Michelson-Morley experiment, the preconceptions of most physicists involved an Absolute Space, an Absolute Time, a luminiferous ether, the velocity of light in ether or "in space" (the two expressions were used interchangeably). Lorenz, a good physical realist in intention, as most experimentalists tend to be, suggested a shortening of rods in the direction of the supposed motion of the earth through ether or in space. *It is all these preconceptions which I challenge.* I see no good reason to believe in ether, or in "space as an associate." In other words, I can see no good reason why we should not expect the non-interference the experimenters found. *They expected something else just because of their preconceptions.* But this is to anticipate.

My thesis is, then, that Einstein as a Machian merely sought to handle the data without bothering about the material universe. His was an elegant, mathematical, postulational set-up. The material universe of the plain man and the experimental scientist tended to drop out of sight, as it always has for the Machian. It is amusing to remember how many have asked, Do the rods shorten for relativity? Or is it as though they shortened? The answer is, of course, the second one. We move into a world of numbers and of *als ob.* Realism is left behind. It is *knowledge* for observers tied to a postulational set-up.

Now this may satisfy the mathematical physicist, moving in a realm of symbols, but it cannot satisfy a materialist. It may also satisfy pious idealistic Englishmen for whom the material universe is a manifestation of Mind or a mathematical God. It may content non-philosophical American physicists who are really only interested in handling magnitudes and making calculations; for it would seem at times as though the joke made by Russell about mathematicians, to the effect that they did not know what they were talking about, has become somewhat applicable to physicists, especially, perhaps, to mathematical physicists. One very able theorist informed me that *things* are not measured but that data are handled consistently in terms of measurement rules.

As I see it, then, materialism is not "metaphysics," but just the usual belief in chairs and tables and in their microscopic constituents. What is needed is a natural philosophy, better than Newton's, to give existential significance to the mensurational knowledge and laws achieved by physics. While I admire the technique of physics, I cannot, for the life of me, see that it is any less, or any more, about the material universe than the other sciences. And so far as the theory of relativity has encouraged a kind of philosophical obscurantism, I am concerned to debunk it, that is, to give it its proper context and range.

iv

I suppose that this is the right moment to bring in my own solution of the results of the Michelson-Morley experiment. After that, I can develop in detail my semantic analysis of "space" and "time," "motion" and "movement."

The essential thesis is a simple one. If we drop out such preconceptions as ether and Newtonian Absolute Space, and even the carry-over of Space with a capital, then we can give up the frame of thought with respect to light, which could think of it only as in motion with respect to a background called ether or Space. It then becomes possible to regard it as an electromagnetic activity, or movement, consisting of self-repeating pulsations spreading out at a determinate speed. And I do not mean by "speed" here the same thing as I mean by velocity. One does not get velocity until one puts the activity "into space," that is, gives it a frame within which it can be measured. Now the peculiarity of light is that it does not exist in a spatial system but in a region. The only contacts it has with a material system are at its source and at its locus of impact upon a material system. In between, it is only a series of spreading pulsations. It is not intrinsically "in space" or in a spatial frame.

But so indurate was the thought-form of the physicist that he just automatically applied to it his scheme of "in space," velocity in space, for example. In the old days light was given a sort of background—to use a *Gestaltist* phrase—against which it occurred. What I have in mind is the flat rejection of such a phrase as "the velocity of light *with respect to* the ether, or space, as a constant regardless of the source of light." But that was the fashion in which the Michelson-Morley experiment was interpreted. The purpose was to detect the motion of the earth with respect to ether and Absolute Space.

In short, I am arguing that the preconceptions are now outmoded, but that something of the thought-form still remains when people think of the velocity of light. They do not fully realize that velocity is a term that requires that light be put "in space," be given a frame of reference, that it does not intrinsically have such a frame since it is only an extensity-activity in a region.

So thought, light is an electromagnetic activity spreading out from a source over a region. Its constancy now becomes the unvarying nature of its pulsations as a series of activities or movements. There is no way in which it can be correlated with *ether* or *Space*. Here we have a clear case of the unobservables about which the positivists so bitterly complain. In my opinion they are not only unobservables; they are myths.

For mensurational purposes, a beam of light must, therefore, be given a frame of reference of a material sort. Only then is it "in space." The obvious frame is the source of light with distances in a material system measured out from it. Only then can we have the necessary context to obtain magnitudes such as s and t. The velocity of light is given by dividing the magnitude distance by the time-interval, t. As we have already noted, time-interval is not a thing in nature but a magnitude obtained by scientific technique. It is clear, therefore, that velocity is knowledge about the speed of light and that the phrase I have seen repeated *ad nauseam, the velocity of light with respect to ether or Space,* is very misleading.

It follows that this unvarying extensity-activity, when put in the material system offered by the source of light, will give a velocity as a scientific magnitude. And this velocity will give us knowledge about the unvarying speed of light in a region. So far as I can see, this velocity should be the same whenever so measured. There would be no reason for expecting it to vary from material system to material system. Hence a theory of light as a type of activity, or movement, having an intrinsic rhythm and extensity involves, when a material setting is given it, a kinematic relativity to a frame of reference built around the source of a light-beam. And this signifies the discarding of the phraseology *the velocity of light with respect to ether or Space.* These are, as I have said, mythical entities.

It follows next that one should expect the noninterference recorded in the Michelson-Morley experiment, and that the tumult was the result of false preconceptions and thought-forms. The light quite inevitably traveled equal distances at the same speed and with the same velocity.

But, historically, the effect was a puzzle and gave rise to artificial explanations. The Fitzgerald-Lorenz theory of the shortening of rods in the direction of movement was one. And, so far as I can see, Einstein merely brought forward a clever Machian set-up and sidestepped the physical angle. If light moved in the ether or in Space, then the method of relative operational simultaneity could be used to account for number assignments. But did the rods shorten or not? Did the light travel equal distances? All that was left vague. It should be remembered that, in those days, Mach and Ostwald did not believe in atoms. The material universe was readily ignored.

As a physical realist this elegant positivistic procedure was not open to me. The result was that I have had to make an analysis of the whole situation and bring out the various meanings of terms.

Let me now ask this question: If the preconceptions had been different and the noninterference of light traveling equal distances in a material system been taken for granted, would all this pother about observers and operational simultaneity, this denial of absolute simultaneity, and so forth have taken place? I doubt it. But this does not deny that it may have been technically useful in physics. In any case, if my analysis is correct, the theory of relativity has no ontological significance whatsoever. Materialism can live very happily with it as a device for physics.

For my analysis, any frame of reference for light, built around its source, is, physically interpreted, only one among many, for physical systems are in changing relations of movement and distance. It follows that there is no preferred frame and no preferred physical system. Note that ether and Space are renounced, and they would be the sole candidates. In place of Space, we should talk of the spatial characteristics of the material universe, including the region in which radiational activities occur. But more of that later.

Hence, we have an empirical justification of Einstein's stipulation that light be considered as traveling at the velocity of 186,000 miles per second for all frames of reference; only now it travels at this velocity for all physical systems with respect to the source of light in each system. As between physical systems moving with respect to one another, there will be at least the Doppler effect. We shall consider later the conditions under which relative motion can be translated into absolute movement.

v

But what is the theoretical import of this analysis? Clearly that it returns us the magnitudes obtained by measurement within each material system as absolute ratios under defined physical conditions. There is no good reason to suppose that the routines of nature vary from region to region just because material systems are in motion with respect to one another. Again, the mythology of an Absolute Time, containing uniform intervals, is removed, for it is realized that time-intervals are not entities in nature but cases of knowledge about durational processes, in terms of defined units, such as the ticking of calibrated clocks or the motion of the earth around the sun. Nevertheless, there is such a thing as absolute simultaneity for the whole universe, and it consists in the co-actuality of events. All actual changes in the universe are necessarily simultaneous.

However, the problem for science is the necessity for, and value of, the device set up by Einstein, once much of its motivation is taken away. I can put it this way: My analysis gives back the one material universe with both a spatial and a temporal unity, whereas the effect of the relativity theory was to break it up into frames of reference, each inhabited by an observer, much as the stars were, for Kepler, the domain of guardian spirits. The temptation was, thereupon, to relegate magnitudes obtained by measurement to the status of relative members, subordinate to the mathematical manipulation determined by relative, operational simultaneity. Note that I am not challenging the logic of the relativity scheme. All I am saying is that it merely generalized a cognitional construction. To this extent, it represented a movement away from realism and existentialism. Scientists were already befuddled epistemologically, as they were torn loose from seventeenth-century intuitionalistic rationalism—quite a time lag for these specialists. Nor was philosophy free from blame. *For cultural reasons* as well as technical ones, it was debating idealism and Humeanism, with only scorn for a frank realistic materialism. In my opinion, it is time to get down to realities, and my recent articles have had that aim in mind.

I well remember how all the idealists, pragmatists, and positivists jubilantly perched on frames of reference having in common only the invariant velocity of light. Quite a pluralistic set-up, relieved only by light signals hurtling back and forth through what they called Space. All measurements suffered a sea-change and became *als ob*. When realists protested and pointed to paradoxes, they replied that magnitudes had now become numbers relative to an observer. And, of course, they were quite right. Twins did not get older differentially. And the reason was that the material universe had been left behind. Clocks did not wear out because they were ideal clocks. Twins did not grow old because they were symbols for number assignments. Scientists did not bother their heads about it all, because they were primarily interested in numbers and equations and not in the proper conception of the material universe. The very development of physics into mathematical symbolization encouraged the perspective. And few Americans knew that Ernst Mach was back of the whole phenomenon. Recently, when I have explained some of my semantic distinctions to astronomers and mathematicians, it was evident that the distinction between knowledge and existence had little meaning for them. With a condescending smile they politely gave to philosophy this mysterious realm of existence by which I seemed to set such store. Numbers were their business and these involved space-time, that is, *s*-numbers and *t*-numbers.

My conclusion is that physics, as a science, must be judge of its own methods and concepts, but that it should not mistake knowledge for existence; and it should not be too certain that relativity theory has the backing that it would have *if it were the only way of explaining the zero result of the Michelson-Morley experiment.* Symbols need interpretation if they are to apply to the material universe; and if the symbols of physicists do not have such application, then you have the blissful autonomy of physics of which operationalists like Bridgman dream, a kind of isolationalism. As a fairly competent epistemologist, my suggestion is that physicists of this sort are just puzzled Humeans. What the realist proposes as a desideratum is a philosophy of nature, backed by an adequate epistemology and ontology. The philosopher has his responsibilities in these cultural affairs. What I have been calling a reformed materialism is my candidate. It is my feeling that our culture needs to have its feet on the ground. I have already pointed out that Einstein does not seem satisfied with positivism and enters a plea for "metaphysics." But the physical realist would prefer to return to the tradition of the Greeks, for whom physics was concerned with a material universe. Of course, as De Sitter notes, Aristotle was just at the beginning of the great Greek scientific development. Hipparchus and Archimedes went far beyond him in astronomy and physics. It was with these that Galileo linked himself. I wish that scientists would stop using the word *metaphysics,* for they seem to give it only a puzzled, emotional meaning. Ontology is a far better word.

In the same Schilpp volume, Russell straddles between materialism

and Humeanism in a typical fashion. Physics gives us our most verified knowledge. Therefore be materialists. But it is a materialism of
space-time, of relativity. On the epistemological side he seems never
to have studied referential critical realism with its distinction between
sensing and perceiving. And I think I am justified in calling attention to the fact that I anticipated Russell's theory of the brain-
consciousness situation in the chapter in *Critical Realism* (1916)
called "Is Consciousness Alien to the Physical World?"

vi

We have now at our disposal all the materials for a semantic
analysis of the various meanings of the terms *space, time, in space,
in time, motion,* and *movement.* Something of a historical context
must be given for each meaning, especially for those outmoded.

Classical mechanics assumed that knowledge was a sort of rational
intuition in which the essential nature of Absolute Space and Absolute
Time was grasped. Euclidian geometry was supposed to be true in an
absolute way and to give the principles applicable to Absolute Space.
As yet, there was no distinction between pure and applied mathematics.

The result was that the expression *bodies in space* tended to be
interpreted quite literally, as though bodies were in an empty receptacle
called Space. And to say that events were "in time" meant likewise
that they could be correlated with moments in an empty Absolute
Time, flowing uniformly. Practical difficulties were recognized by
Newton, but the intellectual framework was of this sort.

It was inevitable that motion should follow suit. There could be an
Absolute Motion set over against Space and Time. The question of
Time seemed less puzzling just because Time seemed simpler in its
nature. I shall show that Time is, if possible, more of an artifact
than Space. Only change is the empirical basis. Intervals are achieved
cases of knowledge in terms of measurement techniques.

In the centuries that succeeded, the struggle between rationalism
and empiricism deepened in philosophy, but seems to have had little
effect upon physics and classical mechanics. It is true that Euler

puzzled over epistemological difficulties under the impact of Berkeley. Kantianism was, as we see today, an impossible compromise. Unfortunately, no adequate form of physical realism was developed by philosophy.

Let us note next what was insidiously happening to mathematics in the meantime and, hence, to the meaning of the phrase *in space*.

As long as geometry had been purely Euclidian, it was natural for a rationalistic set-up like classical mechanics to assume that it dealt with Space as an external reality, having the characteristics of Euclidian geometry, and that the applicability of Euclidian geometry signified the existence of Absolute Space as a medium in which motion took place. And if Space, why not Time? And if Space and Time, why not Motion? These became three absolutes. There might, of course, be difficulty in detecting them. There was, as yet, no clear distinction between motion and movement, that is, relational change of neighborhood within a physical system. Newton himself was a little perplexed, as comes out in the famous case of the swirling pail of water.

With the growth of non-Euclidian geometry, the distinction between pure and applied geometry came increasingly to the front. The result was a gradual reformulation of the phrase *in space*. It was eventually realized that, for science, the phrase must mean "the applicability of a geometrical set of principles to the data of extensive measurement." But this realization came slowly and the old verbal habits lingered.

This prior mental habit clearly operated in the conception of ether, in the nineteenth century. It was conceived as occupying Space and having properties which, unfortunately, were contradictory. I have already indicated the role of such preconceptions in the Michelson-Morley experiment. I find that scientists still tend to think of light-rays as "in Space" apart from the assignment of a frame of reference by which distances and time-intervals can be assigned. What Einstein did was to substitute a stipulational set-up without quite saying that he was disregarding the conception of light traveling in space. Much of the polemics was due to this evasion, which reflected Mach and Avenarius. Lovejoy, for instance, was thinking about a material universe. The translation, into a universe of discourse, of observers and their calculations seemed a begging of the question—as, indeed, it was in some measure, as I have tried to show by giving a realistic solution of the Michelson-Morley experiment. What Einstein did was to define his terms in such a fashion that a kinematic set-up would involve certain number-assignments. It would be entirely reciprocal and it would all be a case of *als ob*. It is a kinematic device. Within the laboratory, measurements are actually made; but these are now tossed into the kinematic framework and so become relative to an observer. In themselves, they are absolute data with the time-interval now connected with the passage of light over a distance. Interpreted as relative to an observer, we now have the s and t numbers linked in terms of relative operational simultaneity. They lose their absoluteness. It is an elegant scheme. But the point is that, for the physical realist, it has little to do with the material universe. It is purely cognitional and developed on the assumption that it was necessitated by the Michelson-Morley experiment. We are told that only in this fashion can time be extended for physics throughout the universe. My query is, What do they mean by time? And why is time-dating so important for physics? Has physics suddenly become historical and curious as to what was going on in Sirius when Columbus was landing on the islands of the New World? I cannot help feeling that there has been a great deal of obfuscation.

vii

There are now several distinguishable meanings relevant to time. For the materialist, time implies, and is built around, the basic fact of change. The actual state of affairs is alone actual, while the past has perished and the future is not yet actual. In short, the universe is a process. To the materialist this fact does not signify what it does to the idealist or the "reformed subjectivist." For a state of affairs is, for him, a condition of existing substances within intrinsically enduring being. His actual is no knife-edge. Moreover, the actual state of affairs is not a present, or now, of the same type as the past and the future. Past, present, and future are cognitional terms and set over against each other. What is the present? The present hour? The present year? The present century? No; one needs an ontological imagination in these matters and I have always written that real time is *in* the universe and not the universe in time. It is just the change characteristic of the material universe. I hope it can be seen why I hold that science has need for philosophy to offer it a good epistemology and an adequate ontology. Otherwise it becomes what the Thomists scall *scientism,* rather bewildered, and yet arrogant because it knows that its methods alone gain verifiable facts. But what are they facts about?

Change as an absolute involves, as I have showed, absolute simultaneity, even apart from human knowledge as to what changes are simultaneous. But science wants the kind of knowledge it gets in measured time-intervals. To obtain these there must be a standard and methods of noting absolute simultaneities after a duration. Classical physics got this far.

Now the danger was to reify this abstraction and talk about Time as homogeneous, isotropic, et cetera, et cetera; and to put events *into* this reified Time. This was, of course, conceptualizing, and very confusing semantically. Scientists asked themselves very gravely whether an event, *other physical conditions being the same,* would be affected by "the time of its occurrence." But such a time has meaning only for cognitional frames.

And then, with the ingenious postulates of Einstein, space-time was ushered onto the scene. Here, a time-interval is so obtained that the ticking of a clock—classical time-interval—is connected with the passage over a distance of light at an invariant velocity. And now, I suppose, scientists and positivists ask whether events are affected, other things being equal, by their position in a space-time world line. Again, when there is no clear epistemology and ontology, nonsense so easily follows. Past, present, and future are often thought of as somehow coexisting timelessly. We are told that we dip into such a timeless time. Well the physical realist can only shrug his shoulders and say that there is need for a natural philosophy to replace Newton's and this phenomenalistic Frankenstein. I remember the period when, surrounded by relativity enthusiasts and the mystagogues of the Wittgenstein revelation, I could only, like poor Galileo, murmur: "And yet there is a material universe and we are parts of it."

viii

Let us turn next to space and its various meanings. In many ways it is simpler than time.

There is, first, the empirical fact that things are extensive in three dimensions. When the constitution of a physical system is not undergoing change, the determinate extensities are characteristics of it. We think of such things as substantive and coexisting. So far as I can see, space is adjectival and has no existence apart from things in their relations. In other words, we should use the adjective *spatial* at the ontological level, just as we should use the words *temporal* or *change* for time. Regions beyond massive material bodies are not Space; they are just regions or fields replete with radiational activities of many kinds.

Spatial things are "in space" when the extensities are measured to give magnitudes that can be handled by geometrical principles. They are in Euclidian space when the principles used are Euclidian. They are in Riemannian space when the principles used are Riemannian. But to ask whether the material universe is, in some ontological sense, in Euclidian Space or Riemannian Space is semantic nonsense. I suppose it is a hangover from Newton's Absolute Space as a receptacle.

And then we come to *space*-time. If my argument has been correct, all we have here are numbers relative to an observer in a frame of reference who can carry on his calculations of *als ob* on the basis of stipulations and relative operational simultaneity. One of my scientific colleagues told me that the last edition of the *Encyclopedia Britannica* had no separate articles on space and time but only on space-time. In my opinion Homer has nodded. It's a scientific age, seemingly. A few minims of philosophy might help to give balance. Some people who have read Jeans and Eddington are hoping to wake up some morning and find themselves in Berkeley Square and far from Hitler. Well, it just won't do. We grow old absolutely and perish. We have cognitional, referential transcendence but no existential transcendence.

Let us now bring existential space and time together. Their existential togetherness consists in the fact that change takes place locally. There is no empty *Time ueberhaupt*. But this plural and local status of time does not signify that time and space are not distinct traits of existence.

ix

Let me turn next to the distinction between motion and movement. Motion is a kinematic term and always involves a frame or background. Motion is cognitional and in respect to something else. It is a way in which movement appears. A ball tossed up from a bus seems to those on the bus to go up and come down; it is, as we say, part of that inertial system. To a person on the sidewalk it traverses a curve. And that is the way the movement *appears* to him.

We saw that scientists sought to give the unvarying extensive movement of light a frame of ether or Space and so think it as motion. I have argued that it was not necessary so to do. But to put it "in space" and measure its velocity it had to be connected up with a material system. Movement, then, is activity, process, change of neighborhood; motion is noted change of position with respect to some frame. It is that sort of knowing about movement. Movement is an absolute, like all change. Motion is relative to a frame.

In kinematics we deal with motion and not with movement. That is why Russell can facetiously assert that a train going from Edinburgh to London corresponds to London going to the train. Everything is reciprocal. In the relativity set-up we have pure reciprocity, for it deals with motion and not with movement. But we know empirically why the train goes to London. It is because of the stoker and his burning coal. Causality comes into play. Wherever there is movement there causality is at work. We are in the material universe.

Now the interesting thing about astronomy is that scientists are pretty well limited to *motion*. Einstein recognizes this fact when he seeks to generalize the principle of relativity, which is kinematic. And he takes his departure from the well-established principle of the identity of inertial mass and gravitational mass. That light is affected by gravitation seems a verified empirical fact, and I do not see why it should surprise the physical realist. And I see no reason why Einstein's equations should not be more adequate to the universe as we know it today than Newton's simpler formula. But to talk about Space as being distorted in the neighborhood of large material masses is, of course, merely a way of speaking. What we seem to have is a gravitational field. The scientific problem is to put it "in space," that is, to handle behavior in it in a mathematical fashion. I shall have something more to say about the difference between motion and movement when I come to touch briefly upon the "expanding universe" conception.

I have argued that wherever there is motion there is movement, that is, causal activity, even if we cannot locate its basis. In other words, a set of frames in relative motion *entails* a case of actual movement in the universe, that is, some change of neighborhood. On this earth we usually have an idea of the energy changes involved. When the scale is cosmic we get confused as between motion (knowledge) and movement (activity). Motion with respect to the stars is not the same as movement, which involves something dynamic and situational. While the universe as a whole (if such a statement is meaningful) cannot be in either motion or movement with respect to, or in changing relations to, something external to it, a body like the earth can be in both motion and movement. All movement is absolute, relational, and dynamic. It can be kinematically *described* as motion with respect to a frame of reference.

I should like, now, to raise some questions with respect to the precise meaning to be given certain terms in physics if we are to work in the direction of a philosophy of nature.

I take it that terms like atoms, electrons, protons, neutrons, photons are denotative symbols which, in intention, designate *forms of being.* My ontology postulates an intrinsic endurance of being, that is, that it does not use itself up. I take it that this basic trait manifests itself in what is called the conservation of energy, where energy is a symbolic quantity connected with the capacity to perform work.

Energy must be regarded as a case of knowledge about being. I judge by my slight knowledge of thermodynamics that it is very general knowledge. And I may say that I am very sceptical of the extrapolation of entropy to the universe as a whole. Eddington may talk about putting away a few conceptions, but a physical realist cannot treat such topics as absolute origins and final states so cavalierly. To him, with his conception of ontological time as change in the universe, absolute origin and end have no meaning; as well talk to a theist about the origin and end of God.

A few words about mass are also in order. It is clear that mass is a factor of proportionality measured in connection with momentum and velocity. It is a quantity, therefore a case of knowledge. In classical physics it was regarded as a measure of a property called inertia. Now, once we give up intuitionalistic rationalism, we are aware that inertia can only be an instance of abstract knowledge about a material system. So far as I can see, it concerns knowledge about causal behavior. This type of behavior is indistinguishable from gravitational behavior. We should, I suppose, give up any notion of "right lines" as *natural lines*. Otherwise there would not be much of an advance upon the Greeks with their natural circular motion. Right, or straight, lines are, clearly, an abstract kinematic conception. In nature itself there are only movements that are always situational. It is, then, a question of how these should be put descriptively into space.

x

As I have constantly emphasized, the postulates of relativity appear to me logically consistent and they seem to be of value to physics, interested, as it is, in the correlation of magnitudes. The very fact that it has helped to free physicists from mechanical pictures has not been without its usefulness. Mass as a magnitude could be correlated with energy, for instance. But it is my conviction that the way it was presented was often misleading. The denial of absolute simultaneity implied a kind of operational pluralism. It was as though frames of reference constituted island universes. The very phenomenalism of the approach weakened the distinction between material systems in movement-relations with one another, and a mathematical projection of frames and observers upon these material systems. And because there was no clear theory of knowledge and ontology, the distinction between knowledge and existence was seldom sharply enough drawn. It is my hope that the semantic contrasts I have developed may clarify the situation.

I have put chief stress upon a conception of absolute simultaneity independent of Newtonian rationalism. But it seems to me that determinate location in the material universe must also be accepted. Thus to say that the material universe is spatial is more accurate than to say that it is "in space." Physically, therefore, two beams of electrons shot out in opposite directions should reach material bodies at equal distances, and together cover a region double that which one of them covers. Here we would have two cases of physical movement. And as motion with respect to the earth, each would, of course, be handled separately and assigned its velocity. But would velocity with respect to one another be meaningful? If the one is taken as a frame, then the other cannot be given a velocity of removal as great as that of light, for the velocity of light is the maximum. At the same time we are empirically aware that a sphere of optical activity spreading out from the center whence the two beams of electrons took their departure would keep ahead of both beams. And I suppose this contrast must signify that the kinematic set-up with its co-called ageless beam of light is postulational. Actual light, as I have argued, has a source, and its velocity should be measured with respect to that source. Two material systems moving with respect to one another could not have quite the same beam of light, for what would be source for one would be effect for the other and the Doppler shift should occur. But then the two frames of reference become material systems in the same universe.

I have said little about the twins, for this paradox follows from the confusion of a kinematic set-up and material systems. I take it that, in both material systems, events would be proceeding much as usual. People would be growing older and clocks would be wearing out. Relativity assignments are affairs of *als ob,* of *knowledge,* within certain assumptions, rather than of existence.

If, then, my solution of the Michelson-Morley experiment is correct, relativity must be judged only in terms of its usefulness for physics. It has no literal significance for the material universe. It is primarily a mensurational scheme.

xi

In conclusion I am going to permit myself some suggestions with regard to cosmology and the expanding universe:

1. All stars and nebulae are material systems in absolute movement in their distance relations. It is a dynamic universe.

2. From the standpoint of motion any one star can be selected as a kinematic frame for motion. Other stars will then appear as in motion with respect to it, though the facts of absolute relational movement cannot be discovered. I take ours to be a circulating universe.

3. Since there is no center to the universe of a static sort and all the stars are in relational movement, the kinematic effect will be that of an expanding universe.

4. The farther the stars are away, the greater will appear to be the motion. This is because movement is additive as it appears as motion. The order will be 1, 2, 3, 4, and so on. Suppose a star is in movement in its relations with the sun, then the next farther star, just not to move but to keep its distance would have to be assigned the same motion. Otherwise we would have a contracting universe. But the first star has no preferential status. Therefore the second star is also in movement, which gives two units for it as against one unit for the first star. The third star must keep up to the second in order not to have a contracting universe and its movement leads to three units; and so on. I take it that a circulating universe would appear kinematically as an expanding universe. If light loses its energy over immense distances, that would be a conflicting factor.

5. The universe cannot be in movement as a whole because it has no environment with which to change its neighborhood. Nor can it be described as in motion, for there is no assignable external frame.

6. I take it that the universe is finite and that it has an internal

dynamic equilibrium. I am skeptical of the time-arrow of entropy for the universe as a whole. Dynamic being causally integrates existents that have emergent properties but only secondary endurance, the endurance of processes.

In some such direction, it seems to me, the adjustment between relativity theory and materialism must be looked for. I see no empirical reason to believe in shortened rods or actually slowing clocks. Give up the preconceptions of the old physics and such theories are unneeded. But Einstein's device must then secure another justification, which may well be its calculative value. To add to clock intervals a *new* interval in which this one is united with the passage of light at an invariant velocity makes possible the use of C as a constant in formulae. The value of this factor must be judged by the physicist. But, once the distinction between knowledge and existence is cleared up and the various meanings of space and time separated, no confusion should result. It is my belief that realistic philosophers should cooperate with scientists in working out a "natural philosophy" continuous with that of the great Greek scientists. Modern physics was long overweighted on the side of rationalism, contrary to ordinary belief, and the development of mathematical physics has revivified this tendency, as can be seen in Eddington and Milne. What I have tried to contribute is philosophical analysis. Needless to say, I have nothing but admiration for Einstein as both man and thinker. But his philosophical affiliations seem to be those of Mach and Kant. Reformed materialism must distinguish, while correlating, the categories of knowledge, s and t, and the categories of ontology or physical existence. I take existence to be simpler in its methods than human symbolic, mensurational, operational, and predictive knowledge.

10
*Querying Whitehead's Framework**

i

There would, I am certain, be general agreement as to the daring, imaginativeness, and sweep of Whitehead's metaphysical system. He brings together, in a selective way, the insights of outstanding thinkers of the past and the texture of recent scientific development. Relativity, quantum theory, the interconnection of things, and the ontological foundation of induction are all included. While the dominant note is a modified Platonism with theistic setting, even Epicurus is not ignored. One has no feeling of eclecticism when incisive comments are made on Aristotle, Descartes, Leibniz, Locke, Hume, Bradley, and Bergson, since the perspective gives point to them.

And yet the whole construction rests on certain premises concerning the nature of perceiving and of conceiving, which are dubious. It is my intention to challenge these and to show an alternative perspective. In so doing I shall develop a referential view of perceiving that gives it objective import, and query his more prehensive stress upon sensory data as terminal. This divergence in the analysis of perceiving will go with a defense of bodies and, thus, of the relevance of a

* Excerpt from *Revue Internationale de Philosophie*, no. 56–57 (1961), pp. 1–32. Reprinted with the permission of the author and publisher.

modified conception of substance, which I speak of as quasi-Democritean. In this, I think I follow in the footsteps of Galileo and Newton, though with due regard to changed ideas of the dynamic texture of bodies. I would put stress on organization, relations, and dispositional properties.

Science marches on, and philosophy must assimilate its conceptual changes in terms of reformations of its categories. In short, I do not follow Whitehead and Russell in giving up the category of substance. Rather do I think it can be made more adequate and be released from the shortcomings of Aristotelian logic and his ontology of "form" and "matter." It can, I believe, likewise be freed from the "psychological nominalism" of Hume with its stress upon impressions and images as terminal for thought.

Now all of this means that any critique of Whitehead must involve an opposing framework of comparable dimensions. One must not only understand Whitehead's motivations and principles but be prepared to counter them.

Looking at the system as a whole, one can only characterize it as in the idealistic tradition. It is a form of immaterialism of the panpsychistic type. It is opposed to positivism, on the one hand, and, on the other hand, to materialism. I shall let positivism fight its own battles. As a matter of fact, it seems to me a little more on the defensive than it was in the thirties. It was always strong in logic and weak in epistemology. And it was fighting battles that had more meaning in Germany than in America with its strong naturalistic movement and its admiration for science. While I have always preferred the term ontology to metaphysics with its transcendentalistic associations, it always seemed to me that the basic question was that of the kind of metaphysics. There is, for instance, nothing particularly obscurantist about a materialistic metaphysics. What it needs is to be brought up to date with respect to its logic and its epistemology. Materialism has always seemed to me to have a bad philosophic press for both technical and cultural reasons, and the cold war had led people to assume that dialectical materialism is the only variety of materialism, whereas materialism goes back to the Greek atomists, as Hobbes well knew.

It goes without saying that an adequate materialism these days requires a satisfactory epistemology, a release from deductive necessitarianism, a recognition of novelty, and, in short, a general enlargement. It is usual in American philosophy to speak of nonreductive materialism in this connection and to point out that it has no implication of what is popularly called "ethical materialism." In general, ontological materialists have been moral reformers with the liberalism of enlightenment. But these are semantic questions.

I have, myself, had debates with the instrumentalists along these lines. They have turned largely on points in epistemology and the mind-body problem. Otherwise, we had much in common since both sides were naturalistic and advocates of scientific method. The divergence came on such matters as the locus of sensations and the import of perceiving. It was my feeling that Dewey substituted "warranted Assertibility"—a good idea in itself—too exclusively for *true* as a term for the endorsement of a knowledge-claim—and I thought of perceiv*ing* as involving knowledge-claims of a referential sort. He, on the other hand, categorized perception as a natural event leading to experiential consequences. As I saw it, this categorization went with his horror of "mirroring" and of the "passive spectator" view of cognition. That is the way things move in philosophy.

Now I always thought of knowing as an *achievement* after its kind and with its conditions, beginning with perceiv*ing*. Of course, it is an achievement that can be put to use and fits into use. It is connected biologically with response and behavior. I shall have much to say about this point later in connection with Whitehead's view of perception. Unlike Dewey, Whitehead makes much of perception in the tradition of British empiricism, but turned inwards, in the mode of causal efficacy. William James was more continuous with British empiricism than Dewey. He made much of "percepts" as cases of *immediate perception* and contrasted them with concepts. That is, he made "percepts" terminal and moved to his "radical empiricism" and neutralism and influenced Russell here, as Russell points out in his book, *My Philosophical Development*. There is a great difference between referential perceiving and [the having of] "percepts." The first makes external things terminal, while the second is "experientialistic" in the tradition of British empiricism.

As I see it, Russell still thinks of "percepts" as *in* and constituting the brain. His approach emphasizes the causal theory of perception and notes a reproduction of structure. That, as I regard it, is all to the good. But he has not done justice to the full, functional unit in perceiving that involves the so-called reflex arc, stimulus and response. Learning plays its role between S and R so that, for man, the unit is S-C-R. That is, meanings, or concepts, develop to improve the response as an affair of intelligent behavior expressible in language. All this is *in* the brain as an organ of behavior. That is, I stress operations and activities. It is the job of the psychologist to study the interconnection of stimulus and response. Humean psychology is altogether too simple an affair.

What I am trying to bring out here is preparatory to my examination of Whitehead's view of perception. As we shall see, Whitehead makes much of the *form* of perception, that is, the activities supplementing the *prehension* of sensory data, and is here more in line with James and Stout and modern psychology. But I do not see that he realizes that sensory data are not the objects of perceiving but cues and guides to perceiv*ing,* as a referential operation. That, I suppose, is why he embraces the subjectivist principle and ties it with his "ontological principle." One must carefully trace out his assumptions.

Since I am concerned here with perspective, I may remark that I am sympathetic enough with the empiricist tradition to be skeptical of what Russell calls "inferred entities." But I query the British tradition of emphasis upon inspection or acquaintance. I take perceiving to be primarily referential and not inspectional. Thus I build on directed reference and not on the kind of *frustrated inference* to an outside world that went with the purely causal approach, characteristic of traditional empiricism. This analysis of perceiving as referential makes the external world cease to be the problem it has been considered. Interestingly enough, I link up here with Dewey and G. E. Moore, though I think my analysis of perceiving gives a somewhat better basis than they had worked out. I shall argue that

Whitehead's *aesthetic* approach goes with retention of inspectionism by way of prehension. It is the Berkeley gambit of immediate perception, to which he adds his theory of transfer and objective immortality. It is all very logical, granted his premises.

One more perspective must be explored, which I think British philosophy has too much ignored. For lack of a better term, I shall call it the *genetic*. The genetic cannot replace the analytic but may operate to give the latter a more adequate starting-point.

Now Dewey and Mead stressed the growth of attitudes and outlooks. All this was within "experience." And they were both biologically and socially inclined. They noted the rise of distinctions and contrasts. In a measure, they were doing what Piaget has since done so strikingly. Baldwin and *even Royce* struck the same note. My old teacher, C. H. Cooley, an able psychological sociologist, worked along the same lines. All this gave a thickness to human experience that British empiricism did not quite have. While James kept an attachment to traditional empiricism and only sought to modify it by a greater stress on the immediacy of relations and a querying of its "atomism," Dewey kept the Hegelian suspicion of it. He moved from Hegelianism to a biopsychological context with emphasis upon reflective thinking and the experimental method. That was all to the good, in my opinion. But, as I indicated above, he carried over certain epistemological phobias. He did not sufficiently note that attitudes and references emerged genetically, which constituted perceiving as of the nature of a referential claim, guided by private sensations. He did not like the idea of the private and tended to deal rather dialectically with experiencing. But into the details of this area I cannot here go. It must suffice to say that I saw this genetic approach feeding into a more adequate notion of perceiving with its distinctions and claims. Put it this way: The emphasis was upon "experience," as it developed, brought out the objective pole of perceiving with its thought of things and persons. Sensations dropped into the background. The result was *a new kind of empiricism,* with stress upon the logic of inquiry and upon consequences. In many ways it was a continuation of Peirce's thought. It was a kind of empiricism that always puzzled Russell. It was biologically and even behavioristically oriented, bypassed epistemology, and thought of ideas as pragmatic instruments rather than cognitive claims. Since I skirmished with it, almost from its beginning, I think I had a fair idea of its affirmations and negations. I was on the outside, as it were, looking in. But I discovered that those on the inside could hardly comprehend any other framework. They were the more inclined that way because of the supposed stalemate between the "new realists" and the "critical realists" in the twenties.

But it is time that we came back to Whitehead. As we shall see, he belongs more to the tradition of British empiricism. He is concerned with the status of sensory data. That is, for him, perception terminates on sensory objects. Out of this arises his doctrine of physical *prehension*. It can, I think, be taken as a modification of Berkeley's reduction of perceiving to the givenness of "ideas," that is, to what is sometimes called "immediate perception." In point of fact, Whitehead does refer to a passage in Berkeley's *Alciphron* in such a way as to imply that Berkeley recognizes a *transfer of content,* the sort of operation that Whitehead calls prehension. In contrast, I shall argue for a causal production of sensations *in the brain* of the percipient and their functioning there as guiding response. This will lead me to a more full-bodied view of perceiving, along genetic lines, which will make the object of perceiving coordinate with the percipient. Perceiving will thus have *objective import* and will be tied in with response, behavior, and language. Sensations will, therein, have guiding and testing functions. The genesis and role of *empirical concepts* in perceiving must be explored. I take it to be evident that they are *not* mere transcripts of sensations and images but more of the nature of constructs developed in the context of dealing with the objective world. There is here an *interplay* symbolized by the triad of S-C-R, stimulus, conception, response. Sensations are information-carrying.

What I am driving at is that British empiricism both got itself into subjectivism and into an inability to do justice to the import of concepts, by making sensations the terminus of perceiving. They are only factors in a larger, biological operation. What I have called the genetic approach had a feeling for this and indicated how such concepts as thinghood and causality emerged. But, as I saw it, there was no adequate revision of empirical epistemology. Here, my thesis is that perceiv*ing* is a case of guided, objective reference concerned with things coordinate with the percipient.

How I am going to query Whitehead's framework is, I hope, becoming apparent. Whitehead moves from perception in the mode of presentational immediacy—largely identified with presentational positivism—to the mode of causal efficacy in which sensory factors are regarded as prehended transfers taken up in actual entities according to the active *form of perception* and subjective aim. At one time, I took these data to be somewhat of the nature of Santayana's essences or Bradley's universals. One reason for this view was that Whitehead rejects the *generation* thesis that would make them *brain-events*. But Johnson has convinced me that they are particulars. There is room for discussion here, since Santayana's essences had the peculiar status of particulate universals and Berkeley's ideas were somehow in many minds and God's mind at once. The position I take, namely, that sensations are particular events located in stimulated brains, has no such ambiguity. It has, of course, its own ontological problem of the mind-body sort.

Let me come back to my argument. Whitehead rejects the adequacy of an outlook in the framework of presentational immediacy, that is, the Humean, positivistic, logical atomism outlook. He then shifts to an activistic subjectivism with data prehended. I, on the other hand, challenge the traditional, empirical view of perception, which makes sensations terminal, and develop perceiv*ing* as a guided operation of objective import concerned with things and constituting the public framework of the language of every day. If you will, causal efficacy works in the texture of S-C-R and not in that of the prehension of sensory data. Objective import leading to material-thing statements and the possibility of an evolutionary materialism is contrasted with the immaterialism of introspective subjectivism. It goes without saying that the referential realist must do justice to the self in his framework. I think that can be done. In fact, I would go farther and argue, with J. B. Pratt, that Whitehead is unable to do justice to the self as an enduring and functioning organization. Here we touch on the status of continuants and dispositional properties.

. . . As I see it, it [Whitehead's position] is a curious blend of British empiricism and Platonism, both modified radically. Sensory data as terminal—not as guides in perceiv*ing*—are regarded as modified transfers that are prehended. They are taken up actively. Whitehead makes much of this activity, which leads into the heart of the concrescent occasion, that is, the new event. "Eternal objects" are conceptually prehended at the other pole in the creative rise of actual entities. All this goes with the rejection of the category of substance as having no empirical foundation.

Now all this is quite logical, and I agree with Professor Johnson that Whitehead has worked it out very consistently. But I do not believe that he can do justice to either things or selves and the language that goes with them. If one makes sensory data terminal in perceiving as Hume, Russell, and Wittgenstein did, then Whitehead's metaphysics is invited. The alternative along this line is *atomic facts,* neutral entities, *ad hoc genus.* That was the path of the new realism, and of logical atomism. Whitehead wanted a more overtly panpsychistic metaphysics. And a positivism that contented itself with *language manipulation* and snarled at metaphysics naturally did not appeal to him.

What a battleground the word *metaphysics* has been! Now, because I had early become a physical realist and evolutionary materialist and a humanist, I had just rejected transcendental metaphysics and adopted the term ontology. It was a question for me of the kind of metaphysics. As I saw it, an adequate epistemology would terminate in ontology. Our human knowledge-claims involve states of affairs to be known. Taking perceiving to be empirically basic, I was led to decipher its referential nature. This meant a *new kind of empiricism* with sensory factors and concepts, functionally interconnected in the job of denoting and characterizing external things. We can call this *realistic empiricism.*

It is a notorious fact that, until a shift in perspective makes itself felt, scientists and philosophers of great ability tend to go around in circles. Russell's handling of proper names is a case in point. It should have been a warning signal to him. The stress on knowledge by acquaintance of what we are concerned with in statements is another case in point. So is Wittgenstein's picturing or correspondence. All this went with the union of the truth-value schematism of logic with an acquaintance sort of empiricism. Nothing could be sharper or more ruthlessly carried through. I have been recently reading Urmson's well-documented examination of the stages through which British philosophical analysis went between the two wars. The moral is: defects will betray themselves and new angles will be explored. It is the hard way. Cultural cross-fertilization—as the anthropologists call it—was too Vienna-wise. Now I think one reason for this was that American thought was too readily identified with pragmatism. Since I have already tried to show the *genetic strength* and *epistemological weakness* of pragmatism, that is quite understandable. Pragmatism was not quite analytic enough. My thesis is that logic is not self-sufficient in these matters but needs the supporting context of epistemology. The best way for a logician to get a feeling for this context is to tackle the problem of perceiving. Now in all this I am merely offering the perspective I think I have gained, for what it may be worth. As I see it, logic, *as more than a calculus,* works in the area where epistemology meets ontology.

I have argued that Whitehead, in common with traditional empiricism and the new realism, makes sensory data terminal. By making them transfers he strengthens the Berkeley motive. And it is to be noted, again, that he rejects the view that sensations are of the nature of events generated *in* the brain. Each gambit has different implications. What Whitehead does with his is remarkable. He gives the data a transcendent function in the mode of causal efficacy. Through them, an actual occasion becomes a participant in the transcendent universe of other things. It is *in* the world and the world is *in* it. Transfer, objective immortality, inclusion, the vectorial movement from the past to the present, organic focusing, all these motives operate. It is clearly an advance on Leibniz in the way of windows. Sensory data are passed on in their glory of color and sound. For him, the alternative is the muddle Locke made of it, of primary qualities separated from secondary ones, the postulation of the "unperceived," and so forth. Well, the best answer is the working out of a different view of perceiving that avoids Locke's bifurcations. This is perceiving in the mode of objective reference. Like Whitehead, I reject perception in the mode of presentational immediacy but, *instead of dropping into subjectivism,* I take the path of *a new kind of empiricism,* which regards sensations as guiding objective reference and the application of concepts. The whole framework is different and must be worked out in detail. The result would be what I would call an *empirical type of materialism.* As I see it, Russell got into the brain but could never get out successfully. By taking the reflex arc as the unit, I try to show that sensations are but units in a return circuit of a behavioral sort, which builds up into pointings, demonstratives, and the development and application of concepts. Lovejoy's "hat" covers this vectorial intake and output. I regard this as a promising alternative to the plunge into subjectivism. I speak here of a *from* and *to* circuit in perceiving.

Let us look at the excellent summary of Whitehead's view of sense perception in his *Adventure of Ideas.* We have, first, his qualified acceptance of the subject-object structure of experience. It is not to be interpreted as simply a knower-known relation. Now, long ago, I fought against this subject-object structure of experience as exhibited by James Ward: no object without a subject and no subject without an object. As I saw it, the referential object could be external, or transcendent. I regard the table I am perceiving as other than what I am acquainted with. I am denoting it and describing it and not "experiencing" it. Traditional empiricism—including logical atomism—never could account for external reference as transcendent in import. It did not understand the biological mechanisms involved. It is response, lifted to reference, that *makes things objects.* Now this is an important point, because it challenges the *aesthetic* view of perception permitted by the subject-object structure of experience, taken inspectionally.

The second point is his *axiom of empiricism,* to the effect that all knowledge is derived from, and verified by, direct intuitive observation. This is, quite obviously, the same perception that operated in Russell's and Wittgenstein's logical atomism. Empirical facts are given and pictured in an immediate way. But, if we take perceiving to be a guided operation leading to the application of concepts, we are led to a more complicated theory of the derivation and verification of knowledge-claims.

Third, all *percepts* are bare sensa mediated by the sense-organs. He writes: "When the direct question as to *things perceived* arises, it seems to me the answer is always in terms of sensa perceived." In other words, sensa are terminal in perceiving. This is more than a matter of definition. It reflects the traditional, causal theory of perception, its neglect of response.

Fourth, the process of experiencing is constituted by the *reception* of entities, whose being is antecedent to that process. Thus an object must be a thing *received* and must not be either a *mode* of reception *or a thing generated in that occasion*. Now as I understand modern psychological theory, the sensory content is not the result of putting together atomic, sensory data but a sort of pattern expressive of processes of analyses and syntheses leading to the goal of discriminative response. A fishing gull out here on Lake Erie flies over a stretch of water intent on noting signs of fish. He does not say "fish" to himself, as a logical positivist would, but dives down into the water. No, I do not think that perceiving is an affair of reception of objects. Nor is it a mode of reception. Rather is it an affair of controlled and responsible operation in which generation of sensory content is tied in with behavior. Human perceiving moves from this level to more complicated levels, but a quick "startle" approaches a throwback. It is clear that I have taken the line of generation as against antecedent objects. Here is one great divide.

Fifth, these *antecedent objects* function to express the point that each new occasion originates by *including* a transcendent universe of other things. Here enters the theory of transfers, objective immortality. It is a *participative transcendence*. Here are the windows. It is all quite logical and represents an improvement on both Leibniz and Berkeley. But it does depend upon the reception notion of sensory data. In place of participative transcendence, my analysis puts guided reference. Russell is, I take it, quite right in stressing causal reproduction of structure. Sensory data are, thus, such that they both guide and verify responsive reference. This is a theory of causally controlled generation as against a theory of transfer.

Sixth, there is nonsensuous perception as well as sense perception. Here Whitehead explores the self and memory and prepares the way for conceptual prehensions. Forms of reception and subjective aims are brought in and the groundwork is laid for teleology and the role of lures. He rightly puts human experience in nature—his one bow to modern naturalism, attacks traditional mechanism, and prepares the way for the upper story of theism by the route of "eternal objects." Now, as an evolutionist, I am not going to defend traditional, deductive mechanism. I have my own "field" notions with stress upon levels of causality, rising to guided and projective teleology.[1] But I am critical of "eternal objects." It seems to me that concepts are functionally developed and applied rather than prehended. It is an affair of working upward rather than from above down. Genesis, function, and analysis are not in conflict. The linguistic approach is helpful. What more do we need than the proper use and understanding of our symbols!

So much for Whitehead's basic assumptions and my objections to them. It goes almost without saying that I agree with his emphasis upon activity in perceiving. The unit, I have argued, is S-C-R or the interplay of stimulus, cortical processes, and response. But I would not regard this activity as a *form of reception,* an expression that goes with Whitehead's thesis that sensory data are *antecedents.* Instead, like Russell, I regard them as arising under causal control. Unlike him, however, I consider them as triggering off responses so that perceiving is a directed operation. As for *subjective aim,* I would stress concernedness and drives and interests, that is, the volitional dimension of the organism, arising to self-consciousness in man. But I cannot see that Whitehead's self-caused subject does justice to this base of operations. Surely we are growths and not simply events. And we get into ontology here. I am for a reformed use of the category

---

1. A paper on levels of causality and the emergence of the normative has recently appeared in the *Journal of Philosophy and Phenomenological Research.*

of substance. There is no reason why it should be tied to Aristotle's ontology of "form" and "matter," or to his subject-predicate logic.

To sum up, at the risk of some repetition: Whitehead seeks the transcendence traditional empiricism blocked, by assigning an antecedent existence to *percepts* and by adding an active form of reception and subjective aim. It is in this way that he is giving windows to his version of Leibniz's monads and even a development to Berkeley. Having turned his back on the unsatisfactory kind of objectivism of positivistic, presentational immediacy, he plunges wholeheartedly into *subjectivism* and seeks to reform it along the lines I have indicated. But can it be doubted that this reform does not harmonize with either language or common-sense beliefs? It is a sort of daring *tour de force*. But, until some alternative was clarified, it had point. Now the alternative I have been suggesting is a reanalysis of perceiving that opens up the objective import of perceiving in a more adequate way than Humean presentationalism. If S-C-R is the unit, then we can understand how sensations play into, and guide, reference and conceptual characterization, as perceiving is lifted to the high level of human dealing with the things around us. This means a break with the subjectivist tradition of modern philosophy to which Whitehead appeals. But it is not a mere return to the Aristotelian type of objectivism, for much has been learned about the mechanism of perceiving that Aristotle and the scholastics did not know. Reference is seen to be developed around response; and meanings and concepts are connected with the ensuing framework and given objective and testable import. The status and role of the various factors can thus be deciphered. Cognitive claims are guided and of objective import. In this *realistic empiricism,* sensations are not terminal but play a role in guidance and in evidential confirmation of statements in the context of referential indication. The crucial point to realize is that "mind" evolves in this *motor framework,* something traditional empiricism did not grasp.

The nature of my argument should now be clear. Whitehead swung from the kind of presentationalism found in Hume, Russell, Wittgenstein of the *Tractatus,* and logical positivism, to the only kind of alternative that seemed to him to have ontological promise, namely, reformed subjectivism. It had long been the gambit of pan-psychism. What he did was to work out a transfer theory of "per-cepts" that gave the new percipient participation in all that had gone before, though selectively. The categorial texture was to be essen-tially intuitively founded and to stress events, concrescence, prehen-sion, aims, and lures. Empiricism was to press beyond the limits of sensationalism and to recognize the role of conceptual prehensions as a door to a modified Platonism and Theism. All this was mag-nificent in its way. But, as I see it, it was threatened by a neglected alternative, a reformed objectivism of the kind I have outlined. Now this neglect was rather indigenous to British thought. It had paid rather scant attention to American pragmatism, to neo-Aristotelian-ism, to dialectical materialism, and to American critical realism. I do not deny that there were good excuses for this neglect. Pragmatism had not been epistemologically and analytically clear. It had slurred over the problem of perception and that of truth. Neo-Aristotelianism had stressed mental *intent* in Brentano but had not connected it up with a genetic, biological matrix and the idea of levels. Dialectical materialism was relatively weak in epistemology and seemed to hover between Hegelian logic and scientific methodology. Critical realism had divergent forms. Something more definite had to crystallize out, as an alternative to Whitehead's plunge into reformed subjectivism-*cum*-panpsychism. All this signifies that Whitehead's gambit was a plausible one. It had to be confronted by a well-worked-out alterna-tive that gave perceiving objective import in another framework.

Now, since I am engaged in scrutinizing Whitehead's framework in the light of an alternative, I must not hesitate to try to make the alternative as clear as possible by looking at it from various angles. The crucial point for me is the generation and locus of sensations and their function in the complex operation of perceiving. The tradi-tion of British empiricism had been to identify perceiving with aware-ness of sensations, with what Russell called knowledge by acquaint-ance. This halfway house was, as we saw, connected historically, through Locke, with the causal, stimulus outlook. As we saw, James was enough of a biologist to ponder the "reflex arc," the stimulus-response complex, but saw no epistemological way out. Hence he took the "radical empiricist" road to neutralism, followed by the new realists and Russell. Dewey moved downward from "experience" to biological behaviorism, shrugging off the role of sensations in perceiving, and truth as a verdict on cognitive claims. Perry was quite logical in following Bergson in denying that sensations could arise in the brain. Needless to say, I thought that Bergson handled perception in *Matter and Memory* very ambiguously. But into that question I cannot here go. Those who have followed my argument will know what points I have in mind. As I saw it, there is only one way out, namely, to take a referential view of perceiving. This outlook gives a function to sensations, a response base for reference, a role to language and concepts, and objective import. And, if this is so, the whole framework of Whitehead's epistemology is undermined. We do not perceive "percepta" but external things.

A few words in this connection about Lovejoy's "under-the-hat" attack. I think he had a point in his criticism of Russell. Accepting the causal approach without the response-completion, Russell got into the brain but could not get out. He is still there. But Lovejoy, himself, was a dualist as regards mind and body. And I confess that I never thought that his epistemology was very clear. I did not see that he stressed directness of reference and explored its biological foundation. But that, also, is a big subject, which the historian will, undoubtedly, take up.

While I am at it, I might well mention a point made by Copleston in his admirable little book *Aquinas,* to the effect that the scholastics would not have felt compelled to deny that sensations are in the brain. It was the *active reason* on which they put their bets, so to speak. And it is this that they must defend. If, as I see it, thought develops in the activity of lifting response to the level of the development and application of concepts and flowers in symbols and language, then reason secures a natural, cortical status in the context of intelligent behavior. I have already mentioned the point that I thought Brentano did not sufficiently explore the basis of *intent*. What seems to be befuddling so many philosophers here is the extreme behavioristic translations encouraged by Carnap. A little more attention to epistemology might have avoided artificial difficulties. I have been tunneling from the side of biology and epistemology, so to speak, while others have been tunneling from truth-table logic and semantics. Perhaps, the meeting will be presided over by "natural-language" analysis. But I have a strong feeling that even these will have to gird up their loins and consider epistemology and ontology. I hope my analysis of perceiving will be of assistance.

Now the upshot of all this is that, while the brain is "under-the-hat," it is the organ of directed response and concerned with pointings and gesturing and with symbolic reference. It is in this referential fashion that the human mind reaches to external things. It cannot intuit them but it can attain tested knowledge about them.

I take it that all these things hang together: perceiving, mind-body integration, evolutionary levels, increasing autonomy, agential causality guided by reason, truth as a tested achievement certifying knowledge and implying correspondence, nonreductive materialism. I shall argue that panpsychism represented a strategy based on the denial of objective knowledge of the material world. We must remember that materialism was crude in former days and that philosophy had its justification for trying to bypass it. Idealism was one method and spiritualism a closely allied one. Berkeley tried to show that all talk about matter and material things was meaningless. Leibniz, on the other hand, sought to get on the inside of an atom as a monad. As I see it, Whitehead tries to reform the Leibnizian move. But, surely, if perceiving and scientific knowledge have objective import, the job is to fit the subjectivist principle into that frame. This, I believe, can be done. But we shall need to take seriously categories like substance and dispositional properties and the self, as a focus of agency, and look askance at self-causation and mere eventism. Nothing can be more stimulating than such a contrast of frameworks and categories.

iii

ESSENTIAL CONTRASTS

Let me now bring my argument to a head. I shall do so by selecting certain crucial topics in Whitehead's system; and I shall work by seeking to bring out the divergent logics of subjectivism and objectivism. It will be my thesis that objectivism can do justice to what is *warranted* in subjectivism but that Whitehead goes beyond these warrants. I shall touch on the following points: 1) the status of primary and secondary qualities, 2) bodies as against objective immortality and self-causation, 3) the reduction of material things to sensory data, 4) the standing of *eternal objects,* and 5) the existence and role of God. I shall conclude by drawing out the import of the famous principle of "vacuous actuality." It is clear that this goes with subjectivism and the traditional axiom of empiricism with its emphasis upon terminal givenness. I met it in an unchristened state in F. H. Bradley, to the effect that it is meaningless to try to transcend experience. In contrast, referential realism turns in the direction of aboutness and the role of concepts. It is no accident that the divergence runs through from top to bottom.

1) As does Berkeley, Whitehead makes much play with sensuous givenness and the aesthetic context. Things are as they seem. *Percepta* shot through with feeling and value are primary. Locke's blunders are adroitly exploited. The *traditional* causal view of perceiving ends in "unperceived material bodies" and bifurcation.

Now I have attacked this older tradition. I have tried to show that sensations guide responsive perceiving and play into the formation of concepts and their application to external things. Such is the working context of perceiving. The aesthetic approach stresses *looks* and *appearances* as terminal. Color sensations and the visual field secure attention as features of what has been called the "aesthetic surface." Our natural languages have room for both vocabularies. But it is the task of epistemology to clarify their import and bases. I have argued that those who start from sensory data as primary in perceiving and try to construct things in terms of them are making a basic mistake. The percipient organism is concerned with using sensations as guides in its objectively directed decipherment of the things to which it is responding and to which it has to adjust itself.

The distinction between primary and secondary qualities, which has played such a role in the history of science and of philosophy, has been a confused one reflecting 1) inadequate ideas of perception, and 2) the stage in science when measurement was of a molar type and electromagnetic phenomena could not be handled. When Galileo interrogated nature, he used experimental manipulation and measurement. He was not measuring his sensations but bodies and their behavior. Measurements are, undoubtedly, guided by sensory coincidences, as when I use a measuring rod, but it is the rod that I am applying to the body being measured. Here, again, a clear theory of perceiving is required, for I find scientists dropping into the phenomenalistic framework urged upon them by the older tradition of empiricism. As I see it, mass, weight, size, and shape are declarations about bodies. And they are not obtained merely by inspecting sensations. They are an affair of the guided application of concepts.

But let us turn to color. As I see it, we do not project our color sensations into things but use them to differentiate things along these lines and to build up color concepts. The appplication of these concepts is guided by a recognition of lighting and atmospheric conditions. Probably color sensations and images tie in with our concepts here more closely even than in our thought of shapes and sizes; for measurement-operations have entered to build up our thought of the characteristics of bodies. But I take it that color charts and talk about optical frequencies are affecting our thought about color. The point I would make is that to say that an object is red is to say something differential about it that can be backed up in various ways and has what I call objective import. Democritus and Galileo did not see how they could explore this objective import. Scientific technique was not far enough advanced. Locke blundered in taking ideas as terminal and Berkeley followed suit. But what Berkeley did was to reduce perceiving to the awareness of sensations and images. Of course, this played havoc with language. But Berkeley made the best he could of it, having Locke's unperceived things and "abstract ideas" as the supposed alternative.

To sum up, the distinction between primary and secondary qualities should be displaced by a recognition of different kinds of knowledges and techniques. Concentration on molar mechanics has given way to electromagnetic measurements and facts. But, in both cases, it is recognized that *a priori* rationalism is not justified. There is always the factor of sensory disclosure and testing. Whitehead's protest against bifurcation is directed against inadequate views of perceiving. All sensory data have the same status and play much the same role in directing perceiving in a referential way. All this will become still clearer in the third section, where I reject Whitehead's reduction of material things to sensory data, a gambit begun by Berkeley. We can, I think, press beyond both "bifurcation" and Cartesian dualism.

It should be obvious now why I think an adequate epistemology essential in all these matters. It has long been my conviction that both American pragmatism and British empiricism lacked the proper epistemological framework. They did not have a view of perceiving that gave it objective import.

2) I have argued for a reform of the category of substance along the line of *bodies* and thus in a semi-Democritean way. Aristotle made advances in logic, though he did not do justice to relations. But his ontology of "form" and "matter" did not fit science, as it developed, as well as did atomism. Eleaticism has, of course, had to give way to empirical knowledge and the categories adjusted to it. It is only of late that the logic of proper names and demonstratives has taken a realistic turn and drawn to itself descriptive and relational terms. A clearer notion of "referring" is arising, which seems to me to fit into my referential view of perceiving. Better linguistic analysis is of help here. But I have not the space to go into logical issues.

Science largely rejected Aristotelianism and went on its own way. The correlatives *form* and *matter,* in terms of which Aristotle had sought to explain change, were replaced by matter in motion. Stress was put on measurement and laws of behavior. In this setting, teleological *lures* and appreciative matter seemed at once mythological and unknowable. All this is relevant to our purpose because Whitehead, in his shift to subjectivism and panpsychism, seeks to give them empirical status. I, on the other hand, approach purpose, or projective teleology, along the lines of levels of causality and emergence, giving intelligence a directive role in causality at the cortical stage of evolution. This, of course, fits in with my guided view of referential perceiving and only takes on from there in what the pragmatist calls the solving of problems. My objection to panpsychism is *not* that it does not have correct, empirical insights but that it has no body and thickness to its ontology. This, we shall see, comes out both in the treatment of perceiving and in the handling of the "self." Surely, the self is not an event. It is a *growth* with dispositional properties and jobs to do. And here, again, we come to the category of substance.

It is recognized that Locke gave a body blow to lingering notions of substance in the old context by his reduction of it to an unknowable *substratum*. Aristotelians are quite correct in their protests. But they must bring in more adequate views of perceiving and of ontology to supplement their protests. In the meantime, the new empiricism took up the tale and focused attention upon sensations and images. The result was the kind of psychologism that Hume developed into a mixture of positivism and agnosticism. The only cure for this is to realize that perceiving and *imaginative thought* are referential and that categorial meanings develop within them. In my opinion, it is best to start with things and bodies in this setting and then work out the logical grammar of substance.

As I see it, Russell and Whitehead were too hasty in their rejection of "substance," following the leads of Hume, on the one hand, and the mistake of Leibniz, on the other. Our knowledge is not an affair of predicative encapsulation; nor is it an affair of a series of sensations and images. Philosophers inevitably work acutely *within preconceptions*. Russell took the path of construction and postulate within the context of presentational immediacy. Whitehead dove down to subjectivism with transfers and objective immortality. Quite rightly, the neo-Thomists are convinced that this does not give the equivalence of substance. I offer my more materialistic version.

3) I do not have much to add to the theme of the rejection of the reduction of material things to sensory data. By his stress on the immediate, or aesthetic, outlook, Whitehead is emphasizing sensory data as terminal and ignoring their use in sense perception as guides to response and directed, referential perceiving. His tie-in with the traditional causal approach is clear. Only he replaces the notion of cause and generated effect by a more Leibnizian pattern of mirroring transfers. It is very ingenious. But it is not the only alternative. I

have argued that the perceptual unit is based on the "reflex arc" or the sensorimotor pattern. This gives the thing with which the organism is concerned as terminal and makes perceiving have objective import. In a way, Whitehead wants "percepta" to have transcendent import, but it is in the way of *participation* through a vectorial transfer. As I see it, this continues the older empirical tradition, which reduces material things to sensory data. Only Whitehead has the startling notion of cosmic concrescence in the monad, or actual occasion, again a Leibnizian motive.

Here we have the watershed between ontological subjectivism and materialism. It must be kept in mind that the motivations against materialism have been strong in philosophy from the time of Plato. These have been connected with the weaknesses of the formulations of materialism and with theistic predilections. Both Peirce and Whitehead rejected materialism because they regarded it as logically tied in with a one-level, deductive type of necessitarianism. I have been assured of this by Peirce experts; and Lowe seems to have the same interpretation of Whitehead's attitude toward materialism, that of dismissal. I do not belittle the job confronting those who seek to rehabilitate materialism as an ontology. It must be, as I have already indicated, a nonreductive kind, able to do justice to *qualia* and qualities as well as to quantities, to valuations and the normative as well as to descriptive knowledge. In these days, any sophisticated materialism must have an adequate epistemology, an evolutionary ontology, and an appreciation of man as an agent. The whole range of analysis should feed into this perspective.

One final comment on this traditional attempt to reduce material things to sensory data. It strikes me as so obviously unable to give meaning to chemical and physical analysis. When I read that scientists have synthesized DNA, the substance that determines heredity in all living things, what meaning can this have for the empirical philosopher? For me, a realistic empiricist, it has the essential meaning of the physical realist, namely, that the complex molecule consists of combinations in various template patterns of six basic nucleotides. The sort of skilled technique that goes on in the chemical laboratory, advancing step by step, achieves this factual knowledge. I cannot *translate* this knowledge of chemical combinations into any assemblage of sensory factors. These may well guide perceiving in the service of external manipulation. But that is all. Concepts must be developed and applied. The role of sensations is that of guiding and testing. The moral I draw is that, in its attempt to get away from *a priori* rationalism and conceptualism, philosophy went to the other extreme of sensationalism, misled by the causal approach of a pre-biological era into the notion that sense-data, or sensations, are terminal for perceiving. The reflex arc or the sensorimotor unit, open to cortical expansion as S-C-R, gives the referential vector connected with behavior and language. My chief objection to behaviorism, as such, as an *escape-mechanism for philosophers,* was that it sought to bypass epistemology rather than to get a new perspective. It was a sort of desperate alternative to Whitehead's dive into subjectivism. I have mentioned another giant, C. S. Peirce. It has been pointed out to me by Professor Goudge that Peirce's view of "immediate perception" is to the effect that a "psychic feeling of red without us arouses a sympathetic feeling of red in our senses," a view akin to Whitehead's "feeling of feeling." In place of "immediate perception" I put referential perceiving, in which the function of sensory factors is guidance and which does not presuppose the identity, or continuity, of "immediate perception." Here is the line of division.

4) I have said little, as yet, of the "mental pole" of Whitehead's actual occasions and of the status of "eternal objects." Now I am just as skeptical of the prehension of universals as I am of the prehension of antecedent sensory data. In point of fact, I agree with Professor Wilfrid Sellars that universals are not psychological entities to be noetically grasped but linguistic functions tied in with the use of symbols. Thus they involve the level of concept-formation and use. Here the genetic approach of Baldwin, Dewey, and Mead is valuable; but it must be supplemented by recognition of how concepts are employed. I have argued that the referential analysis of perceiving gives the correct point of departure and that an understanding of the grammar of language takes on from there. This seems to be the

growing point of Philosophy today. I would argue that concepts are human achievements and have no cosmic status otherwise. There is a touch of this in Aristotelianism in its departure from Plato's noetic intuitionism of Forms.

Let it be recalled that I note at least three kinds of empiricism: 1) *Traditional, British empiricism,* 2) *pragmatic empiricism,* stressing the status of ideas as instruments linked with consequences, and 3) *realistic empiricism,* which regards concepts as achievements concerned not only with consequences but with directed knowledge-claims, guided and tested by sensory data. Human knowing is a very complex, structured activity, starting off with a biological base and raised to cortical and linguistic levels. Concepts connect up with references and applications; and the truth of a statement signifies an endorsement—after testing—of a referential knowledge-claim. Correspondence is an implication and not a test.[1] It is an *achievement* dependent on the information-carrying role of externally controlled sensations.

Since W. T. Stace took violent exception to my contribution to the Whitehead volume in Living Philosophers in a *Mind* review, I feel justified in calling attention to his recent article in *Mind* as an expression of the first kind of empiricism. He writes as follows: "All verbal expressions, whether they consist in single terms or in complete sentences, must if they are to possess cognitive meaning or significance, either refer to some specific but unanalyzable experiential datum, or be amenable to a process of analysis the end-term of which will be such experiential data."[2] But, surely, we are faced with the question of the role of demonstratives and proper names. Do these apply to what we are "acquainted with" or to that to which we are referring? Stace, obviously, follows the Russell tradition. I hold it to be mistaken. Do we observe *through* our sensations? Or do we simply observe our sensations? It is evident that one who still adheres to the traditional type of empiricism will find no sense in my

---

1. See my *Philosophy of Physical Realism* (1932), "Correspondence an implication, not a test," sec. pp. 115 f.
2. *Mind* (October 1958), p. 468.

type of realistic empiricism. But, *when people set out to refute realism,* they should at least study the various kinds.

Returning to Whitehead, it can be granted that he modifies Platonism considerably. His eternal objects are arranged by God and act as lures in lesser actualities. But the realistic empiricist holds that *patterns* are worked out in the material world, as physics, chemistry, and biology show, and the emergent materialist sees reason to believe that these arise through integrative causality. Perceiving involves the deciphering of patterns in an elementary way; and this is taken up by means of scientific method with the invention of new tools and methods. And so we come back to the thesis that concepts are achievements and not ingressions. It strikes me as merely a dogma when Professor Lowe asserts that materialism can find no place for novelty and adventure. This is just a continuation of the tradition operative in Peirce, which *identified* materialism with a one-level, once-for-all, deductive necessitarianism. What good does it do philosophy to continue this kind of semanticism? Is it not historically dated?

Platonism is a big subject and I cannot go into its ramifications. Both the psychological and the logical status of concepts need clearing up. They seem to be achievements rather than ingressions. And they have a cognitive as well as an instrumental function. Being tied in with these kinds of activity, I am not surprised that their linguistic use involves rules and regulations. I suggest that an inadequate view of perceiving did much to retard the recognition of this fact. Once it is recognized as a referential activity with a job to do, the way is open for a comprehension of higher activities. The essential reply to Whitehead's Platonism must be in terms of an analysis of such activities. I do not see how they can help being functional and *normative*. The natural languages must be seen in this context. How to integrate logical calculi with them is one of the moot questions of the moment. An empiricism that did not recognize the presence of such categorial meanings as substance and causality in its statements was relatively helpless before extensional and truth-table logic. I have brought all this in because it indicates the *gap* that is opening between Platonism, on the one hand, and the formal linkage of sensory empiricism and logical tautologies. Logical thought undoubtedly has its rules and structure but, as I see it, these flower out of, and reflect, the needs of veridical thinking and so ultimately have an ontological base. Thus realistic empiricism moves between Platonism and traditional empiricism, while attempting to correct pragmatism's overly instrumental and consequential slant due, as I have argued, to its turning away from epistemology and ontology, too hastily. An adequate analysis of perceiving could, I think, have set pragmatism on a firmer, technical foundation. It would then have taken the material world and cognitive claims about it more literally.

The essential reply to Whitehead must be in the way of such realistic explorations. I have the impression that he is being bypassed by philosophy just because these explorations are going on.

5) The affirmation of God in his primordial and consequential dimensions along with the repudiation of naturalistic humanism follows from Whitehead's architectonic. As I see it, his proof of God is a built-in one. It is of the cosmological variety. God is the primary principle of concretion; his arrangement of "eternal objects" makes them available to the lesser actualities as lures and possibilities. But all this depends upon his modified Platonism. If we take a functional view of concepts as connected with identifications and classification and the finding of connections in what we are perceiving, that is, in this kind of problem-solving, then we have a different cosmology.

If, then, we reject Whitehead's built-in cosmological proof of theism, we are left with the traditional ones; and their philosophical standing is not high. There are various personal and cultural motives that give psychological support to theism. These are by no means negligible; quite the contrary, in fact. And they find linguistic expressions of ingenious types. The result is a sort of semantic battle with the big battalions on the side of traditional forms of religion. I have sometimes had the temptation to envy those who, in clear conscience, could take the popular side. But it was not for me. There is no denying the fact that ontological materialism, by its very framework, is non-theistic. The job is to do justice to man's stature and agency.

VACUOUS ACTUALITY AND PANPSYCHISM

I must now pay my respects to "vacuous actuality" and the "ontological principle, no actuality, then no reason." Being an ontological materialist, I have considerable sympathy with the ontological principle, but not with the identification of actuality with experience or experiencing.

It is quite true that if the terminus of perceiving consists of *sensory percepts,* as Berkeley, Bradley, and Whitehead hold, then it is quite logical to maintain that experience is ultimate ontologically. You then have the idealistic gambit in good conscience and you can condescend in academic ways to common sense and science. But you ought to be pretty sure that there is no alternative. As I see it, logical positivism did much this sort of thing but snuggled up to science by joining it in loud abuse of that mysterious thing called "metaphysics" tied in with obscurantism and impossible transcendence. Now I do not want to be unfair. It helped to initiate good analytic work in logic and language. But I think that those who have followed my argument will see that I hold that both common sense and science are naturally ontological just because they believe they observe and measure *material bodies.* It is a materialist ontology bothered by the mind-body problem and the whole question of the status of purpose, appraisals, and the normative. It is to these questions that I have devoted many years of thought along emergence lines. I think I have cast light upon them in terms of levels of causality and the double-knowledge approach to the mind-body problem. But into all this I cannot here go in detail. . . . The point is that ontological materialism, connected up with an adequate view of the objective import of perceiving, serves to dissipate these phobias about "metaphysics." Russell was nearer right in his early days when he spoke about the belief in things as man's primitive and natural metaphyiscs. He had his warning; but the tradition of Hume and the reduction of perceiving to sensations was too strong a preconception for him to overcome. I have tried to show that the functional unit is S-C-R.

And so the choice is between two gambits. If perceiving is an affair of guided reference and tested conceptualization, there is an *aboutness* that is irreducible to givenness, or acquaintance, or *prehension*. . . .

It is clear that we have here the basic question about the *nature of the reach* of human knowing. Whitehead, moving within his preconceptions in his daring and magnificent way, thinks in terms of transfers of antecedent entities that have objective immortality. I think of sensations as cerebral events linked up with motor responses but the connection intercalated cortically at the human level—and I suppose this intercalation of learning had its antecedent as instinct was replaced—so that attitude, reference, meaning, and language dominated perceiving as an activity. In this setting, sensations could be used as cues and sources of disclosure for concepts and their application. More explicitly, they became evidence. The sense organs had begun biologically as guides to adjustment to the environment; their nervous centers were inevitably linked, as biologists point out, to maintain the unified economy of the organism. Then came the cortex and increasing intelligence directed, of course, to external adjustment. So we humans adjust ourselves to the things around us, point, refer, denote, characterize. The nature of the reach of human knowing must be thought of in these terms. "Mind" is not a substance but a referential activity making use of symbols. It is in this setting that the "I" confronts the "that." And it is in this setting that categorial meanings, such as body and causality, are worked out and applied. Hume had his points against *intuitional* rationalism, but these can be absorbed by realistic empiricism.

Now the import of all this is that Berkeley, Bradley, and Whitehead are wrong in their reduction of perceiving to sensory percepta and in the inference they draw to the effect that experience cannot be transcended, that *being* must be experiencing and that any other domain is *nothing*. Of course, transcendence must have its mechanism and cannot be a new kind of floating over to the object and getting acquainted with it. What impresses me is the method nature adopted. By linking S with R, it got a base to develop that flowered into reference and symbolism with the help of the cortex.

Now the moral of all this is that even geniuses like Russell and

Wittgenstein and Whitehead could not work out an adequate epistemology without *leads,* such as those I have indicated. They made, of
course, their own kind of contribution which, I think, can be assimilated. Philosophy has a wide front and many problems. My quarrel
with Dewey and the pragmatists is that they dropped the problem
of perception despite their interest in biology. My criticism of Whitehead is *not* that he ignored perception, but that he tried to link
British empiricism—scientifically out-of-date—with Leibniz in a new
kind of subjectivism. What was needed was a new kind of objectivism.

The history of science gives the story of the rise of methods of
measurement, questioning, and experimentation that enabled man to
go beyond the qualitative, rather common-sense, realism of Aristotle.
Every one should read Crombie's detailed account. *Bodies* and their
behavior began to take the place of the Aristotelian preconceptions of
"natural places," "natural motion," "forms," and "matter." Mass
and molar mechanics were the first achievement. But philosophy was
unable to reorientate itself. It tried, first, an intuitional kind of
rationalism on the model of mathematics; and then it tried the
way of ideas, which made ideas terminal in perceiving; and, to be
Newtonian, postulated a correspondence with "unperceived things."
It would not do. But it gave birth to positivism, Kantianism, and
idealism. It was not until the theory of evolution came on the scene
that new possibilities were opened up. It is fascinating to note how
Peirce and Dewey envisaged them. Peirce never escaped from Kantianism and sought to unite it with a panpsychistic form of "immediate
perception," not unlike Whitehead's, as Professor Goudge has pointed
out to me. Dewey took the path of behaviorism and *avoided the problem of personal perception,* as behaviorism does. It is a path that also
tempted Professor Ryle. I have explored a referential view of perceiving that gives it objective import and seems to me to fit into
science. Take this path and *true* becomes a term for the endorsement
of tested knowledge-claims as cases of knowledge-about. Correspondence is not a test but an *implication* of the endorsement, backed up
by recognition of the *evidential* role of sensory factors in the genesis
and application of concepts. As I see it, it all hangs together.

I cannot resist, finally, giving some indication of how the realistic empiricist would approach the problem of the atom—that terrible ingredient of the atom bomb—which would make it more than a *"scientific construct."* Since I hold that *bodies* having mass, energy, and internal structure are objects of perceiv*ing,* and not assemblages of colors, apparent shapes, and feels, I am hospitable to the reality of the microscopic in another than a Berkeleian way. It is upon bodies that science began to experiment *physically;* to note, first, their molar behavior—discovering mass and later energy—and then to explore their chemical constitution. New instruments and techniques developed bit-by-bit with new concepts. As Conant explains in his book *On Understanding Science,* this was a gradual advance with difficulties at every stage. And now we have come to cloud-chamber photographs of electron paths and even newer techniques for nuclear particles. As I see it, man has been supplementing his organic, sense-organ technique, used in ordinary perceiving, and thus extending perceiving by the aid of instrumentation. As we should expect, new types of concepts are also added in the extended S-C-R. The referential and objective import of perceiving is kept.

Thus I consider viruses, molecules, atoms, electrons, and nuclear particles to be, in principle, perceivable and, with these new techniques, actually perceived. We must remember that perceiving on this analysis is not an intuiting, or prehending, but a guided denoting and characterizing. It is, therefore, not surprising that frames of reference, measurement, and tested theory play an increasing role in science. But, as I see it, we are still concerned with the perceptible, material world. When I read Dingle, Sherrington, and Jeans I have a strong suspicion that such philosophy as they picked up did them as much harm as good. Or, to put it another way, they were in no position to solve philosophical problems as such.

But were philosophers to blame? I cannot hold so. As we saw, when qualitative Aristotelianism broke down under the impact of new methods and questions, Descartes, Locke, and Hume did yeoman's work, as did Kant later. But, as I see it, they did not have the right cue. Biology and psychology were not advanced enough to suggest the complex mechanism of perceiving. Technical advances were made but they did not quite fit together. It could not be clearly seen how deduction had relevance to nature or what the base of induction was. Whitehead at least had a *feel* for these questions that the positivists did not have. And then the fitting of man into nature *while doing justice to his evolved capacities* was a task of the first magnitude. Mind had to be integrated into nature and the causal role of intelligence indicated. Something like a broad front had to be kept in mind.

What I like about Whitehead is that he took epistemology, ontology, and axiology seriously and made no special parade of his logical and mathematical equipment when it was not relevant. He did not turn his back on the insights of past philosophy as so many logical positivists did, who thus condemned themselves to shift from position to position, under pressure and self-criticism. What I have tried to do in this paper is to present an alternative to Whitehead's subjectivism. It is an alternative that he, as a theist, would not have liked. But I knew him well enough personally to know that he would have intellectually welcomed the challenge involved.

v

[Yet the] gist of the situation is this: if, in line with modern communication theory, we regard perceiving, with its controlled *from* and *to* circuit, as making cognitive use of sensations as information-carrying, we give perceiving objective import. This was the scheme nature worked with, and I can see no alternative.

Whitehead's "reformed subjectivism" is marked by categorial openness of texture—its strong point—but links itself with a questionable speculative framework, though of impressive subtlety.

11

Existentialism, Realistic Empiricism, and Materialism*

i

. . . I have the impression that British and American analysts are so engrossed in specific problems within their frame of reference that they are not always fully aware of their assumptions. Much the same, I think, holds for existentialists and for dialectical materialists. It is just possible that the outlook of a philosopher who does not belong to any of these three movements yet appreciates their emphases may be stimulating. I am going to begin with some introductory remarks in the way of orientation.

My first remark is to the effect that I do not think that analysts have paid sufficient attention to epistemology. Here I speak as a realistic empiricist. I have the impression that many analysts waver between phenomenalism and a kind of behavioristic naïve realism. Queries along these lines seem to me to be in order.

Existentialists pay little attention to the empiricist tradition. Yet it should be plain that empiricism has long opposed *essentialism* along semi-nominalistic lines. Being is not reducible to abstract thought. This point in common between existentialism and empiricism should

Philosophy and Phenomenological Research 25, no. 3 (March 1965), pp. 315–32. Reprinted with the permission of both the author and publisher.

be recognized. Some measure of cross-fertilization between empiricism and existentialism would seem to be called for.

There are two types of materialism in the philosophical world today, dialectical materialism and evolutionary, or nonreductive, materialism. I believe that a debate between these two types would be fruitful. What they have in common is a need for a realistic foundation. Both are opposed to phenomenalism or positivism. I have recently tried to further this demand by bringing out the role of sensation in perceiving. As I see it, perceiving is referential and directed, in a response way, at the external thing but is guided by informative sensations. I speak here of a from-and-to circuit.

The meaning of *dialectic* is under debate. I shall not go into that, for it seems to be the job of Marxism to come to terms with its traditions. On this side, we hear much of the *de-materialization* of matter. This expression would seem to refer to the changed idea of the nature of matter. It is no longer conceived as solid, uniform, and simple. This is certainly an advance. But I would hazard the opinion that it makes a sophisticated materialism more plausible. I do not find the introduction in science of a new type of being. But there is recognition of novelty of organization and of capacities. Geneticists speak of the gene-pool as the basis of cultural evolution.

For all these reasons, I am advocating a debate between empiricists, existentialists and materialists.

ii

In the philosophical sweepstakes of the present, then, there seem to be three main international contenders: 1) Anglo-American empirical philosophy; 2) Marxism in terms of dialectical materialism; and 3) existentialism. Thomism, as a perennial philosophy, operates in the background.

It is my intention to take two steps backward, as it were, and look at these three movements. I am not here concerned with communism as a social movement. It is more closely connected with *historical materialism*. Into the interconnections between dialectical materialism and historical materialism I shall not go here, for it is a complex topic. Sartre is probably right in maintaining that dialectical materialism *tends* to accept the thesis that evolution is in line with progress in a thesis-antithesis-synthesis sort of way. Emergent evolution is less predictive. But I want to register my feeling that Marx thought that stalemate and chaos might be a possibility.

I have the impression that both Anglo-American empiricism and dialectical materialism concern themselves more with science than does existentialism. Existentialism emphasizes the human condition, highlights it. But neither Jaspers nor Sartre completely ignores science. It is thus a matter of emphasis. But Marxism and Anglo-American empiricism have somewhat different slants on the scientific view of the world. I shall try to explain what I mean later. It must suffice to say that I think British and American empiricisms have been too much dominated by positivism and pragmatism, while Marxism has thought too much in terms of Hegel's march from thesis to antithesis to synthesis. These variations in texture are important in the long run. I confess that my own outlook, which I have worked out over many years, beginning before the Russian Revolution itself, is more realistic than either positivism or pragmatism and has been concerned with novelty, or emergence, in nature. I shall try to spell all this out later. It may be enough at this point to say that I have been concerned with evolutionary levels in nature, with the efficacy of mind and consciousness, and with the import of what is commonly called free will or responsible decision.

A few general words about the third member of our trio, Existentialism. I capitalize it because it is that sort of thing.

Now it seems to be the case that, after Sartre called himself an existentialist, some of the others felt uncomfortable with the label. He was a sort of *enfant terrible* with his bold theses of atheistic humanism and absolute commitment. Heidegger did not quite like the emphases and stressed his own interest in Being and a kind of absolute ontology. This is interesting because Heidegger, the German, was, in a manner, a teacher of Sartre. He is the older man. Jaspers, another German, had what I would call a vague, Neo-Kantian outlook and a mild theism in the background. And then there were the overtly religious and theologically inclined existentialists, those who affiliated themselves with the Dane, Kierkegaard. One can, I think, associate here the Protestant Tillich, and the Roman Catholic Marcel.

All in all, then, Existentialism is a term for a cluster of positions. Yet I do think they have something in common against Anglo-American empiricism and Marxism. In many ways, it has functioned as a sort of third philosophical force. This is partly due to *overtones.* Its ethical terminology had an emotive flavor in such ideas as authenticity, commitment, bad faith, the spurning of the impersonal and average. And it had literary expressions in Sartre, in accordance with the French tradition. I doubt that Camus was, technically speaking, an existentialist, but his writings blended with features of the movement.

All in all, then, Existentialism is a movement to be appraised judicially. It has its own dimensions in human life. Perhaps the question, so widely asked these days, of the "meaning" of human life defines its center of interest. This term, of course, needs definition. One can readily talk of the meaning of the word *lion,* but to talk about the *meaning of lions* is something else again. But man is an animal who can ask questions. That is a point that Heidegger makes. And he certainly can ask questions about the relation of the world to what we call purposes and values. Does nature in the large concern itself with these items? Does the old idea of Providence have application?

Of course, these are not new questions. We all remember Ruskin's pathetic fallacy. But it is not surprising that, in this century of wars and revolutions, of an increased tempo of change, these questions should be asked more imperatively. I shall ask the background question: What have the Existentialists done in the way of clarification? By confronting them with Anglo-American empiricism and Marxist materialism, light may be thrown on the issues. I shall try to be as little technical as possible or, better yet, to explain such technicalities as are needful. This can be called an exploratory operation.

I have decided to emphasize Sartre in my study of existentialism just because it is easier to know where he is. Or, to express it better, *just about where he is.* I am reminded here of modern electron theory. It is impossible to tell precisely where the outer electrons of an atom are in a chemical reaction. What we have is a sort of wave phenomenon. There is something of this in Sartre. But I find him fascinating. I shall use the method of contrast. I know pretty well where I stand on the same questions. I find more of a touch of empiricism in his theses than I find in Jaspers or Heidegger. I suppose this expresses the continuing influence of Descartes on French thought. Rationalism and empiricism have, in this regard, something in common. Both tend to be analytic. Descartes, I think, could have understood Locke and Hume, even though he disagreed with them. While I have made great efforts to appreciate Heidegger and Jaspers, I find their modes of thought a little alien. There is a tendency to call on intuition. Heidegger is making a tremendous effort to penetrate to the *revealable depths of Being.* He turns his back on representational, or correspondence, theories of truth, something that, I think, is tied in with scientific achievement.

We have here what I would call another *genre* in philosophical thought. It is well to be acquainted with it and to do justice to it. But it is also well to contrast it with others. That is why I am studying a trio, and for this purpose, I think that Sartre is most useful. His outlook is frankly naturalistic and humanistic, as both Anglo-American empiricism and Marxism tend to be, though he likes to shock the *bourgeoisie,* much as Bernard Shaw did in his day. One must get a firm grasp on his terms. He plays with them dialectically. Being-for-itself has a hankering to be Being-in-itself and can't be. In this fashion he tries to show that the very idea of God is a contradiction. Now I have a quite different notion of Being-for-itself or conscious being, approached along evolutionary and realistic lines. I think the contrast will be interesting.

So much in the way of introductory indications. I have decided that it will be best for expository purposes to begin with an outline, so to speak, of British and American empiricism and then pass to *Diamat.* The study of Existentialism can then come and its genre be all the more appreciated by way of contrast.

iii

REMARKS ON ANGLO-AMERICAN EMPIRICISM

It is well to take two steps back from the controversies of the hour to get perspective. I shall be a little heretical, but then, one has the right to one's own perspective so long as he can offer a justification.

American philosophy, at the beginning of the twentieth century, reflected a transition from an idealism dominated by the thought of Kant and Hegel to the more empirical and pragmatic ideas of James and Dewey. There was a greater stress on time and on action. Much of the controversy turned around the notion of truth. For the idealist, truth had been largely a logical affair. Both its meaning and its tests were tied in with the principle of coherence. The more inclusive a consistent set of ideas was, the more it approached Absolute Truth. Such Absolute Truth was a limit to be approximated. There was a spiritualistic background in this type of philosophy and a tendency to identify Absolute Truth with Absolute Mind. Matter and materialism had been left far behind in these speculations. I have always felt that Berkeley and his doctrine that *to be is to be perceived* had a continuing influence.

Now pragmatism—or, as Dewey came to call it, instrumentalism— represented a definite shift of ground. The emphasis was on time and action. Ideas, William James averred, were *made true* by their consequences. In a broad sense, that is true which works; in the long run and on the whole, of course. The talk tended to be about beliefs, perhaps because James was a psychologist as well as philosopher. He even spoke of the will to believe, or the right to believe, if there was a living option.

It should be noted that James linked himself up more with the British empirical tradition of Locke, Hume, Mill, and Bain than with the German thinkers Kant and Hegel. He wanted to be concrete in his thinking, to keep abstract ideas in touch with perceptual experience. Sometimes his phrasing was a little too concrete, as when he spoke of the cash-value of ideas. At such times, his desire for a vivid style got the better of him. But such lapses were rare. Good writing ran in the James family. His father was a brilliant conversationalist and his brother Henry was a master of prose.

John Dewey, who was to exert such a prolonged influence on American thought, was early trained in Kant and Hegel and only slowly departed from them, partly under the stimulus of William James and partly because of the impact of Darwinian thought. He began to emphasize the role of reflection and of problem-solving. He became persuaded that the job of human thought was not to reproduce a cosmic pattern in a constitutive way but to handle situations as these confronted man. Ideas, he came to hold, were instruments in such adjustments. Experience was something to be *reconstituted*. There was nothing beyond experience, nothing transcendental to be mirrored in thought. Thinking was forward-looking, an affair of plans and projects. Clearly, this is a form of activism and it did agree with the American temperament. American culture is usually regarded as pragmatic; and James and Dewey are considered its spokesmen. And there is a great deal of truth in this assumption.

But we must not oversimplify. There was another current in pragmatism associated with the name of C. S. Peirce. Peirce was a scientist and a mathematician, aware of the importance of scientific method. Something of this emphasis was passed on to Dewey. Hence we must not ignore the element in the pragmatic tradition of the recognition of science.

So much, in broad outline, is the first shift in American philosophical thought from a rather formal idealism, largely taken over from Europe, to novel stresses on ideas as instruments and upon ideas as plans of action. I think it was a healthy development but a little one-sided.

As one might expect, the next generation coming after James, Peirce, and Dewey sought to qualify and add to pragmatism. There was the feeling that something had been left out. Had justice been done to the claims expressed in human knowing? Was there not another dimension to human knowledge and to the idea of truth? How about the vast world of nature, which science was exploring?

Did not human ideas have to, somehow, *correspond* to what is there? Now this was an old gambit but it had apparently been ignored in the controversy between idealism and pragmatism. One reason for this was certain difficulties inherent in an old framework set up by John Locke. It goes with what is usually called the causal theory of perception. We don't perceive unless our sense organs are stimulated. *What, then, do we perceive?* Locke's answer was that we first of all perceive our sensations and images, called, taken together, our *ideas*. How, then, do we get to external things, the sort of objects science talks about? In Locke's day, this was the world of Sir Isaac Newton, the world of mass and gravitation. Today it is the world of electrons, atoms, and genes.

Locke never mastered his dilemma. Roughly speaking, he resorted to a kind of pragmatic inference and the faith that ideas resembled what he called the primary qualities of external things—extension, mass, et cetera—*perception;* that is, that our percepts, which are experienced, represent something other than themselves. But how can we know this? And how can the belief be tested? Berkeley and Hume gave this gambit up as a bad job. What we call British empiricism came to stress sensations and images.

The young men after James and Dewey returned to this problem to test it afresh. There were two groups, called, respectively, the new realists and the critical realists. The first group gave up representative realism as something impossible to revise. The drastic move was, then, to hold that external things are simply presented as they are. This is a form of naïve realism to the effect that there are no such entities as subjective sensations but that the external thing is open to inspection when we respond to the stimulation of our sense organs. That is, we just *see* things. Modern behaviorism has a touch of this kind of realism. Perry, Montague, and Holt took this position, notwithstanding obvious difficulties, because they saw no alternative.

The critical realists—there were seven of them including myself—sought another kind of direct realism. I may mention Santayana, Strong, Drake, and Lovejoy as working along this line. I am the only one left of both the new realists and the critical realists. And I have had a long time to analyze and reflect. The solution to the problem of perceiving I have worked out is, in general, as follows: I take the unit on which perceiving rests to be a circuit *from* the object stimulating the percipient organism *to* a directed response to the same object. This is a guided response and, at the human level, quite clearly, the information coming to the organism enables it to decipher features of the object. This operation is lifted to the level of perceptual judgment in which statements can be made about the external thing. Thus, I say that I *see* this tree with its branches and green leaves. Much takes place before this cognitive claim is made.

I have not the space here to go into details about this view of perceiving. I call it a direct, referential view of a realistic type. And I do think it has promise. There goes with it, quite naturally, a double-knowledge, identity theory of the mind-brain situation. That is, I think that we can know about the brain from the outside as neurology does, and also, as a subject, *participate* in its working. I am inclined to think that sensations guide the activity of the brain and that concepts are developed in the cortex for much the same function. Words like seeing and judging and valuing reflect the *achievements* of the brain-mind. I *see* this thing and *appraise* this possible act. I see no theoretical need for a dualism in these evolutionary days. I may also mention the point that such a functional view can do justice to what is plausible in the notion of "free will" and personal responsibility. We have to work out decisions for they are not predetermined for us. We do so with different degrees of wisdom. What all free men dislike is compulsion from outside. Needless to say, there are many details that I cannot take up here, such as that of neuroses. As I think you can see, there are many fascinating topics. On the whole, then, I think that the realistic, evolutionary approach in American philosophical thought was a promising one. But I must turn to British empirical philosophy.

This is symbolized by G. E. Moore and Bertrand Russell. Moore contributed the *method of analysis,* which later became increasingly linguistic. He was a meticulous thinker. Like the Americans of my generation he laid much stress upon the need to work out a satisfactory view of perceiving. He was a convinced realist but, it seemed to me that what he called sense-data—a sort of *alias* for sensations—

got in his way. He could not manage to connect up sense-data with material things. It will be recalled that I regard them as used, in perceiving, to guide the percipient and to give information about the external thing controlling it. In ordinary parlance, the thing *appears* in the sensations and this *appearing* is used to decipher the object so that we can make statements about it. That, I take it, is why science puts so much stress upon sensory verification.

Bertrand Russell sought to combine symbolic logic with Hume's stress upon sense impressions as the primary objects of our knowledge. He is a very able man and a master of prose. But, as you can see, I did not believe that he understood what I have called the circuit underlying perceiving. British philosophy was not, as a whole, as much in contact with modern psychology as American philosophy was. There are always cultural discontinuities in these matters. While there was more kinship between British and American thought than is usually the case, the divergence was there. As we shall note, German philosophy tended to be intentionally self-isolated. I suppose national pride played a part in this separation, but it is always unfortunate. It has, I am sure, affected the development of Existentialism. The Germans do not like British and American empiricism and its linkage with science. Philosophy is, for them, something apart—speculative and having a tradition and momentum of its own. Sartre came under German influence but, like a true Frenchman, kept up the Cartesian stress on reason.

But a few closing remarks on British thought. What is called *logical positivism* came from Vienna in the twenties and thirties into both England and the United States. The stress here was upon a proposal to define meaning in terms of verification. The meaning of a statement was to be in terms of the method of its verification. Since the perspective was that of Hume, the implication was what we call *phenomenalism*. The world was reducible to actual, or possible, sensations. You can see that this assumption conflicted with my kind of realism, for which sensations are informational about something other than themselves.

The logical positivists created a furor because they held that only scientific and logical statements are, in the strict sense, meaningful.

This implied that theological statements and even moral ones were meaningless. This thesis created, very naturally, much discussion. It had point on its own terms. How can you verify theological statements? On the whole, it forced theologians to reexamine their mode of argument and was, so far, healthy. I suppose that is one reason why religious thought, such as Tillich's, has turned to Existentialism. I shall make some incidental remarks on this topic in the conclusion.

I believe that I am justified in saying that logical positivism has shot its bolt. It has been qualified and qualified. First, it was realized that all sorts of statements are meaningful in their own terms. This line is being developed by the "ordinary language" movement centered at Oxford. The aim here is to clarify statements. And then the phenomenalistic aspect of positivism with its view that sensations are terminal was increasingly challenged. Don't we talk about material things? There are signs that some form of direct realism is in the making. At least, there is a renewed interest in realism. I am rather hopeful that it will take the lines I have here outlined.

iv

WHAT ABOUT DIALECTICAL MATERIALISM?

Americans should know something, *in an objective way,* about dialectical materialism. I have already pointed out that historical materialism with its stress on the economic base of society and its belief in the class struggle in the nineteenth-century form is not identical with it. Most people believe that Marx had a point in stressing the economic side of society but that he was too belligerent. Perhaps that was a matter of his temperament and of the times in which he lived. I used to teach social and political philosophy at the University of Michigan and studied these questions pretty thoroughly. I belonged to a generation of prewar liberals who were influenced by Bernard Shaw, the Webbs, and H. G. Wells. Roughly speaking, we held to what is called today a mixed economy with a public sector, the sort of thing advocated these days by Walter Lippman, Galbraith, and others. We were all for gradualism and for the democratic approach. It seems that today in the United States we hear only of the great *center* of contented persons. I do not think that Americans should be too contented. It is, after all, a changing world with an increased *tempo*.

But I must not pursue this side issue. I may remark that there is a great interest in European circles in what is called the Young Marx, whose writings have been recovered. Some Marxist revisionists anchor their thought on him. That was before he had moved to England and concentrated on economics. The industrial revolution in England in this period was pretty grim. One has only to read Charles Dickens and his novel *Hard Times* to realize that. The economy of abundance had not yet arrived.

Dialectical materialism was, in essentials, a fusion of scientific materialism and Hegelian dialectic. Hegel was *the* philosopher in Germany. He had worked out a logic of a peculiar sort. It was contrasted with traditional logic, which stressed consistency and non-contradiction. This new logic was supposed to reflect, and correspond to, a kind of inner movement in reality, a movement that went with opposition and negation. It was the belief of Hegel that he had seized upon a kind of dynamic in the nature of things. Let us recall that he was an idealist and identified Reason with Reality. He thought he had found a principle of development in Reason, a kind of inner goad leading to growth, a sort of inevitable progression. Hegel's great strength was in history. But this seemed to involve inevitable progress.

Marx and Engels took off from here, but with some aid from Feuerbach, who had queried Hegel's idealism. I think that Professor Sidney Hook is quite right in holding that Feuerbach has been too neglected a figure in the history of philosophy.

The Young Marx had long been influenced by the Enlightenment, just as our Jefferson was. In all this we must have a historical sense. Our forefathers were not too sold on Europe at this time. . . .

But let us return to dialectical materialism. I said it expresses a fusion, of an odd kind, of scientific materialism and Hegelian dialectic, with a stress on development. In his interesting essay *Materialism and Revolution,* Sartre criticizes the note of inevitable progress in Marxism. He is not so optimistic. And yet, as we shall see, he was, himself, much influenced by Hegel and speaks much of negation and negativities. His basic terms, Being-in-itself and Being-for-itself, are translations of Hegel's *An sich* and *für sich*, In-itself and For-itself.

So it should not surprise us that Engels, the companion of Marx, worked out formulae for this tensional progression of reality. He writes of the unity of opposites, of negation of the negation, of quantity at critical points changing into quality, of the unity of theory and practice. This last point has its merits.

The much-disputed question is the relevance of these formulae for concrete investigation. Of what help are they to the sciences? Seeing that they are not used in the West where science has made its greatest strides and have been challenged by physicists in the Soviet Union, it is questionable whether they contribute much. They may be said to symbolize the fact that ours is a restless universe and not static. But, as I have followed international discussion, it is becoming clear that Soviet philosophers are becoming suspicious of mere lists of examples of, for example, quantity turning into quality and want detailed investigation of all that happens when boiling water turns into steam or when a mutation occurs. It is also becoming apparent that both Polish and Soviet thinkers are stressing modern mathematical logic and ignoring dialectical logic. Engels was an able man but reflected the philosophical situation of his time. What we can admit is that he was rightly convinced that change is of the nature of things. Manchester *Laissez-faire* is not an eternal scheme of a fixed natural law. Institutions must be adjusted to new conditions and possibilities. No one who studies the succession of problems faced by Russian managers as they are confronted by the demand for quality in production can doubt this. And our consumer economy has its own problems, as Galbraith has spelled out.

But let us turn back to the materialistic aspect of dialectical materialism. It should be recognized that Marx rejected mechanical and what he called "metaphysical materialism." These, he thought, did not do justice to history, which was his forte. He even criticized

Feuerbach along this line, holding that he had returned too much to physiological materialism.

And now let us look at Lenin, who was forced to do systematic work in philosophy. This was because some of his Marxist contemporaries were being influenced by the Vienna physicist and philosopher, Ernst Mach, who was an empiricist of the Hume type. That is, he wanted to reduce material things to sensations.

. . . Lenin was convinced that this was a wrong move; and so he sought to establish realism. Now I do think that realism in theory of knowledge precedes any materialism, as a condition of it. Materialism is what we call in philosophy an *ontology,* that is, a discourse about what is. I note that Thomists always make this point. Theirs is what they call a *formal materialism,* something that goes back to Aristotle. Its weakness is, I believe, that Aristotle did not, quite naturally, have the modern conception of matter.

It will be recalled that I suggested that perceiving is directly referential and is guided by sensations, so that we, as it were, look *through* our visual field at the things we are responding to. I argued that our senses give us information that we use in deciphering things and making statements about them. Lenin did not quite work this out but he was convinced that positivism was mistaken. There can be little doubt that Lenin was an able man. . . .

But even if a realistic theory of knowledge enables us to get cognitively to an external material world, we still have the problem of working out its constitution. And here we must, I think, take evolution and novelty very seriously. The higher should not be reduced to the lower. If mind and consciousness emerge and become efficacious we should try to work out their technique. I do not believe we can understand human life otherwise. I have long advocated what I have called *levels of causality.* This outlook is called nonreductive. Every attempt is made to do justice to the novel. And, of course, the outstanding features of human life, reason, culture, the achievement of knowledge, and control, must be recognized. The results of physics, chemistry, biology, psychology, and the social sciences must find room in an inclusive perspective. Even philosophy of history has its relevance. I incline to agree with Professor Isaiah Berlin of Oxford that there has been too much impersonalism in history. The tendency is to wait, rather passively, upon mass movements.

I conclude that dialectical materialism aligns itself with science but is in the throes of evaluating the import of dialectical principles largely inherited from Hegel. Just how this will be worked out remains to be seen. It is no simple matter.

v

THE FOUNDATIONS OF EXISTENTIALISM

I am going to pass now to a consideration of the third of my trio, Existentialism. It has a vogue on the Continent, where it developed and has affected religious thinking, particularly, on this side of the Atlantic. It has a hortatory way of stressing individuality, authenticity, anxiety, and freedom. The *human condition* bulks large in its presentations. There is less concern with logic and theory of knowledge and the sciences. For these reasons, it is a sort of *genre* of its own.

Most expositions of it begin with Kierkegaard with his aversion to Hegel's impersonalism and his shift to the subjective and a leap of faith, not altogether unlike William James's "Will to Believe." Curiously enough, Nietzsche is always included, though he was critical of Christianity. I suppose what they have in common is a concern with human life. Existentialism is what the Germans call *Lebensphilosophie,* a philosophy of human life, a concern with the human situation.

I do not want to give the reader the impression that British and American philosophers are not concerned with the human condition. It is only that they want to approach it with as few untested assumptions as possible. On the whole, they are modest and want to cooperate with the relevant sciences. Where they have inherited problems, they want to clarify these as much as possible.

The interaction of empirical philosophy and of existentialism should be stimulating to both. But it will take time. What I shall try to bring out is the need for breaking down international barriers.

It will be recalled that I chose Sartre as my exemplar of Existentialism in place of Jaspers or Heidegger. That is because it is easier, on the whole, to know his assumptions. This comes, in part, from his French lucidity.

Heidegger uses the German language in a very idiomatic fashion. That may be one of his strengths on specific points. But we want to understand his general outlook. Like Sartre, he started from Husserl's descriptive method but got interested in ontology, that is, in *Sein* and *Being*. The influence of Kierkegaard is noticeable here. It is *care* that makes one ask ultimate questions. He began with a sort of descriptive analysis of human life. Time stands out in man's life for he is always looking to the future. He has no fixed essence but is a changing project. He uses tools that are at hand (*zuhanden*). In the background there grows up an awareness of things that are gradually studied by the sciences. But Heidegger does not concern himself with scientific methods.

As has frequently been pointed out, there is some resemblance between this outlook and that of pragmatism. John Dewey is said to have noted it. But Heidegger sought to make his peace with Kant and, under the guidance of anxiety, press beyond Kant's agnosticism. As nearly as I can make out, he sought a kind of intuition of *Being* in a metaphysical way. Truth is an *unveiling* of Being. This outlook involved a rejection of the correspondence theory of truth that had been dominant since Aristotle, in all but pragmatic circles. All this led Heidegger to make researches in pre-Socratic Greek philosophy and in German poetry.

All this represents an intense effort of its kind. And one must put oneself, as nearly as one can, in Heidegger's place. I think it is easier to grasp Sartre's assumptions. And I think that I know just where I diverge from him.

Jaspers is a very prolific writer. There is a good deal of wisdom in his comments on the world situation. But I am concerned here with frameworks. As I see it, Jaspers takes his point of departure from Kant and seeks to pass between the subject-object construction to Something that is All-Encompassing and thus to a mild form of theism. Now I, as a realist, do not accept the traditional notion of the correlation of subject and object. I think we make external things objects of our perceiving and thinking and learn facts about them. So, you see, I have no base for Jasper's Encompassing. The divergence begins right here. It is a matter for theory of knowledge to explore. I shall now turn to Sartre.

Sartre is a brilliant essayist and playwright. In this he belongs to the French literary tradition. I shall, however, devote myself to his great work *Being and Nothingness*. I shall try to get clear in my mind his notion of Being-in-itself and Being-for-itself. And in what sense is consciousness Nothingness? I shall likewise try to understand his middle way between realism and idealism. It will soon become apparent just where I differ from him. To put it briefly, I think of consciousness as a functional activity involving sensations and ideas, while he defines it as a translucent awareness of appearances. He is enabled in this way to define it as a Nothingness and a sort of hole in Being that breaks up any cause-effect continuity. Consciousness is, as it were, the locus of fresh starts and thus of Absolute Freedom. I, on the other hand, think of levels of causality and regard consciousness and mind as ingredients in problem-solving and new integrations. I have a high respect for the brain and hold that the individual participates in its working.

What I shall try to bring out is how Sartre manipulates his terms to get his results. Then I shall offer my alternative.

Sartre starts from Husserl, who focuses on a descriptive logic rather than on theory of knowledge. What he takes from Husserl is the thesis that consciousness is always intentional and is awareness of something other than itself. He then takes the step of seeking a pre-reflective stage that will free consciousness from self-consciousness. At this level, the self becomes an object along with other objects, and one escapes the trap of an isolated subjectivism.

It soon becomes clear that Sartre is seeking to avoid materialism—or shall we call it realism?—on the one hand, and idealism, on the other. As we saw in the study of dialectical materialism, realism is the correct epistemological expression. One can get to materialism, as an ontology, only through realism. As I pointed out, the Thomists are well aware of this requirement and have stressed a certain incompleteness in the Marxist analysis of perceiving. I have met this by showing the use made of sensations in perceiving and their informational function. I shall say something more about this situation shortly.

But let us return to Sartre. How does he endeavor to move between realism and idealism? By a sort of compromise. Cognition is, for him, an affair of intuition or givenness. And we can intuit both "material things" and the "psychical."

But can we intuit material things? Only if they are identified with *appearances*. Sartre is here caught up in the Kantian distinction between phenomena and noumenal things-in-themselves, which are unknowable. And he decides to reject the latter, quite rightly. He does not explore the view I have been defending that perceiving is a directed response in which appearings are used as cues and indications of what is appearing, so that perceiving is referentially concerned with external things that are not so much intuited as *described* on the basis of received information. Not having explored this possibility, Sartre concludes that material things are simply profiles of appearances. Any sense of transphenomenality is due to a sense of resistance and independence.

Here we have, then, *Being-in-itself*. It is a plenitude with no inside. It has no secrets. It is solid and self-identical. I suppose we can call this a form of naïve realism. It links up with Cartesian and Bergsonian matter as extension.

But, in human experience, there is a correlation and fusion. Consciousness, or the For-itself, contributes particularity, order, change, value, and instrumentality. These are, as it were, projected on the massive plenitude. Heidegger's pragmatism and stress on projects come to the front. The idea of the "material world" as a totality is a construct. So is that of the self as a psychical whole. These are *correlates;* and so we escape both materialism and idealism. It is all very ingenious. In a sense, man makes his world. But the *Subject* neither secretes it nor has the job of knowing something completely alien to it. By taking consciousness as, by its very nature, an awareness of something other than itself, Sartre seeks to lay a new foundation. Let us try to understand his manipulations and then offer our alternative.

Consciousness, or Being-for-itself, can hardly be explained in terms of Being-in-itself. It is fundamentally a Nothingness. It is not the Ego, which is a construct. It is a Nothingness that is an activity. It is a hole in Being-in-itself but a hole that has initiative. This initiative is its Freedom.

Here we have a dualism that puzzles commentators. Sometimes Sartre uses metaphors, speaking of an explosion in Being. But we have the flat opposition of massive and inert Being-in-itself and this kind of free activity. It reminds us of Bergson's vitalistic dualism with matter spatial and consciousness active and temporal.

But what is the alternative? Well, a critical type of realism, such as I have outlined, would take the physical world to be patterned and dynamic. It would consider atoms, electrons, chemical combinations, and organic evolution quite seriously. All this would involve the use of sensory information in the context of question and experimental technique. It would be knowledge-about and have its own categories. It would not be condemned to an intuited plenitude.

What could be considered the status of consciousness in this approach? Well, my suggestion is that consciousness is of the nature of an alerted use of sensations and feeling in guiding the organism's adjustment to its situation. New levels of abilities emerge. There is a rehearsal of possibilities and the need for decision. As I have already suggested, external perceiving is supplemented by introspection so that we have a double knowledge of the functioning organism. I can see no basis for a *caveat* against this evolutionary view. Consciousness is to be connected with functional activities. These are both cognitional and valuative. There are levels of causality and human agency represents the highest level we know of causality. I do not see that Sartre's schematism takes evolution into account. His theory of knowledge as an intuition of appearances, as a massive plenitude, is hardly favorable.

Thus far, I have been largely critical. And so I want to stress now my appreciation of his psychology. His emphasis on the imagination is excellent. We do have a sense of what is lacking in situations, the absence of a friend in a *café*. There are frustrations and conflicts and what Sartre calls negativities. All this strikes me as quite empirical. Man is in a situation and has to handle it as best he can. He must commit himself. And I do think that his concept of "bad faith" has point. One seeks to escape responsibility.

Again, the self has no predetermined essence. It is an integrative growth expressive of projects and situations and considered possibilities. All this is to the good. The emphasis upon it has been a contribution of existentialism. It stands out in contrast to Hegelianism but I doubt that it is so different from British and American thought on the subject. Yet new terminologies have their advantages. The idea of the *absurd* brings home man's status and situation. On the one hand, as Sartre says, it stresses a frank recognition of the kind of world we are in and, on the other hand, it draws the inevitable conclusion.

As a naturalistic humanist, I was not shocked by Sartre's atheism. On the other hand, I was somewhat skeptical of his manipulations of Being-in-itself and Being-for-itself to show that the idea of God is contradictory. I, myself, welcome the debate that is going on in theological circles but see no short out. It is an older subject than most Christians realize. And attempts to *prove* the existence of a God have not been too successful.

vi

CONCLUDING REMARKS

My summary of conclusions can be quite brief. I desiderate less cultural separation in philosophy than is the case. It is not that philosophers of different schools do not know, in a general way, where others stand. But it is the case that intensive study in formative years gives a bent and perspective to their thought that is not easily overcome. As a result, they do not see alternatives clearly.

Let me illustrate. I worked within the American realistic movement trying to avoid both Locke's representative realism and Kant's combination of phenomenon and noumenon. The desirable objective was, quite clearly, some way of uniting direct cognitive reference with processes of informational mediation. In the long run, I worked out my present notion of a from-and-to circuit that unites sensory input with its referential use. But, quite understandably, the American new realists had not grasped this possibility and had taken the position that a reform of Hume along presentational lines was the promising move. For them, the critical realists were all bogged down in Locke's schematism. To make matters worse, John Dewey transformed the new realism into a kind of experientialism that aimed at problem-solving and reconstruction.

While this was going on, a movement in Vienna developed called logical positivism, which sought to combine Hume's sensationalism with modern logic. It had a good deal of self-confidence and pro-pounded theses about meaning and verification. It took time to work these out and show whither they led. I offer this as another illustration of the difficulties confronting the young philosopher. He is con-fronted by a sort of jungle.

While all this was happening to analytic empiricism—and this is an oversimplification—dialectical materialism was confronted by the growth of science and developments in scientific method and mathe-matical logic. It was not averse to this growth but found it hard to fit its dialectical axioms into the picture. What, precisely, did these mean?

On the Continent in the meantime, the existentialist development took place. Its roots are to be found in Kierkegaard's criticism of Hegel, on the one hand, and in Nietzsche's *Lebensphilosophie*. Hus-serl also played a part in his stress on logical description. It is to be noted that Anglo-American efforts at a more adequate epistemology were rather ignored.

This is the way philosophy tends to run its course. What I have been arguing for is increased contact, more interaction. First, I tried to offer a realistic epistemology that would fit into science and a naturalistic ontology. In its way, it would undercut Kant. It is the external thing we perceive.

Here I had an alternative to Sartre's ingenious phenomenalism. Its advantage lay in the fact that it did not need to postulate two kinds of Being. Rather its task was to do justice to the emergence of mind and consciousness in the physical world. But one of the clues was to be found in the use of sensory information in the guidance of the organism. Recent theories of feedback as against one-directional causality seemed to support this approach. I had long spoken of the brain-mind. The theory was not unnatural that we have both external knowledge of the brain and inside, participative, knowledge. This way of thinking would lead to a double-knowledge, identity, theory and avoid the two kinds of Being that are on Sartre's hands. As I have suggested, mental activity is an alerted use of cues and symbols in integrative response.

As I have indicated, I have great respect for Sartre's emphasis upon freedom. He connects it with a theory of consciousness as a break in the causal nexus of Being-in-itself. I, on the other hand, regard it as tied in with a high level of causality requiring integrative adjustment. I reject causal *pre*determination and hold that there is a causal job to do that must be worked out. This is what choice and decision imply. I hold that G. E. Moore was perfectly right in stressing the modal phrase: *"He could have done otherwise."* This is categorical and reflects the causal nature of choice.

Thus I have much in common with Sartre's Existentialism and should like to see the differences debated. . . .

12

Foundations in the Philosophy and
Theology of Paul Tillich*

i

Tillich speaks alternately of Abyss and of Transcendence: . . . As
one who stresses levels of nature, I stand out against what I consider
bad [abstract *a priori* and misdirecting] traditions in philosophy
[and] against the denigration of those interwoven realities, matter
and energy, that come to flower on . . . this planet.

There is one feature of Tillich's philosophy and theology to which
I want to direct attention. It is the identification of God with Being
Itself. . . . But what if being itself turned out to be matter and
energy and that it was from this that life and intelligence emerged.
. . . What a dramatic setting the Jews achieved with covenant,
punishment, and mercy from on high. It was a mythopoeic creation
of the highest order. But where was the testing? . . . It is a gambit
that will be replayed many times.

Let me call attention to a statement by Tillich in reply to his

* These statements are a series of excerpts from "Religious Existentialism,
Secularism and Humanism," in *Reflections on American Philosophy from
Within* (South Bend, Ind.: Notre Dame Press, 1969). The title above is the
editor's. Reprinted with the permission of both the author and publisher.

critics. . . . It is on page 334 of . . . *The Theology of Paul Tillich.*
There he asserts "The unsymbolic statement which implies the necessity of religious symbolism is that God is being itself, and as such
beyond the subject-object *structure of everything that is."*

Here we find, in a nutshell, the foundation of his ontology and
of his apparently daring assertions that God does not exist, that is,
that He is beyond existence. He is the abyss, the Ground. It is for
this reason, among others, that he rejects the Thomistic proofs for
the existence of God. God is not a being among other beings. To
set up anything and give it divine status is idolatry. As we well
know, Niebuhr and others have used this schema very effectively in
their political and social rhetoric. . . .

But, from the side of philosophy, these remain the questions, What
is the basis of this ontology? How does Tillich get to Being-Itself,
to this Ground, or Abyss, to which all symbols are tied? Well, as
nearly as I can make out, he moves to it along Platonic and Augustinian lines. A modern realist is immediately suspicious, for he remem-
bers how Plato dealt with sense perception in the *Theaetetus.*
Perceptions are affairs of flux and the impermanent. They are more
nonbeing than being. To get knowledge one must turn to intellectual
apprehension of constants, such as forms. Mathematics is [consid-
ered] a better starting-point than perception.

. . . It is interesting to remember that Protestant thought turned
away from Aristotle and scholasticism to Plato and Saint Augustine.
I think that Professor Randall is right in treating Tillich as belonging to the Augustinian tradition as enlarged by German idealism.
Certainly, Tillich paid little attention to Locke and empirical developments. He was a liberal, however, and valued modern sciences
and art highly.

ii

Tillich began with a theistic ontology . . . in an Augustinian
way and fitted his epistemology to it. Kantian epistemology was to
be subordinated to it as relevant to existing things. What is primary,
then, for a knowledge terminating in basic ontology is a kind of

participation in true being, a participation that unites love and cognition. But this kind of cognition seems to work largely in terms of symbols elicited from encounters. This gives what Tillich called a "belief-ful or self-transcending realism." It is existentialist in that it is tied in with what he called ultimate concern. In its orientation, it is a theocentric religion of the Hebraic-Christian type. Now humanism is often called anthropocentric, though it does not neglect the scientific view of the world and locates man's place in it as indicated by the best knowledge obtained. I do not think that anthropocentric means selfish but what existentialists of the philosophical line would call a recognition of the human situation. Maritain seeks to unite the two orientations in what he calls integral humanism. As we have noted, Tillich identifies being with God. . . . God is the Totally Other, the Unconditioned. And yet his message tells us that he accepts us and becomes a *Thou* to our *I*. Faith must give us the courage to be.

I do not belittle the dramatic intensity of the outlook that has back of it Jewish priestly and prophetic thought and the brooding reflections of Christian saints and theologians. To me, however, it is a mythopoeic creation, a projection of thoughts and feeling in pietistic or in logically systematic form. And, as I shall indicate later, I have great admiration for many of its dialectically patterned constructions. But I want now to contrast the two paths that seem to me open, the naturalistic one and the theistic. Justice must be done to both. It is, after that, a question of personal decision.

The two philosophical entrances are epistemology and ontology; and I want to study both. . . .

The matrix of Tillich's philosophy, if I judge correctly, is a fusion of Kantianism, Platonism, and German idealism with undertones of Husserlian phenomenology. This is a heady mixture, especially when it is suffused with theological motivations. Through it shines a very honest and enlightened personality. But is it valid?

Let us now see to what it leads. Back of phenomenological analysis of essences or structure is to be found a kind of awareness of reality as a whole. Human experience contains encounters that indicate this confrontation with Being-Itself. This is the sense of the Unconditioned, which is analogous to Jaspers's transcending *Umgreifende* and clearly has a similar existentialist provenance. Tillich admits the need of a kind of epistemological "justification by faith." Let us bear in mind the point that Being-Itself, which is thus affirmed, is to blossom into a God beyond the God of Thomistic proofs. This is because it is that which underlies existing things. It is the Ground, the Abyss. It is both transcendent and an underpinning. Boehmean mysticism fuses here with Platonic transcendence to produce something analogous to Anselm's ontological argument. As is well known, there were anticipations of this in Hegelian idealism and in Hocking's version of it in America.

. . . I must confess that I am very skeptical of Tillich's bypassing the world around us, which we deal with in everyday life and which science is investigating so meticulously, to try to peer into something called Being-Itself. I cannot help feeling that Plato and Kant gave bad leads here, which Tillich is following. . . .

What, then, I am calling attention to is that Tillich makes his precarious leap of faith to Being-Itself in the setting of philosophical traditions, very much alive in the Germany of his time, but being challenged in the United States of my era. It is in this way an importation of the postwar period of what is usually called neo-orthodoxy. I met this "wave of the future," somewhat to my surprise as modernism was making its transition to humanism. I taught a course in the Philosophy of Religion at the University and had to keep familiar with religious currents. I must confess that I was rather astonished by Barth, Brunner, and Niebuhr. I tried to size them up as between liberalism and biblical fundamentalism. . . . None of them pretended to be philosophers and Barth had some derogatory remarks to make on philosophy of religion. But Tillich, as I have noted, worked on the boundary line between theology and philosophy. What I am trying to bring out is the divergence between his approach to philosophy and my own. And I think it would hold in some measure for the pragmatists, though as I have tried to show, I was not satisfied with Dewey's use of the word *experience,* and what seemed to me a shying away from epistemology. . . .

But to return to Tillich. I take his Being-Itself as an echo of

Kant's noumenal world beyond phenomenal existence. It is much the sort of thing one has in Jaspers and Heidegger, it comes to a reification of what I have called the *status of existence* apart from existing things. And then he begins to inflate it in terms of what he calls the "depth of reason" and an ontological reason that grasps and shapes reality to attain an approach to an objective Logos, all of which savors of romantic idealism. I would have some hope in his technical reason but that it is too merely instrumental and is of the same vintage as Heidegger's first stage of practical dealing with objects before he is shaken by "metaphysical dread" into his effort at intensive intuition. I would, myself, distinguish the practical and the theoretical in a less ecstatic manner and would have the theoretical play back into the practical. . . .

. . . Tillich turns his back on this kind of orientation with its stress on evidence and proceeds to inflate—I know no better word— a supposed supersensible world of Being-Itself which, as I said, must be regarded as a reification of the status of existence cut off from existing things. As we should expect, this device has its antecedents in both Plato and Kant, though formulated differently. I am convinced that it is a temptation that philosophy must live down. I have always had a respect for Aristotle's effort to do so. And I think that Thomism was a gesture in that direction but burdened too much as yet with the demands of Christian supernaturalism. . . . I suspect that St. Thomas, or his intellectual peer, if living today, would have a different perspective. . . .

. . . As I understand it, he [Tillich] holds that "ecstatic reason"—more or less a term for the emotional leap of faith—takes "sign events" as indications of significance bearing on God's plan and purpose. This is linked with man's "ultimate concern." I take it that Tillich avoids physical miracles in the fundamentalist sense and its view of the supernatural. His emphasis is on God's working in history, much as Niebuhr's is. I, myself, find it hard to see how this belief can be tested in the multiform currents of history. I would stress detailed knowledge of events and circumstances and such light as cultural anthropology, economics, and sociology would add. . . .

A certain wonderment about, a standing back and looking at

nature and life, should be encouraged. It might even take the interrogative form of the question, Why is there anything and not merely "nothingness"? But such an interrogation should not be allowed to get out of hand but be encouraged to lead to disciplined thought. It has its semantics and its logic. . . . [And] there is an alternative that should also be explored, that of the acceptance of nature.

I sense in existentialism a tendency to put assigned significance above historical fact. Even Bultmann and Niebuhr flirt with this propensity. I do not think it has reached the stage of "two truths" but may well encourage an almost unconscious duplicity.

Quite naturally, I am skeptical of the ability of "depth theology" and "encounter theology" to meet the situation arising from cultural development. This is very broadly based.

iii

Depth is, of course, a metaphor. Let us take depth psychology as an illustration. Intellectualism in psychology had too much neglected instinct, feeling, the subconscious, motivations, genesis in favor of sensations, images, and associations. Depth psychology united with psychiatry in prying out genetic factors and odd devices such as rationalization. This is a work of supplementation and was all to the good. It did not seek to escape from biological contexts.

But depth theology and encounter claims seem to me to belong to a different gambit, that of mysticism. The idea is that one can dig down to God and the supernatural. Feeling is, as in mysticism, supposed to have its epistemological disclosures. The dyad *I and Thou* comes into play.

Now, of course, I take feeling very seriously in the economy of living things. It is indicative for reaction. But I would stress its role in adjustment and appraisal rather than in cognition. The "heart" has such "indicative" reasons. Description is not enough for action. One has to note impact and bearing.

Mysticism is a complex topic, which has been much discussed. It must be studied historically and culturally. Orthodoxy has often been rather arid, as has been shown in Islam, Eastern Jewry, and in pietism. But mysticism must also be studied psychologically and epistemologically. Here *processes* and *claims* are involved. I note that critics of Encounter claims have stressed the difficulty of verification. Brought up among psychologists, I would also note studies of the "sense of presence." A child develops expectations with regard to its mother and tends to see her at any signal. We have something analogous in dreams and their apparent objectivity. . . .

What I offer in naturalistic humanism is an outlook that works within the world, stressing explanation and creative mastery. . . . I would . . . stress . . . the quality of life and . . . new levels. . . . What our author [following Schleiermacher] calls a sense of dependence, I call a sense of realities. But a sense of realities does not preclude aspiration and rational enthusiasm. As for serenity, the naturalist . . . gains it by insight and self-mastery . . . and by interest in human life.

PART II
THREE PREVIOUSLY
UNPUBLISHED CONSTRUCTIVE
ESSAYS

13
A Conflation of Philosophical Positions

i

A conflation or "blowing together" of competing philosophical positions in the contemporary world seems eminently desirable, though not easy of achievement. It would involve an active confrontation of divergent positions with some knowledge, historical and otherwise, of the reasons for such divergence.

Let me illustrate in an informal way. Neo-Thomism has a long history resting on modifications of Aristotelianism. I shall concern myself largely with two points, namely, its view of sense perception and its concept of the nature of the physical world. Dialectical materialism developed out of a rejection of Hegelianism on crucial points concerning being and knowing. It will be recalled that Hegel drew no line between thought and being. The real is the rational and the rational the real. Under the influence of Feuerbach, the Marxists turned to the consideration of the sensuous and, as the phrase is, turned Hegel upside down. Just how Hegelian dialectic was to be combined with materialism remained a problem. Science was to be accepted but "vulgar materialism" rejected. There are problems of interpretation here. I shall concern myself with the "reflection" theory of sensation as a good point of departure. Existentialism is, in many ways, dominated by German traditions in philosophy. One hears of Kant and of Hegel and of Husserl. These constitute a kind of technical framework to which are added motivations taken from Kierkegaard and Nietzsche. Naturalism is played down and largely ignored. The stress is on the existential implications of "being human." When we turn, finally, to the movements of British and American philosophy, we find these are internally more diverse. Differences stand out. On the whole, the stress is on empiricism, but this is interpreted in different ways. The range is from phenomenalism through pragmatism to varieties of realism. It is a kind of open affair reflecting developments of all sorts, such as those in symbolic logic. There is no such concentration as we find in Neo-Thomism, dialectical materialism, and existentialism.

Now it so happens that I am an evolutionary materialist and a critical realist. I am, therefore, very interested in both Neo-Thomism and dialectical materialism. Both of these positions stress epistemology and ontology. But I shall be concerned to look at them in terms of points made by British and American thinkers. Here is the conflation I would emphasize. I might put it this way: I feel most at home in British and American thought but I am convinced that it has often avoided fundamental issues. Materialism and naturalism are such issues. And here existentialism comes in in a rather curious way as concerned with man's status in the world. It varies from Sartre's odd dualism between being *en soi* and being *pour soi* to Jaspers's play with Kantianism and Heidegger's search for a new approach to Being. I am inclined to think that, unintentionally, existentialism fits in with Neo-Thomism and dialectical materialism to emphasize issues that empiricism has, in some degree, sidestepped. There are fashions here. The spectrum is rather broad. There is nothing in empiricism as such to limit it to analysis, semantics, and phenomenalism. But I think that it cannot be denied that naturalism, materialism, and realism have been pushed to one side. As I see it, existentialism should be discussed with these as alternatives in mind. And, if so, Neo-Thomism and dialectical materialism come into the picture. What is needed is a concern with basic frameworks.

My purpose in the present paper is to correlate and explore. What I want to do is to open up issues. I shall often limit myself to comments and queries. What I shall be doing, largely, is to stand back and try to work out an adequate perspective.

ii

SOME GENERAL REMARKS ON THE SCENE

Empiricism, I have argued, is not much more than a covering term. Its main thrust was against an *a priori* type of rationalism. But it early got attached to an emphasis upon sensations and images as the primary objects of cognition. Berkeley and Hume were important figures in this development. The moral was drawn by J. S. Mill when he asserted that matter was only the permanent possibility of sensation. As I see it, underlying all this was a blindness to the actual role of sensations in perceiving. The dominant setting was a kind of introspectionism developed in the context of Cartesian dualism. It was assumed that states of mind were the immediate contents given, and that perceiving could be identified with acquaintance with such contents. Out of this approach arose a doctrine of the primacy of sensation and feeling. One finds this assumption in both empiricists of the Hume-Mill tradition and in idealists such as Bradley. Bradley could not see how he could get beyond the immediacy of appearance. What he did was to transform this into universals.

It is really not surprising that, as biological pressure increased, there was an abrupt shift to behaviorism. Consciousness and introspection were simply bypassed. The unexplored *alternative* was a better analysis of perceiving to bring out the importance of response. Sensations could then be seen to play a guiding and informative role in a referential act. The old, epistemological tradition that one must start with subjective states of mind as primary and terminal could then be challenged. One need not swing over to the rather naïve objectivism of behaviorism. As objective in outlook, behaviorism, I have always held, is justified.

Kant and Hegel had intervened for philosophy and had somehow to be absorbed. Kant was closer to the physical sciences than was Hegel. Unfortunately, he did not basically reanalyze perceiving and made its import phenomenal, leaving things-in-themselves as "metaphysical" lures. Hegel erected a kind of immanent panlogism. He simply suppressed Kant's things-in-themselves. His strength was in the historical and social field. As we have already noted, the Marxists challenged his idealism and sought to be more realistic and empirical. It was not easy to improvise a new epistemology but they came up with dialectical materialism, which we shall later study.

It so happened that I began my thinking in the United States in the period of transition from so-called Anglo-American idealism to such movements as pragmatism, behaviorism, and realism. Philosophy had become very much alive. It allied itself with science in an unusual degree. Out of this alliance came a new form of naturalism, which stressed levels in nature. It is my impression that the German existentialists ignored this possibility. Certainly, Jaspers does not consider emergence but keeps to the Kantian-Newtonian framework. This is an example of *the isolationism that has plagued philosophy*. To some extent, it was here motivated by national pride. On the other hand, I am aware that philosophy had become exceedingly technical and that it took a man's full time to become well informed on work going on around him.

I can note that the same causes were at work in England. During the years before the First World War, there was much intercourse with the United States, and James and Bradley debated theses. Bosanquet read and discussed points about the American realistic movement. I had letters from both him and Bradley. In a letter to me, Bradley acknowledged that realism had its appeal but that he could not see how we could get beyond "appearances" to a material world. Now that was the basic point on which I was working. As I saw it, material things appeared in the appearances and were used in perceiving in a referential and informing way. But a change came about in what I might call the *proportionality* of British and American thought. G. E. Moore and Bertrand Russell caught attention in quite an understandable way. The rise of mathematical logic played its part. At the same time, something of the momentum of the philosophical movement in the United States lessened. I have always argued that this was due, in part, to a supposed stalemate on the part of the new realism and critical realism. However that may be, Cambridge and Oxford took over, with the younger generation of Americans more or less sitting at their feet. We began to hear of analysis, of Wittgenstein, of logical atomism, of logical positivism and, finally, of "ordinary language." I do think that much was accomplished technically, though many false leads were followed. What struck me was the neglect of epistemology as a basic concern. Moore never seemed to me to get beyond sense-data, for all his common-sense realism, and Russell remained attached to Hume.

It is within such a scene that I am going to analyze and conflate outstanding philosophical positions. I think that I can contribute most by moving back and forth and making comments. Some repetition may ensue but it will have different contexts. I begin then with a preliminary survey of positions. After that, I shall define, as adequately as I can, my outlook because I shall use it in my conflation. Then I shall explore and criticize in depth.

iii

A PRELIMINARY SURVEY

Suppose I begin with dialectical materialism. I think its history and import have been somewhat neglected. It should be noted that I am not examining historical materialism, which is concerned more with the social sciences. I had studied this latter carefully in connection with my courses at the University of Michigan on political and social philosophy. But I had neglected to examine the "reflection" theory of sensation. I suppose this neglect was natural since it has been fairly common. It is only recently that my curiosity has been aroused.

As I am beginning to see it, Engels, Lenin, and others, just because they rejected idealism, were led to connect sensations with material things as *somehow* reflecting them. I find the same motivation, oddly enough, in Neo-Thomism. Positivism made sensations —called by Mach elements—terminal, but materialism could not accept this resolution. As to Aristotle, the causal theory of perception seemed very plausible. I think it is so to reflective common sense and to science. The traditional problem was that of correlating the internal effect with the object. It must somehow be informational.

Could it not, then, be regarded as a mirroring or reflection? But how, then, get to the object from the internal effect? There was the rub. Representative realism had been analyzed and rejected. One must, somehow get to the object. Here, then, seemed to be the choice. Fall back on idealism and positivism or just affirm that sensations reflected material things. The Marxists grasped the nettle. So far as I can see, they were not able to work out the mechanism involved in referential perceiving and are usually classified as subject to the impasse set up by Berkeley. I shall discuss the problem in detail later. However, it is well to note that Russell, among others, is making much of causally reproduced patterns in camera plates and phonograph records. Not unsurprisingly, I have found V. S. Toukhtin, in Volume 3 of *Soviet Studies in Philosophy,* appealing to isomorphism and transmitted structure and the mathematics of projection along the same lines. Ryle seems to be dubious, but chiefly because he does not see how all this can be connected up with external perceiving. I have long argued that nature has been ingenious enough to complete *the circuit from the causal phase to the guidance and application phase of perceiving.* Were this not so, of what use would the sense organs be?

It is a curious fact that academic philosophy in the West has preferred subjectivism, idealism, and positivism as stances. The exception has been in scholastic philosophy with its traditions of realism and its rejection of Cartesian skepticism. It is to this that I turn next.

In studying Neo-Thomism in more detail, I have found it very logical in its context. But the context is pre-scientific. On the other hand, it has stood by common sense better than did British empiricism. It refused to reduce things to sensations. It is all rather intriguing, if not a little amusing. While Russell was sure that the belief in material things was a holdover from a primitive metaphysics, the Thomists defended the validity of the belief. Let us explore the situation. We shall see that much depends upon an adequate epistemology. I shall continue to argue that we can undercut representative realism and justify a direct realism of reference that recognizes the circuit *from* the object [to the subject and back] *to* the object and makes use of sensations as cues and guides in the operation. Within this setting, empirical concepts arise to perform a descriptive function at the human level.

As I understand it, Neo-Thomism hesitates between a direct presentationalism, or perceptionism, and representationism. Coffey is quite frank about this point in his admirable book on Epistemology. Maritain tries to work out a cognitive-identity theory in terms of intentionality. I shall examine this thesis in some detail when I take up these various positions in depth.

But let us here look at these questions historically. Thomism was rightly skeptical of the Cartesian Revolution. The idea was that Descartes had brushed perceiving aside too readily and had plunged into a kind of intuitive conceptualism. Thus arose the artificial problem of an "external world." Gilson rejects this demarche as artificial. But, of course, it forces us to analyze perceiving more carefully.

Let us look at what happened. Secular philosophers took the path either of sensations and sense-data or that of universals. William James followed Hume and Mill along the first gambit, as did Russell. Mach and the logical positivists did the same. The stress was on the "given" and immediacy. Bradley translated the *given* into an assemblage of universals. Blanshard, in our own day, follows this line and attacks substance as involving an unknowable. It is not surprising that Catholic thinkers are convinced that subjectivism and idealism have dominated modern thought.

But let us look at the other side of the picture. What are the empirical, or sensible, things about which the Thomists talk? They are the things around us that we can "see" and handle. So far, so good. But we soon find that these objects are identified with inherited Aristotelian principles, such as qualitative forms, and *hyle*. And to these is added existence as God-given. As against the empiricists and the logical positivists, the Thomists, like Aristotle, recognize dispositional properties. That is a good point; and we all know how much discussion there has been of late on the logic of solubility.

Returning to history, we all know that the revolution in science involved a stress on measurement. Mass and momentum were behavioral quantities, not qualities seen. The clock and the balance came to the front. Mathematics was developed to take account of laws of motion. It was not long before "forms" were regarded as otiose, as "barren virgins." Corporealism came to the front, as in Boyle.

Now it did not follow that the epistemology of all this was understood. It was not. But language took its course. It was held that measurement gave *facts* about the things measured. These facts could be correlated in terms of laws. But what had all this to do with perceiving? It became clear that perceiving was merely a point of departure for gathering information connected with scientific method. Nature was being interrogated.

In what sense did this development leave us with "sensible things"? People talked about primary and secondary qualities, and so forth. But the underlying question still was that of the nature of perceiving. Until that was cleared up, no satisfactory formulation was possible. [And now] I am arguing that perceiving rests on the referential use of information fed into us by the senses. Measurement and instrumentation give us added information. We must think this through.

To come back to Neo-Thomism, my feeling is that it has not sought to think this through. As I see it, it keeps outworn categories rather than revised ones. But when we follow the sophisticated ingenuities of logical positivism, we are sometimes inclined to admire Neo-Thomism. It is only too true that academic philosophy took the path of sensationalistic empiricism, Kantian phenomenalism, Hegelian rationalism. And, in my opinion, it did all this because it was not able to undercut representational realism. That was the blockage. I uttered a bitter *ha! ha!* when I read that Carnap was ignoring epistemology because he thought there was a stalemate between idealism and realism. It was to be Hamlet with Hamlet left out. Well, the Neo-Thomists never did that sort of thing. At most, Maritain makes use of it to escape the impact of science. He wants, as we shall see, to keep close to *sensible things.*

I conclude that a conflation of dialectical materialism and Neo-Thomism on the question of perceiving should be interesting. Thomistic scholars rightly say that materialism depends on a logically prior realism.

I shall not at this point say much about what is usually labeled British and American empiricism. I am not too fond of the term because it has been tied in philosophically with Hume. Because of this, I have distinguished at least three kinds of empiricism: 1) traditional British empiricism, 2) pragmatic empiricism, such as Dewey's, and 3) my own realistic empiricism. My quarrel with Dewey was that he seldom faced up to epistemological issues but fell back on the word *experience,* in a social and behavioristic setting. There was validity in Santayana's strictures.

As I see it, British and American philosophy has had the value of a forum for the discussion of issues. I have watched it shift from idealism to neo-realism to logical positivism to semanticism. There has been much technical ingenuity in it but too seldom a facing up to fundamental issues, such as scientism and materialism. I must qualify here. There has been a long tradition of naturalism in American thought and scientism has been much discussed. As for England, I would not go so far as to say that G. E. Moore's vague proclamation of a naturalistic fallacy was a disaster for it, but I do not think it was far from it. After that, axiology and an examination of criteria for value judgments became more an American affair. It was my thesis that values are not properties but conditioned *appraisals,* nothing very mysterious. These could be made to fit into the human situation.

I turn, last of all, to existentialism. Here, I take it, one must recognize the context and presuppositions of existentialist thought and the emphasis upon man's uniqueness as one who inquires. Let us look at both of these points.

Existentialist philosophizing works within the methods and ideas associated with Kant, Hegel, Kierkegaard, Nietzsche, and Husserl. Now these were able men, but is there reason to believe that they "boxed the compass"? To disregard other movements and trends was to deprive oneself of possible leads. I have already called attention to the fact that British and American thought moved away from Kant and Hegel and from idealism in general. . . . And one hardly hears of epistemology in existentialist literature. What seems most to stand out is Husserl's phenomenology. I would be prepared to argue that this *methodology needs to be supplemented by epistemology* if it is to escape the idealism into which Husserl fell in the end. Professor Farber, an expert on the subject, so argues. I take it that the horizon of the existentialists needs enlargement.

The second point was man's uniqueness. Man, alone, presses questions about his own being and about being in general. Hence, the justification of such topics as care and dread, the subjective, the import of death. These bring out the *existential* as against the impersonality of science. *Existenz* is a human condition. Man finds himself thrown into the world. He it is who must think, value, and decide.

All this is rightly regarded as a challenge to what is called *scientism*. This moves from the world to man. But man is more than a thing. He is a self, an *I* mingling with *thous* over against *its*. Now I, as a philosopher, have always been acutely aware of the import of man's claim to know, his varied appraisals, and his power of decision. Science can be completed only by means of a clarification of these activities. It, itself, depends on them. That is why I have given so much time to epistemology and axiology. Any adequate naturalism must include them. And that is why I have felt disappointed in existentialism. It has been too inclined to work within accepted frameworks. It needs confrontation with other movements and trends. Then the debate can go on.

I shall, in the main, confine myself to Sartre, Jaspers, and Heidegger. These are the challenging figures. Sartre is keen when he looks upon man in the world and sizes up the present situation. But I do not think his foundations are defensible. He is, essentially, a phenomenalist who digs beneath Husserl's Transcendental Ego to a profile of appearances given to consciousness. Here his argument against material things is much like Ayer's logical positivism. The aim is to escape somehow between idealism and realism. I fear that phenomenology, for all its virtues, encourages such a move. But I must postpone analysis until I take up the question in depth. Jaspers moves within a Kantian framework and seeks to pass beyond the phenomenal world of science to a beckoning region of the Encompassing more symbolized than known. On epistemological grounds

I reject this schematism. I take the material world to be directly perceived, and stress emergent levels in its constitution. Accordingly, justice must be done to the human and subjective along other lines. I take it that room must be found in nature for them. Heidegger's gambit is much the same. He gives an excellent description of *Dasein* and man-in-the-world moving into the future and using tools. But he turns away from nature at large to man's condition and seeks clues to Being in care, *Angst,* and death. It seems to be his hope that this approach will put him in touch with Being, as something more basic than things-as-they-are. He is led to probe pre-Platonic Greek philosophy for linguistic hints of Being's uncovering Itself, and also listens attentively at suggestions in poetry.

One can only respect the zeal and earnestness of these moves. And, of course, one can understand how their commentators follow hints almost breathlessly. It would seem the only way of escape from science and naturalism into what is called the Transcendent. But a realistic empiricist is led to ask whether scientism and modern, evolutionary naturalism are as bad as they are pictured. May it not be that the Kantian-Hegelian framework, which these thinkers take almost for granted, is actually outmoded? Such queries as these are implicated in the conflation I am undertaking.

iv

MY OWN WORKING PERSPECTIVE

I take it to be only fair to bring out explicitly the point of view I, myself, entertain. It will act as a background and, where desirable, I shall defend it. In my contribution to the two volumes, published in 1930, called *Contemporary American Philosophy,* I brought my theses together under the title *Realism, Naturalism, and Humanism.* Since then, I have been concerned to clarify the issues involved, taking account of various movements. My main purpose here will be to bring out perspectives. The above three *isms* seemed to me to interlock.

Suppose we start with humanism. This concerns the human situation. And it is not surprising that we hear of Marxist humanism, of Neo-Thomist integral humanism, of secular, naturalistic humanism, of scientific humanism, of existentialist humanism. The aim of all these movements is to do justice to the place of man in the world while acknowledging what is distinctive about him, such as morality, cognitive achievement, and artistic endeavor. As I saw it, this involved a naturalistic theory of values or, let us say, appraisals. I approached these in an evolutionary, and historical, fashion. Man learned to set up standards and to improve them by noting consequences in a more or less reflective way. Hence, I was neither an absolutist nor a relativist of the skeptical sort. It was a matter of growth, of learning the hard way, of finding out what was most satisfactory. There was no easy way to progress. Society and the individual interacted in complex fashion.

The emphases could be quite different. Maritain sought an integration of humanism with theism. The Marxist stressed the social, economic setting. I was surprised to find Sartre looking upon God as the locus of "absolute values" and dropping back upon rather arbitrary commitments of lonely selves for value decisions. On the whole, I thought Heidegger's stress upon "being-with" truer to the facts. As we shall see, there is a tendency toward solipsism in Sartre's foundation. The job of naturalistic humanism is to see man in the world with his human capacities and achievements. It followed that the naturalism I would embrace would be along the lines of emergence. It strikes me that much recent stress upon "absurdity" in nature is rather rhetorical. *Sartre's sharp dualism,** however, gives it point.

I have the impression that many Continental thinkers do not take the import of evolution seriously. Perhaps, this is, in a measure, due to the Kantian, Hegelian framework within which they move. They tend to reject naturalism as akin to scientism, and they make much of the possibility of some kind of vertical transcendence. This is obvious in Jaspers, and it clearly motivates Heidegger's search for Being. Philosophy must be the gateway to this kind of unveiling.

The working out of an adequate realism was clearly involved in

---

* Italics added.

my quest. One had to break through the barriers set by Lockean representation and Kantian things-in-themselves. How could a direct realism be framed, which made use of sensations but did not make them terminal as Berkeley, Hume, and Mill did? The answer gradually came to me as I studied the whole mechanism of perceiving. The traditional causal approach took just one phase of the operation. Biologically, nature was more ingenious. The information fed into the organism had the function of guiding it. That is, sensations were used in the responsive, referential act. With the cortex, man went on from guidance to language and description. But concepts secured application and aboutness within the basic, referential framework.

Thus I linked up epistemology with ontology. I found that *metaphysics* had become a "dirty" word associated with an endeavor *to go beyond experience*. It was tied in with Kant's things-in-themselves and German, speculative philosophy. Scientists when they move into philosophy usually, I have found, go off at half cock. It is seldom that they see the whole picture.

This is only a brief outline of my working perspective. But it will, I think, serve my purpose. I shall now go on to explorations in [more] depth of competing positions. I shall first take up what is usually called the empirical tradition in its variations. This is not an altogether satisfactory label, but it will do. What I shall be concerned with are the trends and interactions in British and American thought. As Bosanquet once phrased it, there has been the meeting of extremes. I recognize to the full that philosophy is a sort of continuing dialogue, and that new topics are introduced. Just at present the stress is on language. My own concern has been with the extra-linguistic and with certain perennial problems. But I see no conflict. It is all to the good if language throws light on these.

I shall begin with the British scene and then pass to the American. I believe that the Americans showed a good deal of initiative in developing pragmatism, realism, and naturalism. But then they seemed to have lost their momentum. In any case, analysis, Viennese positivism, and the role of language attracted attention. First Cambridge and then Oxford came to the front. Perhaps G. E. Moore and analysis helped to make the transition. Analysis was an attractive term, though I had my reservations. At times, it appeared that one did not need to work for a defensible epistemology and ontology to carry on. With all due respect to the present emphases of Oxford "ordinary language," I shall argue that more is needed. I can hardly confront dialectical materialism, Neo-Thomism, and existentialism on this base alone. So I shall supplement it with ideas taken from American realism and naturalism.

v

THE EMPIRICAL TRADITION

I have already put my reservations on the use of the term *empirical*. The stress is on the experiential foundation of ideas. But it does not exclude concern for logic and mathematics. J. S. Mill gave some bad leads at this point in the direction of what came to be called psychologism. But that belongs to history.

Toward the end of the nineteenth century, Anglo-American idealism was in the ascendent in both England and the United States. Kant and Hegel were points of departure. But there were memories of Berkeley, Hume, and Mill. In the United States, William James cut back to these through Bain. He helped to inaugurate a stress on perceptual experience, which brought him into touch with Bergson and Mach. Out of this grew his *radical empiricism,* so influential in the development of American new realism.

In England, I judge that this move influenced Russell more than it did G. E. Moore. Out of it grew his neutral monism with its attempt to break down the barriers between mind and matter.

It must not be forgotten that F. H. Bradley stressed immediate experience as the starting-point. In a letter to me [I have already mentioned] about my book *Critical Realism* (1916), he stated that he saw many points in favor of realism but could not see how one got beyond *appearances*. Let us bear this question in mind.

As I recall it, one of the first moves in England was in the direction of personal idealism. The aim here was to do justice to human personality. It was a milder and less religiously motivated move than Kierkegaard's earlier one, of which we hear so much in existentialism.

Stout was the only one of the personal idealists with whom I had any contact. In accepting an article of mine for *Mind,* he remarked that his view of perception was similar to mine. I was then stressing the distinction between the content of perception and the object of perception. I understand that he, himself, was being influenced by Brentano's stress on intentionalism, a gambit of medieval, Aristotelian origin that we shall find again in the *esse intentionale* of Neo-Thomism.

There is some point in recalling that Mill worried over the question of how to deal with our belief in external things and tried to solve it by the association of ideas, reducing matter to the permanent possibility of sensations. One should in this connection examine the efforts made by Condillac, Destutt de Tracy, and Cabanis in France to work out the passage from sensations to the belief in things. The stress here was on touch and resistance. When we touch our bodies we have a double sensory experience, which we do not have when we touch other things. Thus a line of demarcation arises. There is point in this. But I do think that a closer examination of perceiving shows us that we do not first observe our sensations in a terminal way and then pass to concern with objects but that we are using our sensations as cues and guides in response. I prefer to speak of reference rather than of intention. And I am quite willing to admit that genetic growth plays its part. There is much learning at work in perceiving. All I would stress is the importance of *directed response* as *completing the traditional causal emphasis.* This framework is important. Otherwise, we have Reid's common-sense intuition of things or an appeal to intentionality. If one begins with a kind of immediate knowledge of mental states (with sensations), how can one pass to the perceiving of external things? A shift of perspective is needed.

But, to come back to the British development, Russell sought first to improve upon Hume by means of new logical techniques. That is, he had the idea of the logical construction of material things out of sensations and sensibilia. This move had its vogue and, in his first period, Carnap followed it. G. E. Moore stressed common sense but could not get sense-data into touch with external things. S. Alexander was influenced by Holt and the new realists in his epistemology. However, with Lloyd Morgan, he sought, on the ontological side, to work out the idea of emergence.

Shortly after this, interest swung to the pronouncements of Wittgenstein's *Tractatus*. Here the stress was not on perceiving but on truth-tables, logical constants, the nature of logic, and language. One must remember that logical positivism hit England about the same time. Within this context, there developed acuity of reasoning. But, as I contemplated it from afar, there was no great interest in epistemology and ontology.

It should be becoming evident that I would approach the so-called problem of the external world in a quite different fashion from the Cartesian and the Berkeley one. I see no good reason to begin with subjectivism and a complex of sensations. Perceiving strikes me as a guided referential activity tied in with response in such a way that we make things our objects and proceed to think and decipher them in terms of indications offered by our sensations. That is, the sensations have a function in perceiving; and perceiving is, from the first, concerned with the things around us. In this setting, the points made by Condillac and De Tracy are quite relevant. Touch and resistance inform response. Even walking toward an object we are "looking at" deepens our awareness of objectivity. The point to bear in mind is that we do not first begin with a contemplation of states of mind. We are, from the beginning, agents in the world. The job of reflection is to clarify the situation.

The reader can understand why I am a little puzzled by Wittgenstein. His logic is good but I can see no adequate grounds for his mysticism. Linguistically, we move back and forth between perceiving and our propositional thought. If need be, we can resort to the technique of meta-linguistics.

We shall find it interesting to study the Neo-Thomist view of perceiving. It rejects the Cartesian move and the sensory subjectivism into which Locke, Berkeley, and Mill got. This, it holds, is the root of modern idealism. But I shall argue that it was enmeshed in the Aristotelian causal approach to sense perception and got back to the world somewhat surreptitiously. It may be well to remark that dialectical materialism solved the problem of perceiving more by *fiat* than by analysis. But it is to its credit that it did not take the shortcut of Berkeley, Hume, Mill, and Russell. I believe that I can fit its "reflection theory" into my analysis of the mechanism of perceiving as a from-and-to operation. As for existentialism, I can see no epistemological advance over Kant. The context of its thought is largely an amalgamation of Hegel and Husserl. Nevertheless, there are accents in it that are very modern. My query will be whether the *existential* cannot find place in an evolutionary naturalism that recognizes man's uniqueness. I shall have something to say in this connection about *transcendence.* Horizontal transcendence can, I take it, be easily accounted for, but I am very skeptical of any *vertical* transcendence, of any Being beyond being, of which Tillich so glibly speaks.

This may be the place to introduce the question why British philosophers turned their backs on materialism. Marxists consider England the sponsoring home of modern materialism. Of course, Hobbes does stand out. It was then France's turn. But I think that it must be recognized that scientists, turned philosophers, spoke for materialism in the nineteenth century, men like Buchner and Haeckel. I always rather admired Tyndall and his famous Belfast Address. I understand that Huxley used to chaff him. And Huxley's stand was, undoubtedly, influential. He did not see how one could meet the arguments of Berkeley and Hume. Yet, *as a scientist,* he was a realist and an epiphenomenalist.

It would seem that philosophy was a somewhat esoteric affair dominated by professors and Churchmen. And it had come to work within empiricist and idealist assumptions. I take it that James Ward, in his book *Naturalism and Agnosticism,* drew the lines pretty well. I wrestled with this book in my early days.

What is the situation now? In his introduction to Lange's classic book, Russell points to behaviorism as akin to materialism. And there are indications that behaviorism is having its appeal to British philosophers. What will come of it remains to be seen. I have always regarded it as a methodological program. But I cannot here go into the situation in psychology. I merely suggest that a good epistemology might help.

So much for British empiricism. It will be recalled that I took this term as largely a label. Had I more space, I should like to take up Cook Wilson and Prichard. I understand that the former held that *appearances* are not entities in their own right but the appearings of objects. I would agree, but I can find in his writings no clear theory of how this comes about. What is the context that leads us to regard sensations as informative of external things, that is, as appearings? . . . [A]bout Prichard, as I understand him, he makes the move of saying that we take our sensations to be physical bodies. We "see" a colored extension and take it to be a material thing. Thus there is a kind of identification. But, surely this does not explain how we come to have the dominating belief in a material thing. As I see it, this belief develops within the setting of an agential activity of give-and-take outlined by guided response. In such a context, interpretative meanings of a categorial type grow up. Russell was quite wrong in discarding these as primitive metaphysics. But what can one do if one starts with a kind of inspectional subjectivism? While we perceive external things we never literally inspect them.* Here I distinguish between natural realism and naïve realism. Natural realism signifies the objective import of perceiving and its foundation, while naïve realism is the belief that one can inspect the very surface of things. As we shall see, American new realism approached naïve realism because it held that indirect, representative realism was the sole alternative. The critical realists were exploring the possibility of a breakthrough to a new type of direct realism.

I turn now very briefly to the American development of empiricism, after which I shall note the semi-fusion of British and American thought.

Scotch common sense was gradually replaced by Kant and Hegel in the form of what came to be called Anglo-American idealism. This varied from what was called objective idealism to absolute

---

* In the sense that we inspect introspectively, as in inspecting memory images, the vividness of sensations, etc.

idealism. Creighton of Cornell may be taken to typify the first, while Royce represented the latter. Bradley and Bosanquet had turned away from epistemology, but Royce tackled it and sought to show the absurdity of realism by definition. If things are completely independent of mind how can they be known? Hence he took the line of "inner meaning" versus "external meaning." The external meaning simply continues the internal meaning. Royce was a very ingenious and able man.

But pragmatism was rising with its stress on time and reconstruction. Workableness was both the test and the meaning of truth. It was my impression that the pragmatists ignored epistemology, much as the idealists had. How could correspondence be tested?

C. S. Peirce, William James, and John Dewey, in succession, developed American pragmatism. C. S. Peirce was a trained mathematician and scientist who made contributions to the development of modern logic. It was not until his *Collected Papers* were published that the range of his thought was fully appreciated. Books on him and essays are coming out in a steady stream. I regret that I did not know more about him while I was working out my own position. William James moved largely within a psychological context, often shocking Peirce. He gradually moved to the position called "radical empiricism," a kind of contextualism within experience. It was not so different from the position of Ernst Mach. I have the feeling that Mill's reduction of matter to mere possibility of sensations along with the dilemmas confronting Kant's things-in-themselves motivated this gambit. Dewey moved between James and Peirce toward instrumentalism and problem-solving.

All this resulted in a new kind of empiricism, which stressed experimentation and reconstruction. I am inclined to call it *pragmatic empiricism.*

But to some men coming on the stage, neither idealism nor pragmatism seemed satisfactory. Why not investigate realism? . . . [Like F. H. Bradley, philosophers generally could see no way of getting beyond the immediacy of appearance.] Here was a challenge. We have already noted that scholastic philosophy blames Descartes for both idealism and subjectivism and the rise of the problem of an external world. We shall study their treatment of perceiving in another section. It will also be interesting to see whether we can straighten out dialectical materialism with its "reflection" theory of sensations. I think it can be done in terms of critical realism with its responsive completion of the act of perceiving.

. . . [T]o come now to the new realists, they followed hints in James's radical empiricism. Why not reject out-of-hand the subjectivistic complication? Why not start with the apparent fact that we see things and respond to them behaviorally? Even Dewey and Woodbridge warned against the danger involved in starting with a preliminary cognition of mental states. How could one then get beyond them? The thing to do was to reform Hume and change his impressions into external objects. This was, of course, in line with the "little black box" stage of behaviorism. But, alas! it was hard to account for error and illusions. In England, S. Alexander wrestled with this difficulty. Now I always thought that R. B. Perry was good in his formal attacks on idealisms but was less strong in his construction. Montague was hardly fair in his exposition of critical realism, holding that it was enmeshed in the mistakes of Locke and Kant. I found this thesis repeated *ad nauseam*. All that it meant was that Montague could see no new approach. Well, he would not have been a presentational realist if he had been able to [envisage a more viable alternative].

I cannot here go into the divergencies among the critical realists. I think they all wanted some new kind of direct realism that would avoid the two-step operation of Locke, yet would give room for subjective items. So far as I can make out, Santayana attracted most attention with his scheme of essences at once intuited and embodied. I worked on different lines, as has, surely, been noted: the idea was that sensations are not terminal in perceiving but play a guiding and informative role in a directed act of response. Thinking is, as Professor Ryle says, polymorphous and begins with a kind of deciphering of cues and indications. In human perceiving, concepts, achieved by such learning, are applied; they are *about* the object perceived. It all becomes linguistically automatic. This analysis undercuts Locke and Kant. It avoids both presentationalism and representationalism. But it also explains why we first tend to be naïve realists or, as Prichard had it, take a colored extension to be a material thing. I do not see how nature could have worked out the use of the sense organs otherwise. They had to supply information and this had to be selectively used. What I call the from-and-to mechanism of perceiving follows.

Let us call this *realistic empiricism*. I take it that *scientific empiricism* develops within this framework by means of techniques of measurement and instrumentation. We interrogate nature and get messages from her. Thus we gain facts about constituents, which we call photons, electrons, atoms, molecules, and so on. Mankind should be very proud of this achievement. But, following very carefully the history of science, I do not find any great mystery in it.

I shall say little about the rise and decline of logical positivism because it is so well documented. It made its technical contributions along the lines of meta-language. But, if my argument is correct, its phenomenalistic stance could not be maintained. I infer that Maritain is leaning on a broken reed when he seeks to reject the microscopic texture of the physical world in favor of "sensible things." I shall have something to say about that later. But, then, even Dewey and Whitehead were somewhat puzzled by the question of the status of "scientific objects." In what sense are they observable?

vi

DIALECTICAL MATERIALISM

As Marxists point out, Great Britain was the starting-point of modern materialism. In fundamentals, Hobbes was a materialist and Locke sufficiently so to help to move French thought in that direction. Hence came La Mettrie, Condillac, Holbach, and Diderot. But while this was going on on the Continent, Berkeley started his Counterrevolution. He feared that Sir Isaac Newton, despite his piety, had brought matter to the fore. After Berkeley came Hume with his skepticism and phenomenalism. Mill reduced matter to the possibility of sensation and Huxley adopted Hume. Soon Anglo-American idealism was in full swing. Kant and Hegel had invaded the tight little island with their complexities and secrets.

It was Marx who gave new vitality to materialism. He had carefully studied Democritus and Epicurus for the Ancient world while listening to Hegel. Hegel had rather displaced Kant to produce a panlogism in his ontology and an institutional ethics in place of the categorical imperative. It is interesting to observe that Kantianism has always been suspect by Marxists. Plekhanov called Kant that "dangerous old man." There is reason to believe that it was Plekhanov who first spoke of dialectical materialism. This was in 1891 in an essay on Hegel. As I understand it, Marx criticized the materialism of the past as not doing justice to change and history, as not dialectical enough. This comes out in his *Theses on Feuerbach,* which we shall consider.

In what follows I am first going to take up materialism as an ontology and show that it involves a realistic epistemology. After this we can note peculiarities of terminology. For instance, Marxists do not like the term *metaphysics,* any more than do the positivists. It is associated with the notion of something transcendent and out of reach. It must be recalled that Hegel drew no line between thought and being. The real is the rational and the rational is the real. What Marx and Engels did was to turn Hegel upside down, to reorient his system. By so doing, they came out with a naturalism. But, I take it, they had no intention of returning to Kant's things-in-themselves or to Cartesian dualism. The result was a kind of immanentism along materialistic lines. Here they had to improvise. Brain and thought had to be brought together and perceiving had somehow to reach the external world. But these were perennial questions, which Hegel had sidestepped. I very well remember that one of my own objections to Anglo-American idealism turned on its neglect of epistemology.

Let us look at the Marxist development historically. It is generally acknowledged that Feuerbach took the first step away from Hegelian idealism. As against the dominantly abstract thought of Hegel with its impersonality he emphasized what he called sensuous thinking.

His epistemology is not clear but it seems that his assumption was that in feeling and sensation we are in touch with reality. To quote: "Truth, reality, sensibility are identical. Only sensible being is a true, a real being; only sensibility is truth and reality." Now this was very vague, indeed, and would hardly do. What Feuerbach proceeded to do was to attack religion as resting on alienation and projection. This had its lasting effect. He ended as a physiological materialist asserting that man is what he eats.

It is historically interesting to contrast this revolt from Hegel with Kierkegaard's. I shall touch upon this in connection with German existentialism.

Now Marx was concerned with history, politics, and economics. He wanted guidelines in this setting and Feuerbach's sensationalism and physiological anthropology did not reach into these fields. Hence his famous theses. In these he emphasized practical activity and history. There is more than a touch of Pragmatism in his approach. Man must prove the truth in practice. The task is to change the world and not merely to interpret it.

After this period on which so much light has been thrown by the publishing of his manuscripts, Marx devoted his energies to politics and economics. No doubt he talked over philosophical points with Engels. But it is to Engels that one must turn in the main. There are indications that both moved to a detheologized Spinoza for suggestions.

It is not surprising that the problem of the relation of thinking to being began to stand out. In an increasingly scientific age perceiving comes to the fore. What is the role of sensations? May not sensations reflect, or mirror, the material things in the external world? This is the reflection theory of perceiving. And it is clearly connected with the causal approach, which goes back to Aristotle. But it is no longer expressed in terms of *forms*. The metaphors used are now more mechanical than aesthetic.

It so happened that, at the end of the nineteenth century and the beginning of the twentieth, interest in philosophical issues had increased. There was the rise of Neo-Kantianism and of what was called empirio-criticism. Mach and Avenarius, among others, had come to the front. Lenin found that Russian Marxists had been impressed by these developments and undertook to examine the issues. The result was his *Materialism and Empirio-Criticism*. I knew little of this at the time. But in 1909 at Heidelberg I encountered a young Oxford philosopher who insisted that I read Avenarius. Returning to Michigan, I went over this literature with Pearson and James Ward for good measure. I had already begun to move in the direction of a critical realism, and my book *Critical Realism* eventuated.

Lenin was, of course, sold on the "reflection" approach. He was convinced that it fitted in with common sense and science in a way that positivism and empirio-criticism did not. But I do not believe he fully appreciated the difficulties. These, as we have indicated, concern 1) direct reference to material things, and 2) the avoidance of traditional representationalism. The perennial problem from Locke on was to do justice to ideas and yet give them a functional, cognitive role. In the course of time I have reanalyzed perceiving to bring in responsive reference to complete the stimulus phase, which has hitherto dominated philosophical thought. From this more complete point of view, we can understand how sensations and ideas function *within* the outwardly directed act of perceiving in the way of guidance and informational cues. In this fashion we move between a simple presentationalism and a suspended representationalism. Nature has been cleverer than the philosophers. And, of course, this enlarged perspective fits in with the role of our sensory equipment in adjusting us to the world around us. We do not need to be dogmatic behaviorists to recognize the logic of the situation. I recognize that the human percipient participates in this referential and deciphering activity. When he uses the pronoun "I," he is both social and objective and personal. . . .

Now, as I read Lenin, he starts from things and moves to sensations as reflecting them. But he does not work out how we get to things in the first place. He is simply convinced that idealists and positivists have made the wrong move. There I think he was right. But the technical result is that he ends with sensations as terminal objects and lands in representationalism. As Passmore puts it: "Berkeley's criticism has to be answered, that if matter is not itself a sensation but only that which gives rise to sensation, we can have no evidence that there is such a thing. Berkeley, Engels admits, is hard to beat by mere argumentation."[2] As I recall it, Diderot made much the same remark. And, in our own day, Russell falls back on Berkeley and Hume while, earlier, F. H. Bradley could not see how we could pass beyond appearances. But, appealing to a better analysis of perceiving, one can see that it involves the use of sensations as informational about what is stimulating us and what we are responding to. Knowing is not an apprehending, as Cook Wilson thought, but a mediated disclosure, an achievement based on sensory appearings. Material things are not presented for inspection (as naïve realists believe) but set off the activities of reference and decipherment. They control response and give information. How else could it have been done?

In a way, then, I commend Feuerbach, Marx, Engels, and Lenin for sticking to their realistic convictions. What was needed further was a better understanding of the from-and-to circuit involved in perceiving. Realistic conviction was not enough. It had to face the gamut of subjectivism, terminal ideas, and things-in-themselves. None of this was silly. There was simply no breakthrough to another perspective. Men like Carnap and Ayer did their best within their assumptions. I have tried to show that these were wrong.

Now I do think that Marxists should distinguish more sharply between realism, an epistemological stance, and materialism, an ontological one. Terminology tends to be inherited. It is interesting that, like the positivists, they dislike what they call "metaphysical thinking." Here we have, in part, an inheritance from Kant and Hegel. But materialism is an ontology that permits the distinction, emphasized by Engels, between thought as a human activity and being or *what is*. Materialism is an old ontology and should not be looked at askance. I recognize the value of semantics and linguistic philosophy,

2. John Passmore, *A Hundred Years of Philosophy* (London: Duckworth, 1957), p. 45.

but science and the extra-linguistic must be studied as well. One final point. Materialism must take evolution and novelty seriously. What a remarkable thing is man.

vii

A few words, in conclusion, about *dialectic*. It is an old term that goes back to the Greeks and there came to be connected with a probing discourse carried on by question and answer. In modern times, it was used by Kant in his exploration of the antinomies of space and time. Hegel systematized it as a logical technique of thesis, antithesis, and synthesis. This was readily formalized as a pattern of thought. One can speak of the minimum use of the term *dialectic* as a term for change through conflict and opposition. Ideas of tension and polarity would be included. I suppose that, in economics, *laissez-faire* would constitute a differing outlook. This accepted a kind of drift. As nearly as I can make out, Marx wanted to stress history and activity. Probably he even thought that there was immanent direction in history, a kind of teleology.

One of the dangers of the time was speculative *Naturphilosophie*. I do not think Engels was immune to this. Why should he have been? I do not think the Marxists are always historically minded enough. Looking at Lenin, *I find he emphasizes interconnections and complexities.* One must press beyond vulgar and any simple kind of mechanical materialism.

. . . I am not here concerned with historical materialism and class conflict. I just want to get the epistemological framework clear. As I see it, Lenin starts from things and moves to sensations, as their "reflection." It is his opinion that the idealists and positivists commence with ideas and cannot get to things. There is point to this latter. But by what right does he start from things? He seems left to the appeal to practice. That does not, of course, satisfy analysts. They classify him under the caption of representative realism. Sensations and concepts are in our heads. If this is true, what is their function? Do they connect up with a referential operation? I would so argue. And, if so, the reflection theory can be supplemented to escape the usual objections. It will be interesting to follow attempts by Soviet thinkers to connect up reflection with isomorphism, transmitted patterns, and projection. I have already referred to efforts along that line made by V. S. Toukhin. In his causal approach to perception, Russell made similar suggestions. The gap lay in the return to the external world. It is this gap that I have sought to fill, taking a hint from nature. A little more animal psychology is suggestive—for instance, the way bats avoid obstacles, the way vipers locate their prey at night by means of heat-sensitive organs, the way dolphins achieve distance location of fish. In all this there is the from-and-to circuit. I suspect that overstress on introspection robbed philosophers of this cue.

I . . . pass to an examination of Neo-Thomism. It has come to intrigue me as a form of realism that often calls itself critical realism. I notice that both Maritain and Wetter use this terminology. I shall now explore the divergence between what they mean by critical realism and what I mean.

viii

NEO-THOMISM

Neo-Thomism is a development of Aristotelianism in its epistemology. Its ontology and metaphysics have a theistic dimension resting on the supposition of the contingency of creaturely existence. For Aristotle, God is simply the Prime Mover. I shall concern myself here chiefly with epistemology but, as a naturalist, will allow myself to consider the question whether nature needs a Ground. Is there anything about it that points beyond it?

We could say that Maritain is a critical realist in the sense that he tries to make explicit what is implicit in Thomism. Gilson is a little more conservative. But I take it that most neo-scholastics admit that the emphasis on epistemology is a modern development associated with Descartes and the rise of modern science. The point they make is that Cartesianism oriented philosophy in the direction of subjectivism and idealism. In Gilson's opinion, the whole problem of an external world is artificial. But, of course, one is still left with the problem of perceiving. *How* do we perceive this external world we accept? . . .

Maritain's first thesis, as presented in his book *The Degrees of Knowledge,* turns on an appeal to immateriality. He holds that there is a rigorous correspondence between knowledge and immateriality. A being is knowledgeable in the measure of its immateriality. Why is this? Because to know is to *become* another thing than oneself. I would myself query this dictum. But it is a good point of departure. Maritain holds that the knower, while keeping its own nature intact, becomes the known itself and is identified with it. But this involves two kinds of existence. The known is *in* the knower in the form of *esse intentionale,* intentional being. This kind of *esse* disengages the thing-object from its natural limits so that it comes to exist in the soul by another existence than its own. And the soul is, or becomes, the thing according to another existence than its own. What, then, is the means to the *union* of the knower and the known? It is the whole world of intrapsychic, immaterial *forms,* which in the soul are like the deputies of the object and which the Ancients called similitudes or *species.* Maritain suggests the term *presentative form* for these, but warns that the notion should be that of *making present* rather than presenting. This, I take it, goes with the idea of union.

It is to be noted that Maritain accounts for errors of sense in a causal way. The form, or sensible quality, is perceived after *it* attains the sense, that is, after transmission through the internal, or external, medium.

Let me comment on this theory and its terms. It is evident that it must grapple with the difficulties of representative realism. That it does so is, in my opinion, to its credit. I have always been persuaded that both British empiricism and Kantianism took the wrong turning in making sensations terminal and seeking to construct things out of them. I could only shrug my shoulders at Russell's ingenuities in logical construction and at Carnap's assumption that the battle between idealism and realism was a stalemate to be ignored. I think he learned the hard way. But, to come back to Maritain, the question, as I see it, is whether *information* about the thing-object can be transmitted to the percipient *in a scientifically understandable way* and there be referentially used. Certainly, information theory is being developed and explored these days. As we saw, something of this was dawning on Russell along causal lines but he did not appreciate the responsive completion in perceiving. He still thought in terms of *percepts* rather than in terms of perceiving. I pointed out that the dialectical materialists were turning their attention to the base of their "reflection" postulate.

One point at issue is whether *knowledge-about* demands the kind of identity, or union, Maritain assumes. I am inclined to hold that nature, in the sense organs, developed receptors able to pick up patterned stimuli and transmit them to the brain. Just how the brain achieved the various sensations correlated with these stimuli and used them as cues to response remains to be seen. Science will do the main work here with its techniques and delicate, electrical instruments. But philosophy can aid in helping to clarify the framework. It seems to me that knowledge is too general a term. We must explore such ideas as information, facts about, iconic signs, indications. Knowledge is an achievement worked up to at the level of concepts and language.

What I feel, then, is that Maritain depends too much on the Aristotelian outlook and terminology. He thinks in terms of "forms" able to break loose from *"hyle."* They are immaterial in this contrast sense and so come to constitute the *esse intentionale* in the soul. Thus knowledge rests on an identity. This is a brave attempt, but I am persuaded that nature had to work it out by stages. Take, for example, the evolution from the eye as a pigment spot to the camera eye.

It would seem that man's camera eye works in with adjusted movement and discrimination. There is, thus, a kind of spelling out, or decipherment, making use of transmitted cues or indications. I fear that I agree with Bacon that "forms" are barren virgins. One other point. I do not think we can get to "immaterialism" so easily. I recognize that the status of sensations in the brain must be worked out. I have given much thought to the question, and I have long argued that we have a double knowledge of the brain: 1) that obtained by external perceiving, extended by scientific technique, and 2) that of participation or acquaintance. Language theorists are just getting to this kind of problem. When I say "I have a pain," what do I have in mind?

Returning to Maritain, I suggest that his assumption that to know a thing is to become that thing misleads him. I would argue for something short of this, for controlled, informational disclosure. And to achieve this I find no need for transmitted *forms*. The way in which the camera eye gathers light to a focus suggests how nature works to get guidance and information. Of course, there are a multitude of problems as to how the brain works. But, fortunately it does work and we use our visual field to explore our world.

I am not one of those who want to project sensory *qualia* into the world. I am concerned with their role in perceiving. Science took the path of measuring and weighing and used sensory cues as guides. But I cannot here enter into questions of the methodology of science. For this section, it is important to note that Maritain wants to keep the qualitative outlook of sense perception as basic for any *philosophy of nature* and is content to take the logical positivisitic defense of phenomenalism as justified for science. Here are strange bedfellows. . . .

Let me turn finally to Coffey. His work on *Epistemology* strikes me as a very scholarly product. He declares that scholastics have been divided between two views, perceptionism, which regards sense perception as a process directly intuitive of external reality, and mediate, or representative, sense perception, which holds the external thing mirrored, or represented, in a mental datum from which, by a process *analogous to inference,* one would attain knowledge of the external reality.

It was the first view that was generally held by medieval scholastics. But, in so doing, they held that the *sensible species* operated but was not that which was perceived.

Now I want to give honor where it is due. I agree that Cartesianism and modern philosophy in general turned away from sense perception too abruptly. I suppose that was, in part, due to the impact of the new outlook on the world. But I have not the space here to go into Cartesianism. I want to return for a moment to Russell. It is clear that, in his latest work, he gave up any construction of the world in terms of sensations and sensibilia—as Carnap also did—and, taking his stand on physics, argued for some *quasi*-inference from sensations to the external world or, at least for vindicable postulates. His position here seems to me quite similar to that of scholastic representationalism, which argues for a process analogous to inference. And, as we saw, the dialectical materialists were in the same boat and were usually accused of representative realism.

What is the answer? I have argued for a reanalysis of perceiving that would bring in the whole circuit, from the object to the [subject and back to the] object, that is, stimulus and guided response. The role of sensations is *within* this operation. Hence the dominant pole of perceiving is referential. I doubt that this feature should be regarded as analogous to inference, though I do think that inference may supplement it. I remember that shortly after the *Essays in Critical Realism* came out, Russell was in Ann Arbor to expound his idea of the logical construction of material things out of sensations and sensibilia and that I advanced the idea of reference in perceiving to him. I fear that his mind was rather closed; it would have required a new orientation. When he thought of sense perception his mind dwelt on the supplementation of sensations by images and memories.

But, to return to Neo-Thomism, when one reads Maritain one recognizes that he thinks the world in terms of Aristotelian "metaphysical principles" plus a permeating existence contributed by God. That, I take it, is not the way we generally think of it today. Mass, momentum, chemical make-up stand out in our thoughts of physical things. In still more penetrative views we pass to electrons and quanta. It can rightly be asked, What is the existential status of these so-called scientific objects? I suppose we should think of them in terms of the contexts in which they are located and tested. Yet I find myself passing to them from perceptually observable material things. It is relevant, I take it, that I do not tend to use the expression *sensible things,* for that could only mean things as sensed. And this could mean only the preliminary knowledge obtained by the use of our sense organs.

As nearly as I can make out, Maritain holds that he intuits the permeating existence [contributed by God]. I am told that most Neo-Thomists stress the judgment of existence. The question then is, What does this entail? [It means] no more, so far as I can see, than that the thing is out there [external to the knower], to be reckoned with causally and logically. But I shall have something more to say on this topic in connection with Existentialism. As I understand Heidegger, he holds that human *Existenz* can understand itself in an ecstatic way. But his is a case of "I am" rather than of "it is."

One other point. I am critical of the traditional contrast between contingent being and necessary being. Both of these terms really apply only to propositions. Instead of contingent being, I would suggest *historical being,* being in time. Unfortunately, the Greeks did not stress time. They did not have much of a historical sense. But what would be the opposite of historical? The term *eternal* seems to play that role. It certainly does in Kierkegaard. But it certainly also calls for analysis. It will be remembered that I pointed to the fact that some people are bothered by the fact of the existence of the cosmos. Could it not have not existed at all? Must we just accept it? But if God existed, could we not ask the same question? The Existentialists have made thinkers conscious of the semantics of nothingness and negation.

A few words, in conclusion, as to what dialectical materialism and formal materialism have in common as against idealism and subjectivistic empiricism.

Both are realistic in intention. Yet both find it hard to escape the difficulties of representationalism. One wants to start from things rather than from ideas, as Berkeley himself saw. But dialectical materialism starts from sensations and Thomism from *sensible species.* I have argued that a better understanding of the from-and-to circuit of perceiving will solve the difficulty. I would further suggest that human knowledge has very humble beginnings in the animal world.

viii

EXISTENTIALISM

I turn, finally, to Existentialism in this conflation of contemporary positions. It is largely a development on the European continent. The great wars seem to have had something to do with its rise, but I believe that this connection can easily be exaggerated. Rather, I have a feeling that a certain tradition in philosophy had come to a dead end. Let us call this the Kantian-Hegelian-Husserlian tradition. This was an abstract, rationalistic outlook, and it did not quite satisfy. Already Kierkegaard and Nietzsche had uttered protests against it. These protests were now to be listened to. The self was to come to the front. There was a touch of romanticism about it, but romanticism in a new framework.

It quickly becomes apparent that naturalism and realism are rejected as not promising. Naturalism is too akin to scientism and does not contain the element of transcendence and openness required. No; a new approach is demanded. It is useless to turn to the pedestrian work of British and American thinkers. One must strike out on new lines.

But I shall try to avoid generalities. It is better to study three outstanding Existentialists, to get their flavor and perspective. I shall take Sartre, Jaspers, and Heidegger. Marcel has his devious points when he tries to explain metaphysics and mystery. But, so far as I can see, there is no clear epistemology back of it. As with Jaspers, there is the attempt to reach Being by escaping the limits set by Kant. But, since I am not a Kantian, this gambit has no thrust for me. My own line is to develop a more adequate naturalism, which will permit justice to be done to the human situation. Man is, of course, no mere object. He is an *agent*, with decisions to make. But what it is desirable to grasp is the divergence of these two approaches. It will not be easy to achieve a dialogue between them.

Let us turn, first, to Sartre. One must distinguish between his foundations and his superstructure with his stress on commitment, self-consciousness, reason, and conflict. He has a role to play in these terms that I admire. I admit that I am somewhat of a fan. There is something brave, sincere, and astringent about his stands. I, also, am an atheistic humanist of long standing. But I suppose I reached this position in a positive way in a growing conviction that I had no need of "the hypothesis." I could not see that it accounted for anything.

But let us look at Sartre's foundations. He seeks to move between idealism and realism by a compromise. He broke with Husserl on the status of the Transcendental Ego, an emphasis that led Husserl ultimately to idealism. Our best American scholar on Husserl, Professor Farber, would keep phenomenology a method. Epistemology would then be a separate discipline. But Sartre moves to what he calls a pre-reflective level and maintains that what stands out here is the intentionality of consciousness. This is presentational. What we intuit is a profile of appearances. Over against this emerges the psychical, the *pour soi*. The contrast, for Sartre, is a sharp one. The profile of appearances turns out to be inert plenitude. He calls it the *en soi*. It is solid and self-identical. Thus we have a kind of basic duality. Founded on this duality we have two constructs, the material world, on the one hand, and the self, on the other. These are *correlates,* and so we escape both traditional materialism and traditional idealism.

We come next to the role of the *pour soi*. This is consciousness as it turns back on itself. It is a Nothingness as against the inert plenitude of the *en soi*. Yet, in its own terms, it is an activity, a kind of hole in being that has initiative. Such is the ontological base of an absolute freedom. Out of this come projects and commitments. Here we find much in common with the teaching of Heidegger. Man in the world is a temporal kind of reality who goes to meet his projected future. Only in relation to projects do things acquire meaning as aids or obstacles. It is in such situations that Sartre finds his negations and negativities. For example, expectations may be thwarted. His language must be understood on this background.

I want next to bring out the role played in this whole cluster of movements by the need to avoid Kant's enigmatic things-in-themselves. Sartre takes a line close to positivism while, if I am not mistaken, Jaspers, Heidegger, and Marcel seek to transcend *things* at the level of human existence in a kind of vertical way. With this motivation, we should expect ingenuities.

I take the realistic, materialistic road, Sartre takes the positivistic road, while the others seek to press between Kant's formulation of the subject-object relation to Being. Sartre makes no such effort. A comparison of his position with regard to material things with Ayer's is intriguing. Ayer writes as follows: "It is true that in talking of *its* appearances, we appear to distinguish the thing from the appearances, but this is simply a linguistic usage. Logical analysis [*sic!*] shows that what makes these appearances the "appearances of" the same thing is not their relationship to an entity other than themselves but their relationship to one another. The *metaphysician* fails to see this because he is misled by a superficial grammatical feature of the language."

Now I have argued that the category of appearing and appearances arises within a referential type of direct realism as an acknowledgment of the informative role of sensations in the operation. It expresses a rejection of both positivism and intuitional, naïve realism. Is the materialist a metaphysician? I prefer to speak of him as an ontologist to avoid the associations of the former term. And I consider both Kant and the positivists as bad epistemologists.

There are other aspects of Sartre, such as his view of God as the traditional source of absolute standards and his defense of humanism, that I should like to take up but have not the room for here. Standards, it seems to me, are worked out as appraisals in terms of long-run consequences of actions. I was always opposed to G. E. Moore's intuitionism and his catastrophic attack on naturalism. I quite understand what he had in mind but his phrasing was very unfortunate. The run-of-the-mill philosophers should not be presented with such red herrings.

Having read considerable of Jaspers and browsed over the material in the *Living Philosopher's* volume, I have come to hold the opinion that, though a man of stature, Jaspers's gambits were determined by the Kantian setting of his thought. I doubt that he was acquainted with the realism and emergent naturalism that I have underlined. I am not too much surprised by this, since even the present generation of American philosophers look abroad for their inspiration. And having met Cassirer and tried him out—and he was a very able man—I had no expectation of cultural interaction.

The ingredients of Jaspers's thought are constituted by 1) a neglect of the whole idea of emergence in nature and thus a retention of Kant's essentially Newtonian philosophy of nature, and 2) an attempt to break through the postulated subject-object framework to a kind of symbolic, or ciphering, glimpse of an Encompassing Being. This gives the dimension of vertical transcendence.

With all due respect to Kant, I am an anti-Kantian. To know, for Kant, is to construct in terms of a very complex machinery. The sense-manifold is worked up in this fashion into phenomenal objects related causally. But Kant hints at another realism of a noumenal sort. It is these hints that Jaspers develops in the form of a more esoteric type of awareness which moves from cipher to Transcendence, yet founders.

Now this entire terminology is a reflection of certain assumptions that I see no reason to accept. I think that knowing presupposes and is directed at what is, being. In this sense, factual knowledge is *about* [something]. Yet knowledge cannot be equated with being. Knowing is, accordingly, transcendent in import and based on controlled reference and disclosure. From this standpoint, there is no need to add a mysterious domain of the Encompassing. As I see it, this schematism reflects Kant's constructed phenomenalism. But one cannot help but admire Jaspers's manifold ingenuities. For him, anguish is the gateway of *Existenz,* as over against empirical existence, and the road to illumination. I, on the other hand, have great respect for nature and the human level attained within it. Human beings are capable of being rational agents with powers of decision and engagement. As much as the Existentialists, I dislike anonymity and impersonality.

. . . But I am, perhaps, less of an individualist, though this is a matter of degree.

I come last . . . to the outlook of Heidegger. I am impressed by the vigor of his thought but wish, above all, to understand his perspective.

As nearly as I can make out, he is primarily an ontologist. He does not concern himself with the traditional problems of sense perception and the mind-body question. Rather he moves from Husserl's framework of description into the world. First, it is the world of practical life, the world surrounding man's active living. Taken thus, it is a world of things at hand. It is by their very nature that they can be made into tools and put to use. But reflection brings a break and we pass to a kind of speculative distancing to what he calls in German *Vorhandenheit*.

It is from this outlook, he argues, that Greek and Western thinking in general have taken their departure. Out of it has come the stress on substance, independence, and impersonal repetition. It is Heidegger's aim to come back to what he regards as the more primary outlook, which centers in man. Here, if anywhere, one can get a new look at Being. And so we find a stress on care, on time as a projective activity, and on death as a disclosure of a Nothingness that brings out an understanding of Being by contrast.

In this fashion, ontology gets a new foundation.[3] It is qualitatively deepened. In the very texture of his life man becomes aware of Being. And here there is the note of vertical transcendence that might point to theism, though Heidegger is reluctant to press it. What awareness of Being should bring in its wake is a kind of authenticity of life. Here enters the element of edification. The average human life is a *falling away* from Being to the things around him. Heidegger's vocabulary is vivid and colloquial. Man is *thrown* into the world, for instance. Being is hidden.

Technically, what is interesting is a turning away from traditional approaches to a search for something more of the nature of intuition.

---

3. Cf. the evaluation of Heidegger's "foundation" in the editor's article "Foundations of Philosophy," *Bucknell Review* 19 (Winter 1971).

Truth is not so much factual correspondence as an unveiling. And this perspective leads Heidegger to explore language and poetry for hints. He turns to early Greek philosophy and tries etymological suggestions. Again, he combs the poems of Goethe, Hölderlein, and Rilke for indications of insight. Thus, in his *Satz von Grund,* he quotes these lines from Goethe:

> Doch Forschung strebt und ringt, ermüdend nie,
> Nach dem Gesetz, dem Grund, Warum und Wie.

It is the old search of philosophy and religion for a path to a transcendent Source of Being. Naturalism is regarded as stultifying. But is this the case? Evolution and progress indicate passage to the new as a possibility. And must this new be already in existence, though hidden?

I have great respect for Heidegger's sustained effort. But an evolutionary naturalism leading to humanism is an alternative that should also be explored.

Thus ends my study of Existentialism. One intriguing feature about it is the sources on which it draws. It moves within the framework of Kant, Hegel, Husserl, Kierkegaard, and Nietzsche. British analytic philosophy and American pragmatism, realism, and naturalism arose in a period critical of Kant and Hegel and hardly aware of Kierkegaard. Nietzsche was interesting, but his doctrines seemed a little alien in import. Was there not too much of the will to power? A generation had already passed. We were inclined to be secularistic and concerned with science. As it turned out, we were too optimistic. European nationalism was riding to its fall, and America would be engulfed. [These were factors that had some effect on the direction and the mood of philosophic effort.]

I have found the effort at a conflation of philosophical positions stimulating. It has disclosed divergent movements but, I think, also a wrestling with genuine problems and some advance to their solution. I would advise partisans some such standing back for a moment and concern for synopsis [and to seek that integral alternative which accounts must naturally for the factors to be acknowledged].

14
A Naturalistic Theory of
Value and Valuation

i

The primary aim of this paper is to clarify issues by introducing
certain needed distinctions.

It has long seemed to me that the philosophy of value had arrived
at a point where it was ripe for basic formulation. The essential
material had been gathered and many relations and conditions pretty
well established. But, somehow, it would not settle down into an
unambiguous perspective. The subjectivists were still fighting the
objectivists and the objectivists were reciprocating. It was clear to
me that I had to move farther back to philosophical fundamentals,
to the headwaters whence spring theory of knowledge, ontology, and
axiology. It was there, if anywhere, that I should find the missing
clue. It might be a very simple clue and yet capable of introducing
order into the subject.

Now I shall make no mystery of the distinction that, in my
opinion, introduces order in theory of value; *it is the distinction between cognition and valuation.* On its face this is an obvious distinction, and yet, it has not been carefully studied to see just what it
implies. What are we trying to do when we seek to *know* things
and events? And what, precisely, are we trying to do when, on the
other hand, we seek to *value* things, events, objectives?

It just happens that philosophy has been so dominated by pragmatic and phenomenalistic trends that it has not of late been asking what human knowing seeks to accomplish. It is, therefore, not at all surprising that it has likewise had no clear idea of what valuing aims at. We should expect the two concepts to develop together and throw light upon one another. As a matter of fact, we should anticipate that the concept of knowing would begin to stand out with some clarity before the concept of valuing commenced to outline itself. It is to be remembered that, in the history of philosophy and psychology, it was not until the time of Tetens and Kant that feeling began to be recognized. The scholastic idea of perfection was dominated by the notion of properties, of which even existence might be one.

However that may be—and I am not now interested primarily in the historical question involved—I think it is true that we should expect a clarification of the concept of knowledge before that of value. We shall, in fact, see that valuation makes use of the framework established by cognition, *but for its own purpose.*

Now I flatter myself that I have, by my persistence in theory of knowledge, helped to get a fairly clear notion of what *explicit cognition* is about. To speak of pure cognition would sound too Kantian. In explicit cognition we are trying to secure concepts that have the capacity to disclose facts about things and events. The denoted objects may be ourselves, other persons, institutions, the inorganic world. What we are trying to do is to grasp their characteristics in this mediated way through propositions. And this involves denotation, reference, description. A study of this kind of operation has led me to a reformulation of the correspondence theory of truth and to the replacement of a supposed "cognitive relation" by denotative selection or referential intent.

I refer to this analysis because it will, I believe, be discovered that valuation uses this framework and even reenforces it. As a matter of fact, I pointed out this situation long ago and treated judgments of value in terms of it in several books and articles, but I suppose it was largely ignored just because of what I have called the dominance of pragmatism and phenomenalism. It had become the fashion

to treat all fundamental philosophical problems, such as the correspondence theory of truth, substance, the mind-body problem, the
problem of an external world, as *pseudo-problems*. Under these conditions, how could one expect a clarification of the contrast between
cognition and valuation! And yet it is my opinion that ethics and
social philosophy wait upon this clarification. In morality the human
self is valuing and preferring, and its activity is conditioned by these
complex operations in which the factual is taken up into the normative.

What I shall try to do in this paper is to distinguish between
these two types of activity while pointing out how they condition
each other. It will be clear that, in valuation, we are nearer to the
springs of overt conduct than in cognition, but that it nevertheless
is other than conduct. There is a decided step from valuation to
volition. The method I shall adopt is to present the broad outlines
of my theory and then to bring it into relief by comparing and
contrasting it with the theories of Perry and Parker. Parker is too
subjectivistic, while Perry is handicapped by the *new realism,* to
which he early gave his allegiance. All the essential facts are to be
found in their books. It is to be noted that both of them reject the
Platonic type of value theory, even in its modern form of intrinsic
validity as advanced by Scheler and Urban. Both of them, likewise,
find insuperable objections to the early Moore-Laird view that value
is a quality of things much after the fashion that red is a quality
of a cherry. Though sympathetic to naïve realism, Perry balks at
this acceptance of tertiary qualities. Red, he thinks, may well be out
there but not the quality of being good. And so he springs back to
the organism and focuses his attention upon interest. Value, he
declares, is "any object of any interest." It is interest that somehow
confers value. Just how it does so remains unclear. And, of course,
it is on this point that Parker attacks him. He wants to know
whether value is a substantive, a relation, or a relational predicate.
Parker, on the other hand, stresses the satisfaction of desire as the
defining essence of value. In this alone is there intrinsic value; and
so the locus of such intrinsic value must be in persons, never in things.
On the whole, Parker pays less attention to judgments of value than
to intrinsic value-experiences. Here is where his tendency to a sort

of idealistic subjectivism clearly manifests itself. He is aware of natural objections to this emphasis and writes as follows:

> That the view which I am defending, that intrinsic value belongs only to experiences, never to objects as such, is a hard doctrine, I do not deny. Prima facie, perhaps, value belongs to objects—the deed is good, the picture is beautiful, the woman is lovely—and this appearance of objectivity is reflected in the judgment of value, which ascribes a worth predicate to the thing itself. But here is a situation where both prima-facie appearance and the usual subject-predicate judgmental form are particularly deceptive.[1]

In what follows I shall develop a theory of value that may be said to lie between Parker's and Perry's. It has this general status because it makes distinctions that their types of philosophy do not so well suggest or admit. It is less subjectivistically inclined than is Parker's and, by means of a subtler epistemology than Perry can avail himself of, it is enabled to explain the nature of two complementary referential judgments about things, events, and possibilities, namely, evaluative judgments and purely cognitional judgments. The point I shall make is that, in assigning values to objects, we are not cognizing them, even though some degree of cognition is presupposed. The act is one of *interpretation* after its own kind and in the light of its own relevant data; *but value is not the sort of quality that could be cognized.* In the strict sense we should not think of it as a quality at all. It is not a characteristic out there to be disclosed by intellectual concepts. Rather, the assessing, or imputing, of value is an act that has a *base* in the powers or capacities of objects in relation to our human interests. It is to me clear that this valuative interpretation of objects is built upon our cognitional selection of them but is different in that it regards them with reference to their bearing upon our human interests.

Ultimately simple as this distinction is, it is, in my opinion, fundamental. Philosophers have been trying to *know* values as supposedly mysterious qualities or entities. What we really have is an appraisal of objects of various sorts in the light of their bearing upon indi-

---

1. *Experience and Substance* (Ann Arbor: University of Michigan Press, 1941 [New York: Greenwood Press, 1968]), p. 295.

viduals and groups. Because such appraisal has, rightly, an objective reference as well as a reflexive reference, it is read as an assignment of something called value, or worth, to the object. And, in my opinion, such assignment is quite justified so long as we do not interpret it cognitionally as implying a value-quality on all fours, with shape, size, power, and potentiality. To me, now, all this sounds a matter of common sense, but I remember how long it took me to get it clear in my mind. Valuing is not cognizing because the purpose and the bases are different.[2]

In everyday life, as we should expect, these two distinguishable aims are operative together just because theory and practice are at this level not yet separated. I, at the same time, know in order to act and value in order to act. Actions depend upon the cooperation of both activities, and nature sees to that because the human being is an organic whole. I do not, of course, mean that my interest and attention may not fluctuate from one to the other of these conjoint phases, but only that they supplement one another and give mutual support. Language reflects this conjoint operation, for we add cognitional predicates to value predicates in the most indiscriminate fashion. We say that our government is a good one, in the main, but too complex and mechanical. We say that a razor has a good cutting edge, We say, again, that an ideal is fine, but too hard to achieve. But such constant mingling of descriptive and valuational predicates is so usual that I need not continue the enumeration.

As I see it, the task of philosophy is to clarify each of these after its kind and then to bring them together again in an intelligent cooperation in ethics, religion, social philosophy, and political philosophy. The attempt to reduce one to the other is, I hold, wrong and misplaced. What is imperative is to grasp the nature of each and its conditions and to help it to play its proper role. Neither the factualistic positivist nor the star-gazing idealist can do this; the pragmatist is so muddleheaded on all fundamental questions that he is of small assistance.

2. Since some of my readers may desire to follow the development of my thinking on this topic, I give the following references: "Valuation and Cognition," *Philosophical Review* 35 (1926), pp. 24–144; *The Philosophy of Physical Realism* (New York: Macmillan Co., 1932).

Such an analysis I consider timely, because what we call *intellectualism* represents a disregard of valuation and its roots. Its original sin was to leave out of consideration feeling, desire, valuation, and volition. Logical positivism, for example, is a form of intellectualism that, for all its logical implementation, is an anachronism. On the other hand, romantic anti-intellectualism tends to express feeling rather than valuation. Hence the job confronting philosophy is to press on to a realism and naturalism that can comprehend knowing and valuing in their intimate relations while not confusing them. [In what follows I shall treat the questions of: 1) value-terminology; 2) the nature and conditions of value; 3) where valuation occurs in nature and the relation of value to existence; 4) the objective reference and functional import of valuation; 5) terminology again! justifiability in valuations.]

ii

First comes the matter of terminology. I have, for fairly obvious reasons, chosen to follow the indications of language and, I think, of our interests and references, and have kept the terms *value* and *valuation* connected with acts and objectives referable to a common external world at once physical and social. We human beings are, in my opinion, evolved material substances of a high order, concerned with both ourselves and others and capable of evaluating objectives in both a personal and a cooperative way. In this sense evaluation is just as objectively intended as is cognition. I do not see how it would be possible to give meaning to ethics and social philosophy without such a perspective. To this extent I would have a different emphasis from Parker's. Besides, we already have excellent words for desires, feelings, and satisfactions, namely, these words themselves, and I can see no adequate reason for turning back on linguistic usage. But, of course, I freely acknowledge that the connection between verbal marks and their meanings is in a sense arbitrary, though not causally, or genetically, unmotivated. I am—it goes without saying—old-fashioned enough to hold that words are not really words apart from meaning—and it did not take the discovery of the mystical potency of semantics to convince me of this elementary fact. After all, I was brought up on traditional logic and not on mechanical calculi whose interpretation—if it had one—came at the end. My principle, then, has been to follow the indications of language and experience, but to do so critically, aware that finer distinctions will need to be made.

A second terminological point is that I prefer to make the distinction between instrumental and terminal, or telic, values rather than the common one between extrinsic and intrinsic values. It is obvious that the term *intrinsic value* does not fit in with value judgments but rather with the more subjective, psychological emphasis— or with Platonism.

A third point is that I have found the generic term *interpretation* employable as covering both cognition and valuation. Knowing is a case of cognitive interpretation, while valuing is a case of valuational interpretation. In everyday life, as I have already pointed out, the two types of interpretation are interfused. Gradually they have been distinguished, though as yet cognition is the more clearly grasped. In fact, it has been so clearly grasped that valuation has been pushed into the background. A scientist thinks that he knows what a fact is, while a value strikes him as ghostly and quite without any respectable status.

And this leads me, as a critical realist, to seek to come to an understanding with my friends, or dearest enemies, the pragmatists. It is important to comprehend just where we differ. My divergence from them is on two scores: epistemological and ontological. Together they make up a full-blooded and significant divergence. I bring it up here because it will play into our whole conception of the status and locus of value. It will be a case of the difference between evolutionary materialism and that philosophical monstrosity called *experientialism*. Existence, being, is a category that is coming into its own again. In short, pragmatism is a veiled form of nineteenth-century agnosticism. But you can't handle religion and politics any longer under such terms. I think the modern mind is getting more incisive and realistic.

The epistemological divergence turns around the concept of cognition. While the pragmatists direct their attention to the validation of ideas within a problematic situation and reinterpret knowledge as essentially validation, the critical realist, though paying full respect to the *testing* of knowledge-claims, holds that knowing aims at the disclosure of facts about actual states of affairs. A true proposition is one that gives such knowledge. As I have recently pointed out, the correspondence of a proposition with its referential object is an *implication* of the fact of knowledge and not itself a test.[3] I have never been a defender of what the pragmatist delights to call the passive, mirror theory of knowing. Cognition is an achievement. We think through tested propositions to their referents. Now this epistemological difference is important for the theory of value, for upon it depends a sharper differentiation of the respective roles of valuing and knowing.

The ontological divergence is equally important, as we shall see in the sequel. As an evolutionary materialist, I would stress the existence of substantial continuants. Such continuants of whatever evolutionary order have structure, powers, and potentialities. I venture to affirm that a revival of interest in the category of substance of a more Ionic than Aristotelian sort is overdue. What I would call realistic empiricism as against phenomenalistic empiricism is certain to have more interest in basic categories, existence, continuance, and potentiality—the heart of a viable concept of substance—among others. It would be a grave mistake on the part of secular philosophy to leave these categories to the neo-Thomist.

iii

We are now ready to examine the nature and conditions of valuations.

First of all, a distinction must be made between individual and group valuations. It is best to begin with individual valuations, while recognizing how much individuals are influenced by the operation

---

3. "A Correspondence Theory of Truth," *Journal of Philosophy* 38 (November 1941) : 645–54.

upon them of group valuations. The French sociologists made much of this influence, as can be seen, for example, in Bougle's *Evolution of Values*.[4] But it is my opinion that the primary philosophical question involved can best be defined in terms of individual valuation. The group status of value waits upon clearer sociological ideas. Since I am now working in the field of social philosophy, I hope to report upon this question before long.

I now come to my second main thesis, namely, that in valuation the individual is reflexive and relational. Whatever is valued—thing, event, person, objective, or possibility—is valued *with respect to its bearing* upon the feelings, desires, plans, interests of the individual himself or of such a *base* as another individual or group. I am more than ever inclined to stress the self as a high-order substance[5] to which these empirical factors must ultimately be referred. Thus an ideal has value to me, a human self capable of striving toward it.

The ontological base is, then, appetency, or conation, and its development with the development of the self through discrimination, intellection, increased sensitiveness, and, of course, accompanying it all, societal intercourse. But I am at present less concerned with genetic questions than with the mechanism of valuation at the level of self-consciousness.

Whether we study valuation from the outside, in the case of another person by noting behavior and language used, or from the inside, in the way of becoming aware of the full context of our own prizings and appraisals, what we may call attitude, decision, outlook, or evaluative judgment, stands out. Just as it is the organic self that believes, so it is the organic self that values. Desire and aversion bear witness to that fact. Hobbes and Spinoza had the root of the matter in them. As conscious persons we experience such desires and aversions and feel drawn to the object or objective, or repelled. This feeling that informs the attitude is diversified and seems to involve a union of affective and kinaesthetic states of the organic self. It is

4. Trans. Helen Maud Sellars; Preface by Roy Wood Sellars (New York: Henry Holt, 1920).
5. Perhaps *continuant* is a good word here.

this matrix, so far as I can make out, which sustains the more specialized activities, which we call wish, desire, and purpose. To be alive is to have urgencies, appetency, desire.

In what can properly be called valuation in any explicit sense, desire and interest are guided by sensations, images, and concepts. These help to give it direction and reference. As is well known, our attitude toward an objective is modified by our idea of it. In this sense valuations are guided and qualified. In ourselves we are quite aware of the living fullness and complexity of such deliberative attitudes of the self. It is clear to us that we are doing something more than knowing and that knowing, as an activity, is itself sustained in such a way. Even a referential proposition involves a mental activity upheld by the desire to know. No teacher is ignorant of this fact. On the other hand, a blind impulse is merely a restlessness, an urgency without guidance. It is clear, then, that valuation as referential implies cognition plus. For it, cognition is directional and informative and yet only a prelude to the final task. The organic self in all its conative complexity must make its decision.

Thus it is because its center is agency, in terms of interest, desire, purpose, and passion, that valuation is necessarily reflexive and referential. Cognition plays its part as it throws light upon the significance of object or objective for the agent. And the property of the object stressed is its capacity to connect up with human life in the way of expression and furtherance. It is for this reason that, in valuation, there are at least two bases of strategic control, the external and the internal. And here it must be remembered that the organic self must take the whole situation into consideration. In this sense valuations are contextual and relational. However much analysis is necessary as a preliminary, synthesis has the final word. This is a commonplace to the ethicist and the social thinker, but even the aesthetician is fully realizing it, as both Parker and Pepper are proving.

Now both the primary bases in situational contexts are variables as well as continuants. On the external side, there may be 1) actual change in the object or new ideas as to the proposed objective, or 2) the individual may learn to know the object better as regards its powers and relations. On the internal side of the agent, the base is a function of many secondary variables such as new experiences, maturation, loss of interest, or shift in preference. It is clear that valuation is a dynamic process to be correlated with the labile equilibrium of living things. It is an expression of the self's apprehension of the object as bearing upon itself, as sized up or adjudged in the light of interests come to consciousness in desire and feeling. The focal center is, as I have said, the agent, with his perspective in the situation he occupies. Valuation is, accordingly, centripetal and reflexive. Interest goes out to return.

So much for the existential setting and operative traits of human valuation. I take it to be as objective as human living itself and as both beginning and terminating in activity. There is nothing subjective in an invidious sense about it. Only because science has been so dominated by cognition alone, a highly developed attitude resting upon social and personal development, does valuation have for it the semblance of subjectivity. But cognition is essentially a substitute for existence. It represents the nearest approach we can get to the thing known. Hence it gives us the illusion of an impersonal objectivity. But to know a thing is never to be it. We can only be ourselves as centers of agency and choice. Ontologically, then, valuation is an expression of being, our being, in its drama of adjustment, manipulation, creative expansion in the midst of things in their own measure and capacity doing likewise. In valuation we are on the inside of being, playing our human role. That is why I would place so much stress upon the role of the substantial organic self in valuation. I shall argue that science will be deepened when it meets with an ontology moving downward from the realities of human living. Positivism, as I understand it, is not doing this, and so the concept of existence remains thin and *sinnlos* for it. But more about this in the sequel.

Each person as a substantial, high-order, existent doing and daring in its environment, human and inorganic, is a center of election and selection, is conative, agential, preferential. It is absurd to think of human life as value-free.

In order to avoid a possible misunderstanding I would point out that an analysis of valuation is not itself a case of valuation but a case of cognition of valuation. The theoretical reason rather than the practical reason—to use a time-honored distinction—is then in operation. Valuations are actualities that can be studied analytically and statistically; and it is my impression that sociologists, for instance, are beginning to realize this fact and its import. Nevertheless, I do think that it is fundamental for the social sciences to grasp the primary ontological nature of valuation and its basis in man's conative and endeavoring nature if it is to escape the etiolating hand that phenomenalism and Humeanism have waved over nature. There is existence; it is dynamic, and man's striving is an expression of it at a high evolutionary level of organized novelty.[6] All of which sums up to my belief that science without an informing philosophy is incomplete, however technologically valuable it may be.

Now, while my outlook is genetic and evolutionary, I make bold to point out that philosophy and the social sciences, particularly, would make a colossal mistake if they merely looked backward on the path we have come. They must have the courage to realize that the past no longer exists, that the substantial reality of men and things is pointed forward. To live is to value, decide, and act; it is to be an agent. What we also need is structured thinking and valuing at the level of existence at which we have arrived. Let us not leave this primary perspective, which comes out so clearly in valuation, to the anti-intellectualist.

iv

It is a debatable question how far down the scale of evolutionary organization anything of the nature of selective valuation extends. It is, I suppose, partly a matter of definition and criteria. Below man behavior and overt attitude must be the empirical test. I am quite ready to admit that the cow *likes* to chew her cud—it would certainly be an awful bore to the poor creature if she didn't—and that the cat likes cream. There are appetencies and satisfiers all down the line of animal existence. And I am even ready to grant some measure of feeling to very lowly agents, together with some slight measure of

---

6. An article of mine entitled "Causality and Substance" will appear in the *Philosophical Review* 52 (1943) : 1–27.

sensory guidance to organic needs. And yet I would be skeptical of any romantic extension of interests and desires and satisfactions below the level of organic life. To use Laird's term, there is *election* throughout nature but, surely, this signifies not much more than well-founded connections between what may be regarded as centers of agency. But anything that deserves the name of interest or propensity seems to me to involve an involution of organization in which there is thickness of potentiality and variability rather than routine.

The upshot of this approach is that I am very skeptical of the downward extension of even such elementary valuations as prizing and liking, below the organic level. If I had been led to embrace panpsychism in any of its forms, either from an idealistic motive or from a too-literal interpretation of the principle of continuity as excluding the emergence of novelty, I would, undoubtedly, have developed eyes of faith and apprehended the spiritual struggles of electrons. If I had been an *experientialist,* without the glimmerings of an ontology, anything would have been possible and I would have mixed up fact and value at my pleasure. As it is, I am not optimist enough to commiserate the electron for having so slight a taste of valuing in its elections, for surely organic life paid its price for sensitivity in exposing itself to evil as well as to good, to pain, frustration, and dissatisfaction as well as to pleasure, success, and satisfaction. He who is too anxious to extend psychological categories to the most elementary agents of inorganic fields seems to me a simple soul with no tragic sense of life. But my primary *caveat* rests on my belief that organized wholes are higher-order substances that have powers and capacities that less differentiated things do not possess. Life I take to be a daring adventure on an open road, an *agony* in the Greek sense, a contest in which success and failure are strangely mingled.

The topic of the correlation of value and existence into which I have been drawn, partly by its inevitability, partly by reading Professor Parker's paper[7] on the subject, deserves more space than I have been able to give it. I have always agreed with Norman Kemp

---

7. This paper was read at the 39th meeting of the Western Philosophical Association as a reply to a paper read by Parker at the previous meeting.

Smith that naturalism signifies that spiritual values emerge and begin to vindicate their reality only at some late stage in the process of evolution.

v

But when one is considering such a fundamental question as the status of value in the universe, it is impossible to avoid the discussion of the concept of value-free existence. As I take it, value here refers primarily to such factors as desire and interest, rather than to such terminal and instrumental values as appraisals and assessments. This emphasis comes out very clearly in both Parker and Whitehead, who both defend the thesis that there is no such conceivable thing as value-free existence.

Since I am more a substantialist than either of them, I think that I can see how our positions diverge. I am no believer in vacuous actuality—to use Whitehead's famous expression. No substantialist could be. But I see no good reason to assign evolved powers and capacities to the inorganic level. Nevertheless, our generic categories of activity and potentiality cover all existence. As we go farther down the scale the analogy with the organic self weakens and, so far as I can see, our agnosticism as regards any glimpse of the "content of being" must increase. We can only fall back on the sort of abstract knowledge science can give, a knowledge, however, to be given the setting of ontological categories like substance and causality. Any critical form of materialism must adopt such a perspective or fall into the illusions of picture thinking. Material actuality is never vacuous, but we can have but abstract knowledge about it. There is dynamism and urgency there; and it is from this base that emergent causality brings forth appetency and finally conscious desire. Conation and interest have their roots in the dynamic nature of matter itself. And, if that were all that was demanded, I also would hold that existence is not value-free. But it is evident that Whitehead and Parker mean far more than this.

Whitehead builds upon the foundations laid by Plato, Leibniz, and Bradley. In so doing he rejects the correspondence theory of truth, substantialism, primary endurance, and objective organization, just the principles that evolutionary materialism accepts. The result is that his actual entities are conceived as *feelings*. What else could they be with this foundation in subjectivism? It is not surprising, therefore, that he makes such statements as the following: "Value is inherent in actuality itself. To be an actual entity is to have a self-interest. This self-interest is a feeling of self-valuation; it is an emotional tone. . . . Each actual entity is an arrangement of the whole universe, actual and ideal, whereby there is constituted that self-value which is the entity itself."[8]

To all this I can only comment to the effect that evolutionary materialism with its quite different principles cannot deduce such conclusions, which seem to it founded on a unique mixture of subjectivism and Platonism. For it, on the other hand, existence is dynamic and its urgencies rise through emergent causality to the level of desire. But this fact by no means signifies that value is alien to existence, the conclusion ontological materialism's opponents seek to draw. Desire is a feature of organic life and, therefore, cannot be alien to existence. As well say that a brain or a stomach is alien to existence. Questions of existence and questions of genesis should not be confused. I do not assert that linguistic intellection is alien to animal life because dogs have not developed that capacity.

Since pragmatists and positivists have no ontology and only a negative sort of epistemology—and take much pride in the fact—it is impossible to discuss the question of value-free existence with them. I turn, therefore, very briefly to Parker.

Now I quite agree with Professor Parker that only what is denotable exists, that to say, that this tree, or even this twinge of pain, *exists* is a tautology. It is my belief that an awareness of existence arises in the self as it apprehends itself in its felt activities and especially, perhaps, in those involving attitudes and actions in relation to other selves and things. The meaning of existence deepens, also, in contrast to experiences of illusion when expectations are thwarted. To say *thing* or *self* is to say "something to be reckoned with," is to admit existence. The critical realist holds that the referential factor

---

8. *Religion in the Making* (New York: Macmillan Co., 1926), pp. 100 f.

in perception is an intentional greeting to what is taken to be co-existent. The Berkeleian greets only his own ideas. Now Parker can never quite make up his mind whether to be realist or Berkeleian. On the whole, he inclines in the Berkeleian direction and falls short of substantialism even with respect to the self, which means, in modern parlance, panpsychism. Were I a panpsychist, I also would correlate being and valuation. As it is, with the best wish in the world I can only grant election and activity to all being. Only as such dynamism works up through the complicated structure of organic and societal life does valuation emerge. When valuation does emerge, it is local and existential, and not subjective in any invidious sense.

vi

The significance of this prior examination of the relation between value and existence is that it brings out the active, striving, conative side of existence, too little recognized by intellectualists today, even though, as I pointed out, Hobbes and Spinoza emphasized it. In the Ancient World the Stoics were the first fully to grasp its importance, though somewhat confusedly because of the enduring influence of the Socratic dictum that virtue is knowledge. But, surely, even knowing must be supported by the desire to know, personal and social.

From this ontological base let us now turn our attention to evaluations of objects and objectives. We are then passing from what Parker calls *intrinsic value*—and what I would prefer to call desires, satisfactions, and value-experiences—to the assignment of worth or appraisal. For the social sciences, this referential activity of evaluation is of prime importance, for institutions are sustained, or allowed to collapse, in terms of it.

What kind of a property is the value symbolized by a value-predicate like good, desirable, right? Here we are dealing with terminal and instrumental values and not with experiences as such. In Perry's terminology, we are concerned with values as the objects of any interest. *Values* in this sense is an elliptical expression for objects, events, and objectives valued.

My primary thesis is, it will be remembered, to the effect that valuation is different from pure cognition. It can be said to appraise the object valued with reference to interest. Interest is dynamic and conative; it is something that tends to pass into action. In valuing we ultimately assess the object, as cognized, in its bearing upon such hormic interest or passion. It is interpreted by the organic self as it is thus cognitively introduced to the interest of the self. It is in this sense that it is reflexive or centripetal, differing basically in this respect from cognition, which is outward looking and factual. It is for this reason that valuing is so closely related to action that it is in some measure its preparation. And action is ontological, an expression of being.

Now both Parker and Perry have arrived at much the same terms for instrumental and terminal values, but they are somewhat puzzled about their formulation. Are values substantive, relations, or relational predicates? To speak of a value as any object of any interest would seem, on the face of it, to make a value a substantive. But the additional phrase surely means "considered as the possible, or actual, object of any interest." The term object is ambiguous, as the critical realist has long pointed out. We make things objects by referring to them. They are not, strictly speaking, objects in their own right. Now, as I see it, Perry as a new realist holds that the selected thing is given along with the interest. They are quite literally brought together. A value would seem then to be an object in a relation to interest and having thereby a relational predicate.

But Parker, being more of a critical realist, recognizes that there is no literal interest-relation. An interest *in* does not for him express a relation but a vector direction of the interest. He rightly points out that what we desire is usually nonexistent. That is, for instance, the characteristic of an ideal. How can we have a literal interest-relation to a nonexistent ideal?

And so we must come back to the capacity of the mind to think through ideas and concepts as actualities and empirical possibilities. Just as in knowing we do not literally apprehend the object but denote it and characterize it through concepts, so in valuing we do not literally apprehend the objects in which we have an interest.

The ability to refer to them rests upon a directed response of the organic self, which is guided by sensations and ideas but which may be dominated by the desire to know, or by the desire to value, or by both intertwined.

But I am led to believe that even Parker has not yet fully realized the difference of intent between cognition and valuation. The essential point is that in valuing we are not trying to find the sort of characteristic, predicative or relational, that knowing, as such, could deal with. What we are doing is to interpret the object or the empirical possibility that we conceive *in the light of the interest.* We are assessing it with respect to the interest. It is for this reason that a value judgment can never be reduced to a factual judgment. The only fact possible in reference to it is the fact that we valued objectives in that way. An ideal must always remain an objective, a possibly realizable state of affairs that we value in the light of our desires and purposes. An adequate theory of knowledge thus makes possible an adequate theory of value. No thing or objective possesses value as a quality that can be known. But it must be *such that* it does, or might, connect up with human interest.

It follows that valuation is a complicated activity, to which knowledge of things and situations, estimations of empirical possibilities, and self-awareness as regards desires and purposes are all relevant. It is a somewhat dramatic affair in which imagination and sensitiveness must play their part. And it is not surprising that those who are primarily trained in the methods essential to pure cognition are apt to be somewhat blind to complexities of this sort. Instrumental values are, of course, more easily handled, because they are primarily a matter of causal means valued for their power to bring about terminal objectives. But even they should not be too simplified.

I would suggest that the social scientist can by special training and effort learn what values have operated in the past in any society, though, if he himself is not open-minded, he will not be able to note and appreciate them. He can, likewise, discover the conditions and efficiencies of instruments and mechanisms. But it would be well for him not to eschew the insights and demands of moralists and artists. In this sense I do not believe that the social sciences are value-free.

vii

Since I have sharply contrasted cognition and valuation as having different intents, I have been led to adopt a different terminology for the validity of the two types of propositions involved. *True* seems to me to mean a case of knowing, and implies that the proposition through which we know corresponds to, and so expresses facts about, the state of affairs known. But a terminal value, for instance, which we call an ideal, that is, a future state of affairs regarded as realizable and desirable, is more of the nature of a *commitment*. The value judgment asserts that such a commitment is justified, that it is founded on knowledge of the facts and upon an awareness of deeply-lying interests of the self. It should not be forgotten that selves are things of a unique sort; growth, choice, decision, and also change are characteristic of them. And it would be foolish to apply to value judgments terms that ignored this primary, reflexive base. We are dealing here with something quick and not dead. A valuation seeks to be responsible to its complex foundations or grounds. For these reasons it would, perhaps, be advisable to speak of a value judgment as valid, or justified, rather than true. For the individual it is a commitment. I prefer this term to that of postulate. But from the side of the logic of ethics it could be called a postulate.

viii

I conclude this attempted clarification of a naturalistic theory of value and valuation by indicating a few points that have significance but cannot be adequately treated here.

The first is, that there are levels of valuation, just as there are levels of cognition.

The second is, that there are kinds of valuation and values involving different interests and different kinds of objects and objectives. We speak of the aesthetic, the political, the moral.

The third is, that values tend to become standardized and even stagnant for both individual and group. The commitments are often too low.

The fourth is, that values and ideals represent a cultural and personal stage between the past and the future. The future is made in part by new commitments. Here is where I would locate the teleological, or creative, source of human living. We are not merely pushed from behind; the self explores and decides.

The fifth is, that valuations are causally effective in that they are a prelude to motivations and action. It must never be forgotten, however, that valuations are complexly conditioned.

The sixth is, that value-predicates are largely symbolic in character because they are not primarily descriptive. It is important to get beneath such symbols to see what interests are finding expression.

The seventh is, that possibilities can be valued as readily as actualities. This fact should drive home the thesis that values are responsible reflexive interpretations rather than literal qualities of things.

The eighth is, that there is no basis for a Platonic theory of values with intrinsic validity. An *ought* is a demand self-imposed or imposed on others.

The ninth is, that we must move beyond traditional utilitarianism to what I would call a humanistic approach. The ultimate criterion for our commitments would seem to be an experimentally discovered well-being and considered satisfaction. I take it that this can be universalized if due regard be given to social and personal differences.

15
Agential Causality and Free Will

INTRODUCTORY REMARKS

What I shall try to do in this paper is to sketch an approach to causality that may throw light on human behavior and, particularly, on those outstanding affairs which we speak of as moral decision. I take these to be high points in the *agential economy* of human beings. I do not, however, regard other practical decisions as generically different, as some seem to do—Professor C. A. Campbell, for instance. Moral decision, as I see it, involves principles of human relations, based on a concern for others and the common good, which may not be primary in other practical decisions. None of these decisions seems to me explicable on purely mechanical principles, but to involve intelligence and its mode of working in the human economy.

What I wish to do, then, is to see human behavior in its natural-history context as representing an emergent level of causality in which the modalities and methods of a temporally extended process of *self-direction* takes place. At the human level, with its unique capacities of learning, memory, and anticipation, the *self* becomes the focus of dominant controls and methods, which we indicate by such terms as character, temperament, attitudes, adopted rules, accepted norms, reflection, giving reasons, et cetera. It is all very complex, as human nature and personality, as going concerns, are.

One of the weaknesses of much of traditional philosophy has been the fixity of its categories. From this has followed something of the formalism so characteristic of its formulation and handling of questions. If I had the space, I could give many illustrations of this freezing of categories. The retention of Cartesian dualism long after it had ceased to be a working hypothesis in biology and psychology is an example. Another instance—and the one that I am going to explore in this paper—is the continued dominance of mechanical notions and models in philosophy while they have lost prestige in the sciences. It is not that science is going in the direction of vitalism and final causes, but that it is opening up its categories and changing their *texture*. I take this analogy from recent work in linguistic philosophy, with which I have sympathy. But it would be a mistake on the part of philosophy to concentrate on the open texture of the words of our natural languages and to neglect the shifts going on in *living science*. Technical terms in science are constantly redefined as concepts, and theories alter. Philosophy must keep in touch with science in this respect. I shall speak of the open texture of categorial meanings.

In connection with causality, I am going to apply the principle of *levels of causality* that I enunciated in 1909 in an article in the *Journal of Philosophy,* then with a somewhat longer name. I was recently heartened by a reference to this article from South America, to be exact, from both Chile and Argentina. This idea was at the base of my interpretation of integrative causality as giving novelty. Those who are interested will find an analysis of my book *Evolutionary Naturalism* by Lloyd Morgan in the appendix to his *Emergent Evolution.* I was then in touch with both S. Alexander and Lloyd Morgan, though more of a naturalist than either. In fact, I called myself a new type of materialist in 1916 in my first book, *Critical Realism,* which gave the name to the famous *Essays in Critical Realism.* I had used this expression [*critical realism*] from 1907. I find that the English associate the origin of the term with Dawes Hicks. I make these historical remarks because the advent of logical positivism and linguistic analysis seems to have blotted out what I still regard as very fruitful developments in American thought, in which philosophy was in close touch with the empirical sciences.

The kind of empiricism I had in mind was what I call realistic empiricism with a referential approach to perceiving as involving both reference and characterization in which sensations function, in the main, as *cues* to adjustment and behavior. At the human level, the *dominance* of concepts, patterns of action, and words in perception indicate that sensations function as cues and guides in behavioral activity, and must be understood in this context. Because man can shift his attention to them, he is led to take them out of this usually dominant context and make them something of the nature of objects of intuition; and, in so doing, he is apt to get himself into difficulties. He wonders about their status, once he has performed this work of isolation. He may then be "stumped" as to how to put things together again.

Now, since I shall be exploring the texture of the kind of causal economy that occurs in human commitment and decision, it is important to get as adequate an idea as possible of the simpler levels from which these emerge. Once these are fairly grasped, the complications involved in human self-direction, where situations have to be sized up and decisions made, can be better understood. It will not surprise us that what we call the "self" functions as a focus in this job of appraisal. Of course, such a self is not a substance but a *locus* of interpretative activity essential to the unified functioning needed by the organism if it is to meet the situation that confronts it. Only so, can the organism remain viable. In other words, decision is an achievement resting on guidance. At this level, the guidance is largely a conceptual affair involving all sorts of summations in the way of knowledge and rules. What has been begun in perception, and the kind of adjustment it mediates, is carried to a level requiring explicit memory, judgments of valuation, awareness of consequences, the use of rules, and related processes. It is guided self-direction at a very complicated level. But, so far as I can see, we have lifted to this level, with its new factors and operations, much of the framework that operates in all biological adjustment. Unless this natural-history context is appreciated, man's practical life cannot be understood. Only so, as I see it, can the mature locus and *role* of the self be grasped. To put it very sharply, the "self" emerges with the kind of job it has to do, that of dealing with demands for making viable decisions at a level characterized by enlarged abilities and confrontation with situations that have grown up with these abilities. I have, myself, found that the genetic approach, made possible by human biology and cultural anthropology, has helped to give me insight into the role of the self as tied in with growing needs and demands. What I have sought to add is the sense of the continuity of this emergent development with the natural-history base.

But, in these introductory remarks, I am chiefly concerned to indicate the philosophical perspective I shall develop in the substance of the paper. And, perhaps, I can best do this in the way of a contrast. I shall reject both traditional empiricism and the abstract and formalized notion of causality employed by philosophers in their discussion of determinism and indeterminism. To take the second point first, I shall seek to enlarge the texture of causality to make it biologically and psychologically adequate to the facts. I shall speak of causal economy and agential causality. And I shall hold that the kind of causality involved in biological, adjustmental response is of a guided sort and not of that *blind kind* which philosophers took over from physics and the era of mechanical models and schematisms. In fact, my thesis will be that philosophy has been too conservative and too dominated by the science of the past. It has thought dialectically in terms of fixed alternatives, called determinism and indeterminism; whereas a proper attention to the relevant facts would have led it to realize that the very notion of causality at the biological level is altering in order to do justice to the texture of the facts. Animal responses are *guided responses;* and the category of causality must be enlarged to include this fact. Here we have the beginning of what I call *guided causality*. Parenthetically, I would remark that my chief objection to the current stress upon *common usage* in linguistic philosophy is its neglect of the open texture of categorial meanings as these reflect advance in science, though, in saying this, I do not for a moment fail to recognize the value of the idea of the logical behavior of words as integral with conceptual patterns. My own generation stressed concepts and did not, perhaps, realize to the full the role of words as tied in with these conceptual patterns and, therefore, expressive of them in their logical grammar. While welcoming this connection as a working base for analysis, I still maintain that the *sights* of philosophy should be kept on developments in the terminology and concepts of the sciences rather than on merely everyday usage. I hope that my forthcoming analysis of agential causality and its *modal categories* will be a good illustration of this point.

So important is the proper setting, that I must include comments on the misleadingness of traditional empiricism. The actual biological unit where the brain-mind is concerned is that of stimulus *and* response. Here we are concerned with the communication and adjustment system of the organism based on the nervous system. The unit is also called sensorimotor. It is this pattern that is the point of departure for guided denotation and characterization, such as operates in perception. And perception is, itself, the condition of directed action. It is in this fashion that a human being is fitted into the world.

Now it was just a misfortune—historically caused—that classical physics had no adequate categories to deal with biological processes. Its schematism led to an emphasis upon a one-directional, causal approach to perceiving, without recognition of response. Empiricism took up the tale in terms of sensations called out in a soul, or mind, which were somehow apprehended. This schematism is so well known that I need not go into detail. With such a framework, epistemology found it hard to escape from subjectivism and introspectionism. It was found that the causal approach was, itself, not justified. Now, so far as I know, American critical realism, at least in the form I gave it, was the first to stress the pattern of guided response and to show that referential meanings and characterizations, developed on this basis, gave a foundation for objective cognition. It can, perhaps, be said that Hobbes's appeal to an *endeavor* outward was, in some slight measure, an anticipation of the present recognition of the stimulus-response pattern as the unit.

But let me repeat that the sensorimotor pattern, as a unit, enables us to understand how sensations act as *cues* to guided responses and so play a part in perceiving that is more that of guiding the application of concepts than that of being the objects of awareness themselves, as traditional empiricism supposed. Man's attention is capable of being shifted to these *cues* operating in perception and he may then speak of "seeing" visual sensations as well as of seeing chairs and tables. When we recall that this way of speaking easily fuses in the philosopher's mind with the schematism of the seventeenth century, it is quite understandable how confused and bewildered he may get. The directed references and conceptual characterizations of actual perceiving, in which sensations operate as *cues,* are replaced by a mythological construction of the mind as constituted of atomic ideas somehow given as *termini* of a mysterious awareness reaching out from a postulated "subject-self." It is, surely, far more empirical to recognize that perceiving is a structured activity of a complex sort capable of developing relevant meanings at both *poles,* that of denotative reference with its sense of the object, or referent, concerned, and that of the percipient perceiving and acting in a guided way. Otherwise, sensations are apt to seem like homeless ghosts with no functional role. Needless, perhaps, to say that the "self" emerges at the percipient pole of the duality and is concerned with a guided behavior that becomes ever more complex both in motivation and in the need for guidance. It is in this context that new levels of causality arise in order to do justice to complexities of situations and their requirements. To be human is to live a life with such conceptual dimensions.

The point of all this is that the schematism of traditional empiricism is completely outmoded and is gravely misleading to philosophical thought, already so given to introspective methods without proper checks. While philosophy has become keenly aware that modern mathematics does not appeal to the intuition of axioms but works with postulates, it does not seem to have paid sufficient attention to developments in biology and psychology. That distinguished philosophers are still trying to construct physical things out of sensations, actual or possible, has long seemed to me bizarre. Only lately has the tide turned away from phenomenalism to the effort to get back to a direct perceiving of physical things, though not an intuition of them. This shift may lead the way to a better understanding of the guidance function of perceiving and how the "self" emerges in the percipient in connection with the job of using guidance for decision, a decision required by the need for unified and viable behavior. Here is the locus of what I call agential causality, with its methods and modalities.

It so happened that, at the University of Michigan, I was in contact with the development of experimental, comparative psychology as this was being pursued by John F. Shepard and Norman Maier. Both were what might well be called *Gestalt behaviorists*. Both stressed sensations as cues to behavior rather than as termini of awareness. That is, they operated functionally as factors in a larger process. Thus, it was the *use* made of these cues in guiding behavioral activity motivated by the dominating goal, the feed-box, that they stressed. Behavior was an affair of selection of patterns that would so fit together. Both regarded rats as capable of "reasoning" in this selective way, though not, of course, of adopting "inference licenses," to use Ryle's expression. Here, I take it, we have something of the nature of the *integration* of patterns, quite akin to the growth of conceptual meanings. It is not at the level of linguistic logic and so cannot be broken up into induction and deduction, both of which concern themselves with the formulation of explicit laws. But it is very important for the understanding of the practical working of the nervous system in its job of guiding the organism.

One of the values of familiarity with such experimental work is that it challenges the intellectual habits of the philosopher, who is apt to be dominated by some historical tradition, and, at the same time, to think of perception in terms of a visual perception dominated by words and concepts and a little set apart from its use in guiding practical activity. That is, the philosopher approaches perceiving as an epistemological problem and not as an activity. So far as the scientific setting of his thought is concerned, it is prone to be that of physics and not so far away from classical physics at that. That is, he is apt to be harking back to John Locke and the like. It is the nature and validity of the knowledge-claim that he has in mind. This other approach stresses, rather, the use made of the knowledge-claim, or, to be more exact, traces the natural-history stages that make possible this level. In short, an animal does not sit down and make judgments about the things around it in terms of verbalized concepts, but relates the sensory cues it receives to patterned tendencies of action. It is in this sense that it "reasons."

Now the moral of all this for my present purpose is that I want to set aside the problems of epistemology, as such, and concern myself with the problem of viable behavior at the human level. What *use* is made by man of both sensory cues and conceptual systems? I take it to be evident that conceptual systems—both cognitional and valuative—dominate practice, though these are always in touch with sensations and feelings. The job before man, as it is the job before the animals, is to act intelligently in given situations. But, of course, it is a human situation, with the possibilities and demands man sees in it, to which the human being responds.

The point of all this *for causality* is that we have here a level of causality that involves this kind of texture and economy. Not to recognize this point is to ignore the actuality of organisms and their natural techniques. In short, it is to be unevolutionary and reductive. It was this thesis that I tried to make over thirty years ago in my book *Evolutionary Naturalism*. There are levels of causality involving different textures and techniques. It is not enough to reject Hume's conjunctive phenomenalism which, of course, had point against intuitive rationalism or the *apprehension* of necessary connections. One must go on to show that categorial meanings arise as factors in one's tested thought of the world and that these meanings have an *openness* of an empirical sort rather than a fixed and dead-level uniformity. Man is an agent with a causal economy tied in with his intelligence. Intelligence must secure causal leverage. Now what I have called the natural-history approach, sharpened by experimental, comparative psychology, introduces us to the kind of patterned, causal economy of animal life upon which man builds his more conceptual superstructure. I shall try to show that the "self" emerges as a necessary focus of selective decision. At this level symbolism and thought are necessary. Man becomes *self*-conscious. I suppose we often look at animals and wonder what they experience in the way of what might be called a *self-feeling* in their modes of selective activity. While we must not confuse levels, it is not necessary to reject some measure of continuity in economy and background.

My introductory remarks are already too extended. And yet I do think that perspective, or approach, is fundamental. What I am attacking in philosophy is sometimes called the intellectualistic fallacy. It is really disregard of the biopsychological setting of decision. It is essential that we turn away from the tradition of British empiricism with its schematism of terminal awareness of sensations for their own sake, a schematism tied in with the old-fashioned, causal approach, which had no grasp of the functional unity of stimulus and response, and immerse ourselves in the modern setting of guided response in which sensations are primarily cues to patterned and, ultimately, conceptual, interpretations, or sizings-up, of the situation confronting the organism. Agential causality with its unification and pressure to viability rises to the *economy* of explicit guidance by judgment and rule. The psychology of this level is a social psychology with cultural norms and methods in operation.

Let me conclude this section by some remarks on naturalism in ethics. There has seemed to me so much misunderstanding, even a little perversity, in the derogatory use of this phrase. Of course, ethics should learn as much as it can from an adequate psychology—and psychology is becoming ever more adequate. But moral judgments, like all judgments, involve the use of criteria in their justification. It is the job of theoretical ethics to make the concepts and logic of morals explicit. Psychology may throw light upon this task, but cultural anthropology seems to me to be as helpful in a supplementary way.

Morality is tied in with appraisals and rules, just as science, in the main, is connected with descriptive statements. But descriptive statements need their criteria and confirmation just as appraisals and rules need their justification. What, in heaven's name, could a reduction to psychology, *as a special science,* mean in either case? And I could never see anything nonnaturalistic about logic and scientific method. These are studies of human discourse and intellectual techniques. And what is nonnatural about them?

Let me speak frankly as an American thinker of an older generation. Taken at its best, G. E. Moore's doctrine of value as a non-natural property was a demand for an adequate theory of appraisal or valuation. What do we do when we assign, or ascribe, a value to an object? Surely, what we are doing is to appraise the *role* the object can play in human lives; we are not *intuiting* a nonnatural property. I judge that the present generation of British thinkers is taking this perspective. In so doing, it is studying the logical behavior of value terms. But the whole terminology of the naturalistic fallacy now loses point. It may be said to have had value as a challenge. But what is unnatural about valuation? How could organisms adjust themselves without being able to *appraise* in an elementary way the objects confronting them? What man does is to make all this conceptually explicit. But, as we shall see, appraisals as well as cognitions are factors in the *decisions* that are terminal in agential causality.

So much in the way of perspective.

KANT AND HUMAN FREEDOM

The reason why philosophers return to Kant is *not* that he solved problems but that he was aware of them.

In taking Newtonianism to heart, he raised the question of the physical status of geometry and mathematics in general. His solution was in terms of a wedding of the *a priori* and the phenomenal. In short, the physical world is a construction; and the principles of the construction are intrinsic to it. Essentially the same thesis is applied to the causal pattern of the world, so that it can be considered a Newtonian machine by reason of its categorial constitution.

The realistic empiricist cannot, of course, accept this constructionist outlook. For him, the categorial constitution of the world is something to be cognitively worked out. If his categorial concepts show inadequacy, they must be developed.

Roughly speaking, even before a realistic epistemology of a promising sort was worked out, scientists began to attack Kantianism on its mathematical side as a result of the rise of non-Euclidian geometries and the consequent decline of intuitional views in favor of postulational procedures. This is a relatively old story with which

I was, naturally, familiar long before the rise of logical positivism or scientific empiricism. It was, perhaps, Einstein who made most definite the distinction between pure and applied, or physical, geometry.

But less had been done about causality. While Kant had tried to answer Hume's conjunctive theory of causality by means of his *a priori* compromise with traditional rationalism, that is, his constructive phenomenalism, this solution had added difficulties of its own which favored idealistic motivations. How could causality apply to things-in-themselves? If not, why postulate them?

There are two points to be made. First, a realistic analysis of perceiving undercuts the debate between Kant and Hume. If physical things are the direct object of referential perceiving, both types of phenomenalism are to be rejected. The question then becomes that of the tested adequacy for our world of our categorial concepts. Are those fixed or capable of development? Now, it is the second alternative that I have defended. Can we not retain the notion of objective connection and involvement—which some call *physical entailment*—and yet acknowledge that the *texture* of this involvement alters with levels of physical organization? It was this idea that I had in mind in setting forth the principle of levels of causality. The traditional models of Newtonian mechanism and Aristotelian teleology seemed to me artificial and outmoded. To employ a Baconian analogy, surely nature had more subtlety than this. Evolution must be taken more seriously. It was this line of thought that I developed in my *Evolutionary Naturalism*. It may have been noted in my introductory remarks that I regarded the behavior of organism as guided by cues and patterns that are functionally integrated. Only so could they adjust themselves to the demands of the environment.

I shall not in this context concern myself with *homeostasis* as an affair of physiological balance. It is very interesting from the causal point of view, and it is clearly something worked out for the body in terms of techniques of self-regulation. The nervous system is, however, an organ specialized along lines of quick communication with the *unit* being that of stimulus *and* response. On both sides, there seem to be both analysis and synthesis at work in a coordinative way. I have been very much impressed by the discoveries of nervous anatomy which show advances from what are practically one-way connections of a stereotyped sort to two-way connections in which there is control exerted in a feedback sort of way, so that the *unit* of stimulus and response becomes functionally developed in an interactive fashion. I have been informed that learning and memory involve the rise of this interactive technique. What we have in the cortex of man is a multidimensional network of centrally aroused patterns, which possess a certain openness and plasticity in the service of viability of response. It will be my thesis that we have here the foundation of the highest level of causality, that guided by conceptual patterns in their selective integration. Here, I take it, we have the emergence of a causality guided and directed by "reason" or, better, by reasoning. If animal psychologists speak of the selective responses of rats as involving reasoning, much more so are we justified in thinking of human action as involving the leverage of intelligence, that is, of the ability to use conceptual patterns. At this level, we have, quite literally, a type of rational causality, that is, a causality guided by *becauses*. All this fits, not only into growing theories of the way in which the brain functions, but into the conclusions of comparative psychology. I might also say that recent emphasis on the logical behavior of words, as functionally tied in with concepts, points in the same direction.

Let us now connect all this with Kant, for philosophers tend to think in historical patterns. I pointed out that Kant owed his importance partly to the fact that he faced problems and tried to go with science as far as he could. But his science was essentially Newtonian. If he went beyond this it was *as a metaphysician,* that is, one who thinks about the whole situation as best he can. His background here was Leibnizian. Now I have great respect for careful metaphysicians. They reflect horizons and problems that are ineluctable. My thesis is, however, that as science expands and takes in the biological, the psychological, and the cultural, anthropological areas, philosophy will find that its metaphysical thought, which has been somewhat of the nature of an extrapolation, will fuse with this more adequate scientific outlook. Thus I would regard myself as having an essentially materialistic metaphysics in harmony with a really up-to-date, scientific materialism, that is, a materialism of levels. The trouble with logical positivism with all its hullabaloo was that it was phenomenalistic and had no adequate epistemology. It was a case of trying to take philosophy by storm with arbitrary slogans. To me, as a realistic empiricist and materialist, it was peculiarly irritating, since its advertised radicalism was essentially Humean and archaic. Materialism is far more radical in its import, as I had occasion to point out. But these are winds of doctrine. The point I have in mind, however, is the cooperation of science and philosophy, in a critical view of the nature of things.

With Newtonian nature a realm of causal necessity of a blind and unguided sort, that is, with mechanics as the model, Kant could only appeal, in a vague way, to the realm of the noumenal. Here the *empirical base* was his recognition that man is a moral creature able to comprehend and respect the demands of reason in its practical form. His famous categorical imperative was the formulation of this demand. Oughtness and rightness are not reducible to the merely affective, as, it seemed to him, English ethical thought wanted to be. To him, it was a categorial question. So far he was, I think, right; though his rationalization of it in obscure, noumenal, and abstract rationalistic terms left much to be desired. I take it that it is only as a more realistic empiricism develops with a more adequate notion of the self that moral rules and categories will arise. But more of that later.

Kant's noumenal self presupposed the phenomenalism of both the physical world and the empirical self. It was, therefore, a part of his metaphysics. If the physical world belonged to the realm of causal necessity *à la* Newton, he could assign *freedom* of a moral sort to the noumenal self. It was all very abstract and dialectical in terms of respect for the universal nature of reason. That only could be right which could be universalized.

Now, I think that the only comment we can make is that Kant made as good a job as he could of an impossible set-up. He was loyal to Newtonianism, on the one hand, and to his moral experience, on the other. But with the obsolescence of Newtonianism, Cartesianism, and associational psychology, a philosopher should be able to achieve a more adequate framework. My suggestion, obviously, is along the line of levels of causality together with a functional notion of the self as the locus of guided decision. I speak of this as involving an enlargement of the category of causality as regards texture and economy, or technique. I do not, in point of fact, see how animals can behave viably without the possession and use of *capacities* of causal import, from instinct to various levels of intelligence. We have already noted that there is neurological correspondence to this causal development. What is desirable is that philosophers should draw back, for a moment, from the inherited controversy, set by Hume, and seek to explore the actual texture of causality at its various levels. *Conjunction* is, surely, a phenomenalistic term opposed to the deductive implications of necessity as conceived by the rationalists. As a physical realist, I do not like terms like *necessity* or *entailment*. They have a deductive aura. And they suggest a dead-level uniformity. Categories are meanings to be achieved and to be made more and more adequate to the discovered facts. In this sense they must be held open. Why should we expect causal processes in the nervous system to be just like those involved in the impacts of billiard balls?

In this task of feeling out an adequate terminology for causality, I long ago started with *involvement* as a point of departure. This was a rejection of conjunction. The next step was to see that the *texture* of the involvements would vary with physical organization. Of course, all this showed that I was temporalistic in my outlook and emphasized processes. The gist of it was that processes varied and had different economies. Evolution was to enter the precincts of causality. It was no longer a question of conjunction versus a rigid, and preordained, necessity but more like that of making adjustments, even solving problems *with the resources at hand*. At least, it could culminate in such exploratory operations, and biological categories would no longer be alien to causality, as they had been when mechanical models dominated thought. Even, as we shall see, intelligence could then secure causal relevance and leverage.

The moral of all this is that Kant faced problems in the scientific and philosophical setting of his period. He opposed freedom to necessity, much after the fashion of Cartesian dualism, that is, in a wholesale way. *If we are to be true to his spirit,* we must make use of developments in science that open up new possibilities. To me, as an evolutionist, this has always meant the exploration of the texture and economy of emergent levels for causality. Causality must be connected with the resources at its command. Shall we, then, speak of necessity? Not if it means being pushed from behind or being deductively entailed in an *a priori* fashion. Laws I think there will be, as corresponding to the *constitution* of the physical system that is functioning. But we must not think of laws as agents in control. I would not myself say that "natural language" has, as yet, worked out the adequate terminology, just because I opine that the categorial meanings have not been adequately achieved. In fact, this paper is, itself, an attempt to indicate directions.

And so good-bye to Kant, while trying to keep in mind his demands. While logic may have no morality—as Carnap affirms— philosophy has the *responsibility* of doing justice to all we know about the world and about the human self functioning in it.

NOT DETERMINISM OR INDETERMINISM

It should be clear by now that what I am driving at is an escape from the traditional disjunction of determinism or indeterminism. If I had to choose between the two I would call myself an indeterminist. But why allow the determinist to entrench himself in outmoded concepts and there to await all assaults? The better policy, surely, is to outflank him by setting up a more flexible and adequate notion of causality. If we can enlarge the notion of causality along the line of levels, we may well be able to rob it of its terrors. We then refuse to allow the determinist of the traditional type to identify causality with his model, which seems to be an archaic confusion of deductive rationalism and mechanical images, and we may well be able to do justice to what is valid about the protests of indeterminism and keep causality. It is this constructive perspective that I wish to investigate. It will be a type of causality at the human level that does justice to *modalities.* Why turn our backs on the fact that human decisions that pass into action arise out of such activities as forecasting consequences, appraising, using tested methods, adopting rules, and so on? In the concrete, this is, I suppose, the sort of activity that gives meaning to "free will." But is not all this a kind of causality with texture and methods appropriate to the job it has to do? How could human beings function viably without it? The natural-history approach shows its antecedents and foundations and the rise of the equipment and resources that makes it possible.

Away, then, with indeterminism as chance. It fits in neither with what we know of the economy of organisms nor with the implications of responsible action. One essential thing is to bring in the *self* as playing, as best it can, a pivotal role in choice. Surely, it is the organ and locus of decision, bringing to bear the resources it has at its command. But this bringing to bear of resources involves techniques of a varied sort if it is to come off. And it is a matter of cultural history that the techniques *made possible* by biological evolution are developed in the course of cultural growth. Thus human causality learns to include tests, methods, and ideals as elements in its texture and economy.

AGENTIAL CAUSALITY AND THE ROLE OF THE SELF

It will, I hope, be recalled that I emphasized the point that the capacity of the nervous system to respond *in a viable way* to situations represented an *evolutionary requirement.* As a network, a communication system, the cortex lifts the stimulus-response unit to a level adequate to its function of unified behavior. Now it is not my purpose—nor is it within my capacity—to make neurological suggestions. I shall argue from the psychological side and postulate an *isomorphism* of a comparable sort in the working of the nervous system. From the philosophical side, I have long maintained the essential identity of the brain-mind and our double-knowledge about it.

The primordial standing of unified response as involving both dominance and inhibition is, I think, generally recognized by biologists. Coghill and Herrick maintain that all integrative processes are directive. Thus we seem to have *dominance, inhibition,* and *directiveness* as characteristics of unified response. To use a very simple illustration by Lorenz, the Austrian ethologist, his dog was swimming the Danube after him for the first time in some trepidation, shown by its looking backward at the receding shore, but kept on with him. Here were dominance of the tendencies to keep with the leader-master, inhibition of impulses to turn back, and a unified, directive behavior. Now I shall not speak of a doggy self and a volition, but only argue that something from which a functioning self with volitions could arise manifests itself. In short, unified response demands dominance, integration, and inhibition at this animal level.

Ethologists tell us that the kind of response set off in strictly instinctual activity follows a fixed pattern. The mark of intelligence is "spontaneity," modification, absence of fixity. It would seem that cortical *resources* are being called on to meet the needs of the situation.

I am arguing that such "spontaneity," or bringing in of resources, to meet requirements involves a new level of causality resting on integrative capacity in the service of directiveness. Thus, between stimulus and response intervenes a delayed process of *sizing up* the situation confronting the organism and adoption of the relevant response. There is, of course, nothing of infallibility in this inserted link. Trial and error, relational insight, and the like, all play their part. Patterns are built up and integrated. Cues of various sorts are used.

Having got this sort of context in a natural-history sort of way, let us next turn to the human self and consider it and its mode of functioning *as reflected in language.* I am not concerned here with introspection taken, as it sometimes is, as an intuition of mental states. I am *not* going to maintain that we can intuit freedom, or "free will," as a sort of counter-causal activity. Rather am I concerned to show that the "self" is thought of as the *focus* of an activity of dominance, inhibition, and directiveness, and that we do not see how our resources, so essential to meeting demands of situations, could be, otherwise, brought to a focus. In short, I am concerned, not with a counter-causal activity, but with a level of causality involving an integrative economy.

It is not surprising that the pronoun *I* symbolizes, at one and the same time, the individual as a whole whose destiny is engaged and the awareness of the level of causality involved with the "self" operating as a focus of judgment and selection. This, I take it, is because the individual cannot but be in the hands of centrally aroused processes concerned with interpreting the situation confronting the individual and that involves considering possibilities and alternatives. As I see it, the "self" arises as the expression of the functional unity required to maintain dominance, inhibition, and exploration. The methods employed are those which help to answer questions. These are discovered and adopted personally and socially. The more complex they are, the more need is there for supervision. I take it that the role of the self is this activity of unifying and guiding direction. It is not that we intuit the self as an entity but that we are aware of the activities and can, in some measure, verbalize them.

From all this it follows that the self is a very complex reality, though not a substance. It had better be called a continuant; and it includes habits, norms, capacities, and methods. For instance, I have argued that the use of criteria to determine the acceptability of ideas is a part of the self-correcting economy of the human self. This point is important, for it implies a type of causality that is no longer blind and merely an affair of push or of predetermined necessity. Much the same holds for appraisals. These, to be effective for guidance, require the use of criteria likewise.

Now the upshot of all this is that the economy of the self, without which it cannot perform its biological job, involves the participation in causality of judgment and the methods that increase the adequacy of judgment. I speak of this causality as a guided and self-correcting causality. And, of course, it is my belief that it emerges with the abilities of the brain-mind and is improved with cultural development. It seems to me unempirical to deny that this level of causality exists. But to recognize it demands a rejection of the models that, in its unevolutionary days, science developed. Man is a rational creature in the sense that he can reason and appraise. And such reasoning and appraisal is required for the kind of life he leads. When we accept such activities as focused and unified in the service of practical action, we have what I call *agential causality*. The higher the mode of agential causality, the more explicit and developed the methods employed. At the same time, there arises a background of achievement and growth that we call character, accepted rules, working knowledge, and so on. These are constituents of the "self."

One more point is important; this kind of causality takes time to eventuate in that terminus which we call decision or choice. It may, in fact, take a long time when the affair is a grave one. Biologists speak of delayed responses. At the human level, such delay may continue until the agent is satisfied that he has the right idea. He will rehearse, anticipate, call to mind similar situations, and ponder, before, as we say, he makes up his mind. As I have said, I see all this in a natural-history context. Man is a learning, appraising, self-correcting animal. And this is impossible without a causal texture and economy isomorphic with it.

Had I the space I would like to make some comments on the current anti-naturalistic terminology of the British philosophers, much of which, I take it, goes back to such traditions as G. E. Moore's conception of value as a nonnatural property, instead of an appraisal, to the retention of Cartesian dualism, to identifying behaviorism with its Watsonian form, and the like. My psychological tradition goes back to functionalism and to a *Gestalt* behaviorism, which took the sensorimotor pattern as a unit and recognized levels of development. As I see it, there is nothing in such a psychology that militates against the functional reality of reasoning and appraisal. In point of fact, as I indicated, Shepard and Maier held that even the rats reason in the sense of using cues to build up patterns of behavior. The point of all this is that philosophy does not gain by trying to draw an artificial line between it and science. I do not see that it has access to information withheld from science. Its job is to clear up muddles and confusions, many of which are the result of traditional perspectives. The enlargement of the category of causality to take in guidance and self-correction is an illustration of constructive thought which both science and philosophy must judge.

THE OPENNESS OF GUIDED CAUSALITY AND FREE WILL

I have always regarded the claim to a "free will" as of the nature of a protest against inadequate notions of causality of the deterministic model. I take it that we can leave fatalism and predestination aside as involving other contexts and assumptions.

Now what I have been working toward is a rejection of the formulation of causality that grew up with classical physics and had its model in something of the nature of the parallelogram of forces. The path taken by a particle was the *resultant* of the direction of impacts upon it. Philosophers often thought of desires as operating in this propulsive way, so strong was the influence of the model. It is hardly needful to point out that modern physics stresses the *field,* and is more inclined to be statistical in its approach with less assurance of fixed mechanisms.

But, as an empiricist, I would lay much stress on the *relative autonomy* of the various sciences while expecting an adjustment between the categories they favor. I have always emphasized the importance of organization and integrative levels, both spelling novelty of pattern and functioning.

The import of this perspective for causality I have already tried to spell out. As I see it, it points to tentativeness, trial and error, exploration, openness, give-and-take, balance, equilibrium. I mention these various terms as indicative of the temporal dimension in causality. The idea is that something is achieved in a causal process and that, in that sense, it is *open.*

But *how* open? And open *in what sense?* These are the questions we must consider. And it is best to take considered choice as the case to analyze. It is fairly clear that we want to avoid the extremes of mere chance and of predetermination, for neither does justice to what I call the methods of guidance in a directed and self-correcting type of causality that uses the resources offered to it by intelligence.

Intelligence secures leverage on causality in terms of learning, appraising, noting consequences, and such. Freedom would seem to rest upon the use of such resources.

It would seem to follow that there are degrees of freedom. But human personality has many dimensions and virtues, and it would be foolish to overstress abstract intelligence. The point is that any individual is freer to the extent that he guides his decisions by the best information he has and uses principles and rules of a well-tested sort. He is then doing to his utmost the sort of thing his mind-brain was evolved to do. In this sense, the use of reason is but the culmination of that guided causality which, we saw, began in perception when action-patterns are guided by cues and sensory factors.

"Free will" is, accordingly, to be conceived as choice and decision, in which the self acts as a focus and locus of the biological need for viable action, in a context in which reflexes and habits are not enough. Responses do not run off in a set way. Judgment, appraisal, and reasoning are needed if actions are to be adequate. In short, the situation is such that it can be met only by intelligence. As I see it, in short, human living represents an evolved constitution of being requiring a texture, economy, and resources that are unique. And yet comparative psychologists are pointing out continuities with the animal world. It is an affair of carrying further, and lifting to a higher level, directive capacities that are rooted in the adjustmental economy of life.

My conclusion is that "free will" is not counter-causal but an enlargement of causality, an enlargement that had humble enough beginnings but was developed in terms of abilities. My argument has been to the effect that this kind of economy had to have such a focus as that we call the self, since there had to be a center for inhibition, dominance, review, and decision. And that, as language clearly indicates, is the role of the self.

I Could Have Done Otherwise. The challenge that brings out to the fullest the nature of agential causality as against the traditions of prefixed determinism is the claim we all tend to make that we could have done otherwise than we did.

Now I take it that this formulation reflects the situation in which the self is as it confronts its task of guided decision. To do its job it *must* reflect and size up alternatives. That is, it is a factor in an operation. The symbol *I* has a performative value, to employ Austin's phrase. It can issue in a decision of moment for the organism and has causal sovereignty or authority. But *before* all the cards are in and it is ready to act executively, it quite rightly regards itself as undecided. We have here a temporal dimension of this type of causal economy. As preceding decision, it naturally has the quality of tentativeness, of awareness of alternatives, of considered possibilities. The modalities of speech reflect this quality. We say to ourselves "We might do this" or "this is a possible action." And if the self is to take itself seriously as an agent, that is, as sovereign so that decisions issue from it, I do not see what other type of language could be used. Looking backward, we reproduce this temporal stage and assert, in its spirit, I could have done otherwise, I was sovereign. It was up to me to decide. That was my job.

But scientific and philosophical reflection shifts to another standpoint, in which stress is laid upon the constitution of the self, its life history, its habits, its working values, its dominant characteristics, and it is argued that the choice expressed all these things.

Of course, it did. I have not been arguing that the self is vacuous. It is a historical growth that develops with the situations it faces and the decisions it makes. All I have been seeking to bring out is that the self ceases to function properly if it ceases to be *open,* that is, ceases to weigh alternatives. It is so easy to stand outside choice and to consider it as something brought about causally in an impersonal sort of way and by an inherent necessity. Our categories then become such affairs as habit, character, tradition. The model in our minds is likely to be that of the dominant science.

But what I have been arguing for is the recognition that this level of causality is one whose very texture involves the meeting of novel situations by means of resources. At the human level, these effective resources include the use of intelligence. True, the working self is a growth; but it is a growth made possible by past uses of intelligence. I am not arguing against causality, but for an appreciation of the texture of this kind of guided and integrative causality so essential to human life. It is a causality that is open, in the sense that we can do things *because*. It is causality at a rational level. Of course, this is not the formal rationalism of Kant, but a concrete and vital rationality. It is a temporalistic rationalism of exploration and appraisal.

The upshot, I take it, is this. The determinists are correct in their rejection of the operation of something chance-like and alien to causality. They are wrong in their disregard of the actual, causal economy of rational beings. They do not appreciate its texture and mode of operation, its relevant openness. The result is that they tend to impress upon choice the model of impersonal predeterminism of a deductive, explanatory sort. The notes of urgency, of trying, of responsibility and answerableness, of the *self* meeting a situation, tend to vanish. And I do not think this is empirically justified. The thing to do, as I see it, is to enlarge our category of causality in accordance with the notion of levels. *If,* after applying our resources and considering various possibilities, we had wanted to do something else than we actually did, we could have done it. The "wanting" here is the guided response of the functioning self. And we do come pretty near indecision at times. But the pressure of our biological make-up is to decision as a prelude to action. It is true, however, that man—more than other animals—can postpone and postpone, in a Hamlet fashion.

The Import of Remorse. It is only as we grasp the role of the self as the focus of decision in agential causality of the human level that we can give its proper meaning to remorse.

Obviously, it does not mean that the past can be changed. What has been done has been done and cannot be done over again. Remorse concerns the *appraisal* of the self as the agent dominant in action. It is both retrospective and prospective, since its object is a continuant. While the self is not a substance, it is substantive.

In remorse, we are normative in intent. We become aware of the kind of self we were—and, perhaps, still are—too selfish and thoughtless; and we don't like it. It is this ability of the self to appraise itself which shows the openness, or modifiability, of the self. Self-knowledge may be very critical, as we all know.

It is the substantive, or continuant, nature of the self that gives point to remorse. Because of this identity, I am challenging myself, as I am, in condemning what I have done. This continuity underlies both memory and appraisal. When we say we *ought* to have done otherwise, we are saying both that we *could* have done otherwise if we had been better selves, and that this different action would have been in accordance with acceptable principles. Just as *ought* implies *can* in the sense that decisions are not fixed apart from moral valuations, so *ought* implies *could have* in a retrospective sense. The contextual setting is that of normative choice. If we are not normative agents, that is, persons whose choices are guided by cognition and appraisal, this language is misplaced. But I have been arguing that the texture and economy of agential causality involves this kind of openness.

Index

Aaron, Richard, 103
Absolute, 27, 236; mind, 277; motion, 231, 232; space, 219, 224, 225, 226, 231, 232, 235; time, 219, 221, 222, 224, 228, 231, 232; truth, 277
Absolutism, 121
Abyss, 294, 295, 297
Actual occasions, 250
Alexander, Samuel, 8, 41, 53, 61, 94, 322, 362
Allen, Ethan, 189
Analysis, 63, 89, 91, 100, 280; linguistic, 362; ordinary language, 57, 307
Analysts, 272
Anselm, 297
Antinomy, 27–39
Archimedes, 230
Aristotelian, 309, 317, 319, 331, 333, 348, 371
Aristotelianism, 254, 260, 303, 329
Aristotle, 120, 230, 242, 254, 260, 285, 287, 298, 307, 309, 325, 329
Atom, 270
Atomism, logical, 89, 100, 249, 251, 307
Atwater, 32
Augustine, 295
Avenarius, 106, 108, 119, 194, 199, 205, 215, 232, 325, 326
Ayer, A. J., 57, 60, 80, 101, 109, 112, 113, 116, 117, 118, 119, 121, 128, 175, 210, 312, 327, 337

Bacon, Francis, 331, 371
Bain, 227, 316
Baldwin, James Mark, 20, 116, 171, 206, 263
Barth, 297
Baylis, 178
Behaviorism, 11, 86, 111, 145, 150, 151n, 263, 279, 305, 319, 367, 379
Bentley, 145
Bergmann, 105, 106, 107n, 109, 111, 112, 114n, 115, 118, 119, 125, 126, 127, 128, 131, 133, 134, 135, 136, 138
Bergson, Henri, 20, 41, 187, 242, 256, 290
Bergsonian, 289
Berkeleian, 114, 128, 356
Berkeley, 53, 56, 63, 67, 77, 88, 116, 120, 149, 156, 169, 170, 197, 202, 205, 211, 218, 219, 232, 246, 247, 250, 252, 254, 258, 259, 260, 267, 268, 279, 305, 308, 315, 316, 318, 319, 323, 327, 334
Berlin, Isaiah, 286
Bernstein, Richard J., 22
Blanshard, Brand, 52, 98–99, 309
Blau, Joseph, 9
Bosanquet, 40, 46, 71, 198, 306, 315, 321
Bougle, 349
Bradley, F. H., 10n, 11, 27ff., 60, 80, 81, 82, 83, 170, 176, 180, 198, 242,

248, 258, 267, 268, 305, 306, 309, 316, 321, 354
Brain-mind, 13n, 125–28, 135, 376, 378
Brentano, 178, 255, 256, 317
Bridgman, 124n, 131, 180, 230
Brightman, 119
Broad, C. D., 51, 53, 57, 66, 76, 80, 81, 86, 93, 94, 95–99, 101, 114n, 200
Brunner, 297
Büchner, 319
Bultmann, 299

Cabanis, 213, 317
Cairds, 198
Calvinists, 125
Campbell, C. A., 361
Camus, 275
Carnap, 56, 68, 78, 94, 109, 110, 113, 117, 256, 310, 318, 327, 333, 375
Carritt, 190
Cartesian, 281, 289, 309, 318; dualism, 50, 62, 76, 155, 198, 199n, 200, 211, 305, 324, 362, 375, 379
Cartesianism, 332, 333
Categories, 90, 97, 118, 122, 138, 139, 174, 210–11, 222, 374, 382
Causal economy, 364, 384
Causal efficacy, 244, 248, 250
Causality: agential, 173, 361–84; emergent, 134, 182; guided, 364, 378, 381, 382, 383; integrative, 134, 362, 378; levels of, 13n, 37, 285, 362, 368, 374
Chisholm, Roderick, 100, 178
Christian Thought, 191
Coffey, 309, 332
Coghill, 127, 377
Cognition, 341, 344, 347, 348, 350, 351
Comte, Auguste, 106, 204, 205
Conant, 179, 270
Conception, 13, 75, 264
Conceptualism, 50
Condillac, 317, 318, 323
Conflation, 303, 340
Consciousness, 28, 34, 79, 85, 115,

136, 171, 200, 290; efficacy of, 35ff.
Contextualism, 153
Cooley, 128, 246
Copleston, 256
Cornelius, 106
Creighton, 321
Crombie, 269

Dalton, 180
Darwin, 141, 187
Darwinism, 99, 278
Decision, 363–64
Democracy, 20, 20n
Democritean, 179
Democritus, 213, 324
Demos, 148
Deontological intuitionism, 163
Descartes, 85, 141, 158, 166, 242, 270, 276, 309, 321, 329
DeSitter, 230
Determinism, 364, 375–76, 383
DeTracy, 317, 318
Dewey, John, 10n, 20n, 21n, 44, 54, 55, 59, 61, 62, 64, 65, 69, 72, 75, 76, 78, 83, 100, 140–61, 172, 174, 176, 180, 181–84, 197n, 200, 213, 244, 245, 246, 256, 263, 269, 277, 278, 279, 287, 292, 297, 311, 321, 322, 323
Dialectic, 273, 283, 328
Dickens, Charles, 283
Diderot, 187, 192, 213, 323, 327
Dingle, 270
DNA, 262
Dobb, 206
Doppler effect, 228
Double knowledge, 85, 171, 213, 376
Drake, Durant, 7, 48, 108, 145, 199, 279
Driesch, 20
Dualism, 290; epistemological, 10, 21, 71, 96, 116; metaphysical, 11. See Cartesian dualism
Duhem, 106

Eddington, 124n, 178, 187, 218, 235, 241
Edwards, Paul, 144

Ehrenfels, 134
Einstein, 124, 215, 219, 220, 223, 224, 227, 228, 229, 230, 232, 233, 234, 236, 237, 241, 371
Eleatic, 185, 190, 191, 260
Emergence, 134, 212
Emergent evolution, 12, 186
Empirical immanentism, 105, 107, 108, 109, 111, 113, 117, 118, 130
Empiricism, 75, 91, 103, 112, 130n, 146, 165, 168, 217, 251, 272, 275, 276, 305, 316–23; Anglo-American, 170, 275, 276, 277–82, 311, 316–23, 369; critical, 67; Humean, 55, 65, 91, 112; logical, 104; phenomenalistic, 164; pragmatic, 54, 55, 56, 65, 321; radical, 84, 108, 114, 322; realistic, 55, 70, 94, 103, 122, 164, 192, 199, 266, 323, 363, 370, 373
Empirio-criticism, 325, 326
Encounters, 296, 299, 300
Energism, 38
Engels, 185, 186, 189, 190, 192, 194, 196, 205, 209, 283, 284, 307, 324, 325, 327, 328
Epicurus, 242, 324
Epistemology, 104, 106, 111, 119, 146, 179–80, 182, 188, 190–98, 210, 296, 315, 365
Essences, 7, 199, 248
Essentialism, 272
Eternal objects, 263
Ethics, 369–70
Euclidean, 231, 232, 235
Euler, 219, 231
Everett, Walter, 147
Evolution, 12, 31, 43
Ewing, 114n, 200
Existentialism, 10, 10n, 22, 57, 79, 101, 272, 274–76, 281, 282, 286–91, 293, 303, 306, 311–13, 317, 334, 335–40
Experience, 87, 91, 148, 158; thickened, 163, 173, 177
Experientialism, 162, 163, 164, 184, 190, 204, 347
Fajans, 135

Farber, Marvin, 21, 312, 336
Feedback, 13, 293
Feigl, Herbert, 56–57, 105, 106, 111, 112, 118, 119, 123, 124, 133, 201n
Feuerbach, 187, 188, 197, 285, 303, 324, 325, 327
Fichte, 193, 197, 202
Fictionalism, 130
Free will, 380–81
Fremdpsychisch, 115, 128–30
From-and-to-circuit, 49–50, 58, 69, 73, 74, 77, 89, 101, 142, 146, 149, 150, 155, 168, 171–72, 271, 308, 333, 372
Fullerton, 29

Galbraith, 282, 284
Galileo, 65, 223, 230, 243, 259
Garnett, 119, 137
Garrigou-Lagrange, 187
Gestalt, 81, 226, 367
Gilson, 309, 329
God, 225, 238, 248, 258, 266, 291, 294, 295, 296, 297, 298, 299, 329, 333, 334, 337
Goethe, 340
Goudge, 263, 269
Green, T. H., 198
Guthrie, W. K. C., 152

Haldane, 124n
Hall, 109
Hegel, 141, 185, 187, 188, 192, 193, 198, 202, 205, 211, 212, 218, 274, 277, 278, 283, 284, 286, 303, 305, 311, 316, 319, 320, 324, 327, 328, 340
Hegelian, 148, 208, 246, 255, 297, 313, 314, 335
Hegelianism, 198, 303
Heidegger, 115, 274, 275, 276, 287, 289, 298, 304, 312, 313, 314, 334, 335, 336, 339–40
Helmholz, 32
Henle, 137
Heracleitean, 34
Heracleitus, 189
Herrick, C. Judson, 173, 377

Hicks, Dawes, 362
High redefinition, 144, 159
Hipparchus, 230
Hirst, R. J., 56, 94, 100
Hobbes, 158, 188, 192, 203, 213, 243, 319, 349, 356, 365
Hobhouse, 100
Hocking, W. E., 297
Hoernle, 11, 40ff.
Höffding, 38
Holbach, 323
Holism, 135
Holt, E. B., 94, 279, 318
Hook, Sidney, 109n, 140, 151, 176, 190, 192, 193, 195, 203
Humanism, 300, 313–14
Humanistic, 360
Humanist Manifesto, 22
Hume, 48, 53, 64, 71, 77, 88, 90, 92, 106, 111, 118, 120, 138, 149, 150, 169, 170, 174, 194, 205, 210, 242, 243, 254, 277, 281, 285, 292, 305, 307, 309, 311, 315, 316, 322, 368, 371, 374
Humean, 53, 76, 84, 98, 112, 132, 138, 204, 211, 219, 229, 230, 231, 248, 254, 261, 267, 268, 270, 317, 319, 323, 327, 352, 373
Huneker, James G., 22
Husserl, 287, 288, 292, 296, 303, 311, 312, 319, 336, 339, 340
Husserlian, 335
Huxley, Thomas, 319, 324
Huxley, Julian, 147
Hypothetico-deductive method, 147

Idealism, 10, 11, 31, 32, 38, 47, 71, 91, 99, 104, 128, 153, 157, 158, 162, 169, 172, 198, 201, 202, 229, 233, 243, 257, 267, 295, 296, 298, 316, 317, 320, 321, 324
Indeterminism, 375–76
Information theory, 331
Instrumentalism, 159, 160, 277
Intellectualist fallacy, 369
Intentionality, 7
Intrinsic endurance, 237
Intuitionism, 111

Isomorphism, 376

James, William, 47, 48, 88, 90, 106, 116, 129, 141, 142, 147, 149, 172, 198, 199, 200, 245, 246, 255, 277, 278, 279, 286, 306, 316, 321, 322
Jaspers, 274, 276, 287, 288, 297, 298, 304, 306, 312, 314, 335, 337–38
Jeans, 124n, 187, 218, 235, 270
Jennings, 134, 135
Joachim, 98
Jodl, 188
Johnson, 248, 249
Joule, 32

Kant, 48, 57, 59, 68, 71, 73, 96, 103, 117, 141, 142, 147, 149, 157, 169, 170, 171, 187, 192, 197, 198, 206, 212, 277, 278, 287, 291, 292, 297, 298, 305, 311, 315, 316, 319, 320, 321, 322, 324, 327, 328, 335, 337, 338, 340, 342, 370, 371, 372, 373, 374, 375, 383
Kantian, 95, 174, 199, 202, 205, 218, 289, 295, 306, 312, 313, 314, 315, 335, 338, 370
Kantianism, 88, 111, 113, 114, 211, 232, 241, 269, 270, 296, 304
Kaufmann, Walter, 57
Kennedy, Gail, 140
Kepler, 229
Kierkegaard, 12, 275, 286, 292, 304, 311, 317, 325, 334, 335, 340
Knowledge relation, 92
Koehler, 126, 134
Kuiper, 179

Laird, John, 343
LaMettrie, 323
Lange, 202, 203, 206, 319
Leibniz, 211, 242, 250, 252, 257, 261, 269, 354
Leibnizian, 262, 372
Lenin, 109, 186, 188, 190, 192, 193, 194, 196, 197, 201, 202, 203, 205, 206, 208, 209, 285, 307, 326, 328
LeRoy, 187
Levy, 124n

Lewes, 134
Lewis, C. I., 112, 113, 144, 160, 162–80
Lippmann, Walter, 282
Little, Ralph S., 135
Lloyd, Alfred H., 147
Locke, John, 48, 51, 57, 59, 62, 71, 78,
    80, 85, 91, 96, 97, 103, 117, 141,
    142, 144, 147, 149, 156, 157, 166,
    168, 170, 187, 192, 198, 208, 212,
    242, 250, 251, 255, 258, 259, 261,
    270, 277, 279, 291, 292, 295, 318,
    322, 323, 326, 367
Lockean, 76, 86, 99, 164, 171, 174, 315
Lockeanism, 111, 113, 169
Lorenz, 224, 227, 377
Lovejoy, A. O., 7, 117, 119, 126, 134,
    143, 145, 232, 251, 256, 279
Lowe, Victor, 262, 268
Lucretian, 179
Lucretius, 213

Mach, Ernst, 48, 84, 90, 106, 108,
    113, 119, 132, 145, 176, 180, 194,
    199, 200, 201, 205, 215, 227, 230,
    232, 241, 285, 307, 316, 321, 325
Machian, 224, 227
Machism, 104, 108, 197, 198, 202
Macintosh, 119
Madden, Edward H., 8
Maier, Norman, 90, 367, 379
Marcel, 275, 335, 337
Maritain, 109, 203, 309, 310, 314, 323,
    329–32, 333
Marx, 188, 192, 193, 197, 205, 212,
    274, 282, 283, 284, 324, 325, 327,
    328
Marxism, 10n, 99, 109, 189, 273, 274,
    276, 284, 306
Marxist, 190, 193, 195, 202, 206, 289,
    303, 314, 319, 324, 327
Mass, 238
Materialism, 38, 105, 109, 113, 119,
    123, 139, 181–84, 189, 193, 207, 208,
    211, 214–41, 266, 267, 273, 307, 327,
    328, 373; dialectical, 11, 185–213,
    274, 275, 282–86, 303, 307–8, 323–
    28, 334–35; evolutionary, 304, 347,

348; historical, 328, 373; reformed,
    8, 12, 14, 21; scientific, 283
Matter, 136, 210, 277
Maxwell, 38
Mayer, 32
McDougall, 100, 134
McGill, Ralph, 21
Mead, 128, 147, 148, 263
Meaning, 117
Metaphysical veracity, 162–80
Metaphysics, 124, 249
Meyerson, 205
Michelson-Morley experiment, 219,
    221, 224, 225, 226, 227, 230, 232,
    233, 240
Mill, 106, 112, 134, 149, 156, 188,
    210, 277, 305, 309, 315, 316, 318,
    321
Mind-body relation, 27–39, 188, 213
Moleschott, 192, 202
Monads, 39
Monism, epistemological, 75, 96; neu-
    tral, 90, 108
Montague, W. P., 21, 21n, 130, 135,
    145–46, 148, 279, 322
Moore, G. E., 53, 54, 57, 58–66, 68,
    73, 82, 83, 85, 87, 101, 107, 143, 190,
    245, 280, 293, 306, 307, 311, 315,
    316, 318, 337, 342, 370, 379
Morgan, Lloyd, 8, 40, 41, 42, 45, 134,
    191, 318
Morris, Charles, 145
Morris, G. S., 147
Motion, 236–38
Movement, 236–38, 239
Mysticism, 297, 299, 300

Nagel, Ernest, 176
Naturalism, 8, 21, 42, 158, 306, 313;
    in ethics, 369–70; evolutionary,
    40ff.; pragmatic, 142; substantive,
    8, 9, 21
Naturalistic fallacy, 163, 311
Nature, 27ff.
Neo-Aristotelianism, 255
Neo-Humean, 104, 110
Neo-Kantian, 189, 274, 325
Neo-Thomism, 175, 187, 261, 303,

304, 307, 308–10, 314, 317, 318, 329–35, 348

Newton, 131, 217, 232, 237, 243, 323

Newtonian, 211, 222, 306, 338, 370, 372, 373

Niebuhr, 212, 297, 298, 299

Nietzsche, 286, 292, 304, 311, 335, 340

Ontological principle, 245

Ontology, 14, 104, 111, 146, 180, 187n, 210–13, 237, 296, 315, 339

Operationalism, 130–33

Organicism, 10

Ostwald, 38, 113, 132, 227

Other selves, 128–30

Paine, Tom, 189

Pan-objectivism, 150

Panpsychism, 136, 257, 260, 261, 267

Parker, DeWitt, 22, 137n, 171, 184, 343, 344, 346, 350, 353, 354, 355, 356, 357, 358

Passmore, John, 53, 327

Pearson, Karl, 108, 326

Peirce, C. S., 14, 48, 67, 147, 246, 262, 263, 265, 269, 278, 321

Pepper, Stephen, 350

Percepta, 252, 258, 262

Perception, 11, 13n, 88, 94, 244, 280, 365; non-sensuous, 253; sense, 47–103, 140–61, 218

Perry, R. B., 109, 116, 146, 148, 149, 152, 201, 279, 322, 343, 344, 356, 357

Phenomenalism, 10, 94, 100, 115, 238, 281, 292, 296, 342, 352, 366, 373; logical, 105, 114, 116, 120, 121

Piaget, 246

Plato, 262, 295, 297, 298, 354

Platonic, 13, 96, 218, 295, 343, 360

Platonism, 95, 107, 182, 242, 249, 255, 265, 266, 296, 355

Plekhanov, 324

Poincaré, 106, 202

Positivism, 99, 101, 198, 201, 203, 204, 207, 212, 229, 274, 307, 351, 355; logical, 10, 10n, 11, 22, 57, 79, 104–39, 148, 153, 254, 267, 281, 282, 362

Pragmatism, 11, 12, 20, 91, 99, 109, 162, 172, 196–97, 229, 250, 269, 274, 277, 325, 342, 347, 355

Pratt, James B., 7, 54, 114n, 117, 119, 133, 166, 173, 203, 248

Prehension, 245

Presentational immediacy, 156

Presentationalism, 52, 54, 63, 96, 143, 146, 160

Price, H. H., 53, 66, 73, 80, 86, 92–95, 96, 97, 101

Prichard, 206, 320, 323

Process, 34, 35, 38

Pseudo-problems, 343

Quine, 78

Randall, 295

Rationalism, 103, 138, 239, 259, 383

Realism, 11, 20, 31, 32, 33, 38, 105, 109, 191, 196, 205, 224, 265, 296, 313; common sense, 45, 138, 172; critical, 9, 45, 46, 47–93, 108, 117n, 145, 149, 155–56, 157, 159, 164, 166, 169, 290, 304, 320, 362, 365; new, 47, 48, 52, 61, 76, 114, 116, 150, 249, 250; perspective, 78, 140–61; physical, 9, 90, 105, 110, 114, 115, 116, 117, 120, 122, 124, 132, 151, 181, 204, 208, 210, 215, 217, 218, 221, 262; referential, 9, 21, 124, 164, 170

Reflection Theory of Knowing, 209, 209n, 303, 322, 326, 328–29

Reid, Thomas, 111, 120, 138, 198, 317

Relativity, 11, 11n, 14, 14n, 130–33, 207n, 214–41

Representationalism, 50, 51, 52, 54, 63

Riemannian, 235

Robinson, 206

Roemer, 223

Rogers, A. K., 7

Royce, Josiah, 27, 128, 246, 321

Rubner, 32

Ruskin, 275

Russell, Bertrand, 53, 55, 57, 60, 64, 65, 66, 67, 76, 78, 80, 81, 82, 84–92, 93, 94, 97, 98, 100, 101, 102, 103,

106, 107, 113n, 114, 116, 124, 127, 135, 143, 144, 150, 165, 169, 171, 173, 178, 199, 200, 210, 225, 230, 231, 236, 243, 244, 245, 246, 249, 251, 252, 253, 254, 255, 256, 261, 264, 267, 280, 281, 306, 307, 308, 316, 317, 319, 327, 329, 333

Ryle, Gilbert, 48, 51, 53, 54, 55, 57, 58, 59, 61, 62, 63, 64, 65, 66–76, 77, 78, 82, 83, 87, 90, 93, 100, 101, 151n, 175, 180, 269, 308, 322, 367

Santayana, George, 7, 48, 67, 87, 145, 199, 248, 279, 322
Sartre, 274, 275, 276, 283, 287, 288, 290, 291, 292, 293, 304, 312, 314, 335, 336–37
Savery, 143, 150, 151
Scheler, 343
Schleiermacher, 119
Schlick, 108, 119
Science, 160–61, 179, 205, 372
Scientism, 312
Self, 115, 366–67, 368, 374, 375, 376–80, 382, 383, 384
Sellars, Ford Wylis, 19
Sellars, Wilfrid, 151, 166, 173, 263
Shaw, Bernard, 282
Shepard, John, 10n, 90, 367, 379
Sherrington, 53, 270
Simultaneity, 222; absolute, 216, 220, 221, 223, 227–28, 234, 238; operational, 220, 233
Smith, Norman Kemp, 353–54
Socialism, 20, 20n
Solipsism, 81, 94, 123, 127
Space, 235–36
Spinoza, 188, 203, 218, 325, 349, 356
Spontaneity, 377
Stace, 169, 264
Stalkers, 19n
Stanley family, 19n
Stebbing, 114n
Stoicism, 191, 211, 356
Stout, 119, 245, 317
Strong, C. A., 7, 48, 279
St. Thomas, 125, 298
Subjective aim, 253

Subjectivism, 10, 107, 321, 344, 355, 365; reformed, 233, 255, 257, 271
Subjectivist principle, 245, 257
Subject-object structure, 251
Substance, 182
Sweezy, 206

Tarski, 160
Taylor, A. E., 29
Tetens, 342
Theism, 255
Thinghood, 173
Thomism, 109, 119n, 273, 298
Thomists, 285, 289
Tillich, 275, 282, 294–300, 319
Time, 233–35
Tolman, 108
Toukhtin, 308, 329
Transcendence, 52–3, 71, 90, 92, 95, 101, 111, 115, 167, 168, 169, 252, 294, 314, 319, 338
Truth, 51–52, 99, 120–23, 195, 209, 269, 340
Tyndall, 319

Uberweg, 189
Ultimate concern, 298
Unified response, 376–77
Unity of Science, 133–37
Universals, 95, 263
Urban, 343
Urmson, 86, 89
Utilitarianism, 360

Vacuous actuality, 267
Valuation, 341, 342, 343, 344, 345, 346, 347, 348–52, 358, 359, 370
Value and existence, 352–56
Verifiability, 117, 150
Vienna circle, 104, 107
Vitalism, 135, 302
Vogt, 192, 193, 202

Ward, James, 10n, 84, 133, 135, 251, 319, 326
Warnock, 51, 63, 67
Warranted assertibility, 159, 244
Watson, John Broadus, 127, 171

Webb, 282

Wells, H. G., 282

Wertheimer, 134

Wetter, 329

Wheeler, 134, 135

White, Morton, 147, 151

Whitehead, A. N., 10, 10n, 145, 170, 179, 180, 242–71, 323, 354

Whiteheadeanism, 22

Wick, Warner, 141, 142n

Wild, John, 95

Williams, Donald, 52, 107, 171

Wilson, Cook, 320, 327

Windelband, 202, 203

Wittgenstein, 56, 106, 131, 249, 250, 251, 254, 269, 307, 318

Wood, David, 19

Wood, Ledger, 117n

Woodbridge, 44, 62, 69, 72, 75, 83, 100, 142, 150, 153, 162, 172, 174, 179, 322

Woodward, 179

Wright, Chauncey, 8